Abortion

Sources for Additional Research

For further information on the religious groups covered in this publication, consult J. Gordon Melton's *Encyclopedia of American Religions,* which contains information on approximately 1,600 churches, sects, cults, temples, societies, missions, and other North American religious organizations.

For additional information on the beliefs held by the religious groups covered in this publication consult the *Encyclopedia of American Religions: Religious Creeds,* a companion volume to the *Encyclopedia of American Religions,* which provides the creeds, confessions, statements of faith, and articles of religion of the groups covered.

To locate organizations concerned with the topics covered in this publication, consult the following terms in the Name and Keyword Index to Gale's *Encyclopedia of Associations:*

- Abortion

- Family Planning

- Pro-Choice

- Pro-Life

- Reproductive Health

- Reproductive Rights

- Right-to-Life

ISSN 1043-9609

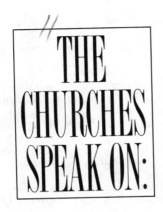

THE CHURCHES SPEAK ON:

Abortion

Official Statements from Religious Bodies and Ecumenical Organizations

J. Gordon Melton
Gary L. Ward, Contributing Editor

Gale Research Inc.

DETROIT • NEW YORK • FORT LAUDERDALE • LONDON

J. Gordon Melton

Gary L. Ward, *Contributing Editor*

Amy Lucas and Bradley J. Morgan, *Project Coordinators*

Aided by:
Susan L. Dessner, Julia C. Furtaw, Jeanne A. Gough, Frances C. Locher,
Annette Novallo, John E. Salerno, and Christine Tomassini

Donald G. Dillaman, *Programming Consultant*

Mary Beth Trimper, *Production Manager*
Marilyn Jackman, *External Production Assistant*

Arthur Chartow, *Art Director*
Cynthia D. Baldwin and Bernadette Gornie, *Graphic Designers*
C. J. Jonik, *Keyliner*

Laura Bryant, *Production Supervisor*
Louise Gagné, *Internal Production Associate*
Sharana Wier, *Internal Production Assistant*

Copyright © 1989 by Gale Research Inc.
835 Penobscot Bldg.
Detroit, MI 48226-4094

ISBN 0-8103-7219-3
ISSN 1043-9609

Printed in the United States of America

Contents

Statements

Roman Catholic Church

Statements in this section are arranged chronologically by issuing date.

Protestant and Eastern Orthodox Churches

This section is arranged alphabetically by individual church, religious
body, or ecumenical organization; the statements issued by each
organization are presented chronologically within that organization.

Jewish Groups

This section is arranged alphabetically by individual religious organization; the statements issued by each organization are presented chronologically within that organization.

Other Religious Bodies

This section is arranged alphabetically by individual church, religious body, or ecumenical organization; the statements issued by each organization are presented chronologically within that organization.

Preface

The Churches Speak is a quarterly series of monographs which systematically brings together the major official pronouncements of North American religious bodies and ecumenical organizations on the issues dominating today's headlines. Each monograph is devoted to a single topic and provides an overview of the topic itself, its historical background, and the full range of opinions found in the individual church statements. The statements themselves provide a unique and conveniently arranged survey of opinion on important contemporary issues, cutting across theological and denominational boundaries to influence the climate of social and political thought in our culture.

The formal statements issued by churches and other religious bodies are intended primarily to inform and guide their members, adherents, and supporters on the issue in question. These statements often attain additional importance, however, since they also exert influence on the actions of the religious agencies, clergy, and church administrators who initiate, direct, and regulate organizational programs. Church statements are also indirectly aimed at nonchurch members in an attempt to alter public policy, mobilize public opinion, or advocate changes in legislation. And they can also become the focal point of intense controversy, functioning as the bulwark against which many people direct their dissent on a given issue. This controversy can become magnified within the issuing organization itself when a significant minority of its members dissent from the positions taken by its hierarchies, judicatories, and boards of social concerns.

Focus is on Contemporary Topics From Major Religious Bodies

Each issue of *The Churches Speak* focuses on a single topic or a few closely related topics chosen for their high current public interest. Topics covered represent a wide range of vital social and political issues, such as AIDS, abortion, racism, the Middle East, euthanasia, capital punishment, and the ordination of women. Statements of major North American churches and religious organizations are included for each topic, providing comprehensive representation of the full range of opinions held on each topic.

The documents included in *The Churches Speak* were obtained through a mailing to all of the religious bodies in North America with more than 100,000 members. On any given issue, additional churches and religious organizations (including some outside of North America), and even some secular organizations known to have a special interest in the topic under consideration, were also solicited for their statements. Other statements have been identified in the files of the Institute for the Study of American Religion in Santa Barbara, California.

While most large churches and religious bodies make formal statements on important issues, it should be noted that many of the more than 1,500 denominations and religious organizations located in North America will not formulate any official statement or speak out on such issues. A number of religious bodies, including some of the largest denominations, do not make such statements as a matter of principle. Rather, they choose to leave actions and beliefs concerning social issues strictly up to individual effort and opinion.

Authentic Texts Used for All Statements

The statements presented in this series are in their authentic form, although obvious typographical errors have been corrected. The original wording, grammar, and punctuation of each statement remains intact. No attempt has been made to introduce foreign material or explanatory notes into the body of the statement's text.

Arrangement and Content

Each issue of *The Churches Speak* begins with an introductory essay which provides an overview of the topic itself and traces its recent historical manifestations. This essay also summarizes, compares, and contrasts the opinions found in the individual statements, allowing the user to place each one in the appropriate context. Each essay concludes with bibliographic citations to sources for further reading on the topic.

The statements presented in each monograph are arranged into four main sections based on broad religious families or traditions: The Roman Catholic Church (which represents the single largest religious body in the United States); Protestant and Eastern Orthodox Churches; Jewish Groups; and Other Religious Bodies.

Within the Roman Catholic Church section, statements are arranged chronologically by issuing date. The remaining sections are subarranged alphabetically by individual churches, religious bodies, or ecumenical organizations; the statements issued by each organization are presented chronologically within that organization.

Each of the four religious family sections is preceded by a note which provides background information on the family and analysis of its perspective on the issue in question. Individual statements contain the following elements:

Issuing organization. The name of the religious body or ecumenical organization issuing the statement.

Statement name. The actual or formal title of the statement. When no formal title is given, a descriptive title has been assigned.

Text of statement. The text of the statement is presented in its original form.

Notes. These appear in italic type following the text of each statement. When applicable, these remarks provide background information on the issuing organization's membership size and geographic distribution, and details about the circumstances under which the statement was made—including when it was passed, why it was passed, and whether or not it is binding on church members.

Index to Organizations, Statements, and Subjects Provided

To facilitate access to the material presented, each issue of *The Churches Speak* contains an Index to Organizations, Statements, and Subjects included in that issue. The index lists, in a single alphabetical sequence, the full titles of all the statements, the names of all religious bodies and ecumenical organizations mentioned in the statements' texts and notes, specifically named individuals, and specific subjects covered within the statements. Statement titles and organization names are also listed by important keywords that appear in their titles/names. Citations in the index refer to page numbers; page numbers rendered in boldface after an organization name indicate the location of that organization's statement(s) within the main text.

Sources of Additional Information

Additional information on many of the religious bodies covered in *The Churches Speak* can be found in the *Encyclopedia of American Religions*. The *Encyclopedia* provides details on approximately 1600 religious and spiritual groups in the United

States and Canada, and is divided into two parts. The first part contains an essay covering the development of American religion, an essay providing a historical survey of religion in Canada, and historical essays grouped by general religious family. The second part contains directory sections listing individual churches and groups constituting the religious families discussed in the historical essays.

A companion volume, the *Encyclopedia of American Religions: Religious Creeds,* provides a comprehensive compilation of 464 religious creeds, confessions, statements of faith, summaries of belief, and articles of religion currently acknowledged by many of the churches or religious groups described in the *Encyclopedia of American Religions.* It also includes extensive notes on the history and textual variations of creeds, reflecting changing social, political, and doctrinal climates throughout the centuries. The material is arranged by major religious families, following, with minor variations, the approach used in the *Encyclopedia.*

Institute for the Study of American Religion

The Institute for the Study of American Religion was founded in 1969 for the purpose of researching and disseminating information about the numerous religious groups in the United States. More recently, the Institute's scope has been expanded to include religious groups in Canada, making it the only research facility of its kind to cover so broad a range of activity. After being located for many years in Evanston, Illinois, the Institute moved to Santa Barbara, California, in 1985. At that time, its collection of more than 25,000 books and its extensive files covering individual religious groups were donated to the Special Collections department of the library of the University of California—Santa Barbara. *The Churches Speak* has been compiled in part from the Institute's collection.

Suggestions Are Welcome

Users with particular questions about a religious group, suggested topics for coverage in or changes to *The Churches Speak,* or other information are invited to write to the Institute in care of its Director:

Dr. J. Gordon Melton
Institute for the Study of American Religion
Box 90709
Santa Barbara, CA 93190-0709

Introductory Essay:

The Historical Context of the Contemporary Abortion Debate

Introduction

Abortion is currently a hot topic of debate, and much of the heat is generated by the various religious groups. This essay will consider some historical and sociological perspectives by which to gain a broader understanding of the debate.

The Rise of the Abortion Issue

Abortion has been legal in this country for about the same span of time as it has been illegal, a fact few people today realize. In almost every state, until the 1860s, abortions could be legally performed up until the time of "quickening" (when an infant's movements in the womb can first be detected). After the 1860s, abortion was progressively criminalized, without much religious fervor one way or another. The subject did not re-enter significant public debate until the 1960s. The earliest official religious statement in the twentieth century touching on abortion is from the Roman Catholic Church in 1959, and it is primarily directed at contraception, mentioning abortion only in passing. The earliest twentieth-century statement in this collection specifically directed to abortion is from the Unitarian Universalists in 1963, though a few religious groups stated their position on the issue prior to that. It was certainly in the 1960s that the volume of interest in abortion increased sharply, a trend that has continued to the point where almost every religious agency that makes public statements on a social issue (many do not) has made one on abortion.

What happened to create this new climate? The 1960 marketing in the United States of the birth control pill and the 1963 publication of Betty Friedan's book, *The Feminine Mystique,* were certainly watershed events. Friedan's book is credited as being the catalyst for the modern women's liberation movement; the "pill" revolutionized not only contraception, but also sexual expression in general and the relationships between men and women in particular. Whereas the women's movement of the late 1800s concentrated on issues such as the right to vote, the movement in the 1960s sought specific constitutional protection for women under an Equal Rights Amendment. Women also claimed the right to decide if a pregnancy would be carried to term.

Why did religious groups get involved? Because abortion so quickly touches upon questions of life and death, the structure of and relations within the family, the relationships between men and women, the power of the government to make moral choices for its citizens, and many more areas in which religions have historically concerned themselves. The religious groups became part of the forces lifting the issue to the prime cultural agenda.

Range of Religious Positions

The positions taken by religious groups have fallen fairly consistently along the conservative/liberal lines established for other topics. For example, a Christian church that is conservative in its theology (i.e., promotes a literal interpretation of the Bible) has likely taken conservative positions on other social topics and will almost certainly be against abortion. A Christian church with a liberal theology (i.e., promotes a more contextual or metaphoric interpretation of the Bible) has likely taken liberal positions on other social topics and will tend to take a pro-choice stance on abortion.

The churches do not cover the entire range of positions on abortion that are theoretically possible. That is, there is no religious group that positively espouses abortion without reservation as the birth control of choice, while there is the extreme position of calling abortion "legalized murder of the unborn" taken by the Bible Missionary Church. Even the Unitarian Universalists, whose statements on this and on many other issues may be considered the most liberal, state that "the issue of abortion is morally complex" and have urged the promotion of "family planning and education for responsible sex." The Unitarian Universalists maintain that the right to choose contraception and abortion are "legitimate aspects of the right to privacy," that women should be able to make decisions regarding their own bodies and futures, and that anti-abortion legislation would merely return abortion to the life-endangering underworld and would impose the religious morality of some onto others.

Several times in this work, more than one document from a single group has been included in order to illustrate how a group's position can evolve over time. Few churches have reversed their initial opinion, but the language of their statements has changed to reflect a different emphasis from one year to the next. An interesting example is the Southern Baptist Convention, which in 1971 allowed for the "possibility of abortion under such conditions as rape, incest, clear evidence of severe fetal deformity, and carefully ascertained evidence of the likelihood of damage to the emotional, mental, and physical health of the mother." In 1974 this was reaffirmed as a "middle ground between the extreme of abortion on demand and the opposite extreme of all abortion as murder." The next several years had more ambiguous wordings, and in 1980, the convention shifted toward a stricter view that favored "appropriate legislation and/or a constitutional amendment prohibiting abortion except to save the life of the mother." In 1982, this position was reinforced with the explicit statement that the possibility of abortion "is not subject to personal judgments as to 'quality of life' based on such subjective criteria as stage of development, abnormality, intelligence level, degree of dependency, cost of medical treatment, or inconvenience to parents." Clearly, there is quite a difference between 1974 and 1982, a difference which may not be noticed when reading the group's 1987 statement, which states that "Southern Baptists have traditionally ... opposed abortion on demand."

One religious group that has clearly reversed itself on the abortion issue is the Presbyterian Church (U.S.A.), and its reversal illustrates the general cultural shift in the last two centuries. As already indicated, abortion to end a pregnancy in its early stages was legal in America in the early 1800s and was not a major concern to the churches. In the 1860s, the American Medical Association began a moral campaign against abortion, though without much participation by churches. The General Assembly (Old School) of the Presbyterians was one of the few bodies to make a pronouncement on the matter when, in 1869, it issued a terse statement against abortion. Then, like almost every other religious group, the Presbyterians were completely silent on the topic for most of the next century. It was during this century that the affects of the cultural shift were seen in the churches, as many of them became more liberal on issues such as alcohol, divorce, dancing, card playing, and abortion. Now known as the Presbyterian Church (U.S.A.), the church reversed itself in 1970 when it came down on the side of personal conscience, claiming it would issue no official church policy on abortion.

Approaches of the Major Traditions

The Roman Catholic Church and the Orthodox churches have come out strongly against abortion, both sharing much of the same early church tradition until the Orthodox break from Rome in 1054. By virtue of its size and emphasis, the Roman Catholic Church has been the single most visible religious commentator on abortion, especially in the United States. Its earliest statement on abortion (which was also the first Christian statement) can be found in the *Didache,* a document of the late first century. It proclaimed "You shall not kill the fetus by abortion or destroy the infant already born."

Two major issues concerned leaders of the church: whether abortion was done to conceal the sin of fornication or adultery, and whether abortion was homicide. The second issue was the more difficult to determine an answer for, and there was disagreement among theologians. St. Augustine, a major theologian in the fourth century, said in the *Enchiridion* that early, "unformed fetuses perish like seeds which have not fructified." The point at which the embryo becomes a human being, called hominization, was said to happen at some point after conception—forty days for males and eighty days for females. The judgment of homicide, therefore, could only be applied to the abortion of "fully formed" fetuses after that time period. Augustine still held, however, that abortion in the early stages was a sin because it broke the necessary connection between intercourse and procreation.

St. Thomas Aquinas, a thirteenth-century theologian who became a major doctrinal authority for the church, followed Augustine's position about delayed hominization and supplemented this with the notion of hylomorphism, which suggested that humans are an indissoluble unity of both body and soul, matter and substance. Until the fetus attains a human shape, therefore, it cannot be fully human; it not only does not yet have a human form, it does not yet have a human soul. Agreeing with a position held by the philosopher Aristotle, Aquinas believed that the fetus began with a vegetative soul, then gained an animal soul, followed finally by a rational soul.

Varying opinions on hominization persisted, however, and in 1588 Pope Sixtus V declared that abortion of a fetus at any stage was homicide. This more rigid stance was problematic, however, and in 1591 Pope Gregory XIV reversed it. Echoing Aquinas's ideas of naturalistic ethics, Gregory XIV stated that abortion was not always homicide, but abortion was still wrong if it were covering up sexual sin. Furthermore, abortion could not be used as birth control since that would interfere with the "natural" connection between sexual relations and conception.

Between 1588 and 1869 various developments brought the idea of delayed hominization into question, a key one being the increase in popular observance of the Immaculate Conception of Mary. Defined as dogma (no longer a matter of optional belief) by Pope Pius IX in 1854, this doctrine held that Mary, the mother of Jesus was, from the moment of her conception, specially preserved from the stain of original sin. This implied immediate ensoulment or hominization, which by extension might apply to others besides Mary. Uncertainty grew about the forty- and eighty-day periods previously accepted for hominization, and there was the sense that perhaps abortion should be prohibited almost always, just in case it might be homicide.

Uncertainty regarding abortion was ended in 1869 when Pope Pius IX issued a statement that sidestepped the problem of hominization. He stated that "the fetus, although not ensouled, is directed to the forming of man. Therefore, its ejection is anticipated homicide." Abortion under all circumstances was prohibited, and this has remained the church's position on this issue to date.

This statement is an example of the Vatican's efforts to restore the power of the papacy. Due to such events as the French Revolution and the dismantling of the Papal States of Italy to form modern Italy, the temporal power of the papacy decreased drastically in the 1700s and 1800s. As the papal authority over the secular world decreased, papal authority over the church was increased. In fact, in 1869, Pius IX convened a church council that is now known as Vatican I; it began on the day of the Feast of the Immaculate Conception. During the course of Vatican I, which was the first full council since the Council of Trent in 1563, the doctrine of papal infallibility was proclaimed as applying whenever the pope spoke officially *(ex cathedra)* on matters of faith and morals.

The council also increased the power of the church by further using the veneration of Mary to its advantage. At the time, Mary was credited with numerous miracle healings and visitations and was a very popular figure; the church thus enhanced its position by supporting this popular devotion to Mary. By lifting up the image of Mary, the council gave more credence to the ideas of Immaculate Conception and immediate hominization, which in turn increased the authority of the church's prohibition against all abortion. The abortion prohibition served a number of purposes at once: 1) it was a channel for increasing control over the private lives of the faithful when control over their public lives was declining, 2) it was an issue on which the papacy could safely assert its ability and authority to regulate the terms of belief, and 3) it aided the increase of Catholic population when the loss of position as state church was decreasing its population. Thus, the consolidation of papal power over the church, the loss of secular papal power, the official elevation of the popular veneration of Mary, the decrease in Catholic population, and the total prohibition of abortion are all intricately related.

In 1917, the *Code of Canon Law* prescribed excommunication for the sin of abortion, not only for the woman involved, but also for any doctors and nurses who took part. Though the church has continued to hold to this and to Pius IX's position of de facto immediate hominization, it does not usually perform baptism, extreme unction, or the funeral mass for stillborn babies or in cases of miscarriage.

Abortion was not mentioned in official statements by the bishops of the American branch of the Roman Catholic Church until a brief reference in a 1959 paper on contraception. There was no direct American Catholic statement until after Vatican II, which, in 1965, condemned abortion on the basis of protecting life. In 1968, Pope Paul VI issued the encyclical *Humanae Vitae,* which condemned abortion both on the basis of protecting life and on the necessary connection between sexual union and procreation, meaning that every sexual act must be open to the life that may result.

Protestants do not have much of a tradition specifically relating to abortion. Since the original Lutheran break (in "protest") from the Roman Catholic Church in the 1500s, Protestants have appealed to the Bible alone for authority (superseding church tradition) and believe that individuals are responsible for relating to God without intervening mediation and must be free to interpret for themselves what the Bible says. The Bible, however, is basically silent on the issue of abortion. Exodus 21: 22-25 does deal with the penalty for miscarriage: "When men strive together, and hurt a woman with child, so that there is a miscarriage, and yet no harm follows, the one who hurt her shall be fined, according as the woman's husband shall lay upon him; and he shall pay as the judges determine. If any harm follows, then you shall give life for life, eye for eye, tooth for tooth, hand for hand, foot for foot, burn for burn, wound for wound, stripe for stripe" (Revised Standard Bible). This Hebrew code of behavior was similar to legal traditions of other, earlier peoples, such as the Code of Hammurabi (209 and 210) and the Hittite Laws (1:17), which held that the loss of a fetus was not considered as great as the loss of an existing human being.

Protestants also refer to Psalm 139, Isaiah 49:1b, and Jeremiah 1 when they consider abortion. "The Lord called me from the womb, from the body of my mother he named my name" (Isaiah 49:1b, Revised Standard Edition) is interpreted as indicating God's concern with the fetus, but how this applies to abortion is ambiguous, as is the passage from Proverbs 24:11, "Rescue those who are being taken away to death; hold back those who are stumbling to the slaughter" (Revised Standard Edition). Therefore, Protestant positions on abortion are generally tied to biblical passages having to do with women, the family, social order, ethics, etc. This is why a church's stand on abortion can become central to the polemics of its particular theological/social agenda.

The Jewish tradition also uses many of the same passages from the Hebrew scriptures, including Exodus 21:22-25, but beyond that considers its strong heritage of tradition and interpretation for its stand on abortion. According to the Talmud, an authoritative commentary on the Bible, the fetus is not a person but is considered to be as an appendage to the mother's body. Personhood is traditionally related to the Hebrew word *nephesh,* the characteristic mark of which is breathing. This idea comes from Genesis 2:7, "Then the Lord God formed man of dust from the ground, and breathed into his nostrils the breath of life; and man became a living being" (Revised Standard Version), and is also found in Ezekiel 37:8-10. Rabbis debated the moment of ensoulment and developed answers ranging from the moment of intercourse to when the child learns to speak. The issue was, for the most part, given up some time ago as a secret not privy to mortals.

The Jewish tradition is fairly clear that abortion is justified in order to save the life of the mother, as her life takes precedence. There is, however, much diversity of opinion about the degree to which the mother's life takes precedence if the intended abortion is to save her from mental, emotional, or spiritual anguish. In Israel today, abortions to save the mother's life or to prevent serious physical or mental injury are permissible, and terms such as "mental injury" are given broad interpretation. The Reform, Reconstructionist, and Conservative Jewish movements in the United States oppose governmental restrictions on abortion, affirming the decision as a private matter. Orthodox Jews tend to take a stricter position against abortion.

The Islamic sacred text, the Holy Quran, does not say anything directly about abortion. It does admonish against killing children for fear of not having enough material abundance to care for them on the basis that Allah, who provided for the parents, will also provide for the children. This thinking is usually extended to a prohibition against abortion on the basis of fear of want. If the pregnancy threatens the life of the mother, then the mother, as the established life with responsibilities, takes precedence; abortion may then be performed as the lesser of two evils. The fetus is traditionally accorded a different status depending on the stage of its development; aborting it is less of a crime when first conceived and more of a crime if it is completely formed and viable, with a soul. Muslims traditionally believe that life in the fetus really begins after 150 days. Generally, however, Muslims take a fairly strict stance against abortion for reasons other than to save the mother's life.

Buddhist tradition is not one prone to definitive statements on moral issues, partly because its faith is a pragmatic one that has no recourse to divine pronouncements. The Buddhist position desires both to protect fetal life and to have compassion for the people involved who must make difficult decisions in a complex world. The statement in this collection, from the Buddhist Churches of America, supports the right of the woman carrying the fetus to decide what to do.

The Place of Abortion in the Social Order

From the earliest times, governments, religious bodies, and individuals have been interested parties in the matter of abortion. Sometimes their concerns overlap and complement each other, but often they are at odds. The interests of the government typically cluster around the desired *functions* of citizens, e.g. soldiers, slaves, growers, producers, etc. Many people in eighteenth century France, for example, were concerned about the general decline in birth rates; hence they considered the use of birth control and abortion as "a terrible and secret cause of depopulation that imperceptibly drains the nation" and as "deadly to the state."[1] From this point of view, what mattered was the *loss* of people and production to the state, not the *manner* of loss (contraception or abortion).

The state has also been concerned with maintaining an equilibrium in the power relationships among its citizens, so that the government does not become unstable. The state's interest in reproductive practices has often been ethnic- or class-specific, as when the first century Roman Empire was concerned about the falling birthrate of the upper class. This trend undermined the ability of the state to control the ever more numerous lower classes, so procreation was declared the civic duty of members of the privileged class, and midwives who administered contraceptives or abortifacients to them were exiled. This kind of ethnic- or class-specific interest is not limited to the state, but rather is often enacted within parts of a population acting with or without the state's blessing.

Historically the role of the state has coincided with the role of men in regulating women's autonomy in all arenas, from sexual activity to voting rights. From this perspective, prohibiting abortion may also be viewed as an attempt by men (and the state) to impose compulsory child-bearing on women. The political nature of abortion and contraceptive issues is thus of great concern to women's rights groups.

Indeed abortion has never been merely a personal or family matter. A wide assortment of power-wielding groups, including church, government (and the military), men, women, the law, medicine, eugenicists, futurists, and population experts, have managed to exert their influence on the issue. The relative strength (or even existence) of these groups and the degree to which they work in tension or collaboration with each other have varied in different historical periods. Views on abortion today are influenced heavily by the women's movement as well as the political and social clout currently claimed by Catholics and conservative Protestants.

Abortion in the Early United States

Between 1800 and 1900, the birth rate among white married women in the United States dropped from an average of 7.04 children per woman to 3.56. This decline began as early as 1810 and affected not only women in urban locales who were affected by the beginning industrial economy, but also women in rural areas. Among the many factors involved in this phenomenon, a crucial one is a shift in the definition of family and motherhood. Whereas earlier motherhood was a more pragmatic business of creating children, the new motherhood was veiled in the "cult of domesticity." Mother became the divinely ordained keeper of the home and was responsible for shaping the morals of the young. This led to an emphasis on "fewer and better" children, an ideology intimately tied to racial, class, and other issues. Fewer children became evidence of a chaste and spiritual (hence "ladylike") life, especially in contrast to the large families of immigrants, the poor, and black Americans.

The Historical Context of the Contemporary Abortion Debate

With access to physicians and medicines, middle- and upper-class women desiring small families were able to obtain contraceptives and substances that would induce abortions. Always a fact of life, abortions did not present legal or moral problems, since abortion prior to "quickening" was, following British Common Law, generally considered morally neutral and was legal in almost all states in 1860. The churches were not concerned with the issue in any significant way. Papal pronouncements had not yet taken a hard line about abortion, and, in any case, the Roman Catholic Church was not yet strong enough in America to take on such a controversial social issue.

The Criminalization of Abortion

In the 1860s and 1870s, opposition to the practice of abortion was led by the American Medical Association (AMA), and eventually most states criminalized it. The AMA presented its first official statement against abortion at its 1859 convention, and from that point on "regular" doctors pressed the issue at all levels, to the extent that they became "the single most important factor in altering the legal policies toward abortion in this country."[2] Interestingly these physicians did not present abortion as a medical or health problem, especially since new techniques made it at least as safe as childbirth. The AMA instead insisted that its campaign was a *moral* one in which they tried to enlist the clergy of various denominations, though without notable success. Churches may have agreed with the AMA, but apparently were not interested in giving the topic much time or energy.

Founded in 1847, the AMA was a new organization, and its member physicians did not yet have the monopoly on health care that they currently claim. Nineteenth-century health care was oriented toward middle- and upper-class women, who were already being served by midwives who assisted at births and abortions and were consulted for other health problems. Thus, the AMA's anti-abortion campaign, which attacked midwife activity, was part and parcel of its rise to hegemony in the health care arena.

Claiming a moral desire to protect the fetus as a living being, AMA physicians were also acting to establish themselves as defenders of the social order. They felt that abortion clearly contradicted the ideology of "true womanhood," since an unwanted pregnancy was proof that sexual activity had occurred without a desire to propagate—that is, abortion highlighted the existence of "lustful" sex, which was not condoned.

Higher class women having abortions contradicted the chaste image being cultivated for (and by) white women of means. So, with statements enforcing the idea that "female chastity is necessary to protect the family and its descent; that female chastity must be enforced with severe social and legal sanctions, among which fear of pregnancy functioned effectively and naturally,"[3] physicians took it upon themselves to correct the situation. The connection to class consciousness was made more explicit by warnings that "respectable" women could find themselves outnumbered by "the ignorant, the low-lived and the alien."[4] Implicit was the idea that abortion may be appropriately used by some but not by others. Of course this line of reasoning reversed the "cult of domesticity," in which racial superiority could be supported by "fewer and better" children. The AMA's actions seemed to suggest that racial superiority would be served by white women having many children and everyone else having fewer children.

While the AMA's ultimate goal may have been to exclude abortion and contraception from upper-class circles only, it became obvious that this was not feasible. There was no way the group could provide abortions, contraception, and sex education to the lower classes while excluding the upper, so instead it created a climate in turn-of-the-century America where almost no legal abortion existed. This reflected a growing trend worldwide, as abortion was, by this time, illegal almost everywhere, including the United Kingdom.

The Birth Control Movement

The first half of the twentieth century saw a great many changes regarding contraception and abortion. The first country to legalize elective abortion was the Soviet Union in 1920, followed in the 1950s by several other eastern European countries. In western Europe, Latvia in 1932 was the first to change, soon followed by most of the Nordic countries.[5] In the United States and elsewhere there was a groundswell of interest in getting sex education material in general before the public. The forces behind this shift were many and complex. Ideas based on the work of English economist Thomas Malthus (1766-1834) were popularized and played a very influential role. He believed that the increase of population is greater than the increase in the means of subsistence, and that population growth must be restricted either artificially or by the "natural" means of poverty and war.

Neo-Malthusian sentiment became widespread, and its affects were various, depending on the agenda of the interpreting parties. The eugenics movement, which believed in the science of improving the hereditary quality of a race or breed, promoted a campaign to reduce the "unfit" portion of the population by various means, including involuntary sterilization. Harry Loughlin (1880-1943), a leading advocate of eugenics, estimated that 10 percent of the population was "socially inadequate," a category that included the insane, criminals, orphans, paupers, etc. These ideas so pervaded the culture that involuntary sterilization was legalized and performed on over 45,000 persons in the United States between 1907 and 1945, most of them poor women.[6] One such sterilized woman, Carrie Buck, took her case to the Supreme Court in 1926 *(Buck v. Bell)*. In a landmark decision the Court defended the sterilizations, the government's right to intervene directly in reproductive decisions, and the government's interests in maintaining, by these measures, a high caliber of population.

Other pioneers in the birth control/contraceptive movement, who occasionally made use of the overpopulation argument, had more liberal, popular-based agendas. These were often "free thinkers" who made their major reputations in unconventional arenas—people like Robert Dale Owen, Charles Bradlaugh, Annie Besant, and others. A major pro-contraceptive pioneer who coined the term "birth control," Margaret Sanger (1883-1966) was involved in the movement in an attempt to combat poverty, reduce religious prudishness, and protect women. Her own mother died at the age of forty-eight, after bearing eleven children. In an era when sex was considered shameful, Sanger and others regarded it as healthful and pleasurable. Her interest in providing the poor with birth control information was not so much racist as helpful—to enable more choice for the allotment of their scarce resources. Not free from racist overtones, however, Sanger occasionally made comments like, "More children from the fit, less from the unfit—that is the chief issue of birth control."[7] She felt that contraception would help all women for many reasons, one being that fear of pregnancy negatively affected sexual enjoyment.

Like the other pioneers, Sanger faced massive opposition from those who felt that open discussion or promotion of such information led to promiscuity. In order to make birth control more available, therefore, she needed to court powerful friends, such as the AMA. She also thought that only experts in physiology and biology were qualified to deal with the technology of birth control. Sanger and others pursued legislative bills which would legitimize birth control measures if a physician were in charge. She was not an advocate of legalized abortion, however, and pursued the politically advantageous path of placing contraceptives in a positive light by

The Historical Context of the Contemporary Abortion Debate

contrasting them with the "cruel" alternative of abortion. The association with the AMA led eventually to a medical model of birth control, with the physician, not the woman, given the decision-making power. Some of the more liberal members of the AMA were willing to work with Sanger, both for personal reasons and in the pragmatic recognition that the desire for birth control was not going to disappear and might lead to rival care-giving organizations. Sanger's organization, the American Birth Control Federation of America, became the Planned Parenthood Federation of America in 1942. Its name continued the strategy of giving birth control "an aura of scientific and medical respectability by assimilating it within the framework of social engineering ('planning') and public policy."[8]

The birth control movement that Sanger led was not a feminist movement; major women's rights activists were not involved, nor were organizations like the National American Woman Suffrage Association, the Woman's Party, or the Woman's Trade Union League. The issue for them at that point did not have sufficient attraction to overcome the backlash that would come with involvement in it. Sanger herself did not aspire to legal or economic equality for women, but rather to the development of the "intuitive forward urge within," which she associated, ironically enough, with the maternal urge. She felt that birth control would liberate the "feminine spirit" to produce a spontaneous, free womanhood and motherhood.[9]

Social Change in the Late Twentieth Century

The birth rate had fallen to 3.56 births per woman by 1900, and by the late 1930s there were only about 2.2 births per woman. The figure jumped somewhat after World War II, then fell to below 2 births per woman from the 1970s through the 1980s. This more recent drop had different reasons from those which caused the decline in the 1800s. In the twentieth century, the cult of domesticity was replaced by such factors as later marriages, more women in college and in the work force, more women heading their own households, and the availability of more reliable birth control—especially since the Pill was introduced in 1960.

By 1980, 82.8 percent of women aged 18-19 years had never married, compared to 67.7 percent in 1960; 50.2 percent aged 20-24 years had never married, compared to 28.4 percent in 1960; and 20.8 percent aged 25-29 years had never married, compared to 10.5 percent in 1960.[10] Thus many more women were spending more of their lives outside marriage and without a focus on childbearing/childrearing. Presuming that heterosexual activity remained intact, it is logical to expect that during the post-1960 years there should have been an increased demand for safe contraception/abortion options. Although better contraceptives were becoming available, there was still a high incidence of illegal abortions. Exactly how many abortions were being performed is difficult to know; one estimate made in the mid-1950s was between 200,000 and 1.2 million per year. Another estimate suggested that when abortion was first legalized in 1973, two-thirds of the legal abortions simply replaced formerly illegal procedures.

Women's new roles effected a significant change in the beliefs of the American public about abortion. A 1965 National Fertility Study showed that, while the vast majority would allow abortion under some circumstances (such as danger to the mother), only five percent would allow elective abortion. By 1969, a Gallup Poll indicated that 40 percent favored elective abortion during the first trimester of pregnancy. In the same year, a nationwide Harris poll recounted that 64 percent "believed that the decision on abortion should be a private one," and even though the AMA still officially took a conservative stand (softened only slightly by a statement in 1967), polls revealed that most physicians favored legalizing abortion.

In the 1950s demographers began talking about the dangers of the "population explosion." The Population Council was founded in 1952 by John D. Rockefeller III to arouse support for population control; it was followed in 1954 by the Hugh Moore Fund, created by the owner of the Dixie Cup Corporation. Much of their attention was directed to the populations outside the United States (often with racist overtones). Within the United States, population groups, medical organizations, and other interests began to converge on a set of reasons to legalize abortion: 1) making abortions illegal is unenforceable and the need for them will not go away, 2) licensed physicians would oversee proper conditions, both sanitary and otherwise (i.e., would reject "inappropriate" reasons for the abortion), and 3) the unborn child has a right to a life of dignity, presumably not possible if the parents do not want to give birth.[11]

The rising modern feminist movement, however, disagreed with the medical profession's decision-making position, focusing instead on women's rights to control their bodies and their pregnancies. Feminists opposed the distinction between therapeutic (medically indicated) and elective abortion, and they supported the woman as the final judge of action. The organized feminist movement's pro-abortion rights activities were a significant factor in pressing legislative and cultural change. Feminists not only testified about the horrors of illegal abortions and conducted demonstrations, but they also created a powerful network of sympathetic doctors and clinics that put pressure on the mainstream legal and medical groups to alter their stance.

Following the examples of countries like Denmark and Sweden, the American Law Institute in 1962 proposed legislation permitting abortion if a physician believed that continued pregnancy presented a mental or physical risk to the mother, or if the pregnancy resulted from rape or incest, or if the child would be born with a severe defect. About a dozen states, beginning with Colorado in 1967, adopted laws based on this proposal. By 1973, Alaska, Hawaii, New York, and Washington had even more liberal abortion laws.

The Supreme Court Decisions

The movement to decriminalize abortion came to a climax with the Supreme Court's 1973 decision in the case of *Roe v. Wade.* Roe was the pseudonym used by a pregnant single woman who brought a class action suit challenging the constitutionality of abortion laws in the state of Texas which prohibited abortions except to save the mother's life. Wade was the district attorney of Dallas County. The Court decided that the abortion laws in Texas violated the due process clause of the Fourteenth Amendment, which protects the right to privacy against state action. The Court said that the woman has a qualified right to voluntarily terminate a pregnancy, but that the state may also have legitimate interests in protecting the potentiality of human life. The judgment was that up to about the end of the first trimester of pregnancy the abortion decision is left in the hands of the attending physician (thus following the pattern of medicalizing abortion). After the first trimester the state may regulate abortion in ways reasonably related to maternal health. After the time when the fetus is viable (capable of living outside the mother), the state may regulate and even prohibit abortion (except to save the life of the mother) if it chooses. Justices Blackmun, Burger, Douglas, Brennan, Stewart, Marshall, and Powell were the supporting justices, while White and Rehnquist filed dissenting opinions.

In another 1973 case, *Doe v. Bolton,* the Court struck down a number of procedural obstacles to abortion, such as authorization by an abortion committee in a hospital, and state residency requirements. The Court stressed that the doctor's "medical judgment may be exercised in the light of all factors—physical, emotional, psychological, familial, and the woman's age—relevant to the well-being of this patient." In 1976 *(Danforth v. Planned Parenthood)* the Court rejected state laws requiring spousal and parental consent. In 1977 *(Maher v. Roe)* the Court stated that public hospitals are not required to provide abortion services; it also asserted that states do not have to pay for elective abortions. Also in 1977 the first Hyde Amendment curtailing federal Medicaid funding for abortion was passed in Congress. The Hyde Amendment was upheld by the Supreme Court in 1980 *(Harris v. McRae)* in a vote of five to four, stating that the Constitution "affords protection against unwarranted government interference with freedom of choice," but "does not confer an entitlement to such funds as may be necessary to realize all the advantages of that freedom."

The Response to Legalization

After the passage of *Roe v. Wade* in 1973, the drive to recriminalize abortion was taken up by a rising right-wing Protestant coalition in an unusual partnership with the Roman Catholic Church. In 1975, the U.S. Catholic Conference presented its "Pastoral Plan for Pro-Life Activity," calling for a parish network that would 1) help passage of a pro-life amendment to the Constitution, 2) elect local pro-life officials, 3) monitor the abortion stands of elected officials, and 4) work for pro-life candidates generally. The "New Right," meanwhile, tried to consolidate groups devoted to the preservation of the traditional roles of the family, the churches, and the schools into a single coalition organized around the planks of pro-life, pro-family, pro-moral, and pro-American, with family as the central theme.[12] Feminists were portrayed as among those who, like the communists, desire to break down the family and its values by fostering abortion or "the contraceptive mentality" and by the "downgrading of the male or father role in the traditional family."[13] Feminists and members of the New Right may concentrate on abortion, but that is because it is symbolic of a whole range of social and theological positions. Abortion easily becomes the litmus test of these other issues as well.

The similar positions taken on abortion by the Roman Catholic Church and conservative Protestants of the "New Right" make for a tenuous bond at best. The National Conference of Catholic Bishops has taken many social stands contrary to the New Right's agenda, and the theology behind Catholic opposition to abortion is somewhat different from that of the Protestants. The National Right to Life Committee, established in May 1973, provided an anti-abortion focus outside an explicitly Catholic approach to the issue. The anti-abortion position, however, tends to temporarily unite groups that otherwise would disagree with each other. Even within evangelical Protestantism, the traditionally liberal *Sojourners Magazine* has made statements that are anti-abortion *and* anti-New Right agenda.

The one national pro-choice religious group, the Religious Coalition for Abortion Rights, was formed shortly after the *Roe v. Wade* decision in an effort to maintain the rights won in that case. Among moderate or liberal religious groups, abortion tends rather to temporarily separate groups that otherwise would agree with each other. The Orthodox Church in America, the Greek Orthodox Archdiocese of North and South America, and other members of the National Council of Churches have taken strong stances against abortion, as opposed to many of the other member churches. By and large, the moderate and liberal religious groups tolerate much greater variety of opinion on abortion than do the others. Most religious groups that take an official pro-choice stand have minority lobby subgroups that offer a dissenting view. Religious groups that take an official anti-abortion stand do not have minority, pro-choice groups. The one exception to that is the Roman Catholic Church's Catholics for a Free Choice group, which was formed in 1970.

Some conservative religious groups have begun demonstrations at abortion clinics in an attempt to obstruct business and to witness to their conviction that the legality of abortion is an unjust law that deserves civil disobedience. Randall Terry, founder of Operation Rescue in Atlanta, Georgia, performed his first "rescue" in 1986 when he and six others locked themselves in an inner room of an abortion clinic, effectively shutting it down for the day. In 1988, more than 8000 persons were arrested in similar demonstrations around the U.S., and support for this group has come from well-known leaders such as Jerry Falwell. Sidewalk counselors have confronted women entering clinics to try to persuade them to make other choices. In 1982 protesters began bombing abortion clinics. By February 1985, 30 bombings had been reported, and the incidents have continued to the present. Most anti-abortion leaders condemn the violence but some suggest that such acts are similar to the unlawful civil rights protests of the 1960s that resulted in sweeping social change.

There are also racial overtones to some aspects of the anti-abortion movement, a recurrent part of positions on various sides of the birth control issue, as noted earlier. Jack Willke, who has been president of the National Right to Life Committee, the country's largest anti-abortion organization, has expressed concern that "western civilization is dying," noting that current population growth in the United States is due primarily to immigration and to longer life spans. The U.S. average of only 1.8 births per woman is not a replacement rate. "At current birth and immigration rates," Willke claims, "the indigenous Anglo race (white, European ancestry) in the U.S. will be a minority by the middle of the next century." If immigrants continue to have more babies, "the population could even grow, but the ethnic composition will be far different from today." Willke believes that the solution "would require a dramatic increase in the birth rate in the near future within our present population. There is no sign of this happening. Furthermore, the increase would have to happen soon if it is to replenish the indigenous population. If too many years pass before another 'baby boom,'... they would not be able to 'catch up.'"[14]

The Immediate Future

The Supreme Court had affirmed its stand on abortion by refusing to hear other cases that attempted to challenge the *Roe v. Wade* decision until *Webster v. Reproductive Health Services* came before it in 1989. By this time, appointments of conservative, anti-abortion justices by President Reagan shifted the balance of power on the abortion issue. The *Webster* case challenged a 1986 Missouri law specifying that "human life begins at conception," requiring doctors to test 20-week-old fetuses for viability, prohibiting abortions in public facilities, and barring public employees from "encouraging or counseling" a woman to have an abortion. The case energized both pro-choice and anti-abortion forces. The Court's July 3, 1989 decision upheld the Missouri law, and while it did not explicitly overturn *Roe v. Wade,* it did broaden the powers of the states to legislate the matter, thus weakening federal protection of the woman's right to end her pregnancy.

The Court has also agreed to hear additional challenges to *Roe v. Wade* in its forthcoming session, and further challenges to current abortion rights are expected. Decisions on several key cases could drastically alter the status of abortion in America.

Meanwhile, technology may be pressing the issue beyond its previous setting. There is now an abortion pill, RU486, that is used for about 15 percent of the elective abortions in France. The National Right to Life Committee has made it clear to corporate officials that boycotts would be the response to any attempt on their part to market the pill in the United States. It is difficult to know how the abortion conflict would manifest itself if safe, legal abortion were to become something women could go to any drug store for and perform in their own home.

The recent decision of the Supreme Court and the potential availability of an abortion pill have made it unlikely that the divisions over the topic will resolve themselves anytime soon. Studies continue to show that the issue derives its intensity not so much from differences in theology as from the very different social circumstances of the debaters. It is an issue intimately interrelated to deeply embedded views on sexual behavior, the care of children, family life, technology, the importance of the individual, women, men, etc. In our volatile, mobile society, there is always the possibility of major, rapid change, but there are also deep currents that this issue seems to touch, and these currents change their course much more slowly.

Where is the weight of religious opinion on abortion today? That is very nearly impossible to answer. One cannot simply add up the members of each group and then arrange them according to the official stance of the group's governing body. The statements of many groups are only representative and not binding on each member. A recent survey of Roman Catholics, for example, indicates that 79 percent favor abortion in case of rape, and 37 percent favor it in the case of a married woman who chooses to have no more children. Religious opinions reflect the opinions registered in general national surveys, which differ greatly, depending on how the question is asked. In March 1989, a *Los Angeles Times* poll reported that 74 percent of those questioned believed abortion was "morally wrong" but that the decision had "to be made by every woman for herself." Two weeks later a *Boston Globe* poll found "an overwhelming majority" opposed abortion in most circumstances. We remain a divided people.

Endnotes

1 Petchesky, p. 68

2 Mohr, p. 157

3 Gordon, Linda, p. 261

4 Mohr, p. 167

5 Tietze, pp. 8-17

6 Haller and Haller, pp. 133, 138

7 See Weeks, pp. 136, 192-193; and Petchesky, p. 93

8 Petchesky, p. 92

9 Kennedy, pp. 134, 135

10 Petchesky, p. 110

11 Petchesky, pp. 122, 123

12 Crawford, p. 36

13 The ideas of Paul Weyrich are quoted in Petchesky, p. 245

14 Willke, pp. 156-159

Selected Sources

Cott, Nancy F., and Elizabeth H. Pleck, eds. *A Heritage of Her Own: Toward a New Social History of American Women.* New York: Simon and Schuster, 1979.

Crawford, Alan. *Thunder on the Right: The "New Right" and the Politics of Resentment.* New York: Pantheon Books, 1980.

Fryer, Peter. *The Birth Controllers.* New York: Stein and Day, 1966.

Gardner, R. F. R. *Abortion: The Personal Dilemma.* Grand Rapids, MI: William B. Eerdmans, 1972.

Gordon, Linda. *Woman's Body, Woman's Right: A Social History of Birth Control in America.* New York: Grossman, 1976.

Gordon, Michael, ed. *The American Family in Social-Historical Perspective.* New York: St. Martin's Press, 1973.

Hall, Robert E. *Abortion in a Changing World.* New York: Columbia University Press, 1970.

Haller, John S., and Robin M. Haller. *The Physician and Sexuality in Victorian America.* New York: Norton, 1974.

Hardin, Garrett. "Abortion—Or Compulsory Pregnancy," *Journal of Marriage and the Family* 30 (May 1968), 246-251.

Kennedy, David M. *Birth Control in America: The Career of Margaret Sanger.* New Haven: Yale University Press, 1970.

Lader, Lawrence. *Abortion.* Indianapolis: Bobbs-Merrill, 1966.

Luker, Kristin. *Abortion and the Politics of Motherhood.* Los Angeles: University of California Press, 1984.

Mohr, James C. *Abortion in America: The Origins and Evolution of National Policy, 1800-1900.* New York: Oxford University Press, 1978.

Morgan, Robin, ed. *Sisterhood Is Powerful.* New York: Vintage, 1970.

Noonan, John T. *Contraception.* Cambridge, Massachusetts: Havard University Press, 1965.

Noonan, John T., ed. *The Morality of Abortion: Legal and Historical Perspectives.* Cambridge, Masschusetts: Harvard University Press, 1970.

Petchesky, Rosalind P. *Abortion and Woman's Choice: The State, Sexuality, and the Conditions of Reproductive Freedom.* New York: Longman, 1983.

Rothman, Barbara Katz. *Recreating Motherhood: Ideology and Technology in a Patriarchal Society.* New York: W. W. Norton ; 1989.

Tietze, Christopher. *Induced Abortion: A World Review,* 1981. 4th ed. New York: The Population Council, 1981.

Weeks, Jeffrey. *Sex, Politics and Society: The Regulation of Sexuality Since 1800.* London: Longman, 1981.

Westoff, Leslie A., and Charles F. Westoff. *From Now to Zero: Fertility, Contraception and Abortion in America.* Boston: Little, Brown & Co., 1968, 1971.

Willke, Dr. and Mrs. Jack C. *Abortion: Questions and Answers.* Rev. ed. Cincinnati, Ohio: Hayes Publishing Co., 1988.

Abortion

Roman Catholic Church

The Roman Catholic Church, which is the largest Christian church in the world, is headquartered in Vatican City. With more than 50,000,000 members in the United States, it is also the single largest religious body in North America. Its tremendous size, influence, and resources have both required and enabled it to make statements offering guidance upon many of the pressing issues of the world, including abortion. Its highly centralized, hierarchical structure has allowed these statements to be particularly powerful in their ability to speak on behalf of the whole church. In the United States, the National Conference of Catholic Bishops and the U.S. Catholic Conference are the policy-setting bodies, following the guidelines set by the Pope and other officials in the Vatican. Authoritative statements may come from the U.S. Catholic Bishops as a whole, from a committee, or from prominent officials, such as Cardinal Joseph Bernardin of Chicago.

The Pope has not spoken ex cathedra (infallibly) on the issue of abortion, yet the teaching on it is powerfully unified and has the impact of a doctrine that is not open to debate. However, in the United States and elsewhere, the teaching on abortion has created significant dissent, dissent which has reached the public at large. Because of the importance of the Roman Catholic Church's role in the abortion debate and because of the well-publicized dissenting positions within the church, this collection of documents contains the official statements of the hierarchy and other significant documents which follow this highly charged intra-church dialogue.

ROMAN CATHOLIC CHURCH— U.S. CATHOLIC CONFERENCE

EXPLOSION OR BACKFIRE? (1959)

1. For the past several years a campaign of propaganda has been gaining momentum to influence international, national, and personal opinion in favor of birth prevention programs. The vehicle for this propaganda is the recently coined terror technique phrase, "population explosion." The phrase, indeed, alerts all to the attention that must be given to population pressures, but it also provides a smoke screen behind which a moral evil may be foisted on the public and for obscuring the many factors that must be considered in this vital question.

2. More alarming is the present attempt of some representatives of Christian bodies who endeavor to elaborate the plan into a theological doctrine which envisages artificial birth prevention within the married state as the "will of God." Strangely too, simply

1

because of these efforts and with callous disregard of the thinking of hundreds of millions of Christians and others who reject the position, some international and national figures have made the statement that artificial birth prevention within the married state is gradually becoming acceptable even in the Catholic Church. This is simply not true.

3. The perennial teaching of the Catholic Church has distinguished artificial birth prevention, which is a frustration of the marital act, from other forms of control of birth which are morally permissible. Method alone, however, is not the only question involved. Equally important is the sincere and objective examination of the motives and intentions of the couples involved, in view of the nature of the marriage contract itself. As long as due recognition is not given to these fundamental questions, there can be no genuine understanding of the problem.

4. At the present time, too, there is abundant evidence of a systematic, concerted effort to convince United States public opinion, legislators, and policy makers that United States national agencies, as well as international bodies, should provide with public funds and support, assistance in promoting artificial birth prevention for economically underdeveloped countries. The alleged purpose, as already remarked, is to prevent a hypothetical "population explosion." Experts, however, have not yet reached agreement on the exact meaning of this phrase. It is still a hypothesis that must stand the test of science. Yet, pessimistic population predictors seizing on the popular acceptance of the phrase, take little account of economic, social, and cultural factors and changes. Moreover, it would seem that if the predictors of population explosion wish to avail themselves of the right to foretell *population increases,* they must concede the right to predict *production increases* of food as well as of employment and educational opportunities.

5. The position of United States Catholics to the growing and needy population of the world is a realistic one which is grounded in the natural law (which, it should be made clear, is not the law of the jungle, as sometimes erroneously supposed) and in respect for the human person, his origin, freedom, responsibility, and destiny. They believe that the goods of the earth were created by God for the use of all men and that men should not be arbitrarily tailored to fit a niggling and static image of what they are entitled to, as conceived by those who are more fortunate, greedy, or lazy. The thus far hidden reservoirs of science and of the earth unquestionably will be uncovered in this era of marvels and offered to humanity by dedicated persons with faith in mankind, and not by those seeking short cuts to comfort at the expense of the heritage of their own or other peoples.

6. United States Catholics believe that the promotion of artificial birth prevention is a morally, humanly, psychologically, and politically disastrous approach to the population problem. Not only is such an approach ineffective in its own aims, but it spurns the basis of the real solution, sustained effort in a sense of human solidarity. Catholics are prepared to dedicate themselves to this effort, already so promisingly initiated in national and international circles. They will not, however, support any public assistance, either at home or abroad, to promote artificial birth prevention, abortion, or sterilization whether through direct aid or by means of international organizations.

7. The fundamental reason for this position is the well-considered objection to promoting a moral evil—an objection not founded solely on any typically or exclusively Catholic doctrine, but on the natural law and on basic ethical considerations. However, quite apart from the moral issue, there are other cogent reasons why Catholics would not wish to see any official support or even favor given such specious methods of "assistance."

Social Development

8. Man himself is the most valuable productive agent. Therefore, economic development and progress are best promoted by *creating conditions* favorable to his *highest development*. Such progress implies discipline, self-control, and the disposition to postpone present satisfactions for future gains. The widespread use of contraceptives would hinder rather than promote the acquisition of these qualities needed for the social and economic changes in underdeveloped countries.

Immigration

9. Immigration and emigration—even within the same country—have their role to play in solving the population problem. It has been said that migration to other countries is no ultimate solution because of difficulties of absorbing populations into other economies. But it is a matter of record that migration has helped as a solution. Sixty million people migrated successfully from Europe to the Americas in the last one hundred fifty years. When the nomadic Indians roamed the uncultivated plains of North America before the coming of these immigrants, the entire country with its estimated Indian population of only 500,000 and its shortage of food, would have been regarded as "overpopulated" according to the norms of the exponents of Planned Parenthood. Yet, the same plains today are being retired into a "land bank" because they are overproductive in a land of 175 million. It is, therefore, apparent that to speak of a population explosion in the United States in these circumstances is the sheerest kind of nonsense.

Political and Psychological

10. The Soviets in their wooing of economically underdeveloped countries do not press artificial birth prevention propaganda on them as a remedy for their ills. Rather they allure them into the Communist orbit by offering education, loans, technical assistance, and trade, and they boast that their economic system is able to use human beings in constructive work and to meet all their needs. The Russian delegate to the relatively recent meeting of the United Nations Economic Commission on Asia and the Far East proclaimed, "The key to progress does not lie in a limitation of population through artificial reduction of the birthrate, but in the speedy defeat of the economic backwardness of these countries." The Communist record of contempt for the value of human life gives the lie to this hypocritical propaganda, but to peoples aspiring to economic development and political status, the deceit is not immediately evident. Confronted on the one hand by the prospect of achieving their goals without sacrificing natural fertility and on the other by the insistence that reducing natural fertility is essential to the achievement of such goals, how could these peoples be reasonably expected to reject Communism? Yet, the prophets of "population explosion" in alleging that contraception will thwart Communism naively emphasize its specious attractiveness in these areas.

Food and Agriculture

11. United States Catholics do not wish to ignore or minimize the problem of population pressure, but they do deplore the studious omission of adequate reference to the role of modern agriculture in food production. The "population explosion" alarmists do not place in proper focus the idea of increasing the acreage or the acreage yield to meet the food demands of an increasing population. By hysterical terrorism and bland misrepresentation of data they dismiss these ideas as requiring too much time for the development of extensive education and new distribution methods and for the elimination of apathy, greed, and superstition. Such arguments merely beg the question, for the implementation of their own program demands the fulfillment of the same conditions. It seems never to dawn on them that in a chronic condition where we

3

have more people than food, the logical answer would be, not to decrease the number of people but to increase the food supply which is almost unlimited in potential.

12. We make these observations to direct attention to the very real problem of population pressures. Such remarks are not intended to exhaust this complex subject, nor to discourage demographers, economists, agricultural experts, and political scientists in their endeavors to solve the problem. Rather, our intention is to reaffirm the position of the Catholic Church that the only true solutions are those that are morally acceptable under the natural law of God. Never should we allow the unilateral "guesstimates" of special pleaders to stampede or terrorize the United States into a national or international policy inimical to human dignity. For, the adoption of the morally objectionable means advocated to forestall the so-called "population explosion" may backfire on the human race.

Signed by members of the Administrative Board, National Catholic Welfare Conference, in the name of the bishops of the United States

Francis Cardinal Spellman, Archbishop of New York

James Francis Cardinal McIntyre, Archbishop of Los Angeles

John Cardinal O'Hara, C.S.C., Archbishop of Philadelphia

Richard Cardinal Cushing, Archbishop of Boston

Aloisius Muench, Cardinal Designate, Bishop of Fargo, North Dakota

Albert Meyer, Cardinal Designate, Archbishop of Chicago

Karl J. Alter, Archbishop of Cincinnati

William O. Brady, Archbishop of St. Paul

Patrick A. O'Boyle, Archbishop of Washington

Leo Binz, Archbishop of Dubuque

Emmet M. Walsh, Bishop of Youngstown

Joseph M. Gilmore, Bishop of Helena

Albert R. Zuroweste, Bishop of Belleville

Joseph T. McGucken, Bishop of Sacramento

Allen J. Babcock, Bishop of Grand Rapids

Lawrence J. Shehan, Bishop of Bridgeport

Notes: *This statement on birth control contained the first reference to abortion in the*

4

official positioning of the U.S. Catholic Conference. It foreshadowed the increasing interest in abortion that came in the 1960s, and illustrated the Catholic objection to abortion in the context that it artificially breaks the natural connection between sexual activity and pregnancy.

ROMAN CATHOLIC CHURCH—POPE PAUL VI

EXCERPT FROM "HUMANAE VITAE" (1968)

Illicit Ways of Regulating Birth

14. In conformity with these landmarks in the human and Christian vision of marriage, we must once again declare that the direct interruption of the generative process already begun, and, above all, directly willed and procured abortion, even if for therapeutic reasons, are to be absolutely excluded as licit means of regulating birth.[14]

Equally to be excluded, as the teaching authority of the Church has frequently declared, is direct sterilization, whether perpetual or temporary, whether of the man or of the woman.[15] Similarly excluded is every action which, either in anticipation of the conjugal act, or in its accomplishment, or in the development of its natural consequences, proposes, whether as an end or as a means, to render procreation impossible.[16]

To justify conjugal acts made intentionally infecund, one cannot invoke as valid reasons the lesser evil, or the fact that such acts would constitute a whole together with the fecund acts already performed or to follow later, and hence would share in one and the same moral goodness. In truth, if it is sometimes licit to tolerate a lesser evil in order to avoid a greater evil or to promote a greater good,[17] it is not licit, even for the gravest reasons, to do evil so that good may follow therefrom;[18] that is, to make into the object of a positive act of the will something which is intrinsically disorder, and hence unworthy of the human person, even when the intention is to safeguard or promote individual, family or social well-being. Consequently it is an error to think that a conjugal act which is deliberately made infecund and so is intrinsically dishonest could be made honest and right by the ensemble of a fecund conjugal life.

Licitness of Therapeutic Means

15. The Church, on the contrary, does not at all consider illicit the use of those therapeutic means truly necessary to cure diseases of the organism, even if an impediment to procreation, which may be foreseen, should result therefrom, provided such impediment is not, for whatever motive, directly willed.[19]

Licitness of Recourse to Infecund Periods

16. To this teaching of the Church on conjugal morals, the objection is made today, as we observed earlier that it is the prerogative of the human intellect to dominate the energies offered by irrational nature and to orientate them towards an end conformable to the good of man. Now some may ask: in the present case, is it not reasonable in many circumstances to have recourse to artificial birth control if, thereby, we secure the harmony and peace of the family, and better conditions for the education of the children already born? To this question it is necessary to reply with clarity: the Church is the first to praise and recommend the intervention of intelligence in a function which so closely associates the rational creature with his Creator; but she affirms that this must be done with respect for the order established by God.

If, then, there are serious motives to space out births, which derive from the physical or psychological conditions of husband and wife, or from external conditions, the Church teaches that it is then licit to take into account the natural rhythms immanent in the generative functions, for the use of marriage in the infecund periods only, and in this way to regulate birth without offending the moral principles which have been recalled earlier.[20]

The Church is coherent with herself when she considers recourse to the infecund periods to be licit, while at the same time condemning, as being always illicit, the use of means directly contrary to fecundation, even if such use is inspired by reasons which may appear honest and serious. In reality, there are essential differences between the two cases; in the former, the married couple make legitimate use of a natural disposition; in the latter, they impede the development of natural processes. It is true that, in the one and the other case, the married couple are concordant in the positive will of avoiding children for plausible reasons, seeking the certainty that offspring will not arrive; but it is also true that only in the former case are they able to renounce the use of marriage in the fecund periods when, for just motives, procreation is not desirable, while making use of it during infecund periods to manifest their affection and to safeguard their mutual fidelity. By so doing, they give proof of a truly and integrally honest love.

Endnotes

[14] Cf. *Catechismus Romanus Concilii Tridentini,* part II, ch. VIII; Pius XI, Encyc. *Casti Connubii:* AAS XXII (1930), 562-564; Pius XII, *Discorsi e Radiomessaggi* VI (1944), 191-192: AAS XLIII (1951), 842-843, 857-859; John XXIII, Encyc. *Pacem in Terris,* Apr. 11, 1963: AAS LV (1963), 259-260; *Gaudium et Spes,* no. 51.

[15] Cf. Pius XI, Encyc. *Casti Connubii:* AAS XXII (1930), 565; decree of the Holy Office, Feb. 22, 1940: AAS L (1958), 734-735.

[16] Cf. *Catechismus Romanus Concilii Tridentini,* part. II, ch. VIII; Pius XI, Encyc. *Casti Connubii:* AAS XXII (1930), 559-561; Pius XII: AAS XLIII (1951), 843, AAS L (1958), 734-735; John XXIII, Encyc. *Mater et Magistra:* AAS LIII (1961), 447.

[17] Cf. Pius XII, Alloc. to the National Congress of the Union of Catholic Jurists, Dec. 6, 1953: AAS XLV (1953). 798-799.

[18] Cf. Rom. 3:8.

[19] Cf. Pius XII, Alloc. to Congress of the Italian Association of Urology, Oct. 8, 1953: AAS XLV (1953), 674-675, AAS L (1958), 734-735.

[20] Cf. Pius XII: AAS XLIII (1951), 846.

Notes: *This statement is an excerpt from* Humanae Vitae *(meaning "human life"), which was Pope Paul VI's reaffirmation of the church's long-standing condemnation of the use of artificial means to prevent pregnancy and reiteration of the prohibition of abortion. Vatican II, which met in the early 1960s, spoke harshly of abortion and infanticide as "unspeakable crimes," but the generally liberal atmosphere of that council produced the anticipation among many that this statement would also be more liberal in the area of birth control. It was not, however, and since then, the American church in particular has encountered heavy opposition to the Pope's stance.*

ROMAN CATHOLIC CHURCH—
U.S. CATHOLIC CONFERENCE

ABORTION (1969)

April 17, 1969

1. In recent years there has been a growing concern for the dignity of human life. The crisis of conscience that has gripped the country over the war in Vietnam, the re-examination of the question of capital punishment, the ethical questions raised by newly developed

skills in the transplantation of vital organs are all indications that our people continue to place a high value on human life. Moreover, our society recognizes that it must increasingly guarantee the basic rights of every person, particularly of those who are least able to defend themselves.

2. At the same time, we face a widespread effort to "liberalize" the present laws that generally prohibit abortion. Initial efforts to liberalize these laws focused on specific problem situations—some of which have already become less problematical due to scientific discovery and advance. During the past year the emphasis has begun to change, and we are now facing a determined effort to repeal totally all abortion laws—thereby resulting in abortion-on-demand.

3. In previous statements on this question we have drawn upon our Judaeo-Christian heritage of concern for the person and have stressed the intrinsic value of human life—a value that bridges the gap between man's temporal existence and his eternal destiny.

4. In a pastoral letter on Human Life in Our Day (November, 1968) we urged that "society always be on the side of life," that "it never dictate, directly or indirectly, recourse to the prevention of life or to its destruction in any of its phases." Our concern is heightened by the awareness that one of the dangers of a technological society is a tendency to adopt a limited view of man, to see man only for what he does or produces, and to overlook the source of man's dignity, the fact that he is made in the image of God, and that from the moment of his conception he is worthy of the full support of the human family of which he is a member.

5. Consequently, we have frequently affirmed as our own the teaching of the Second Vatican Council, that "whatever is opposed to life itself, such as any type of murder, genocide, abortion, euthanasia or willful self-destruction, whatever violates the integrity of the human person . . . all these things and others of their like are infamies indeed. They poison human society but they do more harm to those who practice them than those who suffer from the injury. Moreover, they are a supreme dishonor to the Creator" (Pastoral Constitution on the Church in the Modern World, n. 27). At the same time, we have emphasized that society has an obligation to safeguard the life of every person from the very beginning of that life, and to perfect a legal-political system that assures protection to the individual and the well-being of the community.

6. We restate with strong conviction and growing concern our opposition to abortion. In so doing, we do not urge one ethical conviction as the sole basis of public policy, but we articulate the concerns that are also held by persons of other faiths and by specialists in the field of medicine, law and the social sciences.

7. Fully aware of problem situations that may exist at times, such as illegitimacy, great emotional stress, possible disadvantage for the child after birth, we find no evidence that easy abortion laws will solve these problems. In fact, the termination of life in these particular situations violates our whole legal heritage, one that has always protected the right to life. Moreover, it allows for an extension of the principle that may well endanger the lives of persons who are senile, incurably ill, or unable fully to exercise all their faculties.

8. We strongly urge a renewed positive attitude toward life and a new commitment to its protection and support. We affirm our social responsibility, together with all society, to bring encouragement, understanding and support to the victims of rape, to intensify our scientific investigation into the causes and cures of maternal disease and fetal abnormality, and to provide to all women adequate education and material sustenance to choose motherhood responsibly and freely in accord with our basic commitment to the sanctity of life.

9. We are certain that respect for human dignity and the reverence for human life are such widely shared values in our society that the discussion by lawyers, doctors, ethicians,

social scientists and all concerned citizens of ethical questions like abortion will lead to a deeper understanding of the eminent value and inviolability of human life.

Notes: *This is the first full statement by the U.S. Catholic Conference on the subject of abortion. The assurances that they would pay attention to the need to protect individual rights and the avoidance of urging "one ethical conviction as the sole basis of public policy," illustrate some of the sensitive areas the Catholic bishops have had to deal with in America.*

ROMAN CATHOLIC CHURCH— U.S. CATHOLIC CONFERENCE

PASTORAL PLAN FOR PRO-LIFE ACTIVITIES (1975)

All should be persuaded that human life and the task of transmitting it are not realities bound up with this world alone. Hence they cannot be measured or perceived only in terms of it, but always have a bearing on the eternal destiny of men. . . . For God, the Lord of life, has conferred on men the surpassing ministry of safeguarding life in a manner which is worthy of man. Therefore from the moment of its conception, life must be guarded with the greatest care, while abortion and infanticide are unspeakable crimes.

Constitution on the Church in the Modern World

1. Respect for human life has been gradually declining in our society during the past decade. To some degree this reflects a secularizing trend and a rejection of moral imperatives based on belief in God and His plan for creation. It also reflects a tendency for individuals to give primary attention to what is personally rewarding and satisfying to them, to the exclusion of responsible concern for the well-being of other persons and society. These trends, along with others, have resulted in laws and judicial decisions which deny or ignore basic human rights and moral responsibilities for the protection and promotion of the common good. In this category are efforts to establish permissive abortion laws, the abortion decisions of the United States Supreme Court in 1973 denying any effective legal protection to the unborn child, and the growing attempts to legitimatize positive euthanasia through so-called "death with dignity" laws.

2. In the Declaration of Independence, our Founding Fathers point to the right to life as the first of the inalienable rights given by the Creator.

3. In fulfillment of our pastoral responsibilities, the members of the National Conference of Catholic Bishops have repeatedly affirmed that human life is a precious gift from God; that each person who receives this gift has responsibilities toward God, toward self, and toward others; and that society, through its laws and social institutions, must protect and sustain human life at every stage of its existence. Recognition of the dignity of the human person, made in the image of God, lies at the very heart of our individual and social duty to respect human life.

4. In this Pastoral Plan we hope to focus attention on the pervasive threat to human life arising from the present situation of permissive abortion. Basic human rights are violated in many ways: by abortion and euthanasia, by injustice and the denial of equality to certain groups of persons, by some forms of human experimentation, by neglect of the underprivileged and disadvantaged who deserve the concern and support of the entire society. Indeed, the denial of the God-given right to life is one aspect of a larger problem. But it is unlikely that efforts to protect other rights will be ultimately successful if life itself is continually diminished in value.

5. In focusing attention on the sanctity of human life, therefore, we hope to generate a greater respect for the life of each person in our society. We are confident that greater

respect for human life will result from continuing the public discussion of abortion and from efforts to shape our laws so as to protect the life of all persons, including the unborn.

6. Thus this Pastoral Plan seeks to activate the pastoral resources of the Church in three major efforts:

   1. an educational/public information effort to inform, clarify, and deepen understanding of the basic issues;

   2. a pastoral effort addressed to the specific needs of women with problems related to pregnancy and to those who have had or have taken part in an abortion;

   3. a public policy effort directed toward the legislative, judicial, and administrative areas so as to insure effective legal protection for the right to life.

7. This Pastoral Plan is addressed to and calls upon all Church-sponsored or identifiably Catholic national, regional, diocesan, and parochial organizations and agencies to pursue the three-fold effort. This includes ongoing dialogue and cooperation between the NCCB/USCC on the one hand, and priests, religious, and lay persons, individually and collectively, on the other hand. In a special way, we invite the continued cooperation of national Catholic organizations.

8. At the same time, we urge Catholics in various professional fields to discuss these issues with their colleagues and to carry the dialogue into their own professional organizations. In similar fashion, we urge those in research and academic life to present the Church's position on a wide range of topics that visibly express her commitment to respect for life at every stage and in every condition. Society's responsibility to insure and protect human rights demands that the right to life be recognized and protected as antecedent to and the condition of all other rights.

9. Dialogue is most important—and has already proven highly fruitful—among churches and religious groups. Efforts should continue at ecumenical consultation and dialogue with Judaism and other Christian bodies, and also with those who have no specific ecclesial allegiance. Dialogue among scholars in the field of ethics is a most important part of this interfaith effort.

10. The most effective structures for pastoral action are in the diocese and the parish. While recognizing the roles of national, regional, and statewide groupings, this Plan places its primary emphasis on the roles of diocesan organizations and the parish community. Thus, the resources of the diocese and parish become most important in its implementation.

I. Public Information/Education Program

11. In order to deepen a respect for human life and heighten public opposition to permissive abortion, a two-fold educational effort presenting the case for the sanctity of life from conception onwards is required.

12. The first aspect, a public information effort, is directed to the general public. It creates awareness of the threats to human dignity inherent in a permissive abortion policy, and the need to correct the present situation by establishing legal safeguards for the right to life. It gives the abortion issue continued visibility, and sensitizes the many people who have only general perceptions of the issue but very little by way of firm conviction or commitment. The public information effort is important to inform the public discussion, and it proves that the Church is serious about and commited to its announced long-range pro-life effort. It is accomplished in a variety of ways, such as accurate reporting of newsworthy events, the issuance of public statements, testimony on legislative issues, letters to editors.

13. The second aspect, an intensive long-range education effort, leads people to a clearer

understanding of the issues, to firm conviction, and to commitment. It is part of the Church's essential responsibility that it carry forward such an effort, directed primarily to the Catholic community. Recognizing the value of legal, medical, and sociological arguments, the primary and ultimately most compelling arguments must be theological and moral. Respect for life must be seen in the context of God's love for mankind, reflected in creation and redemption, and man's relationship to God and to other members of the human family. The Church's opposition to abortion is based on Christian teaching on the dignity of the human person, and the responsibility to proclaim and defend basic human rights, especially the right to life.

14. This intensive education effort should present the scientific information on the humanity of the unborn child and the continuity of human growth and development throughout the months of fetal existence; the responsibility and necessity for society to safeguard the life of the child at every stage of its existence; the problems that may exist for women during pregnancy; and more humane and morally acceptable solutions to these problems.

15. The more intensive educational effort should be carried on by all who participate in the Church's educational ministry, notably:

    a. Priests and religious, exercising their teaching responsibility in the pulpit, in other teaching assignments, and through parish programs.

    b. All Church-sponsored or identifiably Catholic organizations, national, regional, diocesan, and parochial, carrying on continuing education efforts that emphasize the moral prohibition of abortion and the reasons for carrying this teaching into the public policy area.

    c. Schools, CCD, and other Church-sponsored educational agencies providing moral teaching, bolstered by medical, legal, and sociological data, in the schools, etc. The USCC Department of Education might serve as a catalyst and resource for the dioceses.

    d. Church-related social service and health agencies carrying on continuing education efforts through seminars and other appropriate programs, and by publicizing programs and services offering alternatives to abortion.

16. Although the primary purpose of the intensive educational program is the development of pro-life attitudes and the determined avoidance of abortion by each person, the program must extend to other issues that involve support of human life: there must be internal consistency in the pro-life commitment.

17. The annual Respect Life Program sets the abortion problem in the context of other issues where human life is endangered or neglected, such as the problems facing the family, youth, the aging, the mentally retarded, as well as specific issues such as poverty, war, population control, and euthanasia. This program is helpful to parishes in calling attention to specific problems and providing program formats and resources.

II. Pastoral Care

18. The Church's pastoral effort is rooted in and manifests her faith commitment. Underlying every part of our program is the need for prayer and sacrifice. In building the house of respect for life, we labor in vain without God's merciful help.

19. Three facets of the Church's program of pastoral care deserve particular attention.

20. 1) *Moral Guidance and Motivation.* Accurate information regarding the nature of an act and freedom from coercion are necessary in order to make responsible moral decisions. Choosing what is morally good also requires motivation. The Church has a unique responsibility to transmit the teaching of Christ and to provide moral principles consistent with that teaching. In regard to abortion, the Church should provide accurate information regarding the nature of the act, its effects and far-reaching consequences, and should show that abortion is a violation of God's laws of charity and justice. In

many instances, the decision to do what is in conformity with God's law will be the ultimate determinant of the moral choice.

21. 2) *Service and Care for Women and Unborn Children.* Respect for human life motivates individuals and groups to reach out to those with special needs. Programs of service and care should be available to provide women with alternate options to abortion. Specifically, these programs should include:

   a. adequate education and material sustenance for women so that they may choose motherhood responsibly and freely in accord with a basic commitment to the sanctity of life;

   b. Nutritional, pre-natal, childbirth, and post-natal care for the mother, and nutritional and pediatric care for the child throughout the first year of life;

   c. intensified scientific investigation into the causes and cures of maternal disease and/or fetal abnormality;

   d. continued development of genetic counseling and gene therapy centers and neo-natal intensive care facilities;

   e. extension of adoption and foster care facilities to those who need them;

   f. pregnancy counseling centers that provide advice, encouragement, and support for every woman who faces difficulties related to pregnancy;

   g. counseling services and opportunities for continuation of education for unwed mothers;

   h. special understanding, encouragement, and support for victims of rape;

   i. continued efforts to remove the social stigma that is visited on the woman who is pregnant out of wedlock and on her child.

22. Many of these services have been and will continue to be provided by Church-sponsored health care and social service agencies, involving the dedicated efforts of professionals and volunteers. Cooperation with other private agencies and increased support in the quest for government assistance in many of these areas are further extensions of the long-range effort.

23. 3) *Reconciliation.* The Church is both a means and an agent of reconciliation. As a spiritual entity, the Church reconciles men and women to God. As a human community, the Church pursues the task of reconciling men and women with one another and with the entire community. Thus all of the faithful have the duty of promoting reconciliation.

24. Sacramentally, the Church reconciles the sinner through the sacrament of Penance, thereby restoring the individual to full sacramental participation. The work of reconciliation is also continually accomplished in celebrating and participating in the Eucharist. Finally, the effects of the Church's reconciling efforts are found in the full support of the Christian community and the renewal of Christian life that results from prayer, the pursuit of virtue, and continued sacramental participation.

25. Granting that the grave sin of abortion is symptomatic of many human problems, which often remain unsolved for the individual woman, it is important that we realize that God's mercy is always available and without limit, that the Christian life can be restored and renewed through the sacraments, and that union with God can be accomplished despite the problems of human existence.

III. Legislative/Public Policy Effort

26. In recent years there has been a growing realization throughout the world that protecting and promoting the inviolable rights of persons are essential duties of civil authority, and that the maintenance and protection of human rights are primary

purposes of law. As Americans, and as religious leaders, we have been committed to governance by a system of law that protects the rights of individuals and maintains the common good. As our founding fathers believed, we hold that all law is ultimately based on Divine Law, and that a just system of law cannot be in conflict with the law of God.

27. Abortion is a specific issue that highlights the relationship between morality and law. As a human mechanism, law may not be able fully to articulate the moral imperative, but neither can legal philosophy ignore the moral order. The abortion decisions of the United States Supreme Court (January 22, 1973) violate the moral order, and have disrupted the legal process which previously attempted to safeguard the rights of unborn children. A comprehensive pro-life legislative program must therefore include the following elements:

   a. Passage of a constitutional amendment providing protection for the unborn child to the maximum degree possible.

   b. Passage of federal and state laws and adoption of administrative policies that will restrict the practice of abortion as much as possible.

   c. Continual research into and refinement and precise interpretation of *Roe* and *Doe* and subsequent court decisions.

   d. Support for legislation that provides alternatives to abortion.

28. Accomplishment of this aspect of this Pastoral Plan will undoubtedly require well-planned and coordinated political action by citizens at the national, state, and local levels. This activity is not simply the responsibility of Catholics, nor should it be limited to Catholic groups or agencies. It calls for widespread cooperation and collaboration. As citizens of this democracy, we encourage the appropriate political action to achieve these legislative goals. As leaders of a religious institution in this society, we see a moral imperative for such political activity.

Means of Implementation of Program

29. The challenge to restore respect for human life in our society is a task of the Church that reaches out through all institutions, agencies, and organizations. Diverse tasks and various goals are to be achieved. The following represents a systematic organization and allocation of the Church's resources of people, institutions, and finances which can be activated at various levels to restore respect for human life and insure protection of the right to life of the unborn.

1. State Coordinating Committee

30. A. It is assumed that overall coordination in each state will be the responsibility of the State Catholic Conference or its equivalent. Where a State Catholic Conference is in process of formation or does not exist, bishops' representatives from each diocese might be appointed as the core members of the State Coordinating Committee.

31. B. The State Coordinating Committee will comprise the director of the State Catholic Conference and the diocesan pro-life coordinators. At this level, it would be valuable to have one or more persons who are knowledgeable about public traditions, mores, and attitudes and are experienced in legislative activity. This might be the public affairs specialist referred to under the Diocesan Pro-Life Committee, or, e.g., an individual with prior professional experience in legislative or governmental service. In any case, it should be someone with a practical understanding of contemporary political techniques.

32. C. The primary purposes of the State Coordinating Committee are:

   a. to monitor the political trends in the state and their implications for the abortion effort:

b. to coordinate the efforts of the various dioceses; and to evaluate progress in the dioceses and congressional districts;

c. to provide counsel regarding the specific political relationships within the various parties at the state level.

2. The Diocesan Pro-life Committee

33. a) *General Purpose*

The purpose of the committee is to coordinate groups and activities within the diocese (to restore respect for human life), particularly efforts to effect passage of a constitutional amendment to protect the unborn child. In its coordinating role, the committee will rely on information and direction from the Bishops' Pro-life Office and the National Committee for a Human Life Amendment. The committee will act through the Diocesan Pro-life Director, who is appointed by the bishop to direct pro-life efforts in the diocese.

34. b) *Membership*

1. Diocesan Pro-life Director (bishop's representative)

2. Respect Life Coordinator

3. Liaison with State Catholic Conference

4. Public Affairs Advisor

5. Representatives of Diocesan Agencies (priests, religious, lay organizations)

6. Legal Advisor—representative of pro-life groups

7. Representatives of Parish Pro-life Committees

8. Congressional District Representative(s)

35. c) *Objectives*

1. Provide direction and coordination of diocesan and parish education/information efforts and maintain working relationship with all groups involved in congressional district activity.

2. Promote and assist in the development of those groups, particularly voluntary groups involved in pregnancy counseling, which provide alternatives and assistance to women who have problems related to pregnancy.

3. Encourage the development of "grassroots" political action organizations.

4. Maintain communications with National Committee for a Human Life Amendment in regard to federal activity, so as to provide instantaneous information concerning local senators and representatives.

5. Maintain a local public information effort directed to press and media. Include vigilance in regard to public media, seek "equal time," etc.

6. Develop close relationships with each senator or representative.

3. The Parish Pro-life Committee

36. The Parish Pro-life Committee should include a delegate from the Parish Council, representatives of various adult and youth parish organizations, members of local Knights of Columbus Councils, Catholic Daughters of America Chapters, and other similar organizations.

Objectives

37. (a) Sponsor and conduct intensive education programs touching all groups within the parish, including schools and religious education efforts.

38. (b) Promote and sponsor pregnancy counseling units and other alternatives to abortion.

39. (c) Through ongoing public information programs, generate public awareness of the continuing effort to obtain a constitutional amendment. The NCCB, the National Committee for a Human Life Amendment, and the State and Diocesan Coordinating Committees should have access to every congressional district for information, consultation, and coordination of action. A chairperson should be designated in each district who will coordinate the efforts of parish pro-life groups, K of C groups, etc., and seek ways of cooperating with nonsectarian pro-life groups, including right-to-life organizations. In each district, the parishes will provide one basic resource, and the clergy will have an active role in the overall effort.

40. (d) Prudently convince others—Catholics and non-Catholics—of the reasons for the necessity of a constitutional amendment to provide a base for legal protection for the unborn.

4. The Pro-life Effort in the Congressional District

41. Passage of a consitutional amendment depends ultimately on persuading members of Congress to vote in favor of such a proposal. This effort at persuasion is part of the democratic process, and is carried on most effectively in the congressional district or state from which the representative is elected. Essentially, this effort demands ongoing public information activity and careful and detailed organization. Thus it is absolutely necessary to encourage the development in each congressional district of an identifiable, tightly-knit, and well-organized pro-life unit. This unit can be described as a public interest group or a citizen's lobby. No matter what it is called:

    a. its task is essentially political, that is, to *organize people* to help persuade the elected representatives; and

    b. its range of action is limited, that is, it is focused on passing a constitutional amendment.

42. As such, the congressional district pro-life group differs from the diocesan, regional, or parish pro-life coordinator or committee, whose task is pedagogic and motivational, not simply political, and whose range of action includes a variety of efforts calculated to reverse the present atmosphere of permissiveness with respect to abortion. Moreover, it is an agency of citizens, operated, controlled, and financed by these same citizens. *It is not an agency of the Church, nor is it operated, controlled, or financed by the Church.*

43. The congressional district pro-life action group should be bipartisan, nonsectarian, inclined toward political action. It is complementary to denominational efforts, to professional groups, to pregnancy counseling and assistance groups.

44. Each congressional district should have a chairperson who may serve as liaison with the Diocesan Coordinating Committee. In dioceses with many congressional districts, this may be arranged through a regional representation structure.

5. Objectives of the Congressional District Pro-life Group

45. (1) To conduct a continuing public information effort to persuade all elected officials and potential candidates that abortion must be legally restricted.

46. (2) To counterbalance propaganda efforts opposed to a constitutional amendment.

47. (3) To persuade all residents in the congressional district that permissive abortion is harmful to society and that some restriction is necessary.

48. (4) To persuade all residents that a constitutional amendment is necessary as a first step toward legally restricting abortion.

49. (5) To convince all elected officials and potential candidates that "the abortion issue"

will not go away and that their position on it will be subject to continuing public scrutiny.

50. (6) To enlist sympathetic supporters who will collaborate in persuading others.

51. (7) To enlist those who are generally supportive so that they may be called upon when needed to communicate to the elected officials.

52. (8) To elect members of their own group or active sympathizers to specific posts in all local party organizations.

53. (9) To set up a telephone network that will enable the committee to take immediate action when necessary.

54. (10) To maintain an informational file on the pro-life position of every elected official and potential candidate.

55. (11) To work for qualified candidates who will vote for a constitutional amendment, and other pro-life issues.

56. (12) To maintain liaison with all denominational leaders (pastors) and all other pro-life groups in the district.

57. This type of activity can be generated and coordinated by a small, dedicated, and politically alert group. It will need some financial support, but its greatest need is the commitment of other groups who realize the importance of its purposes, its potential for achieving those purposes, and the absolute necessity of working with the group to attain the desired goals.

Conclusion

58. The challenges facing American society as a result of the legislative and judicial endorsement of permissive abortion are enormous. But the Church and the individual Catholics must not avoid the challenge. Although the process of restoring respect for human life at every stage of existence may be demanding and prolonged, it is an effort which both requires and merits courage, patience, and determination. In every age the Church has faced unique challenges calling forth faith and courage. In our time and society, restoring respect for human life and establishing a system of justice which protects the most basic human rights are both a challenge and an opportunity whereby the Church proclaims her commitment to Christ's teaching on human dignity and the sanctity of the human person.

Notes: *This pastoral plan was a response to the Supreme Court's 1973 decision in Roe v. Wade. It attempted to organize the church's resources, to raise individual awareness, and to influence public policy toward a reversal of the decision. The plan also endorsed passage of a constitutional amendment to protect the rights of the unborn. In 1985, this pastoral plan was reaffirmed and expanded in the statement "Pastoral Plan for Pro-Life Activities: A Reaffirmation."*

ROMAN CATHOLIC CHURCH— CATHOLICS FOR A FREE CHOICE

A CATHOLIC STATEMENT ON PLURALISM AND ABORTION (1984)

A Diversity of Opinions Regarding Abortion Exists Among Committed Catholics.

Continued confusion and polarization within the Catholic community on the subject of abortion prompt us to issue this statement.

Statements of recent Popes and of the Catholic hierarchy have condemned the direct termination of pre-natal life as morally wrong in all instances. There is the mistaken belief in American society that this is the only legitimate Catholic position. In fact, a diversity of opinions regarding abortion exists among committed Catholics:

- A large number of Catholic theologians hold that even direct abortion, though tragic, can sometimes be a moral choice.

- According to data compiled by the National Opinion Research Center, only 11% of Catholics surveyed disapprove of abortion in all circumstances.

These opinions have been formed by:

- Familiarity with the actual experiences that lead women to make a decision for abortion;

- A recognition that there is no common and constant teaching on ensoulment in Church doctrine, nor has abortion always been treated as murder in canonical history;

- An adherence to principles of moral theology, such as probabilism, religious liberty, and the centrality of informed conscience; and

- An awareness of the acceptance of abortion as a moral choice by official statements and respected theologians of other faith groups.

Therefore, it is necessary that the Catholic community encourage candid and respectful discussion on this diversity of opinion within the Church, and that Catholic youth and families be educated on the complexity of the issues of responsible sexuality and human reproduction.

Further, Catholics—especially priests, religious, theologians, and legislators—who publicly dissent from hierarchical statements and explore areas of moral and legal freedom on the abortion question should not be penalized by their religious superiors, church employers, or bishops.

Finally, while recognizing and supporting the legitimate role of the hierarchy in providing Catholics with moral guidance on political and social issues and in seeking legislative remedies to social injustices, we believe that Catholics should not seek the kind of legislation that curtails the legitimate exercise of the freedom of religion and conscience or discriminates against poor women.

In the belief that responsible moral decisions can only be made in an atmosphere of freedom from fear or coercion, we, the undersigned, call upon all Catholics to affirm this statement.

Notes: *This full page ad in the* New York Times *was signed by dozens of prominent Catholics, including 27 priests and nuns. It brought to full public awareness the controversy growing within the Roman Catholic Church on its strict stand against abortion. This sort of advertised dissent from organized loyal opposition within the Catholic church was an unprecedented move. The ad appeared in the closing weeks of the presidential election campaign of 1984, in which abortion was a prominent issue.*

ROMAN CATHOLIC CHURCH—
U.S. CATHOLIC CONFERENCE

STATEMENT ON ABORTION (1985)

In both our private and our civic roles, all of us frequently face the questions, Whose side am I on? With whom do I take my stand?

These questions can be painful for anyone, but especially for a Christian. Following Christ obliges us to defend the weak, the voiceless, those who suffer injustice. Following Christ obliges us to do so out of love, not out of a desire for conflict. Following Christ even obliges us to love those whose actions we oppose, ready always to forgive as God forgives us. To "hate the sin but love the sinner" is essential to Christian life.

The church seeks to respond to these imperatives whenever it addresses issues which involve threats to human life and dignity. Called to defend the innocent against attack in war or violent crime, we also ask that even the attackers be treated justly, without hatred or a thirst for vengeance. Committed to a preferential option for the poor, we urge justice for the victims of economic injustice, but we reject violence between social classes while calling upon those who have more to share with those who have little.

Nowhere is this combination of justice and charity more necessary than in dealing with the national tragedy of abortion.

The church has always rejected abortion as a grave moral evil. It has always seen that the child's helplessness, both before and after birth, far from diminishing his or her right to life, increases our moral obligation to respect and to protect that right.

The church also realizes that a society which tolerates the direct destruction of innocent life, as in the current practice of abortion, is in danger of losing its respect for life in all other contexts. It likewise knows that protecting unborn human life will ultimately benefit all human life, not only the lives of the unborn.

Some misunderstand or deliberately distort this concern for the unborn. They say that the abortion controversy requires one to choose between the rights of women and the rights of the unborn. To stand in solidarity with the innocent victim of abortion, they say, pits one against not only abortion but women's rights and dignity.

This is a misunderstanding of the Christian message. Christian love extends to all God's children without limit or exception. It does not mean choosing one over the other, but loving all and treating all with respect.

We therefore stand with the child who has no voice of his or her own, and we also stand with the woman facing problems in pregnancy, doing all we can to provide her with effective, morally acceptable assistance. Mourning with those who have been involved in abortion, we extend to them God's healing forgiveness. Opposing those who seek to justify the destruction of the unborn, we wish at the same time to serve them by helping them see that what they advocate expresses not liberation but a failure of love.

Much has been made lately of statements by persons who, emphasizing that they are Catholics, assert that they are not bound by what the church says about abortion. In reply, we wish to make a very simple point: The church's teaching in this matter is binding not only because the church says so, but because this teaching expresses the objective demands placed on all of us by the inherent dignity of human life. A Catholic who chooses to dissent from this teaching, or to support dissent from it, is dissenting not only from church law but from a higher law which the church seeks to observe and teach. Such dissent can in no way be seen as legitimate alternative teaching.

Through the Respect Life Program, which begins on the first Sunday of October, the church recommits itself at every level to the Christian message of unconditional love for all human beings. This program addresses a broad range of issues involving the sanctity and dignity of human life, while giving special attention to the current situation of virtually unrestricted abortion. It provides resources and suggests programs to enable parishes, schools and church-related organizations to contribute to the church's long-range effort. We urge all Catholics to participate in this effort by finding out how they can help make the Respect Life Program a success in their area.

Respect for life requires us to speak a firm no to all that threatens or diminishes life both before and after birth. We must say no unequivocally to abortion, to euthanasia, to nuclear war, to degrading poverty and to many other violations of human dignity. But these noes express the church's positive attitude of love for all human life as a precious gift of the Creator. Every Catholic has the awesome responsibility of understanding this message more clearly and communicating it to others, so that all God's children may have life and have it more abundantly.

Notes: *This statement, issued in conjunction with the annual Respect Life Sunday event, was a response to an advertisement in the* New York Times *almost a year earlier and to the discussion the advertisement had engendered. The chair of this committee was Cardinal Joseph Bernardin, who displayed part of his "consistent ethic" belief urging a consistent regard for life, not just with abortion, but in the areas of war, poverty, and euthanasia. The statement asserted that dissent on the issue of abortion was not legitimate within the church.*

ROMAN CATHOLIC CHURCH—
COMMITTEE OF CONCERNED CATHOLICS

DECLARATION OF SOLIDARITY (1986)

We Affirm Our Solidarity with All Catholics Whose Right to Free Speech Is Under Attack.

On October 7, 1984 at the height of the 1984 presidential campaign, an advertisement containing the "Catholic Statement on Pluralism and Abortion" appeared in the *New York Times*.

Ninety-seven leading Catholic scholars, religious and social activists signed the Statement. Since that time, many of the 97 signers and their families have been penalized by segments of the institutional Roman Catholic Church.

- Members of religious communities have been threatened with possible dismissal from their orders if they do not retract.

- Academics have been denied the right to teach or lecture at Catholic colleges and institutes.

- Social activists have been disinvited from participation in programs on issues of peace and justice.

- Signers and their families have been harassed in their workplaces.

Such reprisals consciously or unconsciously have a chilling effect on the right to responsible dissent within the church; on academic freedom in Catholic colleges and universities; and on the right to free speech and participation in the U.S. political process.

Such reprisals cannot be condoned or tolerated in church or society.

We believe that Catholics who, in good conscience, take positions on the difficult questions of legal abortion and other controversial issues that differ from the official hierarchical positions act within their rights and responsibilities as Catholics and citizens.

We, as Roman Catholics, affirm our solidarity with those who signed the Statement and agree to stand with all who face reprisals. "The ties which unite the faithful are stronger than those which separate them. Let there be unity in what is necessary, freedom in what is doubtful and charity in everything." (Second Vatican Council, Church in the Modern World: 92)

Notes: *This second* New York Times *ad, this time by a different group expressing solidarity with the dissenting views held by Catholics for a Free Choice, further revealed the lack of unity within the Roman Catholic Church on the abortion issue. It also showed how that controversy was also raising the related issues of intellectual/moral freedom, which had a part of the broader abortion discussion.*

ROMAN CATHOLIC CHURCH—
SISTERS PATRICIA HUSSEY AND BARBARA FERRARO

STATEMENT ON ABORTION (1986)

In September 1984 we signed the Catholic Statement on Pluralism and Abortion which was published in the New York Times on Oct. 7, 1984. Since that time we have been engaged in discussions and negotiations with our general government group in an attempt to respond to the demand of the Vatican Congregation for Religious and Secular Institutes that we retract our signatures from the statement on pluralism and abortion or face dismissal from the Sisters of Notre Dame.

On March 22, 1986, for the first time we met representatives of the Congregation for Religious and Secular Institutes in the persons of Archbishop Vincenzo Fagiolo and Sister Mary Linscott. The meeting was described to us as a "pastoral," not a juridical or canonical visit. During that meeting Fagiolo clearly told us that no one could be or remain in religious life if they dissented from the hierarchical magisterium's teaching on abortion. In addition, we were told that the resolution of our case required that we declare our adherence to that teaching.

One formulation suggested to us was that attested to by the Sisters of Loretto on the preceding day. Because this demand in content and in process is in our opinion inappropriate within the Catholic community and does not reflect the truth as we know it, we are compelled to make the following statements.

We believe that the Vatican in characterizing the New York Times ad as a pro-abortion statement has deliberately chosen to misconstrue it.

1. The ad spoke of a diversity of opinions on abortion among committed Catholics and called for dialogue.

   We regret that the official church has taken part in repressing open discussion within the church and demanding obedience to authoritative rule without allowing legitimate dissent.

   We believe that dialogue is essential for the very life of the church. If we are serious about the search for truth, this can only happen when true dialogue occurs. Dialogue needs to happen in an atmosphere free of fear and coercion.

2. The statement alluded to legitimate Catholic positions on abortion other than that held by the hierarchy.

   We regret that the male, celibate church is ignoring and trivializing the experiences of women. We regret that the official church cannot deal with women as full persons and moral agents in our own right. We regret that the official church is neutralizing and negating the serious reflections of Catholic theologians and theologians in other faith traditions on the issue of reproductive rights.

   We regret that the official church is continually repressing dissenting voices and seems to be acknowledging only the view of the religious right within Catholicism.

   We believe that women are to be affirmed in their reproductive decisions on the basis of individual conscience and personal religious freedom.

   We believe that by the official church's inability to deal with birth control that in practice it promotes the high abortion rate it claims to abhor.

   We believe that Catholic theological reflections and ecumenical exchange on the most conflictual subjects including reproductive rights are essential for the life of the church.

   We continue to believe that there are other legitimate positions on abortion that are theologically and ethically defensible within the framework of Catholic tradition.

Theological inquiry and ecumenical exchange even on the most difficult issues are essential for the life of the church.

We believe that dissent on all controversial issues, including reproductive rights, is essential for the life of the church. We believe that dissent falls within the rights and responsibilities of all Roman Catholics. The official church has a responsibility to foster a climate in which faithful dissent is incorporated into the ongoing life of the community.

3. The statement said that those who publicly dissent from hierarchical statements and explore areas of legal and moral freedom on the abortion question should not be penalized by their religious superiors, church employers or bishops.

We regret that the official church is prepared to and has used force, threats and violence to obtain submission. We regret that the official church, which speaks of religious liberty, freedom to dissent, equality of persons before the law in society, fails to apply these same human rights to the church itself.

We believe that the integrity of legitimate church authority has been threatened. We believe that the hierarchy has given scandal by: their disruption of and intervention in women's religious communities; extracting what amounts to loyalty oaths; attempting to compromise the integrity of many religious signers; and deliberately misinterpreting and miscommunicating nun-signers' statements to the public.

We are also concerned by the punitive actions taken against many lay signers affecting their economic livelihood and academic freedom.

The cornerstone of the Catholic tradition is the search for truth. Unfortunately, the actions of the official church thwart that goal and are totally contrary to our "vision of church as a discipleship of equals."

Our statements come as a result of both reflection and challenges from: the experiences of women we have known and worked with; the Scriptures and our studies of theology and the history of the Roman Catholic Church. They are also the result of 19 years of Pat's experiences and 24 years of Barbara's experiences as members of the Sisters of Notre Dame.

We stand with those in the church who believe in all women's rights to make moral choices; who value integrity and do not compromise it; who respect conscience and do not undermine it and who seek the truth and do not fear it.

Notes: *This statement was a letter sent to the Vatican and made public in late June 1986. Its authors, Sisters Hussey and Ferraro, ran a shelter for the homeless in Charleston, West Virginia, as part of their work within the order of the Sisters of Notre Dame de Namur. Of the 27 priests and nuns who had signed the 1984* New York Times *ad, only these two had unresolved cases within the hierarchy.*

ROMAN CATHOLIC CHURCH— SISTERS OF NOTRE DAME DE NAMUR

STATEMENT ON THE HUSSEY-FERRARO CONTROVERSY (1986)

Up to the present time (June 1986) we sisters of the general government group (of the Sisters of Notre Dame de Namur) have made no general statement on this matter, though our opinion on various stages of its development has been expressed in correspondence with Sisters Barbara Ferraro and Patricia Hussey, and this has been published within the American provinces. We think that the time has come to make known our position on the situation as it now stands and the action we propose to take in the immediate future.

Developments from October 1984

The advertisement, published Oct. 7, 1984, in the New York Times, was titled "A Diversity of Opinion Regarding Abortion Exists Among Committed Catholics." It contained these two sentences: "Statements of recent popes and of the Catholic hierarchy have condemned the direct termination of prenatal life as morally wrong in all instances. There is the mistaken belief in American society that this is the only legitimate Catholic position." It appeared during the presidential election campaign in the United States and in the context of controversy within the church there on the right of political candidates who were professed Catholics to uphold the state's right to legislate in favor of abortion.

A letter, dated Nov. 30, 1984, from Cardinal (Jean Jerome) Hamer and Archbishop (Vincenzo) Fagiolo, prefect and secretary respectively of the Congregation for Religious and Secular Institutes, requested Sister Catherine Hughes, as general moderator, to direct Sisters Barbara and Patricia to make a public retraction in regard to the controversial section quoted above. If they refused to do this, they were to be warned, in accordance with Canon 696.1 and Canon 697, with an explicit threat of dismissal. A copy of this letter was sent to Sisters Barbara and Patricia, and a meeting with them was promised for March 1985, when the five of us would arrive in the United States from Latin America. This meeting took place and also a further one in Worcester, Mass., during part of which members of the Boston and Connecticut provinces were present. After that meeting the major superiors of the two provinces wrote letters, forwarded to the Congregation for Religious and Secular Institutes by Sister Catherine Hughes, in which they contended that the advertisement was "not a pro-abortion statement." Cardinal Hamer, in his reply of May 14, 1985, disagreed with this opinion and stated that "the wording of the statement . . . . was a source of confusion and even 'scandal' to many Catholics and (the sisters) are therefore subject to Canon 696.1, unless they retract." He then went on to say what this retraction should consist of—for each sister to write to her provincial to say that she supports or adheres to the authentic teaching of the church on abortion and for the provincial to communicate this statement to the sisters of the province. "This would de facto constitute a retraction and satisfy the requirement of the Holy See." A copy of this letter was sent to the sisters, and Sister Catherine wrote on behalf of the general government group to say that we thought the cardinal's request was reasonable, i.e., for the sisters to say that they adhere to the church's teaching on abortion—and that we could not support the opposite view. In their reply to us Sisters Barbara and Patricia said: "You need to know that we will not retract nor will we put anything in writing."

During the summer of 1985 Sister Elizabeth Bowyer was in the United States and met Cardinal Hamer with other concerned major superiors and with Sisters Barbara and Patricia. Later in the same year in Rome, Sister Catherine and other members of the general government group met Cardinal Hamer and continued the dialogue. At an interview on Feb. 18, 1986, the cardinal asked that the question, Do you accept the authentic teaching of the church on abortion? should be put to the sisters. If the answer were yes, then the whole affair would be over. The sisters were not willing to give an affirmative answer to this question.

Later, in March 1986, Archbishop Fagiolo, secretary of the Congregation for Religious and Secular Institutes, accompanied by Sister Mary Linscott, SND, went to the United States and interviewed the sisters who had signed the original advertisement. With the exception of Sisters Barbara and Patricia, all those interviewed explained their position in a way that enabled the matter to be closed, so far as they were concerned.

Sisters Barbara and Patricia wrote a statement which was sent to the Congregation for Religious and Secular Institutes on April 24, 1986. Before that date, on April 15, 1986, Sisters Peggy Loftus and Catherine had met the two sisters in Charleston, W. Va., and they told us that this statement represented their final petition. They reiterated their refusal to make a statement regarding their belief in the sacredness and inviolability of life because they felt it could be used to compromise their true position; and they confirmed that should the occasion present itself they would again take the kind of public and vocal pro-choice stance which they had done at the demonstration in support of legalized abortion on March 9, 1986, in Washington, D.C.

Because the five of us were known to be meeting together in late May for the first time since November 1985, many members of the two sisters' provinces have been writing to them and to us during April and May 1986, to make known their opinions on our respective positions and responsibilities.

Commentary: The Times Advertisement

We believe that many of the signers see the advertisement as a call for dialogue about the church's teaching on abortion and not as a pro-abortion statement. We understand the political context in which it appeared on one day during the immediate run-up to the U.S. presidential elections, in a charged atmosphere which it is difficult to imagine so many months after the event. We recognize also the American tradition of open discussion in the press, a tradition which is not necessarily the same in other nations, even those with a free press. We do not see in this action sufficient cause to initiate a process for dismissal.

Nevertheless, we question the prudence of using this particular medium to initiate such a dialogue: There was a lack of clarity in the language which gave some readers the impression that it was a pro-abortion statement and that it was calling into question the legitimate teaching authority of the church. A public press statement becomes the property of its readers as well as its authors, and since the Roman Catholic Church is international, the signers of the advertisement had less control than usual over different interpretations of the advertisement made in good faith.

Congregation for Religious

The interpretation by the Congregation for Religious and Secular Institutes was that the statement denied the authoritative teaching of the church, and retraction or the penalty of dismissal was demanded through the general moderator. During 17 months of correspondence and dialogue, this demand has been reduced to a request for the sister to say that she accepts the authentic teaching of the church on abortion. We believe, and appreciate, the fact that the congregation has moved progressively from a juridical to a pastoral mode of action, culminating in a personal visit of the congregation's secretary to the sisters concerned.

The Sisters

Sisters Barbara and Patricia work in an ecumenical project in Charleston, W.Va., in which they deal every day with poor people in trouble. They are particularly concerned in their work with the problems of sexually abused women. It is natural that they should be highly aware of the problems faced by such women and strongly committed to improving their chances of leading lives of human dignity. We regret, however, many aspects of the way in which they have tried to do this from October 1984 onward.

The sponsorship and funding of the advertisement led to a suspicion that other strategies were operating besides those of the signers. A costly advertisement seems an inappropriate way to begin to help the dispossessed. A public stance by Sisters of Notre Dame would seem to demand prior consultation with the members of their congregation. But beyond these considerations is the fact that from the very beginning of our discussions, the sisters have stated that their position is "non-negotiable."

We have found this attitude a block to genuine dialogue. Their frequent use of the media has been characterized by statements which are derogatory to persons in the church and reflect a lack of respect for the church's teaching authority. They appear to have ignored the fact that as women who have public vows and who belong to a religious congregation, they are not free to act in public as though they were private individuals.

We are conscious of our covenant relationship with Sisters Barbara and Patricia. We are sisters who have made a common commitment and have accepted to be in communion with one another in carrying out that commitment. We think that they have shown little awareness of their responsibility to the congregation in their public statements and actions.

At the present time we see the sisters' position to have changed from their original request for open dialogue on the subject of abortion. At this point they are taking a public pro-choice stance with no reference to the sanctity of life or the place of moral responsibility in decision making and action. We believe that Sisters Barbara and Patricia's present position has serious potential for the giving of scandal and continues to reflect an attitude of intransigence rather than dialogue in regard to the teaching authority of the church. We have grave concern in regard to the public pro-choice position which they have taken and plan to begin a process of clarification of their full position and examination of their stance in the light of the church's teaching and of our congregational statement of mission.

Notes: *This statement from the order to which Sisters Ferraro and Hussey belonged was issued at about the same time the sisters wrote their letter to the Vatican. The statement showed the continued escalation of the conflict and the perspective held by the order's headquarters at the Vatican.*

ROMAN CATHOLIC CHURCH— SISTERS PATRICIA HUSSEY AND BARBARA FERRARO

RESIGNATION STATEMENT (1988)

Dear Sisters of the Boston and Connecticut teams and members of the provinces,

It is now six weeks since the leadership informed us of their decision not to dismiss us. We have used this period to reflect on the political importance of this decision for all women, for the church and for Notre Dame and to evaluate our own future relationship with the Sisters of Notre Dame. We have also listened for reactions from others in the community and the Vatican.

The past four years have been extremely painful for us. We have found it difficult to reconcile our vision of community and mission with the actions of the leadership. We have also been disturbed and disheartened by the canonical relationship that Notre Dame wishes to maintain with the Vatican as we submit our constitutions for CRIS' (Congregation of Religious and Secular Institutes) approval. CRIS demands that radical changes be inserted in our constitutions which do not reflect our lived reality. Compliance with their demands will only deepen the canonical relationship with Rome.

However, we decided to put these questions and concerns aside until such time as we had defended the right to be members of the community and hold a public pro-choice position, or for that matter, any public position on non-infallible teachings that differs from the official church teachings.

We now believe that the leadership has affirmed that right to be member and hold public positions on non-infallible teachings that differ from official church teachings. This act benefits Notre Dame and all other canonical communities. We are also grateful that Rome has not acted to overturn the leadership's decision.

Now, for the first time in four years, we are able to address the question of our future in the community in a free and non-coercive atmosphere. Our reflections have led to our decision to resign from the community, effective upon your receipt of this letter.

Two factors have most influenced this decision:

1. The past four years have shown us that to truly stand with people who are struggling, one must be in a relationship of equality with them. Thus for us to stand with women, we

need to renounce the differences, privileges and even limitations that are part of membership in a religious community in a patriarchal church.

2. We also find that the violence of the process used with us by the leadership, the lack of respect and understanding of our motivation for the good of the whole church by many in the community are for us insurmountable barriers to the reconstruction of a positive covenant relationship.

In closing, we want to express our deepest thanks to the Sisters of Notre Dame who have voiced their support and questions to us openly and honestly. We pray that fears do not paralyze any of us in the future.

Notes: *In this resignation statement, Sisters Ferraro and Hussey state their decision to resign from their order, despite being informed on June 4, 1988 that they would not be dismissed. This illustrates how deep the abortion controversy runs.*

Protestant and Eastern Orthodox Churches

While the Roman Catholic Church is the single largest religious body in North America, the Protestant and Eastern Orthodox churches together contain more than half of the religiously affiliated individuals in North America. These churches have a wide variety of approaches and responses to the issue of abortion. Those taking a "liberal" or "pro-choice" stance tend to emphasize both the importance of giving the woman involved primary say in the matter, and the importance of maintaining personal freedom when an issue with such diversity of religious opinion is involved. Those taking a "conservative" stance against abortion tend to emphasize the "right to life" of the developing embryo, and the importance of defending it as a helpless life against acts of aggression. The most difficult area for the conservative groups to agree upon is the precise list of legitimate reasons for abortion. Most would include "to save the life of the mother," but some would not. Of those that would, many would go on to include "in cases of rape, incest, or severe deformity," but many would not.

While not all statements from each group are included, where ever possible a number of different statements from the same group (or from minority units within that group) are given in order to show the continuing interest in the issue and to show how a group may deal differently with the issue at different times. Some groups issue longer statements on abortion, and a few of those (Church of the Brethren, Lutheran Church-Missouri Synod, Presbyterian Church in America, and the Presbyterian Church (U.S.A.) are included to illustrate the thought some groups have devoted to the issue. Also included are statements from two groups outside the United States—Methodist Conference (England) and the United Church of Canada—and an ecumenical body (the National Association of Evangelicals). The National Council of Churches has not issued a statement on abortion.

AMERICAN BAPTIST CHURCHES IN THE U.S.A.

RESOLUTION ON ABORTION (1988)

American Baptist Resolution Concerning Abortion and Ministry in the Local Church

The General Board of American Baptist Churches, in the U.S.A. has solicited and received significant response through hearings, letters and questionnaires from individuals and congregations across the country. The response indicates that American Baptists believe that ministry to persons in situations of crisis pregnancy and abortion is a concern that primarily affects the local churches and therefore the topic needs to be addressed at that level. The General Board concurs with this and calls upon local churches to continue studying these issues, prayerfully seeking, under the guidance of the Holy Spirit, to come to a position that will direct them in ministry. The role of the General Board in this matter is not to speak for churches but to assist them in carrying out ministry and advocacy according to their convictions. Therefore, as a reflection of American Baptist thought, this resolution is offered to assist our churches.

As American Baptists, members of a covenant community of believers in Jesus Christ, we acknowledge life as a sacred and gracious gift of God. We affirm that God is the Creator of all life, that human beings are created in the image of God, and that Christ is Lord of life. Recognizing this gift of life, we find ourselves struggling with the painful and difficult issue of abortion. Genuine diversity of opinion threatens the unity of our fellowship, but the nature of covenant demands mutual love and respect. Together we must seek the mind of Christ.

As American Baptists we oppose abortion,

> as a means of avoiding responsibility for conception, as a primary means of birth control, without regard for the far-reaching consequences of the act.

We denounce irresponsible sexual behavior and acts of sexual violence that contribute to the large number of abortions each year.

We grieve with all who struggle with the difficult circumstances that lead them to consider abortion. Recognizing that each person is ultimately responsible to God, we encourage women and men in these circumstances to seek spiritual counsel as they prayerfully and conscientiously consider their decision.

We condemn violence and harassment directed against abortion clinics, their staff and clients, as well as sanctions and discrimination against medical professionals whose consciences prevent them from being involved in abortions.

We acknowledge the diversity of deeply held convictions within our fellowship even as we seek to interpret the Scriptures under the guidance of the Holy Spirit. Many American Baptists believe that, biblically, human life begins at conception, that abortion is immoral and a destruction of a human being created in God's image (Job 31:15; Psalm 139:13-16; Jeremiah 1:5; Luke 1:44; Proverbs 31:8-9; Galatians 1:15). Many others believe that while abortion is a regrettable reality, it can be a morally acceptable action and they choose to act on the biblical principles of compassion and justice (John 8:1-11; Exodus 21:22-25; Matthew 7:1-5; James 2:2-13) and freedom of will (John 16:13; Romans 14:4-5, 10-13). Many gradations of opinion between these basic positions have been expressed within our fellowship.

We also recognize that we are divided as to the proper witness of the church to the state regarding abortion. Many of our membership seek legal safeguards to protect unborn life. Many others advocate for and support family planning legislation, including legalized abortion as in the best interest of women in particular and society in general. Again, we have many points of view between these two positions. Consequently, we acknowledge the freedom of each individual to advocate for a public policy on abortion that reflects his or her beliefs.

Respecting our varied perspectives, let us affirm our unity in the ministry of Christ (Colossians 3:12-17):

- Praying for openness and sensitivity to the leading of the Holy Spirit within our family,

- Covenanting to address both the causes and effects of abortion at the personal and social levels.

WE CALL UPON

- *American Baptist Congregations*

    To challenge members to live in a way that models responsible sexuality in accordance with biblical teaching,

    To expend efforts and funds for teaching responsible sexuality,

    To provide opportunities for intergenerational dialogue on responsible sexuality and Christian life,

    To provide relevant ministries to adolescents and parents of adolescents in and outside the church.

- *Pastors and Leaders*

    To prepare themselves to minister compassionately and skillfully to women and men facing problem pregnancies, whatever their final decisions.

- *American Baptist Regions*

    To provide leadership and support for appropriate programs and ministries to aid the local churches in these tasks.

- *Seminaries and Institutions of Higher Education*

    To provide courses that will enrich the theological understanding and counseling skills of American Baptist leaders so that they will be able to assist persons facing decisions regarding responsible sexuality and abortion.

    To assist churches by production of a new study packet on abortion which could be helpful to any church's ministry regardless of its position on this subject.

    To prepare, identify and make available other appropriate materials relating to responsible sexuality at all age levels.

WE ENCOURAGE CONGREGATIONS AND INDIVIDUAL MEMBERS

- To engage in meaningful dialogue on abortion with openness and Christian compassion,

- To initiate and/or become involved in creative community ministries in their communities that provide alternatives to abortion for women with problem pregnancies and for their loved ones,

- To provide appropriate financial and emotional support for those women who carry their pregnancies to term and further to maintain contact and provide loving community for them after birth,

- To acknowledge that men are equally responsible for the creation of problem pregnancies and to help them recognize their responsibility for the social, medical, moral and financial consequences of their behavior,

- To minister with love and spiritual counsel to those who choose to terminate their pregnancies,

- To be actively involved in caring for children who are potentially available for adoption, including those with special needs, and to assist agencies in order to facilitate placement for them, and

- To participate in organizations addressing abortion issues in ways that are consistent with their beliefs, and witness to the reconciling love of God.

BEYOND OUR OWN HOUSEHOLD OF FAITH, WE CALL UPON:

- Government, industries and foundations to support the research and development of safe, reliable, affordable and culturally appropriate methods of contraception for both men and women worldwide.

- Our governmental institutions to continue to pursue the goals of economic justice, social equality and political empowerment without which the painful human dilemmas now being faced will continue without relief. We are concerned that many women receiving abortions are themselves adolescents who are often economically disadvantaged.

- Public media (television, cinema, audio and print) to stop the depiction of sex outside of marriage as normal and desirable, the portrayal of women, men and children as sex objects and the elevation of sex as the source of all happiness. We particularly oppose print and cinematic pornography.

We acknowledge that we often lack compassion, insight and the necessary commitment needed to serve our Christian community and the wider society adequately. We affirm our commitment to continue to counsel and uphold one another, to maintain fellowship with those whose opinions differ from ours and to extend the compassion of Christ to all.

Adopted by the General Board of the American Baptist Churches - June 1988.

161 For, 9 Against, 2 Abstentions.

Notes: *This 1988 resolution on abortion was a result of the special task force assigned to study the American Baptist position. The results were so divided that they decided not to take a particular stand as a whole, but to allow individual members to support whatever public policy they thought best.*

AMERICAN FRIENDS SERVICE COMMITTEE

STATEMENT ON ABORTION (1970)

On religious, moral, and humanitarian grounds, therefore, we arrived at the view that it is far better to end an unwanted pregnancy than to encourage the evils resulting from forced pregnancy and childbirth. At the center of our position is a profound respect and reverence for human life, not only that of the potential human being who should never have been conceived, but that of the parent and the other children in the human community.

Believing that abortion should be subject to the same regulations and safeguards as those governing other medical and surgical procedures, we urge the repeal of all laws limiting either the circumstances under which a woman may have an abortion or the physician's freedom to use his or her best professional judgement in performing it.

Notes: *The American Friends Service Committee is an intra-family Quaker group founded in World War I to show national loyalty through war-alternative activities. It has been maintained as a primary social action agency to which many different Friends groups contribute. This statement excerpt is as published in* We Affirm, *a brief collection of such statements published by the Religious Coalition for Abortion Rights. This statement, which supported liberalization of abortion laws, had particular interest given the well-known pacifist and humanitarian stances taken by Quakers.*

ASSEMBLIES OF GOD

A BIBLICAL PERSPECTIVE ON ABORTION (1985)

Just a few years ago the term *abortion* in law implied criminality in producing miscarriage. An abortionist was one who practiced producing criminal abortions.

Today when the word *abortion* is used, it almost immediately brings to mind the legal practice of destroying unborn children. Even though abortion on demand has been legalized, it is still immoral and sinful.

Change of Medical Definitions

Proabortionists have done everything in their power to promote abortion on demand. They have adopted expressions by which they describe the unborn child and the abortion process to try to make the practice respectable.

Dr. C. Everett Koop is surgeon-general of the United States. When he was surgeon-in-chief of the Children's Hospital of Pennsylvania and professor of pediatrics and pediatric surgery at the School of Medicine, the University of Pennsylvania, he wrote: "We who as a people always knew that abortion was the killing of an unborn baby were brainwashed to believe that the destruction of the 'products of conception' or the destruction of a 'fetus' is not the same thing as killing an unborn baby. Traditional medical definitions were deliberately changed in order to do away with our moral repugnance toward abortion."[1]

Proabortionists refer to the abortion process as "interrupting" rather than terminating a pregnancy. They talk of "evacuating the contents of the uterus" or of removing "post-conceptive fertility content." They refer to the unborn baby as "potential human life" when it is obvious the organism is human and alive before birth. Human life is potential only before the male sperm and female ovum join to form a new living human being.

Christians must not be deceived by inaccurate, deceptive medical terminology. They must be guided by the principles and precepts of Scripture.

What the Bible Says About the Unborn Child

While some have tried to justify abortions before the unborn child can sustain life outside the womb, the Bible does not make such a distinction in the life process. The term *viable fetus* may properly indicate, as a scientific fact, the time when life can be sustained outside the womb; but it does not indicate that life as a person fails to exist prior to that. Those who may be tempted to accept abortion at some early stage just because it is declared legal would find it helpful to consider several Biblical truths.

1. The Bible recognizes that a woman is *with child* even in the first stages of pregnancy.

   When the virgin Mary was chosen to be the mother of Jesus, this announcement was made to her: "Thou shalt conceive in thy womb, and bring forth a son" (Luke 1:31). The angel then informed Mary that her cousin Elisabeth was pregnant. The words used were: "She hath also conceived a *son* in her old age" (Luke 1:36). Scripture makes it clear that in the prenatal phase John the Baptist was recognized as a son even though it was 3 months before the time of delivery.

   In Luke 1:41, 44 John before birth is recognized as a "babe." This translates a Greek word used of children both before and after birth (Acts 7:19). The words "she hath *also* conceived a son" indicate Jesus was recognized as a son though Mary's pregnancy was in the earliest stages.

   The Bible always recognizes the prenatal phase of life as that of a child and not as a meaningless product of conception. There is no distinction made in the value of life between the born and unborn child.

   Even when pregnancy in Bible times was due to an illicit relationship, the quality of that life was not questioned. The daughters of Lot were pregnant by incest (Genesis 19:36), but this was not considered a condition that called for abortion. Bathsheba recognized she was pregnant by adultery (2 Samuel 11:5), but this was not viewed as being encumbered with a mere appendage of matter to be removed from the mother's womb.

   John Calvin made a very significant observation concerning abortion in commenting on Exodus 21:22, 23: "The fetus, though enclosed in the womb of his mother, is already a human being, and it is a monstrous crime to rob it of life which it has not yet begun to enjoy. If it seems more horrible to kill a man in his own house than in a field, because a man's house is his place of most secure refuge, it ought surely to be deemed more atrocious to destroy a fetus in the womb before it has come to light."[2]

2. The Bible recognizes that God is active in the creative process of forming new life. To abort a pregnancy is to abort the work God is doing.

Concerning Leah, the wife of Jacob, Scripture indicates, "When the Lord saw that Leah was unloved, He opened her womb. . . . So Leah conceived and bore a son" (Genesis 29:31, 32, NKJV).

When Job compared himself to his servants, he asked, "Did not He who made me in the womb make them? Did not the same One fashion us in the womb?" (Job 31:15, NKJV).

In pointing out God's impartiality Job said: "Yet He is not partial to princes, nor does He regard the rich more than the poor; for they are all the work of His hands" (Job 34:19, NKJV).

Isaiah speaking for God wrote: "Thus says the Lord who made you and formed you from the womb, who will help you: 'Fear not, O Jacob My servant'" (Isaiah 44:2, NKJV). And again, "Thus says the Lord, your Redeemer, and He who formed you from the womb: 'I am the Lord, who makes all things'" (v. 24).

David summed it up well when he wrote: "For you created my inmost being, you knit me together in my mother's womb. I praise you because I am fearfully and wonderfully made, your works are wonderful, I know that full well. My frame was not hidden from you when I was made in the secret place. When I was woven together in the depths of the earth, your eyes saw my unformed body. All the days ordained for me were written in your book before one of them came to be" (Psalm 139:13-16, NIV).

Concerning Psalm 139:13-16, Donald Shoemaker wrote: "This passage can only evoke holy caution and respect for unborn life. God is at work, and as we observe we must worship, for the place where we stand is holy ground. Such respect for the divine origin of life is not to be found among the proabortionists. Theirs is an unholy intrusion into the divine laboratory to interrupt and to destroy the handiwork of the blessed Creator! God loves the unborn. This psalm will never let us forget it."[3]

The omniscient God who knows what happens to persons after their birth also knows what happens to these persons before birth. He is creatively active in the birth process, and to terminate a pregnancy is to destroy the work of God. Abortion is evil man's defiance of the Almighty. It is an indication of the depths to which a consenting society has fallen.

3. The Bible recognizes that God has plans for the unborn child. Only He knows the potential of this new life.

When God called Jeremiah to his prophetic ministry He indicated the ordination was prenatal when He said: "Before I formed you in the womb I knew you, before you were born I sanctified you, and I ordained you a prophet to the nations" (Jeremiah 1:5, NKJV).

When Zechariah the priest was ministering at the altar of incense, an angel announced that his wife Elisabeth would give birth to a son who should be called John. Then it was revealed that God had definite plans for this child. He was to be a forerunner of Jesus (Luke 1:11-17).

To destroy the life of an unborn child is flagrantly to disregard the plans God has for that life. It robs the unborn person of the privilege of choosing to be an instrument of God's design.

4. The Bible recognizes that God is sovereign in all things, including the quality of life of the unborn child.

When people reject God, eventually they make human life relative. Some are considered worthy of life, others are considered expendable.

A study by Dr. Leo Alexander of Harvard University, a psychiatrist at the Nuremburg trials for Nazi war criminals, showed the beginnings of the holocaust were found in the belief that some human life did not deserve to exist.

As a result of this belief they killed the unwanted, the lame, the crippled, the retarded, and eventually even disabled veterans who served Germany in World War I. From there it was just a small step to the holocaust.[4]

When people set themselves up as God to determine if a life is worth living—whether before or after birth—they are rejecting the sovereignty of the Creator of all things.

There are things finite humans cannot understand. God's ways are above man's ways. While today's medical technology makes it possible to know that less than desirable conditions sometimes exist in unborn children, it is important to remember they are still God's creations.

When Moses complained of his lack of eloquence, God said, "Who has made man's mouth? Or who makes the mute, the deaf, the seeing, or the blind? Have not I, the Lord?" (Exodus 4:11, NKJV).

When man establishes criteria for what constitutes unworthy lives, he is invariably wrong because he fails to recognize the plan and purpose of God. Who but God knows whether someone destroyed in the holocaust might not have discovered a cure for cancer. Who but God knows what blessing millions of children killed before birth might bring to improve the quality of life.

In the course of an impressive address before the House of Representatives, the following quotation was included from a person who was born as a result of a rape: "Some people disclaim their natural habitat. I always name my origin. It didn't hold me back, and neither has my color. I was born in poverty. My father raped my mother when she was 12. Now they've named a park for me in Chester, Pennsylvania."[5]

The quotation was from Ethel Waters who ministered to millions through the medium of gospel song. Had abortion been legal at that time, quite possibly someone would have suggested it. If this had happened, the world would have been much poorer. The work of evangelism would have been deprived of a great gospel singer.

When Pregnancy Threatens the Life of the Mother

In earlier years mothers sometimes died as a result of pregnancy. Today because of advances in medical science, this condition rarely occurs. Should such an isolated situation develop, and if after prayer for healing God in His wisdom does not miraculously intervene, the individuals involved would need to look to God for further guidance. The diagnosis of attending prolife physicians will be helpful in arriving at the proper conclusion.

God's Attitude Toward Killing Innocent Persons

God's Word is very explicit concerning the taking of innocent human life. "You shall not murder" (Exodus 20:13, NKJV) is not only one of the Ten Commandments, but also a dictate which reoccurs throughout Scripture.

God instructed Moses to set a law before the Children of Israel which brings the sanctity of life of unborn children into focus. "If men strive, and hurt a woman with child, so that her fruit depart from her, and yet no mischief follow: he shall be surely punished, according as the woman's husband will lay upon him; and he shall pay as the judges determine. And if any mischief follow, then thou shalt give life for life, eye for eye, tooth for tooth, hand for hand, foot for foot" (Exodus 21:22-24).

Dr. Stanley M. Horton, professor of Old Testament and Hebrew at the Assemblies of God Theological Seminary, stated the opinion of many when he wrote the following concerning Exodus 21:22-24: "The situation here is of two men who are fighting as a result of a quarrel. The same Hebrew verb is used in Exodus 2:13 of the two men Moses saw fighting. Somehow as they are fighting, they hit a pregnant woman, and her child 'comes out,' that is, is born prematurely. If there is no 'mischief,' no 'mortal accident,' to the child or the mother, then the man who struck the woman must pay a fine as determined by her husband and ratified by the judges. But if there is 'mortal accident' causing the death of the child or the mother, then the law of a 'life for a life' takes over.

"'Her fruit' is the Hebrew *veladeha*, translated 'her children' in this same chapter (v. 4), as well as everywhere else it occurs in the Old Testament. The plural is used here because it would not be known in advance whether more than one child was in the womb.

"'Mischief,' Hebrew *ason*, is used in Genesis 42:4 where Jacob is afraid something might happen to Benjamin (as he thought had happened to Joseph), that is, death. (See also 42:38; 44:29.)

"It is clear from this that the fetus is recognized as a child and has the same rights as older children.''

God's attitude toward the killing of innocents is clear. Except in capital punishment decreed through the judicial process (Numbers 35:12) or protection of property at night probably involving self-defense (Exodus 22:2), no one is guiltless who takes the life of another.

Concerned Christians and the Abortion Issue

When the evil of abortion on demand for convenience is considered, it is obvious concerned Christians must act as they would in the case of other evils of commensurate magnitude. There are steps Christians can take to restrain and hopefully reverse immoral trends.

1. Christians should pray earnestly for divine intervention in the affairs of men. This would eliminate degrading national moral standards and consequently the laws that permit evils such as abortion on demand for convenience.

   The power of a spiritual awakening can be seen in history. France and England both had revolutions in the 18th century. France has a political revolution which resulted in untold suffering and bloodshed. England had an industrial revolution. The difference between the two is that England enjoyed a spiritual awakening. It elevated the quality of life in the land, possibly averting a violent revolution such as France experienced.

   A spiritual awakening in our country could have a salutary influence on today's moral climate. Not only would the sanctity of human life be honored, but moral standards in general would be lifted.

2. Concerned Christians should help provide for Biblical moral instruction in all possible forums. Instead of the standards of the church being influenced by humanistic and even atheistic philosophies, a church thoroughly rooted in the eternal truths of God's Word can lift the standards of society. When people accept the absolutes of Scripture rather than the relative values arising from speculative human reasoning, all levels of living will be greatly improved.

   When disregard of Biblical standards of righteousness is recognized as sin, when refusal to acknowledge the sovereignty of God is recognized as sin, when rejection of Jesus' salvation and lordship is recognized as sin, the condition of society will be vastly improved. Then problems such as abortion will be greatly reduced.

   Biblical instruction must be given its proper emphasis both in the church and the home. Believers must be so thoroughly rooted in Scripture that they can give a reason for convictions based on God's Word.

3. Concerned Christians should counsel those with unwanted pregnancies about the alternative of adoption. They should support Christian agencies. They should lovingly assist in every way possible those wishing to give their children up for adoption. Such parents find themselves in a very confusing role.

4. Concerned Christians should actively support prolife legislation and oppose any legislation designed to destroy the moral fiber of society. As citizens of our country they

should express their opinions to governmental representatives. They should become influential in determining the kind of people who will be placed in public office. They should encourage committed Christians to seek positions of influence.

5. Concerned Christians should compassionately minister to those who suffer overwhelming remorse and guilt from having had, or having participated in producing, abortions. These people need to be reminded that when they confess their sin to God, He forgives and cleanses. They need to be reminded that Jesus said, "Him that cometh to me I will in no wise cast out" (John 6:37). They need the prayerful, moral support of those who are strong in the Lord.

Endnotes

[1] C. Everett Koop, "A Physician Looks at Abortion," in *Thou Shalt Not Kill,* ed. Richard L. Ganz (New York: Crown Publishers, Inc., 1978), p. 8.

[2] John Calvin, *Commentaries on the Four Last Books of Moses,* trans. Charles William Bingham, 4 vols. (Grand Rapids: Wm. B. Eerdmans Publishing Co., 1950), 3:41-42.

[3] Donald Shoemaker, *Abortion, the Bible and the Christian* (Grand Rapids: Baker Book House, 1976).

[4] Francis Schaeffer and C. Everett Koop, *Whatever Happened to the Human Race?* (Old Tappan, N.J.: Fleming H. Revell Co., 1979), p. 106.

[5] Thomas J. Bliley, Jr., of Virginia, *Congressional Records,* Extension of Remarks (Washington, D.C., House of Representatives, July 25, 1983).

Notes: *This statement by the Assemblies of God (approximately 2,135,104 members in 1986) emphasizes Bible passages which show God's care for the fetus and for innocent life.*

ASSOCIATION OF FREE LUTHERAN CONGREGATIONS

RESOLUTION ON ABORTION (1978)

BE IT RESOLVED, That we continue to oppose the sins of abortion and homosexuality and that our position upon those two subjects be as follows:

INASMUCH as the government of the beloved United States has allowed the use of abortions as a means of birth control, AND WHEREAS the indiscriminate taking of a human life, including that of a human fetus, is against our understanding of the Word of God,

BE IT RESOLVED, That the Annual Conference of the AFLC stands opposed to abortion as a means of birth control.

BE IT FURTHER RESOLVED, That each congregation and individual within the AFLC is encouraged to protest in writing to their respective legislative officials.

WHEREAS, Due to the increased moral decay of our society, specifically regarding the gay rights movement, we heartily support those who on the basis of the Bible oppose homosexuality.

BE IT FURTHER RESOLVED, That we offer the hand of Christian love to those homosexuals who wish to be helped by God's power: We have love for the sinner but hate the sin.

BE IT RESOLVED, That we support and pray for government, and law enforcement agencies in their effort to control terrorists, ". . . that we may lead a quiet and peaceable life in all godliness and honesty." (I Tim. 2:2)

Notes: *This second statement continued the sentiment of the previous year but more distinctly linked the resolutions on abortion and homosexuality, which were also coupled in*

1977. This pairing shows a presumed shared characteristic between the two (most likely sexual immorality), though that is not discussed in the abortion portion of the statement.

ASSOCIATION OF FREE LUTHERAN CONGREGATIONS

RESOLUTION ON ABORTION (1986)

WHEREAS, the 1977 Annual Conference of the Association of Free Lutheran Congregations resolved to oppose therapeutic abortions as a means of birth control and to encourage each congregation and individual to protest in writing to their respective legislative officials; and

WHEREAS, the 1978 Annual Conference resolved to continue to oppose the sin of abortion; and

WHEREAS, the 1980 Annual Conference reaffirmed the "conservative stand taken by the AFLC based on the Word of God and His Laws concerning the moral issues of our day;" and

WHEREAS, the destruction of millions of lives by means of abortion which began with the 1973 Supreme Court decision still continues; therefore be it

RESOLVED, that the Annual Conference of the Association of Free Lutheran Congregations affirms that

a. the unborn children are persons in the sight of God from the time of conception (Job 10:9-10; Psalm 51:5; 139:13-17; Jeremiah 1:5; Luke 1:41-44);

b. the unborn children stand under the protection of God's command against murder (Genesis 9:6; Exodus 20:13; Numbers 35:33; Acts 7:19; I John 3:15); and

RESOLVED, that we encourage a clear witness on behalf of the sanctity of unborn life, including the support of responsible pro-life groups in our communities, such as "Lutherans for Life;" and be it further

RESOLVED, that we encourage prayerful support for the development of alternatives to abortion programs, providing compassionate help for those in need; and be it further

RESOLVED, that we boldly proclaim Law and Gospel, which alone can change the sinful hearts of men and women and turn them from sin to salvation.

Notes: *This 1986 resolution showed that the abortion issue had been separated from the homosexuality issue. Additionally, the church's stand on abortion was now supplemented by biblical passages showing God's concern for the unborn.*

BAPTIST GENERAL CONFERENCE

RESOLUTION ON ABORTION (1971)

Abortion (Adopted 1971)

Being very much aware of the current concern about the liberalization of existing laws related to abortion; and, recognizing the necessity of periodic re-evaluation of laws which are so intimately related to human well-being;

Be it resolved that:

We exhort our people to be guided by these basic Christian principles as they relate themselves to the controversy and concern surrounding the abortion problem:

1. The Stewardship of Life

   Human life is a gift from God and as such is a sacred trust. In those areas of human experience where life is so basically involved such as conception and abortion we ought always to be governed by our awareness of the sacredness of life; and,

2. Individual Responsibility

   We as Christians ought not to regard abortion as a means of evading individual responsibility; and,

3. Christian Morality

   Since many abortions are sought as a result of an immoral sexual relationship, we must submit that the most effective solution to the abortion problem is the revival of the Christian concept of morality wherein the fruits of sexual relationships are accepted as a trust from God and not an inconvenience to be disposed of; and,

4. The Christian community should respond in sympathetic understanding to the individuals immediately involved, whatever action is taken in regard to abortion.

Notes: *In their 1971 statement, the Baptist General Conference (about 136,688 members) took a moderate stance that affirmed the sacredness of life but did not take a definitive stand on how abortion should be evaluated.*

BAPTIST GENERAL CONFERENCE

RESOLUTION ON ABORTION (1981)

Abortion (Adopted 1981)

Recognizing the critical nature and complexity of the issue of abortion, be it resolved that the Baptist General Conference opposes abortion on demand and encourages its members to influence public opinion in this regard and that our attitude toward those involved in abortion and abortion decisions, be able to speak the truth in love, seeking to bring to bear the forgiveness of God and healing through Christ's body, the church.

Notes: *In this 1981 statement, the Baptist General Conference shifted from its 1971 position and took a very strong stance against "abortion on demand."*

BIBLE MISSIONARY CHURCH

RESOLUTION ON ABORTION (1983)

5. We strongly oppose the modern day ideas of abortion and consider such as legalized murder of the unborn.

Notes: *The Bible Missionary Church (unknown membership) has strongly condemned abortion as "legalized murder."*

CHRISTIAN CHURCH (DISCIPLES OF CHRIST)

RESOLUTION ON ABORTION (1975)

General Assembly, 1975

WHEREAS, the Christian Church (Disciples of Christ) has proclaimed that in Christ, God affirms freedom and responsibility for individuals, and

WHEREAS, legislation is being introduced into the U.S. Congress which would embody in law one particular opinion concerning the morality of abortion. . . .

THEREFORE BE IT RESOLVED, that the General Assembly of the Christian Church (Disciples of Christ). . . .

- Affirm the principle of individual liberty, freedom of individual conscience,/ and sacredness of life for all persons.

- Respect differences in religious beliefs concerning abortion and oppose, in accord with the principle of religious liberty, any attempt to legislate a specific religious opinion or belief concerning abortion upon all Americans.

- Provide through ministry of the local congregation, pastoral concern, and nurture of persons faced with the responsibility and trauma surrounding undesired pregnancy.

Notes: *The Christian Church (Disciples of Christ), which claimed approximately 1,116,326 members in 1985, affirms freedom of conscience and opposes legislation restricting abortion on the basis of particular religious beliefs. This excerpted 1975 statement is printed as it appeared in a brochure published by the Religious Coalition for Abortion Rights.*

CHRISTIAN AND MISSIONARY ALLIANCE

STATEMENT ON ABORTION (1981)

The church, as well as the general public, is confronted with the moral issue of abortion. Because of the importance of this issue to our society, the General Council of The Christian and Missionary Alliance has chosen to make a statement concerning its position on the subject of abortion.

The moral issue of induced abortion ultimately involves a decision concerning those circumstances under which a human being may be permitted to take the life of another. We believe that life begins at conception and that this life is to be considered as human at that time.

We believe that abortion on demand is morally wrong. We cannot allow the current social climate of moral relativism and sexual permissiveness to dictate our responses to moral and social dilemmas.

The Word of God teaches that each individual is known by God from before the foundation of the world (e.g. Jeremiah 1:4, 5; Psalm 138: 13-17). Our omnipotent, omniscient, omnipresent God has pronounced His blessing upon the life of a child according to Psalm 127:3-5.

Since all life exists for God's purposes and all human lives are equally sacred, it is our belief that the life of the unborn person is blessed of God and must be preserved and nurtured. We, therefore, are opposed to induced abortion.*

Endnote

*Only in the rarest instances, when it is impossible to save both the mother and the unborn child alive, should the question of an induced abortion be considered.

Notes: *This 1981 statement by the Christian and Missionary Alliance (approximately 238,734 members in 1986) equated "abortion on demand" with "moral relativism and sexual permissiveness." All human lives were "equally sacred," and induced abortion was opposed under almost all circumstances, including when the life of the mother depends upon aborting an unviable fetus.*

CHRISTIAN REFORMED CHURCH IN NORTH AMERICA

RESOLUTION ON ABORTION (UNDATED)

A. Abortion

Three overtures requesting synod to define the position of the church on abortion were presented to the Synod of 1971. Synod in response appointed a committee "to search out and set forth the scriptural teaching relative to (induced) abortion and recommend a statement to synod for adoption" (Acts of Synod, 1971, p. 48).

The following year a report was submitted and acted upon.

These recommendations were adopted *regarding induced abortion:*

1. That synod affirm the unique value of all human life and the special relationship of man to God as his image-bearer.

2. That synod, mindful of the sixth commandment, condemn the wanton or arbitrary destruction of any human being at any state of its development from the point of conception to the point of death.

3. That synod affirm that an induced abortion is an allowable option only when the life of the prospective mother is genuinely threatened by the continuation of the pregnancy.

The following recommendations were adopted *with reference to the role of the believing community:*

1. That synod call believers to a recognition of the need for Christian compassion and understanding accompanied by positive Christian action for the unwed pregnant girl, for families for whom the birth of another child looms as a very special burden, for those who are pregnant because of rape or incest and for those families who already have abnormal children or who face the likelihood or possibility of having an abnormal child.

2. That synod call the churches to offer their full resources of counseling, encouragement, acceptance and material and financial support to any girl or woman faced with the burdensome reality of an unwanted pregnancy. The churches should offer this support joyfully and without recrimination in the name of Jesus Christ by whose grace we all must daily live.

3. That synod declare that when a person has taken an action in regard to induced abortion which is contrary to the decision of synod, we should be careful to deal with such a person with loving concern rather than judgmental pronouncements.

4. That synod call believers to a ringing testimony against the evils of abortion as practiced in our society, encourage them to promote action and legislation that reflects the teaching of Scripture.

References: Acts of Synod, 1971, p. 48.
Acts of Synod, 1972, pp. 63-64.

B. Birth Control

In response to an overture from Classis Grand Rapids West synod first spoke out on this matter in 1906. Later in 1936 synod having heard the report of a special committee previously appointed to study the matter of birth control, adopted a two page testimony.

Birth Control Testimony

In view of the increasing sensualizing of marriage in our day, the steady decline in the birth rate not only in the world at large but also in the church of Jesus Christ, and the alarming prevalence of practices which are contrary to the ordinances of God and violate the Christian ideal of marriage and parenthood, the synod of the Christian Reformed Church, assembled at Grand Rapids, Michigan, June, 1936, feels constrained to address the following testimony to the churches:

According to the teaching of Holy Writ marriage is a creation ordinance instituted by God with a twofold purpose: the loving companionship of husband and wife in a lifelong physico-spiritual union, and the begetting of children in and through this marital love life. Scripture expresses both these aims in solemn words of the Almighty himself. The former in Genesis 2:18 and 24, where we read: "It is not good that man should be alone; I will make him a help meet for him. . . . Therefore shall a man leave his father and his mother, and shall cleave unto his wife; and they shall be one flesh." And the latter in Genesis 1:28, where, following the statement that God made man male and female, we read the divine injunction: "Be fruitful, and multiply, and replenish the earth. . . ." Implied in the former passage are the duties and privileges of marital love, companionship, and mutual helpfulness; and in the latter those of reproduction, fatherhood, motherhood, and Christian nurture.

In a fallen world the sinful inclination of the human heart is to trample upon these ordinances of God and to pervert the functions of holy wedlock to selfish and unholy ends. In this way the sacred marriage union may deteriorate, and in many cases has deteriorated, into a life of sensuality and selfish indulgence. One such form of perversion of the marriage ordinance of God is seen in the refusal on the part of physically normal married people to beget children, or in their failure, when able to do so, to reproduce the race adequately. Many look upon childbearing as an incidental instead of a primary function of marriage, and the idea that the size of one's family is to be determined by mere considerations of personal preference, instead of by the ordinances of God, is apparently making headway even among Christian people.

In the face of conditions and practices occasioned by these perverted views, the synod desires to re-assert the Christian, the biblical, view of marriage and parenthood. In the light of the twofold scriptural principle stated above there can be no doubt that it is the duty as well as the privilege of normally endowed married people to produce as large a number of children as is compatible with the physical, mental, and spiritual well-being of the wife and mother on the one hand, and of the children on the other. To be sure, the mother may at no time be sacrificed to the production of a numerous progeny. She is a spiritual personality and, together with her Christian husband, a "joint heir of the grace of life" (I Peter 3:7). But it is equally true that her supreme glory as woman lies in motherhood. In the words of the apostle, "she shall be saved through her childbearing" (I Tim. 2:15).

The synod has no desire to define the specific duty on this score of any given husband and wife. This is, in the last analysis, a distinctly personal matter, which husband and wife must settle in the presence of their God and in the light of the best medical advice—Christian medical advice—available. Living as we do in a world suffering from the ravages of sin, certain conditions and circumstances may demand of Christians that they forego parenthood, or that the voluntary limiting of the number of their offspring becomes their duty before God. While making full allowance for this personal and medical angle of the matter, synod is convinced that it is the solemn duty of the church to bear testimony against the growing evil of a selfish birth restriction and to hold up the sacred ordinances of God and the Christian ideal of marriage and parenthood, which are increasingly being ignored and flouted in our day. Childbearing and parenthood are to be held up as a basic aim of marriage. The glory of fatherhood and motherhood, which Scripture stresses so repeatedly, should be made real upon proper occasion in the preaching and teaching of the church, and especially in the thought, the conversation, and the life of all who name themselves after Christ. Disparaging remarks about large families as such should not be heard among Christian people. "Lo, children are a heritage of Jehovah; and the fruit of the womb is his reward" (Ps. 127:3).

In this connection the synod raises its voice in protest against the growing evil of the indiscriminate dissemination of contraceptive information, an evil against which even the American Medical Association has in its 1936 annual session gone on record on moral grounds, (*Journal of the A.M.A.*, May 30, 1936, pp. 1911, 1912). Let Christian married people who are genuinely perplexed as to their specific duty at a given time rather consult their pastor, and, especially, some Christian physician, of whom it may be expected that his advice will be not only medically sound but also in harmony with the demands of Christian morals in the light of the Word of God.

Finally, the synod would urge all Christians in the words of the Apostle: "Be sober, be watchful" (I Peter 5:8). In these days of growing worldliness let Christian people be on their guard lest ways of ease and luxury undermine their morals. Let young people who name themselves after Christ fight manfully against the subtle temptations of our day and in the strength of God live chaste lives. As they look forward to marriage, let them cherish truly Christian ideals in the light of the two-fold purpose for which marriage was instituted by God. Let parents seek to mold the thoughts and ideals of their growing sons and daughters, so that these in sex matters may think and speak and live as becomes Christian young people. Let our ministers at the opportune time and in the light of God's Word speak words of wisdom and discretion to their people on the subject of marriage and parenthood. And let those who live in the state of wedlock by the grace of God make all things, also childbearing, parenthood, and Christian nurture, subservient to the coming of the kingdom of our God and his Christ.

References: Acts of Synod, 1906, p. 53.
Acts of Synod, 1936, pp. 136-138.

Notes: *In this statement from the Christian Reformed Church in North America (approximately 219,998 members in 1985), abortion was allowable only when the life of the mother was threatened. Abortion was viewed negatively in light of the scripture and in the context of "the increasing sensualizing of marriage in our day, [and] the steady decline in the birth rate not only in the world at large but also in the church of Jesus Christ." The mother was not allowed to be sacrificed to numerous progeny, but at the same time, "she shall be saved through her childbearing" (I Tim. 2:15).*

CHURCH OF GOD (JERUSALEM ACRES)

STATEMENT ON ABORTION (1968)

F. Abortion

Prominent theological teachings of many religious organizations have been that abortion is a sin in any circumstances, even if abortion would save the life of the mother. The position of The Church of God is one of sound scriptural backing as follows:

Jesus said in Matthew 18:8: "Wherefore, if thy hand or thy foot offend thee, cut them off and cast them from thee: it is better for thee to enter into life halt or maimed, rather than having two hands or two feet to be cast into everlasting fire. And if thine eye offend thee, pluck it out, and cast it from thee: it is better for thee to enter into life with one eye, rather than two eyes to be cast into hell fire." The situation of the unborn child is very much the same as the situation in this scripture in that it is not an entity (separately sustained being). It is actually part of the body of the mother and is totally incapable of independent existence. To remove the fetus in any stage of the pregnancy for the sake of the health of the mother that she may enter into life could be no more considered feloneous than the amputation of any other part of her body which threatens her life through disease.

As with the Church's decision on birth control, it is the entrance of breath which determines the existence of a human being. Although abortion could in no case be called a murder, such an act carried out for motives other than for the health of the mother is an offense to God of another category, for God looketh on the heart.

The Church of God, therefore, maintains that abortion should be resorted to only when the health of the mother is endangered. The aborting of the development of a fetus is in no way immoral in such cases. Again, the final determination in these matters must be based on the conscience of the believer who may not be judged by anyone for making either decision.

Notes: *This statement by the Church of God (Jerusalem Acres), which has approximately 10,000 members, affirmed individual judgment on the issue of abortion, although abortion should only be resorted to when the mother's health was in danger. It saw the fetus as an appendage of the mother's body and not alive as a human being until the entrance of breath. This statement was taken from the* Manual of Apostles Doctrine and Procedure.

CHURCH OF GOD AT ANDERSON, INDIANA

RESOLUTION ON ABORTION (1981)

After years of activity in the United States directed at passage of an Equal Rights Amendment (ERA) to the national Constitution and related decisions of the Supreme Court, the General Assembly decided to speak on the major social concern of the legal availability of abortion to almost anyone for almost any reason. The Assembly action read:

WHEREAS, the United States Supreme Court has declared unconstitutional all state laws regulating abortion, and has opened the way for abortion on demand for any reason; and

WHEREAS, the rights of the unborn child are being stripped away by reinterpretation of the Constitution by the Supreme Court; and

WHEREAS, this opens the door to possible elimination of other unwanted or undesirable human beings; and

WHEREAS, the Bible contains reference to God's personal acquaintance with children prior to birth, inferring the fetus has life, such as

1. In Jeremiah 1:4, 5 ''. . . the Word of the Lord came unto me saying, 'Before I formed you in the womb I knew you, and before you were born I consecrated you; I have appointed you a prophet to the nations.''' (NASV);

2. And in Psalm 139:13, King David inspired by God, wrote, ''Thou didst form my inward parts; thou didst weave me in my mother's womb. I will give thanks to thee, for I am fearfully and wonderfully made.'' (NASV); and

WHEREAS, abortion on demand, we believe, greatly diminishes the moral values, not only of the one seeking abortion, but of this whole nation; and

WHEREAS, the unborn child cannot plead in its own defense;

BE IT THEREFORE RESOLVED that the General Assembly of the Church of God go on record as opposing abortion on demand, recognizing that the unborn fetus is a living human being and thus should be protected by the laws and Constitution of the United States of America; and

BE IT FURTHER RESOLVED that the General Assembly of the Church of God urges all congregations to express our compassion and concern not only to protect life before birth but to work to assure that the lives that are preserved may receive the care, attention, and help that God wants for all persons; to provide family life and marriage education that will foster such a reverence for God-given life that both the causes and consequences of unwanted pregnancies may be diminished; and that the resolution be publicized.

Notes: *In this 1981 resolution from the Church of God at Anderson, Indiana, (approximately 185,593 members in 1985), an explicit link was made between the enacting of this resolution and the attempts by others to pass the Equal Rights Amendment, though it did not explain this link. The reasons given against abortion focused on God's care for the unborn and the devaluation of human life implied in abortion.*

CHURCH OF ISRAEL

STATEMENT ON ABORTION (1982)

10. We believe that Abortion is murder of the unborn and innocent children of God. Life begins at conception and to destroy that life through any type of abortion amounts to an act of murder. Since abortion is an act of overt violence and terror of the unborn we oppose abortion and believe it is the duty of the family and the Church to oppose the murder of the unborn. (Exodus 21.22-25, Exodus 20.13, Deut. 5.17)

Notes: *This statement by the Church of Israel (approximately 500 members) sharply condemned abortion in all circumstances as murder.*

CHURCH OF THE BRETHREN

STATEMENT ON ABORTION (1972)

Biblical Teaching

A Christian ethic regarding abortion begins with the biblical teaching about the sacredness of life and about love for persons, two of the central themes of scripture. Abortion as used hereafter refers to any intentional interference with embryonic or fetal human life that results in the termination of that life prior to birth. When considering the biblical teaching about abortion one should remember that there are few scriptural passages directly related to the question and that the direction of scripture is not so clear that anyone can be dogmatic in his interpretation. No biblical passage condemns or approves of abortion as such. Nevertheless the Bible teaches that God is the creator of human life in its biological form as well as its distinctly personal qualities. Therefore we turn first of all to passages about life and then to passages about love and compassion.

The Bible teaches that human life is a sacred gift from God. This does not mean that human beings have no part in the creation of new life, for God has clearly entrusted the cultivation and propagation of human life into the hands of persons (Genesis 1:2). Nevertheless, it remains a sacred gift from God and is at center a mystery beyond definition. Science can describe the development of the fetus, but is cannot penetrate the mystery and uniqueness of the person who is brought into being by the hand of God.

The mystery of the creation is heightened by the fact that it is difficult to prove from the scriptures just when personal existence begins. Many passages seem to suggest that personal existence begins long before the time at which a fetus may be born and live. Heart, blood, mind, and breath are all signs of personal life. Biblically the "heart" refers to the center of personal being. "You shall love the Lord your God with all your heart, with all your soul, and with all your might" (Deuteronomy 12:23). The mind and the strength, thinking and moving, are evidence of personal life. Soul and breathing are closely associated, suggesting that full personhood comes with breathing. Body and personhood are so joined that the latter does not exist without the former. Thus the Bible seems to suggest multiple signs of personal human life, many of which are present long before viability.

At the same time it is difficult to prove from the scriptures that conception is clearly the beginning of personal human life. While in Psalm 51:5 the psalmist speaks personally about his own conception ("In sin did my mother conceive me"), Jeremiah 1:5 speaks of being called of God before conception ("Before I formed you in the womb I know you"). Reference to "conception" in scripture is nearly always accompanied by reference to "bringing forth" as in the phrase "conceive and bear." Although the growing fetus may occasion personal reference, the beginning of personal existence remains shrouded in the mystery of God's call.

In the Bible the creative act of loving God and the response of a caring community is decisive in calling forth personal human life. The announcement of a child to be born is normally a time of joy and thankfulness. Signs of quickening and movement within the womb heighten expectancy for the coming child (Luke 1:44). Sensitive persons are moved with reverence in the presence of a growing fetus (Psalm 139:13-16). Thus many passages suggest that the growing fetus is precious in God's sight and that the bodily signs of personhood are distributed throughout fetal development.

A comparison of the value of fetal life and the life of the mother seems to be implied in Exodus 21:22-25. There one who accidently hits a pregnant woman and causes a miscarriage may have a fine imposed upon him by the husband. Should the expectant mother die, the guilty party may be required to compensate by giving up his own life. Interpretations of the passage vary, but it would seem to suggest that while the life of the fetus is precious, it is not so precious as the life of the mother, and therefore an accidentally caused miscarriage is not necessarily treated as manslaughter. We must remember however that the passage is not considering voluntary abortion. We must also remember that Jesus tremendously heightened the commandment not to kill, even including an admonition against anger (Matthew 5:21-23).

Everything we know of Jesus from the scripture indicates his love and compassion for persons. He did not consider that the law was to be applied without regard for the persons involved. For this reason, Scribes, Pharisees, and Saducees considered Jesus to be a lawbreaker. An important example is that of the woman taken in adultery (John 8:1-11). Her sin was so serious that she was on the point of being stoned to death. Jesus did not abolish the high requirements of the moral law, but suggested that those without sin carry out the punishment. He then forgave her, asking her not to sin again. From Jesus we learn that when we espouse high moral principles with harsh consequences for many, we must be ready to forgive such persons and to offer them every opportunity to make their own responsible decision. Jesus did not weaken the moral law against adultery; he rather set it within a context of compassion for persons.

Over the years Brethren sought to follow the example and teaching of Jesus that religion and morality are ultimately voluntarily decided before God. Believing that the heart and soul of morality is the free choice of persons who love other persons, Brethren generally have been unwilling to rely upon military force, capital punishment, religious inquisition, or punitive legislation. Brethren have sought rather to develop helping institutions and service for those who suffer, to introduce a note of compassion.

Social Considerations

The biblical affirmation that human life is sacred does not easily resolve the ethical dilemmas concerning the quality as well as the fact of human life. Such a dilemma is obvious when the life of a mother is threatened by her pregnancy. Most Brethren have been willing to allow that a fetus may be aborted to save the life of the pregnant woman. This seems to be within the direction of biblical teaching although we marvel at the love of a mother who voluntarily risks her life in order that her child might be born. Surely no one should be required to do so.

The dilemma is posed in another form when the threat of world overpopulation is considered. Various population estimates indicate that the world will be intolerably overpopulated within two or three generations if present population trends continue. The human reproductive potential is increasingly coming into conflict with the lives and quality of life of those already born. Is the threat of overpopulation with attendant starvation and death sufficient reason to resort to abortion? Reverence for human life should lead Christians to use medically safe and effective contraceptive methods rather than resort to abortion.

The moral dilemma of abortion is complicated by the fact that abortion is not so available to the poor as it is to those who are not poor. It is hardly just to retain strict abortion laws that are only enforceable against those who cannot afford to do anything but comply. The dilemma is also complicated by the fact that abortion is so prevalent, even in the face of great danger and degradation. Thousands of women each year willingly risk their lives and many die because of self-induced or illegally obtained abortions. Their decisions to abort could hardly have been made for the sake of mere convenience or whim, but must rather have been accompanied by severe mental anguish and despair. Even though abortion is not an acceptable means of solving problems, there are many situations in which a woman finds no alternative that she feels she can bear. In such cases, condemnation is destructive and does nothing to relieve misery; it only makes a woman less capable of coming to a rational decision.

Merely condemning abortion is self-defeating. In our concern for the well-being of the fetus, we may add to the despair that has already driven the mother to seek a "way out" of her problems rather than find a constructive solution. On the other hand, merely condoning abortion is equally self-defeating. In our concern for the mother, we run the risk of encouraging her too easily to make a decision that is callous of all human life in its destruction of the unborn. We must not allow ourselves simply to voice a position and then be satisfied that we have met our responsibility. Rather, as Christians we must actively and compassionately share in the burdens that lead women to seek abortions.

In seeking to preserve the life of a woman and the fetus she carries, we need to understand the life-destroying situations that drive her to abortion. Her family may already be so large and so poor that they are starving. The fetus may be defective and require expense and care, both emotional and physical, that she and her husband are unable to give. Faced with these and other difficulties, a couple must sometimes make an extremely difficult decision. When they prayerfully and maturely wrestle with all available alternatives and choose personal sacrifice for the sake of their unborn child, we celebrate God's compassionate spirit.

Medical/Counseling Considerations

The range of individual choice regarding pregnancy and family planning is much broader than it used to be and modern medical developments promise to make it even more so. Modern contraception has made pregnancy a relatively deliberate and free option for many persons in our society. The risk to life and physical health of the mother as a consequence of pregnancy and delivery is now small; the physical risk accompanying medically ethical abortion procedures in the first trimester of pregnancy is much smaller. This risk increases, however, as pregnancy progresses. By way of contrast, the risk to health and life due to clandestine, unhygienic, often desperate abortion procedures at the present time is exceedingly high, and there are many hundreds of needless deaths yearly. Further technological advances in the utilization of intrauterine devices (IUDs), the "morning-after" pill, and the seemingly imminent appearance of effective oral medication that will abort by chemical means in the earliest stages of pregnancy promise to make it increasingly difficult to delineate contraception from abortion. Existing public laws with respect to abortion, therefore, may well become increasingly irrelevant and unenforceable.

Technical discoveries about the genetic and congenital abnormalities of human development have increased the possibility of detecting carrier states of defective genes and chromosomal defects and of predicting such disease in potential offspring. Such conditions may occasionally be diagnosed as early as midpregnancy. Genetic counseling considers the degree of risk involved, the seriousness of the possible defect, the parents' willingness to care for a defective child, the possibility that a defective child might be helped by medical or surgical procedures to achieve a more nearly normal life, the possible result of the defect on the life of the child, on other members of the family, and on society.

Psychological studies of women who undergo abortion by acceptable medical procedures have not supported generally held beliefs regarding the emotional stress of such an experience. In the majority of cases, general relief or a brief and mild depressive reaction is reported. Rarely do more severe disturbances appear. The emotionally disturbed woman who undergoes abortion seems to experience no loss of stability and, sometimes, even improves. Frequently expressed beliefs regarding the occurrence of involuntary infertility, difficulty in sexual functioning as well as depression, are not substantiated by the presently available evidence. There is, however, continued expression of concern by psychiatrists and psychologists about adverse effects, short-term or long-term, individually or collectively, of repeated resort to abortion.

Effective research has yet to be done to clarify the real psychological and social efforts of changing social codes regarding abortion and the response that large numbers of persons are making to these changes. Clinical experiences with persons who have sought an illegal abortion, usually in a context fraught with tension, secrecy, fear, and real risk to life and health, reveal frequent important emotional trauma and suffering from the experience. It appears that condemnatory attitudes, compassionlessness, profound insensitivity, and lack of understanding in ourselves and those around us lie at the heart of this distress. Even when no longer expressed in legal prohibitions, these attitudes tend to be preserved in the larger community, and often in the church as well, by keeping distant from the problem and by isolating responsibility within the hands of the medical profession. Professional people, as well as their patients, have need for persons of compassion and insight who will undertake to share the burden of moral decision and thereby bring a fuller humanity into the lives of all. The meeting of minds, whenever possible, of caring persons most involved and most to be affected by any decision brings dignity, moral sensitivity, and support to persons in crisis.

Psychological studies of children and of family life have brought a new and increasing concern of behavioral scientists for the problems of the ''unwanted child.'' Nearly everyone agrees that being unwanted in early childhood is devastating to the development of personality and is the cause of many behavioral and emotional problems.

The physician is committed to the preservation of life. When faced with a request for abortion, he is placed in a position of felt conflict that is often keen. Along with his commitment to life he and other counselors are also called upon to care about and relate to individual persons in their choices, conflicts and needs. He is asked to care enough that instead of controlling, dominating, or manipulating, he seeks rather to set persons free to grow and to discover their own highest purposes.

A Position Statement

Brethren oppose abortion because it destroys fetal life. Let is be clear that the Brethren ideal upholds the sacredness of human life and that abortion should be accepted as an option *only* where all other possible alternatives will lead to greater destruction of human life and spirit.

However, we confess that we are part of a society that contributes to abortion by denying parents the support and assistance they need. We further confess our lack of compassion, our condemnation of those who differ with our view of morality, and our need to coerce and compel others to our way of thinking.

Thus, our position is not a condemnation of those persons who reject this position or of women who seek and undergo abortions. Rather, it is a call for Christlike compassion in seeking creative alternatives to abortion.

We support persons who, after prayer and counseling, believe abortion is the least destructive alternative available to them, that they may make their decision openly, honestly, without the suffering imposed by an uncompromising community.

We oppose any action, direct or indirect, by parents, physicians, the state, or anyone that would compel a woman to undergo an abortion against her will.

All who seek abortions should be granted sympathetic counsel about alternatives available as well as the health and safety of publicly available physicians and hospital care.

It is vital to the spiritual and social well-being of the Brotherhood that it educate its members about the sacred spiritual quality of human life and human sexuality, family planning, and the meaning and practice of responsible parenthood. This effort should be both an individual and collective responsibility. The Brotherhood should also support organizations such as Planned Parenthood and Clergy Consultation Service in their educational efforts.

Christian parents must seriously consider limiting family size, since over-population poses a very real threat to the whole of human life.

However, this should be achieved by contraception and voluntary preventive measures, such as male or female sterilization, rather than by abortion.

The Brotherhood should do everything it can to assist and encourage mothers and fathers to want and care for all their children. For example, Brethren can show their concern and compassion by providing homes for unwanted children or by giving of their time and resources to families who cannot afford the care of another child or cannot bear the physical strain of an additional infant.

For many Brethren, situations such as threat to the life and health of the mother, rape, incest, or possible fetal deformity are considered sufficient to warrant abortion. However, such situations need not necessarily lead to abortion unless they threaten serious destruction of the life or spirit of the family. The precise definition of circumstances must be left to the mother, father, physician, pastor, and other significant persons who are well informed and in whom the mother and father have confidence.

Counseling should encourage the mother and father to work through the decision in view of the value of human life, the options available, including adoption and foster care, the consequences of options, and the well-being of those most directly affected.

Physicians are urged not only to consult with their medical colleagues, but also to seek other ways to share the burden of moral responsibility so frequently thrust upon them. They are encouraged to resist the inclination to shoulder the weight of decision in isolation from others who are involved and concerned. Any physician or attendant who, because of personal moral conviction, chooses not to perform or participate in an abortion, however legal, should be free to do so in good conscience, and should receive the full support of the church. We urge a physician with such convictions to refer patients who may desire an abortion to another competent certified doctor.

Laws regarding abortion should embody protection of human life, protection of freedom of moral choice, and availability of good medical care. Brethren should work for laws that uphold these principles, even though there are differing opinions as to how such principles may be achieved. Brethren are asked not to try to enforce their highest ideal of morality by strict civil law.

Recommendations

1. That the Brotherhood make available a course of study on human sexuality and responsible parenthood. Such a course should be designed to assist congregations and families in their teaching and individuals in personal growth.

2. That a "fellowship of families" be organized in a network throughout the brotherhood for the purpose of helping those families who need support and assistance in wanting and

caring for their children. Examples of such assistance include taking in an unwanted child, sharing in the care of a handicapped child, sitting with children so that parents can renew their own relationship, or giving material and financial aid. The strength of such a fellowship should be in its ability to respond creatively to any situation in which families need help in wanting and caring for children.

3. That, at the joint initiative of the Brotherhood and of interested physicians, a group of physicians, informed pastors, and knowledgeable laymen be called together to consider ways to promote sharing the burden of responsibility for moral choice, so often left to the physician alone.

—Adopted by the Church of the Brethren Annual Conference, 1972

Notes: *This longer statement by the Church of the Brethren (approximately 159,184 members in 1986) gives a greater indication of how a church decides policy on a single issue. The Brethren ideal stated that abortion would be accepted only when other options were more destructive. The statement did not seek to coerce, through civil law, those who disagree with the Brethren moral position and supported those who have decided on abortion, even if others felt their reasons were insufficient. This position was basically reaffirmed in 1984.*

CHURCH OF THE NAZERENE

STATEMENT ON ABORTION (1985)

C. Abortion

35. We believe induced abortion to be permissible only on the basis of sound medical reasons that give evidence of life-endangering conditions for the mother. We oppose induced abortion for personal convenience or population control. We also oppose liberalizing the laws which allow induced abortion on demand. There may be pregnancies that require deliberate termination by therapeutic abortion, but such a decision should be made only on the basis of adequate medical and spiritual counseling [Exodus 20:13; Job 31:15; Psalm 139:3-16; Isaiah 49:5; Luke 1:31, 41-44; Romans 12:1-2].

    We further believe that responsible opposition to abortion requires our commitment to the initiation and support of programs designed to provide care for mothers and children.

Notes: *This 1985 statement by the Church of the Nazarene (approximately 543,762 members) opposed laws which allowed "abortion on demand." Interestingly, it also said that, by taking this position, the church was required to work toward support systems for mothers and children.*

CONSERVATIVE BAPTIST ASSOCIATION

RESOLUTION ON ABORTION (1981)

Abortion - 1981

WHEREAS, the entire abortion issue may well be the most demanding question of our day involving response on social, political, moral and religious levels, and

WHEREAS, we believe that the Scriptures teach an unmistakable sanctity of the womb (Psalm 139:13-17; Isaiah 44:2; Jeremiah 1:5),

BE IT THEREFORE RESOLVED that Conservative Baptists reaffirm that the most basic of all human rights is the right to life, and

BE IT FURTHER RESOLVED that in light of this reaffirmation, we declare ourselves to be opposed to abortion, believing it to be the taking of innocent human life.

Notes: *This 1981 resolution by the Conservative Baptist Association (approximately 250,000 members) condemned abortion in favor of the "right to life" of the fetus, whose life God made sacred.*

CONSERVATIVE BAPTIST ASSOCIATION

RESOLUTION ON ABORTION (1983-84)

Abortion - 1983 and 1984

WHEREAS, the most abused, defenseless, and un-cared-for segment of our society is composed of the unborn infants who are ripped from the womb by induced abortion, and

WHEREAS, it has become socially acceptable for men to repudiate their paternal responsibilities by acquiescing to the destruction of their own unborn children, and

WHEREAS, Biblical Christianity commands respect for all human life, born and unborn,

BE IT THEREFORE RESOLVED that we declare once again our unqualified opposition to abortion performed in disregard for the life of the unborn person, their rights and their worth, and that we encourage all medical personnel within our constituency to refuse to take part in any such abortion procedure, and we further urge that Conservative Baptists protest by every legitimate method this wanton attack upon human life in which the life of every person is denigrated and injured, and

BE IT THEREFORE RESOLVED that we support the efforts of those who would be executive, legislative, and judicial means attempt to curb this monstrous evil in our society, and

BE IT THEREFORE RESOLVED that in order to demonstrate not just hatred for evil but sacrifice for truth, we urge the people in churches of our fellowship to be aggressive in their concern for those considering abortion, and to be active in the love and care of unwanted children, and

BE IT FURTHER RESOLVED that recognizing our responsibility to all lives, the born and the unborn, we guard and cherish the life of every person and most particularly the handicapped, the depressed, the neglected, the injured, and the unwanted.

Notes: *It is interesting to note the shift in language from the Conservative Baptist Associations' 1981 statement to this statement, which is far more colorful and angry in its tone (e.g. "ripped from the womb," "monstrous evil"). It implicitly spoke of a particular understanding of the structure of the family when it castigated men for repudiating their "paternal responsibilities" in this matter.*

CONSERVATIVE BAPTIST ASSOCIATION

RESOLUTION ON CRISIS PREGNANCY CENTERS (1986)

Crisis Pregnancy Centers - 1986

SINCE Conservative Baptists have consistently opposed abortion, and

SINCE abortions frequently result from the frustration of women who feel trapped by overwhelming circumstances,

THEREFORE we encourage Conservative Baptists to support crisis pregnancy centers and to become actively and helpfully involved in the lives of women facing crisis pregnancies.

Notes: *This statement on crisis pregnancy centers reflected the growing concern on the part of those who opposed abortion that they needed to support those with problem pregnancies by offering them practical alternatives to abortion.*

EPISCOPAL CHURCH

RESOLUTION ON ABORTION (1967)

House of Deputies—Eighth Day

The said Committee reported and recommended that the House concur with the House of Bishops, with Amendments, the amendments taking the form of the following Substitute Resolution:

Whereas, Several Dioceses of the Episcopal Church have joined with civic, social, and welfare groups in urging that State laws governing abortion be amended along the lines recommended by the American Law Institute and the American Medical Association; therefore be it

Resolved, the House of Deputies concurring, That the Sixty-Second General Convention of the Church support abortion-law reform, to permit the termination of pregnancy, where the decision to terminate has been arrived at with proper safeguards against abuse, and where it has been clearly established that the physical health of the mother is threatened seriously, or where there is substantial reason to believe that the child would be born badly deformed in mind or body, or where pregnancy has resulted from forcible rape or incest.

The House concurred, with Amendments
(384 aye—189 no)

[Communicated to the House of Bishops by Message No. 150.]

Notes: *This 1967 statement from the 62nd General Convention of the Episcopal Church (approximately 2,739,422 members in 1985) followed the lead of the American Law Institute and the American Medical Association in recommending legalized abortion with safeguards against "abuse."*

EPISCOPAL CHURCH

RESOLUTION ON ABORTION (1988)

Resolved, the House of Deputies concurring, That the 69th General Convention adopt the following statement on childbirth and abortion:

All human life is sacred. Hence, it is sacred from its inception until death. The Church takes seriously its obligation to help form the consciences of its members concerning this sacredness. Human life, therefore, should be initiated only advisedly and in full accord with this understanding of the power to conceive and give birth which is bestowed by God.

It is the responsibility of our congregations to assist their members in becoming informed concerning the spiritual, physiological and psychological aspects of sex and sexuality.

The Book of Common Prayer affirms that "the birth of a child is a joyous and solemn occasion in the life of a family. It is also an occasion for rejoicing in the Christian community". As Christians we also affirm responsible family planning.

We regard all abortion as having a tragic dimension, calling for the concern and compassion of all the Christian community.

While we acknowledge that in this country it is the legal right of every woman to have a medically safe abortion, as Christians we believe strongly that if this right is exercised, it should be used only in extreme situations. We emphatically oppose abortion as a means of birth control, family planning, sex selection, or any reason of mere convenience.

In those cases where an abortion is being considered, members of this Church are urged to seek the dictates of their consciences in prayer, to seek the advice and counsel of members of the Christian community and where appropriate the sacramental life of this Church.

Whenever members of this Church are consulted with regard to a problem pregnancy, they are to explore, with grave seriousness, with the person or persons seeking advice and counsel, as alternatives to abortion, other positive courses of action, including, but not limited to, the following possibilities: the parents raising the child; another family member raising the child; making the child available for adoption.

It is the responsibility of members of this Church, especially the clergy, to become aware of local agencies and resources which will assist those faced with problem pregnancies.

We believe that legislation concerning abortions will not address the root of the problem. We therefore express our deep conviction that any proposed legislation on the part of national or state governments regarding abortions must take special care to see that individual conscience is respected, and that the responsibility of individuals to reach informed decisions in this matter is acknowledged and honored.

Resolved, the House of Deputies concurring, That this 69th General Convention call on the Presiding Bishop and the Executive Council to provide and promote the use of materials on human sexuality, birth control and family planning for all age groups as part of this Church's on-going Christian Education curricula as reflective of God's creation; and be it further

Resolved, That the topic of abortion be included in the Church's education curricula and that these materials be explicit, with a full understanding of the physical, emotional and spiritual realities and risks involved in abortion; and be it further

Resolved, That we encourage the members of this Church to give strong support to responsible local public and private school programs of education in human sexuality.

Notes: *This statement from the 69th General Convention of the Episcopal Church reaffirmed and shared the tone of previous statements which had been issued since 1967. It clarified the idea that abortion should not be resorted to for "mere convenience," and that legislation on the issue would not resolve the "root of the problem." It also pressed for more complete sex education within the church in an effort to prevent the need for abortions.*

EVANGELICAL CONGREGATIONAL CHURCH

STATEMENT ON ABORTION (1983)

143.1.2.5 Abortion

The moral issue of abortion is more than a question of the freedom of a woman to control the reproductive functions of her own body. It is a question of those circumstances under which a human being may be permitted to take the life of another.

Since life is a gift of God, neither the life of an unborn child nor the mother may be lightly taken. The value of life prior to birth is seen throughout the Scriptures (Psalms 139:13-16; 51:5; Jeremiah 1:5; Luke 1:41-44). Divine blessing is conferred upon an unborn infant (Luke 1:42, "Blessed is the child you will bear!"). The strife-filled lives of Jacob and Esau are shown already in process prior to birth (Genesis 25:22-23).

It is neither right nor proper to terminate a pregnancy solely on the basis of personal convenience or sociological considerations. Abortion on demand for social adjustment or to solve economic problems is morally wrong. On those rare occasions when abortion may seem morally justified the decision should be made only after there has been thorough and sensitive medical, psychological and religious consultation and counseling.

Notes: *This statement by the Evangelical Congregational Church (approximately 35,584 members in 1985) counseled against abortion as the taking of another life, except in the rare cases when it was possibly justifiable.*

EVANGELICAL FREE CHURCH OF AMERICA

STATEMENT ON ABORTION (1977)

Committee on Social Concerns

Resolution of the Social Concerns Committee of the Evangelical Free Church of America presented to the Annual Conference in June 1977.

A Declaration for Life and Morality

We hold an unborn child to have the rights of a person from conception and that these rights may not be properly abrogated by law.

We hold that it is the responsibility of parents to protect the rights of an unborn child and that abortion as commonly practiced today is not a legitimate means of handling unwanted, inconvenient or embarrassing pregnancies. We further hold that the rights of marriage should not be taken out of the context of marriage, but, even when they are, any resulting child is not to be viewed as having any less right to life and liberty from conception than any other child.

We hold that the state should guarantee the rights of the unborn child as it would guarantee the rights of any of its citizens, but that where the state adopts a lesser morality it is the duty of the Christian to adhere to and foster a higher morality.

We also hold that the eclectic morality upheld by the courts relative to abortion forbodes ill, not only for the defenseless, but also for the aged and the infirm, and represents an over-all trend which, if persisted in, will have repugnant consequences in the lives and consciences of every individual in our nation and in our national heritage and destiny.

The Social Concerns Committee also recommends the following paragraph concerning the action of the church to the individual:

Recognizing that the underlying social impetus to the abortion movement is the problem of unwanted children; we encourage our churches to take positive action in ministering to those situations where this problem of unwanted children exists. This could be done through counseling services, personal assistance to families where there is inability to provide for the means of children, and to become an agent of grace and support to the mother and her child.

Notes: *This 1977 statement by the Evangelical Free Church of America (approximately 110,000 members) opposed abortion as a means of handling unwanted pregnancies and* *viewed its legalization by the courts as a sign of "eclectic morality" that did not bode well for the future. It encouraged the church to assist those facing problem pregnancies.*

EVANGELICAL LUTHERAN CHURCH IN AMERICA

STATEMENT ON ABORTION (1978)

The 1970 convention of the church adopted the Social Statement on Sex, Marriage and Family. That statement provides basic principles on abortion based on theological grounds with socio-ethical considerations to be taken into account. Specific decisions are to be dealt with in counseling situations.

The statement opposes

a. Abortion on demand—"Earnest consideration should be given to the life and total health of the mother, her responsibilities to others in her family, the stage of development of the fetus, the economic and psychological stability of the home, the laws of the land, and the consequences for society as a whole"; and

b. Use of abortion as an alternative form of contraception— ". . . the fetus is the organic beginning of human live, . . ."

The Division for Mission in North America provides helpful interpretation in its study book "The Problem of Abortion after the Supreme Court Decision."

The Committee on Memorials from Synods recommends that the above minute be transmitted to the Nebraska, Central Pennsylvania and Wisconsin-Upper Michigan Synods as the response to their memorials.

Notes: *This statement from the 1978 Lutheran Church in America convention reaffirmed a 1970 statement that opposed abortion "on demand" and as an alternative form of contraception. On January 1, 1988, the Lutheran Church in America merged with the American Lutheran Church and formed the Evangelical Lutheran Church in America.*

EVANGELICAL LUTHERAN CHURCH IN AMERICA

RESOLUTION ON ABORTION (1980)

Abortion

A Statement of Judgment and Conviction

A resolution adopted by the Tenth General Convention of The American Lutheran Church (GC 80.4.46) "as a statement of judgment and conviction," which "expresses its corporate voice on an issue as its contribution to a public debate on that issue" of abortion. Ballot vote tally: Yes-609 (65%); No-323; Abstain-11.

Resolved, That The American Lutheran Church

a. affirms that human life from conception, created in the image of God, is always sacred;

b. understands that an induced abortion ends a unique human life;

c. advocates responsible exercise of sexual and procreative acts so as to prevent the temptation to turn to abortion;

d. deplores the alarming increase of induced abortions since the 1973 Supreme Court decision and views this as an irresponsible abuse of God's gift of life and a sign of the sinfulness of humanity and the brokenness of our present social order;

e. acknowledges that there may be circumstances when, all pertinent factors responsibly considered, an induced abortion may be a tragic option;

f. rejects the practice in which abortion is used for personally convenient or selfish reasons;

g. recognizes that guilt is a common consequence of abortion and applies to all involved-fathers, mothers, doctors, counselors, and the society in which abortion is so readily tolerated;

h. believes that because abortion has not only legal and medical, but also theological, ethical, moral, psychological, economic, and social implications, it is therefore too important a decision to be left solely to one person;

i. regards civil law as a significant factor in shaping the judgments of citizens concerning that which is moral or immoral, good or evil, in the social order; this church therefore deplores the absence of any legal protection for human life from the time of conception to birth;

j. urges those dealing with problem pregnancies to avail themselves of competent Christian guidance to help them explore the entire issue, including long-range effects and options other than abortion;

k. declares that life is not only under sin but also under grace and urges pastors, medical personnel, and parishioners to exercise their priestly and healing role under Christ.

Notes: *The Evangelical Lutheran Church in America (approximately 5,300,000 members) was formed on January 1, 1988 by a merger of the American Lutheran Church and the Lutheran Church in America. It has not yet created a new statement on abortion, so the statements presented here are those of the formerly separate bodies. This resolution from the 10th General Convention of the American Lutheran Church rejected abortion because it was "selfish". It further stated that it "deplored the absence of legal protection" for the fetus.*

EVANGELICAL MENNONITE CONFERENCE (KLEINE GEMEINDE)

STATEMENT ON ABORTION (1973)

5. Abortion

We believe that human life is precious to God, our Creator; that God's interest in the individual goes back beyond his birth as a baby; that human life begins at fertilization and that abortion is not in principle an acceptable solution for relieving personal and family distress; that abortion (the willful termination of a life) is a violation of God's will (Psalm 139:13-16).

Notes: *This statement by the Evangelical Mennonite Conference (Kleine Gemeinde) rejected abortion as a "violation of God's will."*

FUNDAMENTALIST BIBLE TABERNACLE

THANKSGIVING FOR BURGER'S RETIREMENT— AND A PRAYER FOR GOD TO ACT AGAIN (1986)

The famed Presbyterian theologian Dr. Francis A. Schaeffer has said, "The last sixty years have given birth to a moral disaster, and what have we done? Sadly, we must say that the evangelical world has been part of the disaster. More than this, the evangelical response itself has been a disaster . . . we must say that very few Christians have understood the battle we are in. Very few have taken a strong and courageous stand against the world spirit of this age as it destroys our culture" (*The Great Evangelical Disaster*, pp. 141,23). These quotations from a fundamentalist of a denomination other than mine, reveal the lack of concern evident by many Christians in the face of the abortion holocaust in America.

Bible-believing Baptists, Presbyterians, Lutherans, and others, lived by the thousands in Germany during the decade of 1929 to 1939. One of the great tragedies of history is this: the evangelicals and fundamentalists of Germany made virtually no public protest against the ever-increasing Nazi holocaust, which eventually destroyed the lives of six million Jews and six million non-Jews. The lack of concern by the churches in Hitler's Germany and elsewhere has been described in a recent best-selling book, *The Abandonment of the Jews*, by David Wyman. Dr. Wyman reveals that the churches, including the fundamentalist churches, in Nazi Germany did virtually nothing to stop the systematic murder of the Jewish people and others.

In America, the response of Bible-believing Christians has been almost the same as it was in Hitler's Germany. Those who claim to believe their Bibles have responded to the abortion holocaust in America by doing little if anything. Thus, Dr. Schaeffer can say that the response of Bible-believing Christians to the moral disaster of our nation, including the disaster of abortion, has been almost nonexistent, and that Christians have failed to take "a strong and courageous stand against the world spirit of this age as it destroys our culture."

The reasons for the churches in Nazi Germany not speaking out against the atrocities of fascism were many. Church leaders were caught up in politics. They knew that a strong stand against fascism would be unpopular. They refused to speak out in favor of the Jews for fear of losing their own popularity. Pastors of congregations feared what the middle-class people in their churches might say. Many feared a church split or the loss of membership. They, too, refused to speak out in support of the Jews. The failure of the churches in Germany to support the Jews is one of the greatest moral tragedies of the twentieth century.

The American church scene has been virtually the same regarding our failure to have any meaningful confrontation with the proponents of abortion on demand. In 1973, with the Roe vs. Wade decision, America entered into an era unprecedented in human history. Ours became the first culture with a Judeo-Christian heritage to fully endorse abortion on demand into the third trimester of pregnancy, so that a woman in our nation could have her baby aborted even into the ninth month. All of this was done by order of the Burger Court, a decision in which seven out of nine men on the Supreme Court declared abortion to be a woman's right. This same decision ensured the view that the pre-born child had no constitutional right whatever. Supreme Court Chief Justice-designate William Rehnquist called this decision a raw use of judicial power in his dissenting vote. Today, he is happily joined by three others, including Supreme Court Associate Justice-designate Antonin Scalia.

Many pastors and church leaders will gladly say, "I am against abortion." Of course, in the early years of fascism, the pastors of Germany would have said almost the identical words, "I am against the persecution of the Jews." Yet these same pastors failed in Germany to put their private beliefs into any sort of public practice; thus, the evangelical disaster of Germany once again parallels that of America.

Happily, there are a few exceptions, a few men of God who have actually joined the picket lines, started pregnancy hotlines, and opened homes for unwed mothers. These men deserve our admiration.

But the vast majority have done nothing of any practical nature. Most of them have not so much as walked in a picket line or counseled a single young woman to save her baby. They may have given a private prayer in their bedroom or closet for the end of the American holocaust, but they have failed to have the moral courage to sally forth and do even one practical deed to stop the extermination of the American Jews—the pre-born children. As a result, over 18 million children have now been sliced, pickled, mauled, dismembered, crushed, and boiled alive in stinging chemical solutions. All the while, the ministers have done virtually nothing to stop the new Hitlers of America—those who have supported abortion on demand in the Supreme Court of the United States of America.

I have seen this disaster. I have beheld the moral and spiritual apathy and pietism which has caused so many Bible-believing pastors to betray the children by failing to speak out. And I have determined that I must not join their cowardly ranks. The blood of pre-born children must not be upon my hands.

My sadness over the abortion holocaust was turned from moral indignation to moral outrage with the ''Baby Doe'' decision of Monday, June 9, 1986. This decision of the Supreme Court must go down forever as one of the most infamous judicial acts in human history. On this day of infamy, five members of the Supreme Court invalidated the regulations imposed by our godly pro-life President, Ronald Reagan, that were designed to require life-prolonging medical treatment for newborns with severe handicaps. *As a result of this decision, babies born handicapped can now be killed if the parents and the doctor so decide. The government of the United States is now prohibited by our highest court from saving babies who are born alive. The majority of the Court said that these living babies have no constitutional right to life, liberty, or due process, rights guaranteed them by the Fourteenth Amendment to the Constitution. We are not speaking here of pre-born infants. We are speaking of children two and three days old, and perhaps even several weeks old. The Court has said that these handicapped children are not protected by the Constitution of the United States. The Court has said that they can be starved to death, denied water until they die of dehydration and thirst, that they can be denied medical treatment, however slight, that might prolong their tiny lives. Even the most callous person must shudder at the Orwellian implications of this monstrous decision.*

But we say the court is wrong. We, the God-fearing conservative people of America, reject totally their morally hideous and insane decision. We say that ''Baby Jesse'' and all other handicapped children should have the same rights, guaranteed by the Constitution, which we had when we were born. We say that no human being has the right to discriminate between which of his fellow men should live or die.

To some, it may seem incongruous, or perhaps even hypocritical for those of us who are pro-life to pray for the death of a Supreme Court Justice. They will ask, ''How can those who are pro-life pray pro-death?'' Notice two fallacies in their argument. The first fallacy is this: we are *merely praying*. The Supreme Court Justices are *acting*—to kill people. Prayer may or may not be answered by the all-knowing, self-existent God. People are not killed by prayers. People *are* killed by the decisions of the Supreme Court. Secondly, we are not praying for *just anyone* to die. We are praying that men who formulate the laws of society be thus removed, and then only as a last resort. Thus, a pro-life advocate in Hitler's Germany certainly would have prayed for Hitler's removal, and done so on moral grounds.

Again, some would argue to support their view that those who prayed for Hitler's removal were wrong. To them, praying the words of Psalm 109:8-9 is immoral. The Psalm declares,

> ''Let his days be few; and let another take his office. Let his children be fatherless, and his wife a widow . . . because he remembered not to show mercy, but persecuted

the poor and needy man, that he might even slay the broken in heart. As he loved cursing, so let it come unto him'' (Psalm 109:8-9, 16-17)

But it is *never* immoral to pray the very words of Scripture, provided that they are applied as the writer originally intended. The Psalmist was praying for God to intervene and remove an evil ruler who "persecuted the poor" and was even responsible for "slay(ing) the broken in heart." This is a prayer directed to an all-knowing God for the removal of an evil leader.

The above prayer in Psalm 109 is quoted in the New Testament in Acts 1:20. Thus the Holy Spirit of God incorporated it into the New Testament, and it becomes a thoroughly Christian Psalm and prayer.

Christ said, "Love your enemies, bless them that curse you, do good to them that hate you, and pray for them that despitefully use you, and persecute you" (Matthew 5:44). To the uncritical thinker, the above-quoted Psalm may seem at first to contradict this statement. But the careful Biblical student who understands the science of hermeneutics (Bible exposition) will realize that the two thoughts in no way contradict each other. First, the Psalm is a prayer for the removal of an evil leader, while the words of Christ are applied to personal enemies (see verse 43, "neighbor"). Secondly, the Psalm is directed toward God, while the words of Christ are directed toward man. Christ told us to act lovingly in our personal relationship to people. The Psalm is not telling us to do anything in contradiction to the words of Christ; it is merely a prayer for God to take things into His own hands. And let it be remembered that God does not have to answer prayer. If our prayers are wrong, He can simply ignore them. A Christian prayer is in no sense a curse. God can choose to ignore our prayers if He so desires.

A CBS reporter in Los Angeles, Mr. Bill Stout, quoted Romans 2:1, and said that this verse could be used against us. But Mr. Stout conveniently left off the last few words of the verse, "for thou that judgest doest the same things." Since I do not kill babies or vote for them to be killed *myself*, Romans 2:1 has *no application of any kind to me*. After hearing Mr. Stout misquote this verse and attack me on television, an aged Roman Catholic priest wrote to me calling this CBS reporter, "a moral idiot." He went on to say, "I thoroughly approve of your prayer. I will join you in it . . . the moral morons at CBS simply do not fathom in any way your moral indignation. Of course, we have a higher Court than the unprincipled relativists of the news media. When we check in with the True Judge of all (God Himself), we are sure that you are on the right side."

God answers prayer. He knows who to answer when we pray. There can never be any confusion in God's mind, even though human beings may not have such understanding. Both sides prayed for victory during the American Civil War. God had the intelligence to answer the prayers of those in the North who opposed slavery. And this same God is able to decide whether or not to answer prayer today.

On Monday, June 16, 1986, God answered our prayers and the prayers of others who have joined us across the nation. God answered our prayers by bringing about the retirement of pro-death Supreme Court Justice Warren E. Burger. Burger was one of the supporters of the original Roe vs. Wade decision, and voted several times in favor of abortion. Burger voted to deny live-born children their constitutional rights in the "Baby Doe" decision. Thus, he was in favor of starving and denying medical treatment to handicapped infants.

We have prayed for the Repentance, Retirement, or Removal of those justices who have voted death to children.
We pray first and foremost for them to Repent.
In the event they are unwilling to Repent, we
pray that God will move them to Retire.
Only as a last resort, we pray that they will
be Removed by God.

Why does such a prayer enrage some people to such a degree? Is it because they unconsciously know that we are morally correct and that God is on our side? Or, is it because they feel that God will answer us? Or perhaps it's because they are on the same side as the pro-death justices, and are themselves fearful of eternal retribution.

It is more likely that all three of the above reasons are combined in some camouflaged and subconscious form in the minds of those who through vocal violence attack we who have committed a matter of national importance into the hands of God our Father.

Regardless of their turbulence and anger, we continue to pray what we have prayed previously. WE CONTINUE TO PRAY THE THREE R'S FOR THOSE PRO-DEATH JUSTICES WHO REMAIN ON THE COURT: REPENTANCE, RETIREMENT, OR REMOVAL. Let us pray:

> God of our fathers, who didst take the side of the poor and rejected Negro after the Supreme Court ruled him less than human in the Dred Scott decision one hundred years ago, hear our prayer.

> We give thanks that Thou hast acted in human history and brought about the Retirement of Chief Justice Burger, the infamous supporter of Roe vs. Wade, that monstrous decision which has permitted the murder of eighteen million pre-born children, and the supporter of the "Baby Doe" decision with its horrible implications for children born alive. We thank Thee that Thy hand has moved in answer to our prayers and removed Warren Burger from the court and into the oblivion of Retirement.

> Now we pray that Thou wilt act once again. John Paul Stevens, Thurgood Marshall, Harry Blackmun, and Lewis F. Powell, Jr. still remain in active positions on the Court. They have authored the "Baby Doe" decision. William J. Brennan, Jr. has joined these black-hearted villains in reaffirming abortion on June 11, 1986.

> These men do not deserve the love or admiration of the American people. God of Washington and Lincoln, we know that they do not deserve to represent the Constitution of our nation.

> We pray that Thou wilt act decisively and forcefully to bring about their Repentance, Retirement, or Removal. Only as a last resort, in the event that they refuse to Retire or Repent, we pray that Thou wilt Remove them in any way that Thou dost see fit.

> We, under no condition, will advocate that anyone rise against them in any form of violence. Instead, we commit them into Thy hands and pray that they will Repent, Retire, or be Removed by Thee. Thus, we pray that our land will be freed of these tyrants, through Thy providence and care. Through Jesus Christ our Lord, Amen."

THE LEADERS OF THIS PRAYER MEETING DO NOT ADVOCATE VIOLENCE OF ANY KIND AGAINST ANY HUMAN BEING, INCLUDING MEMBERS OF THE SUPREME COURT. WE ARE AGAINST THE BOMBING OF ABORTION CLINICS, AND THE USE OF VIOLENCE IN ANY FORM AGAINST THE SUPREME COURT OF THE UNITED STATES OF AMERICA, OR ANYONE ELSE. BUT WE DO RESERVE THE RIGHT TO PRAY IN THE ABOVE MANNER, AND WE ENCOURAGE OTHERS TO JOIN US IN PRAYING FOR TYRANNY TO END AND FREEDOM TO REIGN ACROSS AMERICA.

Notes: *Dr. R.L. Hymers, Jr., leader of the Fundamentalist Bible Tabernacle in Los Angeles, (a part of, but not an official spokesperson for, the Baptist Bible Fellowship of some 1,024,000 members) has developed a widespread reputation for his anti-abortion activities, including the controversial prayer for the death of certain Supreme Court justices mentioned in this document.*

GREEK ORTHODOX ARCHDIOCESE OF NORTH AND SOUTH AMERICA

STATEMENT ON ABORTION (UNDATED)

The most divine gift bestowed by God upon mankind is the gift of life itself, and throughout the centuries the sacredness of human life has been indisputed by responsible men and women of all persuasions.

We are currently confronted with a controversy surrounding the liberalization of abortion statutes stemming from the initiative of various groups and individuals whose actions, although predicated upon sincere and humanitarian motives, are nevertheless in conflict with divine law. Their position evolves from the general contention that the termination of unborn human life is justifiable when medical opinion believes there is substantial risk that continuance of the pregnancy would impair the physical or mental health of the mother, or that the child would be born with grave physical or mental defects, or if the pregnancy resulted from rape or incest.

It has been the position of the Orthodox Church over the centuries that the taking of unborn life is morally wrong. This is based upon divine law which is the most difficult law for man to comprehend for it transcends the boundaries of human frailty due to its source of divine authority. No law is perfect, and man in his diverse interpretations of the law is continually reminded of his human limitations. Even in such basic law as "Thou Shalt Not Kill" we can take no pride in its exceptions which justify war and self-defense, for they serve only to becloud our unceasing efforts toward shaping man in the image of God. This same principle of exception also extends to the unborn child. When the unborn child places the life of its mother in jeopardy, then and only then can this life be sacrificed for the welfare of its mother. To move beyond this exception would be transgressing man's duty in the protection of human life as understood and interpreted by the Orthodox Church.

We are profoundly aware that the discipline of divine law sometimes creates inequities that are difficult for human comprehension to accept, but the eternal values of divine law were not created for *a* man, but for mankind.

The solution to our vexing problem of an increasing need for abortion does not lie in reinterpreting the law to meet the needs of our present day morality, but rather challenges us to find more effective means of living up to the high standards of divine law which is the eternal protector of human life.

We give glory to God for creating man in His image, and we offer humble thanksgiving that in his unending search for knowledge and truth man is proving worthy of this divine gift. With the great advances in human achievement, especially in the realm of medical science, we are fully confident that the welfare of both the born and unborn are being drawn closer to the day when complications of pregnancy and abnormal birth will go the way of many diseases which have been overcome and are now conspicuous by their absence.

Notes: *This statement by the Greek Orthodox Archdiocese of North and South America (approximately 1,950,000 members in 1977) strongly condemned abortion and allowed it only if the life of the mother was in jeopardy.*

INTERNATIONAL PENTECOSTAL CHURCH OF CHRIST

RESOLUTION ON ABORTION (UNDATED)

BELIEVING that the moral issue of abortion is more than a question of the freedom of a woman to control the reproductive functions of her own body; and

BELIEVING that it is rather a question of those circumstances under which a human being may perform the sovereign right of taking the LIFE of another; and

BELIEVING that ALL LIFE is an expression of God's love, so that neither the life of the unborn fetus nor the mother may be taken lightly; and

BELIEVING that God Himself, in Holy Writ, has told us what our attitude must be towards the unborn through the specifically stating in Psalms 139:13,16, and in Luke 1:31,32,33,41, that He conferred Divine blessing upon unborn infants and provides penalties for actions which result in the death of unborn babies;

The INTERNATIONAL PENTECOSTAL CHURCH OF CHRIST issues this statement of its basic position addressing this subject; and

CONDEMNS in the strongest possible terms the role and influence of the Federal Judiciary which has made it legal to terminate a fetus for no better reason that personal convenience or sociological considerations up to and including the last trimester of pregnancy:

AFFIRMS our conviction that abortion on demand for social adjustment or to solve economic problems is morally wrong, and expresses its firm opposition to any legislation that will legalize abortion for those reasons;

ASSURES the Christian community that at the same time we recognize the necessity for therapeutic abortions to safeguard the health or life of the mother, as for example, the possibility of tubular pregnancies, which are considered by most doctors to be fatal unless terminated;

CALL UPON the committed Christian who may experience other pregnancies, such as those resulting from rape and incest, which may require deliberate termination, to arrive at the decision only after there has been extensive medical, psychological and religious counseling of the most sensitive kind realizing the final decision remains that of the woman, and when such determination has been reached, the individuals involved should not be subjected to censure; and

CHALLENGES our pastors and church leaders to speak out strongly in favor of the Biblical standard that upholds the sanctity of life.

Notes: *This statement by the International Pentecostal Church of Christ (approximately 3,500 members in 1985) objected to laws which allowed abortion for reasons of personal convenience, and it affirmed abortion as a moral alternative only when the life of the mother was at stake or in cases of rape or incest.*

JEHOVAH'S WITNESSES

RESPECT FOR THE GIFT OF LIFE (1973)

DEEP respect for the gift of life is a foundation of true peace and security. But such respect is sadly lacking among many people. As is well known, men can take away life by killing; but no man can restore life once it is gone.

[2]We should show respect for life as a sacred obligation. To whom? To the Giver of life, the one to whom the psalmist said: "For with you," namely, Jehovah God, "is the source of life." (Psalm 36:9 [35:10, *Dy*]) We owe our lives to him, not only because he created man, but also because he has allowed mankind to continue reproducing till now and has provided the means for sustaining life. (Acts 14:16, 17) More than that, he caused his Son to become the Repurchaser or Redeemer of the human family, buying it with his own precious lifeblood. (Romans 5:6-8; Ephesians 1:7) As a result, he now extends to all who will accept it the grand hope of life in his righteous new order. That is something that we really want, is

it not? In view of all this, should we not deeply respect and appreciate God's gift of life? How can we do so?

³For one thing, if we are serious about showing respect for life, we will not join with those who, simply for entertainment, feed their minds on programs that feature violence. Accepting violence as "entertaining" has caused many to become hardened and unfeeling toward human suffering and loss of life. They learn to live just for the present and show little concern for their own or anyone else's future welfare. But if we are grateful for God's goodness and the hope he gives, we will resist such spirit. We will cultivate appreciation for life as a gift from God. This will affect how we use our own lives, how we treat other people, even how we view those who have not yet been born.

Respecting the Life of the Unborn

⁴The power to pass on life is a grand privilege, divinely given. That life is passed on, not at birth, but at the time of conception. As the *Encyclopoedia Britannica* states, it is then that "the life-history of the individual, as a distinct and biological entity begins." Similarly, God's interest in a human life begins before birth. The psalmist David wrote, saying to God: "You kept me screened off in the belly of my mother. . . . Your eyes saw *even the embryo of me,* and in your book all its part were down in writing."—Psalm 139:13-16 [138:13-15, 16, *Dy*]; Ecclesiastes 11:5.

⁵In modern times the lives of millions of unborn children are deliberately being ended by abortion. Is this right? Some argue that the unborn baby has no conscious appreciation of what life is and is incapable of a separate existence outside the womb. But that is also basically true of a newborn baby. At birth it has no grasp of life's meaning, nor could it continue existence apart from constant care of parents or others. The living cell formed in the womb at the time of conception has every possibility of becoming a baby if not interfered with. Taking the life of a newborn baby is viewed as a crime nearly everywhere. Even where babies are born prematurely, great effort is made to save them. Why, then, should it not also be viewed as a crime for anyone to take the life of the unborn to prevent its further development and birth? Why should life be viewed as sacred only after it leaves the womb and not also while inside the womb?

⁶The important thing is not just how men may view matters but what God, the Giver of life, says. To Jehovah God the life of the unborn child is precious, not to be trifled with. He gave a law to ancient Israel specifically protecting the life of the unborn child. If, in a struggle between two men, a pregnant woman was injured or a miscarriage resulted, this law set forth strict penalties. (Exodus 21:22,23) Manifestly the deliberate taking of the life of an unborn child would be even more serious. According to God's law, whenever human life was taken deliberately, the guilty one was sentenced to death as a murder. (Numbers 35:30, 31) God maintains the same high regard for life now.

⁷Deep respect for God's will regarding the life of the unborn child works to real benefit. By his making parents fully responsible for the life of the unborn, he provides a curb to sexual promiscuity with all its bad effects—venereal disease, unwanted pregnancies, illegitimate children, broken families and the mental strain of an unclean conscience. This can contribute to family peace now and is an important factor in our gaining future blessings.

Endnotes

² Why should we show deep respect for the gift of life?

³ How does one's watching violence for entertainment affect his attitude toward life?

⁴ (a) When is life passed on to one's offspring? (b) What shows whether God is interested in a human life before birth?

⁵ Why are the arguments put forth in an effort to justify abortion not sound?

[6] How does the Bible indicate God's view toward the deliberate taking of the life of an unborn child?

[7] Against what are we protected when we respect God's will regarding the life of an unborn child?

Notes: *This statement from the Jehovah's Witnesses (approximately 588,503 members in 1982) was taken from the book,* True Peace and Security—From What Source?, *which is published by the Watch Tower Bible and Tract Society of Pennsylvania. It took a strong anti-abortion stance and indicated that its position of making parents responsible for every pregnancy would be God's way of curbing "sexual promiscuity with all its bad effects— venereal disease, unwanted pregnancies, illegitimate children, broken families and the mental strain of an unclean conscience."*

LUTHERAN CHURCH-MISSOURI SYNOD

ABORTION IN PERSPECTIVE (1984)

Except when otherwise noted, Scripture quotations in this publication are from the Revised Standard Version of the Bible, copyrighted 1946, 1952, © 1971, 1973. Used by permission.

Citations from The Lutheran Confessions are taken from *The Book of Concord,* translated and edited by T.G. Tappert (Philadelphia: Fortress Press, 1959).

Introduction

More than a decade has passed since the Commission on Theology and Church Relations issued its report, "Abortion: Theological, Legal, and Medical Aspects." Much has happened since then. While the principles and warnings issued in that document are still valid today, it would at that time have been difficult to anticipate the 1973 Supreme Court decisions which, by striking down many of the legal restrictions which surrounded abortion, made possible a dramatic increase in the number of abortions performed in this country. Since then abortion has been and continues to be an issue creating deep divisions within our society.

As groups supporting and opposing a right to abortion emerge within our nation, as the number of abortions performed yearly grows astonishingly, and as courts consider cases which may involve all citizens in the public funding of abortion, the Christian community must struggle with the moral and spiritual issues raised by such a rapid transformation of our public policy with respect to abortion. Controversy over abortion will probably continue in our country. As Lutheran citizens we seek to participate in this national debate—a participation which should be informed by the discoveries of medicine and science, be familiar with the legal situation which now exists in our country, and be guided by a vision of human life which is grounded in God's Word.

This report—intended as an aid to such informed participation—results from a request by the Commission on Theology and Church Relations that its Social Concerns Committee prepare a resource document for use by members of The Lutheran Church-Missouri Synod. While drawing on the theological principles presented in the Commission's 1971 document, this new report seeks to respond in greater detail to the changed political situation we face and to the moral problem which abortion continues to present.

I. The Medical Perspective

A. The Beginning and Development of a New Human Life

Christian vision, even in a prescientific age, has always been shaped by words like those of Psalm 139:

> For thou didst form my inward parts,
>   thou didst knit me together in my mother's womb.
> I praise thee, for thou art fearful and wonderful.
>   Wonderful are thy works!
> Thou knowest me right well;
>   my frame was not hidden from thee,
> when I was being made in secret,
>   intricately wrought in the depths of the earth.
> Thy eyes beheld my unformed substance;
>   in thy book were written, every one of them,
> the days that were formed for me,
>   when as yet there was none of them.

Such words have not only moved us to wonder at the marvel of new life; they have persuaded us that the dignity and value of human lives depend on no special achievement, for God has set His hand upon us and taken care for our days even "when as yet there was none of them."

We are prepared, therefore, to accept with continuing wonder and delight what medical researchers have begun to learn about the formation of a human being. The development of a new individual begins with fertilization. Sperm and ovum, in themselves incapable of growth, unite to form something new: a cell which carries the genetic characteristics of both parents and which establishes many characteristics of a new human being (e.g., sex, color of the eyes, blood type, facial features, some elements of intelligence and temperament). Given time and the proper environment this new cell will undergo constantly changing yet continuous development marked by the terms embryo, fetus,[1] infant, child, adolescent, adult. If the fertilized ovum, already undergoing cell division, successfully implants itself in the spongy lining of the mother's womb, a "bag of waters" will begin to form in which the embryo will float freely within the womb. Around 14 days after the time of fertilization this new cell—now multiplied to thousands of cells—may mysteriously "segment" or "twin" into two or more individuals with identical genetic inheritances. After this happens or fails to happen, the individuality of the new life (or lives) is clearly established.

The rate and magnitude of change and development which follow are astonishing. After a mere three and a half weeks the tiny heart begins to beat. Backbone, spinal column, and nervous systems are taking form—as are the kidneys, liver, and digestive tract. When the embryo is four weeks old, though he/she is only the size of an apple seed, his/her[2] head and body are clearly distinguishable. By the end of six to eight weeks of gestational development electrical activity from the developing brain can be detected (a fact of some significance, since it is now common to use cessation of brain activity as a criterion for determining death). By the end of two months of development the limbs (including fingers and toes) have begun to appear and the unborn child—now technically called a fetus—can hear, respond to touch, and make his first movements (though the mother will probably not feel such movement for several more months). By the end of the first trimester of a pregnancy the baby is fully formed. He can change his position, respond to light, noise, and pain, and even experience an attack of hiccups. In possession of his own set of fingerprints, the child now need only continue to develop size and strength until he is born.

B. Abortion

Abortion may occur spontaneously or may be induced. Not every fertilized ovum develops and matures according to the schedule outline above. Pregnancies may end at many points in this course of development. Spontaneous abortions occur most frequently at the time when implantation must take place if the new life is to survive. For any of a number of possible reasons—improper hormone levels in the mother, some abnormality in the uterus caused by infection or scar tissue, an incapacity due to genetic defect of the fertilized ovum to sustain itself, an incomplete process of fertilization—abortion will often occur at this point. Spontaneous abortions, usually referred to as miscarriages, are less likely after the first three months of gestational development.

Today, however, the word "abortion" is used most often to refer to action aimed at bringing pregnancy to an end. During the first trimester of pregnancy an induced abortion will usually be done by means of dilatation and curettage (D & C). The cervix opening is forcibly dilated, and the embryo and placenta are cut and scraped, or vacuum suctioned and scraped, in order to empty the uterus.

After the first trimester induced abortion is more difficult and less safe for the mother. Dilatation and extractions may be used—which requires dilating the cervix, inserting a forceps to dismember and remove the fetus, followed by curettage to be certain the uterus is emptied. A different method—known as saline abortion—is also used for second trimester abortions. A needle is inserted through the woman's abdomen into the amniotic sac ("bag of waters"), and some amniotic fluid is drawn off and replaced with a concentrated salt solution. This poisoned solution asphyxiates the fetus. Normally the mother will then go into labor and deliver a (usually) dead fetus. A more recent version of a similar method involves the injection of prostaglandins, which also induce labor and delivery. This method is considerably more likely than the saline method to result in the delivery of a living (and if the pregnancy is advanced enough, possibly viable) child.

An induced abortion beyond the second trimester will often require a surgical procedure called hysterotomy. The procedure is technically similar to a Caesarian section—except that the intent here is abortion rather than delivery of a child. It is complicated by the fact that a fetus aborted by hysterotomy may possibly still be viable when he or she is removed from the womb and the placenta is severed. Hence, this procedure raises serious legal questions about the physician's responsibility not just to the mother but to the possibly viable infant.

While some abortion procedures involve less risk than others, any abortion may involve complications. Immediate complications may include infection, hemorrhage, cervical damage, perforation of the uterus—any of which could endanger the life of the mother or prevent future pregnancies. Delayed complications may include sterility, greater chance of premature delivery in subsequent pregnancies (which may, in turn, cause physical or mental defects in the prematurely born child), and an increased incidence of ectopic (tubal) pregnancies. Finally, we should note that complications are not merely medical or physiological; they may also be emotional and psychological, for even a carefully considered decision for abortion can later be cause for intense guilt and deep regret.

C. Amniocentesis

Amniocentesis is a medical procedure in which amniotic fluid is withdrawn from the amniotic sac by means of a needle inserted through the abdominal wall of the mother. Fetal cells within this fluid can then be studied, and from such study much can be learned about the condition of the developing fetus. The procedure is not without some risks, chief among them an increase in the rate of miscarriage. (The risk of fetal death from infection or puncture is one in 200. If miscarriages are included, then the fetal death rate is at least 3 percent.)[3]

Amniocentesis was first developed in the 1950s with the intent of detecting and treating problem pregnancies (e.g., when the mother's blood was Rh negative and the fetus's Rh positive). However, from amniocentesis we can also learn the sex of the fetus and information about chromosomal abnormalities and neural tube defects (spina bifida). As a result, the most common use of amniocentesis today is in the second trimester to detect defects, especially the possibility of chromosomal abnormalities such as Down's Syndrome when the mother is in her late childbearing years. Abnormalities are very rarely found—on an average, fewer than 0.5 percent[4]—but if an abnormality is found, such pregnancies will often, then, end in induced abortion. Since amniocentesis cannot be successfully done before about 14 weeks gestational age, any abortion which is determined upon because of information gained through amniocentesis will necessarily be a relatively late second trimester abortion (perhaps, even, of a possibly viable fetus).

D. The IUD

The intrauterine device, discovered and developed in the late 1950s, calls for brief comment here. There has been disagreement about the precise way in which it prevents pregnancy. Some have held that the IUD prevents fertilization of the ovum, others that it prevents a fertilized ovum from implanting in the uterine lining, still others that either may be the case on different occasions. It is generally agreed, however, that the IUD's effectiveness is due mainly to prevention of implantation. Of course, precise determination of what an IUD does solves no moral problems. If an IUD prevents fertilization, the moral issue raised by its use would be that of contraception. If an IUD prevents implantation, the moral problem raised by its use would be abortion, even if it could be shown that *individual* human life does not begin until the time of implantation or before the possibility of "twinning" has passed.[5]

E. Fetal Therapy

In California surgeons have successfully operated on a fetus (by inserting a catheter through the mother's uterus in order to drain fetal urine) to treat a congenital defect that prevents normal growth of the ureter, obstructs the passage of urine, and can lead to serious brain damage. In Colorado physicians have inserted a brain shunt in a fetus to relieve pressure from accumulating fluid, a condition which could have resulted in brain damage and abnormalities of head and face. Even more remarkable is the case of a 21-week-old fetus partially removed from the uterus while congenital defects in both ureters were repaired and then returned to the uterus to be carried to term. (In this case the child died after birth, but from cause unrelated to the surgery.)

The fetus, bearer of an uncertain legal status at best, has suddenly become visible through fetoscopy (using instruments to see the fetus *in utero*) and sonography (the "picturing" of fetal size and shape by sound waves). Fetuses have become patients, some of whose illnesses can be diagnosed and treated even while they remain within the womb. Increasing recognition of such possibilities will make more glaring the difficulties raised by medical advances for our society's attitude toward abortion.

The basic moral principle of justice is that we should treat similar cases similarly. But we now face the possibility that one fetus could be given therapy while *in utero* and another fetus, with similar problems in similar circumstances, could be aborted—the only difference being that in one case the mother would choose to sustain fetal life and in the other she would choose to end it. Indeed, we find ourselves in circumstances in which the legal right to abortion recognized in *Roe v. Wade* means that a woman has no legal duty to ensure that a fetus is born alive but, if she intends to carry the fetus to term, the law might in some circumstances impose upon her a duty to assure that the fetus receives the therapy needed to be born as healthy as possible.[6] Not only a moral but an emotional juggling act is required when in one moment we consider the most advanced medical techniques for fetal therapy and in the next moment, in a similar case, regard the status of another fetus as wholly dependent upon the will and choice of his mother. These difficulties will have to be faced, however, if we consider what the medical perspective has to teach us.

F. The Doctor's Dilemma: Medical Ethics and Abortion

In almost all professions, ethical standards frequently—perhaps usually—exceed those laid down by law. It is not unusual, for example, for physicians who are found not guilty or are exonerated in criminal or civil proceedings to be disciplined for precisely the same act because the act is deemed unethical by their professional colleagues. One may well despair of defining "medical ethics" with any precision; but in ordinary usage the term refers, albeit somewhat loosely, to the *moral*, as opposed to the *legal*, obligations of a physician in his/her professional practice. The difference is not, admittedly, always clear; some standards which are commonly regarded as being in the province of medical ethics in fact have legal effect. Physicians may, for instance, be barred from practice if found guilty of "infamous conduct," i.e., some sort of professional behavior which can, by professional associates of good repute and recognized competence, be reasonably regarded as being disgraceful or dishonorable. Indeed, when there is a code of ethics and an association of physicians who recognize it as "approved," any violation of such a code may be regarded as infamous conduct, as decided in 1955 in the Supreme Court of Massachusetts.[7] But disputes arise when medical ethics and the law do not coincide, especially when rules in the former are very widely recognized and accepted. Then the question arises: what should take precedence, the rules of ethics or of domestic legislation and judicial pronouncements?

Professional consensus is at present inclined to regard abortion as a borderline case. Or, to say the least, it is, in the context of profoundly and rapidly changing attitudes in the religious, legal, and scientific communities—and in the "public philosophy" as well—under relentless pressure to minimize the purely ethical component in decisions relating to abortion.

Much recent domestic legislation and a sizable number of judicial determinations now permit abortions upon request of the mother; and medical practitioners in growing numbers perform the procedure simply by virtue of the permission that is now granted by law. While it remains true that significant numbers of physicians still decline, out of professional, religious, or personal scruples, to perform or assist at abortions—except in very extraordinary circumstances—and many others participate with varying degrees of reluctance rooted in mental and moral reservations, we are nearing the day when a majority of physicians regard abortion from a neutral ethical perspective. Or many, preferring not to face it at all, relegate these agonizing ambiguities to others for resolution.

A surprising symbol of the reversal of older attitudes and usages is the steady abandonment of the Hippocratic Oath and the Declaration of Geneva (both of which explicitly prohibit abortion) as an incident in the life of the physician at the moment he takes up his profession.[8] There is, moreover, the related dilemma of those physicians, surely still a majority of those now practicing in the United States, who took the oath before the current retreat from it began. May the pledge-bound physician violate the Oath? The problem is more poignant when it is recalled that the Oath has always been taken by individual physicians, not corporately or in their behalf by an agent or agency.

Indeed, in reviewing the literature bearing upon this sensitive issue, it is difficult to overcome the feeling—or to rebut the evidence—that in the everyday practice of medicine physicians spend little time in systematic, deep, and critical reflection upon their work. They evidently take for granted a few moral principles, writes the distinguished medical scholar John Walford Todd in the current *Encyclopedia Britannica,*

> whether they believe these are derived from Hippocrates, from the natural law, from the divine law, or just from plain common sense. They do their best to benefit their patients, by curative methods, if possible, and otherwise by relieving symptoms and by kindness or reassurance; they tell the truth (except when the truth is too wounding); and they do not reveal their patients' confidences.[9]

But there persists, even among those physicians who profess no religion (except perhaps the "civil religion" of secular sanctions for "human decency"), as well as among committed Christians, a deeply troubled pathos haunted by the sense that the startling increase in abortion in our time involves special and unique considerations. *A profession whose peculiar function has always been the fostering and preservation of life is increasingly applying its skills to the termination of life;* so much so that abortion is fast becoming a leading cause or form of death. The bearing of medical ethics upon such considerations is, one would suppose, decisive. But many physicians, whose number it is impossible to guess, find uneasy reassurance in the consoling premise that they are, after all, only technicians, laboring in a field clouded by agonizing uncertainties and imperfect knowledge, whose shadows it is the responsibility of others—theologians, theoretical scientists, philosophers, ethicists, mystics, and justices of the Supreme Court—to dispel.

The relatively sudden introduction of so large a number of respectable physicians into a field so lately served almost exclusively, and more or less clandestinely (to say nothing of illegally), by a small number of physicians looked upon by their colleagues as pariahs,[10] is still of too recent development to have permitted the accumulation of substantial studies of the ethical implications for the medical profession itself. Evidence on the point is not wholly wanting, however.

An example is the pioneer study of Nathanson and Becker, published in 1977. The paper, heavily statistical in form and based on telephone interviews with 473 obstetrician/gynecologists, is introduced by a summary:

> Although religion is the most powerful predictor of whether a doctor will perform any abortions, satisfaction with his or her patients and emotional reaction to the abortion procedure powerfully affect the physician's practice. Doctors who are most satisfied with their patients are less likely to ask unmarried teens for parental consent and to charge lower fees. Physicians who are severely disturbed over abortion perform terminations less frequently and more often ask spousal or parental consent—but charge lower fees and are more likely to accept Medicaid patients.[11]

The paper, like others which have canvassed American physicians more generally, also notes that inquiries of this sort demonstrate "substantial support" among physicians for "a liberal abortion policy once that policy has been enacted into law." The studies emphasize, moreover, that the "liberal" physicians are found to be "younger, non-Catholic, and from specialities other than ob/gyn."

Religion aside, Nathanson and Becker found that few responses were expressed primarily, or even incidentally, in explicitly ethical/moral terms; and they concluded that "obstetrician-gynecologists . . . remain ambivalent about various related legal and moral issues." Thus it is not surprising to find that physicians' personal feelings about the patient and the procedure become major determinants of their response to women seeking abortion. And, given the high degree of control and influence physicians have over whether, how, and where abortion services are performed, it is also not surprising that the structure of abortion services in this country appears to have developed largely in accommodation to these doctors' feelings.[12]

Many doctors appear to have accepted as at least a provisional answer for themselves the view that a living (i.e., *post partum*) human being is in a crucially significant way more fully human than any fetus, that a fetus's rights to life is in some important sense minimal at conception but becomes progressively stronger as birth approaches, and that the morality of a particular abortion is determined by weighing the various rights of the mother against the fetus's right to life. Especially since *Roe v. Wade* brought doctors a measure of peace of mind, questions which probe more deeply have uneasily, and perhaps understandably, been tacitly referred by physicians to others for resolution, while they themselves go about their business as technicians primarily, and, more diffidently, as friends and counselors of their patients, in a social context which lawmakers and judges have altered drastically in recent years.

II. The Legal Perspective

A. *The Legal Status of Abortion*

In this section we offer a brief overview of the legal status of abortion and the legal problems it continues to raise in the United States.[13] We recognize, of course, that Christians often differ in their political judgments, and, since moral principles cannot always be translated into legal requirements, such differences are not ordinarily a matter for concern. However, on issues of great moral significance like abortion, it is imperative that we take more than the usual amount of care to understand and reflect upon what the law permits and prohibits.

Certainly the most important legal decisions in the matter of abortion have been the 1973 decisions of the Supreme Court in *Roe v. Wade* and *Doe v. Bolton*.[14] Although it is incorrect to say that these decisions permit abortion-on-demand, their practical effect has approached that. In the case of *Roe v. Wade,* the structure of the Court's decision can be outlined fairly simply. The Court held that abortion could not simply be prohibited, such prohibition being a violation of the woman's constitutionally guaranteed right of personal privacy. The Court also held, however, that this right was not unqualified but was limited by other important interests of the states, if such could be shown to be pertinent here. The question then arises, are there such compelling state interests which should limit the woman's right to abortion?

The Court found two compelling state interests which might justify regulation of and restrictions on abortion: (1) the states' interest in protecting the health of the pregnant woman; and (2) the states' interest in protecting the potentiality of human life.

With respect to (1) the Court, maintaining that in the first trimester of pregnancy mortality rates in abortion are less than in normal childbirth,[15] held that the states' interest in safeguarding maternal health could justify no regulation of abortion during the first trimester. After that point the Court permitted states to establish regulations designed to protect the health of the pregnant woman—e.g., a requirement that abortions be performed only in licensed medical facilities.

With respect to (2) the Court held that states could have no compelling interest in protecting the potentiality of human life prior to the time of viability (when the fetus can exist outside the uterus of the mother). The Court set the time of viability at 24 to 28 weeks of gestational development—that is, approximately the end of the second trimester of pregnancy.

Thus, the force of the Court's decision was to divide a pregnancy into trimesters and to see the potential for regulating abortion grow as each trimester passed. In the first trimester of pregnancy the Court held, in effect, that no restrictions could be placed on a woman's right to procure an abortion (assuming she could find a doctor willing to perform it). In the second three months states could pass regulations designed to protect the health of the pregnant woman but not to protect fetal life. And in the last trimester of pregnancy the states could, *if they wished,* protect fetal life by going "so far as to proscribe abortion during that period except when it is necessary to preserve the life or health of the mother." (However, *Doe v. Bolton* [1973] at the same time extended the term "health" far beyond the mere physical well-being of the mother.[16]) Hence, the Court's decision in *Roe v. Wade* did not require that the unborn child be given protection at any time during pregnancy. It merely permitted such protection to be given during the final three months of pregnancy.

In the decade since *Roe v. Wade* state legislatures have passed laws regulating abortion, the federal government has been involved in questions concerning the funding of abortion, and new cases have made their way to the Supreme Court. New issues of substantial significance have arisen, issues which had not been specifically addressed in *Roe v. Wade*.

In *Colautti v. Franklin* (1979) the Court appeared to modify one determination made in *Roe v. Wade*. The Court now recognized that the time when the fetus is viable outside the womb is relative to the progress of medical science and cannot be set forever at 24 to 28 weeks gestational development. Hence, in *Colautti v. Franklin* the Court specifically recognized that relativity and left the determination of viability to the judgment of physicians. The potentially explosive force of this seemingly minor modification becomes apparent when we consider the likelihood that development of an artificial placenta will, in the near future, permit fetuses to live outside the womb earlier even than 20 weeks of gestational development. When that becomes possible, the Court's division according to trimesters will seem increasingly untenable. The question as to whether a physician has an obligation only to the pregnant woman or whether the well-being of the fetus (when it is viable) must also be considered has not yet been resolved.

This issue quickly arose in one of the most important decisions to follow *Roe v. Wade*. In *Planned Parenthood of Central Missouri v. Danforth* (1976) the Court considered and rejected a Missouri statute which prohibited use of the saline method after the first trimester and required, instead, the newer method of prostaglandin injection. The Court overturned this, holding that it was a requirement not reasonably related to maternal health. Of interest, however, is the fact that the Missouri law clearly sought to view abortion primarily as a "severance procedure" intended to permit the woman to be relieved of carrying the child, but not necessarily intended to result in a dead child. If, especially in the second trimester, some methods of abortion offer greater hope that the fetus may survive the abortion procedure, and if medical advance increasingly makes such fetuses possibly viable, it may be possible to seek legal ways to encourage the use of these methods and to stress the responsibilities of physicians and other medical personnel toward possibly viable infants who may survive an abortion.

The Court has not, however, been eager to face such questions. In *Akron v. Akron Center for Reproductive Health* (1983) the Court took note of the increasing safety of *second* trimester abortions and overturned an Akron ordinance which—seemingly in accord with the *Roe v. Wade* schema—required that second trimester abortions be done in hospitals. The Court held that, because these abortions could now be safely done in abortion clinics, an interest in maternal health could no longer justify a requirement that they be done in hospitals. The Court did not, however, take notice of the other side of medical advance: namely, that viability has been pushed back into the second trimester and that, therefore, greater regulation to protect potential life might be needed. In a related decision, *Planned Parenthood Association of Kansas City, Mo., Inc. v. Ashcroft* (1983), the Court did uphold a Missouri statute which required the presence of a second physician—to protect the interests of a possibly viable fetus—in *third* trimester abortions. The day is surely at hand, however, when clear thinking will force the Court to ask whether a similar requirement is not appropriate also in the second trimester.

Another important issue which has arisen in the years since *Roe v. Wade* concerns government responsibility to *fund* abortions just as it funds other medical procedures (in particular, childbirth) for people receiving government assistance. In *Maher v. Roe* (1977) the Supreme Court upheld a decision by the Welfare Department of the state of Connecticut not to fund an elective abortion unless it was medically necessary to safeguard the mother's life or health. In a related case, *Poelker v. Doe* (1977), the Court upheld the city of St. Louis' decision that its municipal hospitals were not required to provide nontherapeutic abortions, even though they provided care for childbirth. Three years later, in *Harris v. McRae* (1980), the Court upheld the constitutionality of the "Hyde Amendment" and, in doing so, extended its ruling in *Maher v. Roe*. The Court now held that the federal and state governments had no obligation to pay even for certain medically necessary abortions. And the Court reiterated its view, first expressed in *Maher v. Roe*, that the issue of funding was a political question to be settled in the legislatures of the several states and that it was even within the power of the states to seek to make childbirth a more attractive option than abortion. In its decisions about funding, therefore, the Court has made clear that the right of a woman to seek an abortion—a right enunciated in *Roe v. Wade*—is a liberty, not an entitlement. The distinction is important and is one we should affirm and support. It says nothing, however, about the many abortions which are not publicly funded.

In *Roe v. Wade* a woman's liberty to seek an abortion was grounded in her right to privacy. The Court began, therefore, by viewing the woman as an isolated individual. It was inevitable that this starting point should raise difficult questions about the relation of a pregnant woman to her husband or (if she is a minor) to her parents. In the decade since *Roe v. Wade* the Court has also struggled with this issue. In *Planned Parenthood of Central*

Missouri v. Danforth (1976) the Court ruled unconstitutional any attempt to require consent of the pregnant woman's husband to an abortion. Given the starting point of *Roe v. Wade*, with an individual right to privacy made central, it was no surprise that the Court refused to permit the husband what, from its perspective, would appear to be veto power over a woman's constitutionally guaranteed right. At the same time, we cannot avoid noting that the Court's starting point undercuts the sharing and mutual responsibility inherent in the "one flesh" bond of marriage as enunciated in Scripture.

The issue of parental consent for a minor daughter to have an abortion has proved intractable. In *Planned Parenthood . . .* the Court overturned a Missouri statute which had required the consent of one parent before an abortion could be performed upon an unmarried woman under 18 years of age (unless the abortion was necessary to preserve her life). In *Bellotti v. Baird* (1977) the Court considered a slightly more complicated Massachusetts law—which required parental consent for a minor's abortion but also provided for judicial recourse if the parents refused their consent. This too the Court found unconstitutional, holding that it still too nearly granted the parents a veto power. However, in *H.L. v. Matheson* (1981) the Court upheld a Utah statute which required physicians to notify (not to seek the consent of) parents before performing an abortion on a pregnant minor. The Court held, in addition, that the minor must always have the option of going directly to court to argue that she is mature enough to make the decision herself and that parental notification is unnecessary or damaging. This issue has proved so intractable precisely because the Court has been unable to deny the importance placed upon the family bond in our society. Yet the Court's original decision in *Roe v. Wade* had recognized the importance only of a woman's right to privacy and of the states' interests in protecting maternal life and the potential life of the fetus. Given that starting point in an ideology of individualism, it has been difficult to find ways to support the family bond within the bounds set down in *Roe v. Wade*. There may, in fact, be no way to offer such support, short of constitutional amendment.

B. Possibilities Worthy of Christian Support

The legal decisions discussed above, of course, are not to be viewed as providing moral determinations for decisions regarding abortion. However, the legal struggles of the past decade have suggested several possibilities for reducing the impact of these decisions. (1) We should stress the fact that the Court in *Roe v. Wade* does not in any way attempt to justify abortion morally. The Court only speaks to the issue of whether a *state* can constitutionally interfere with or impose restrictions on abortion. (2) We should emphasize that the Court has specifically held in *Roe v. Wade* that abortion on demand is *not* a protected constitutional right. (3)We should affirm that the grant of power to the woman recognized in *Roe v. Wade* is a liberty, not an entitlement, and that the government has no obligation to fund abortion. (4)We should work toward recognition of an earlier date for viability, since *Roe v. Wade* recognizes the power of the state to give some protection to the fetus from the date of viability. (5)We should learn to think of a woman's court-established ability to obtain an abortion as the right to a "severance procedure" aimed not at procuring a dead infant but at relieving her of the burden, perceived or otherwise, of carrying a child she does not wish to carry. That is, even if a woman may have the ability to terminate a pregnancy, she may well not have the right to terminate the life of a child. Thus, a state may impose obligations on all concerned to do all in their power to enable the fetus to survive. (6)We should encourage legislative and administrative attempts to involve parents in abortion decisions made by a minor daughter. The moral requirements of the Fourth Commandment apply here as well as the prohibition given in the Fifth Commandment. (7)We should strive for greater change in the structure of *Roe v. Wade*, recognizing that such change may be accomplished by means of constitutional amendment, by change in the views of the membership of the Supreme Court, by legislative actions, or by changes in medical knowledge, e.g. earlier viability dates.

III. The Theological Perspective

Christians in this country have been blessed with a political heritage and system which acknowledges their need and right to shape their lives in accordance with their religious convictions. Such a blessing is not without its dangers, however, one of which is the tendency to regard religious belief as restricted to the private realm. A proper theological perspective will never acquiesce in the notion that Christian faith can be that narrow. Christian love shapes our understanding of what care and concern, justice and equity, for the neighbor must mean. Christian love moves us to serve the needs of neighbors, and sometimes those needs can be served only in the public sphere. Moreover, the properties protected under the First Amendment, sometimes called the preferred freedoms, are an invitation to speak out in exercise of the privileges these freedoms confer. Thus, the expression of Christian judgment is not only countenanced but invited in a society which believes that public policy should emerge from the clash of opposing views in the public sphere. The framework of this service to the neighbor in society must, of course, be the distinction between the two kingdoms (AC and Ap. XIV), which reflects the distinction between Law and Gospel.

The Bible is not a code book which enables us to dispense with theological and ethical reflection, but Christian belief and action are decisively shaped and governed by Scriptural teaching and narrative. The great Christian truths of creation and redemption, and the dark shadow cast by sin, inform everything Christians say and believe about God's will for human life and the meaning of human personhood. Naturally, these truths remain somewhat abstract as they are stated below in the form of theological principles. They become more concrete as they lead, also below, to ethical reflection. And when they influence the values we share in our families and use in the nurturing of our children, the policies we espouse in the public sphere, and our common life within a worshiping congregation, they cease to be abstract and begin to form Christian character. We offer here four Scriptural principles, with accompanying brief discussion, to assist in the shaping of Christian belief, character, and action.

A. Theological Principles

1. *Human life, at every stage of its development, is valued by God*

The Scriptures do not specify the moment at which a new individual human being comes into existence—we have already indicated what science and medicine have taught us, namely, that the development of a new individual begins at fertilization—but the Scriptures do make clear that every human being is valuable because valued by God. It is truly an act of *procreation* when a man and woman, participating in the blessing of God spoken to the creation, conceive a child. This unborn child, like all human beings at every stage of their development, is made in God's image—made for life with God, made to respond in love and obedience to the mercy and grace of God.[17]

The God in whose continuing creative activity parents are given a share is no respecter of persons. He values the weak and the lowly, and with Him achievement does not count for more than potential. Human dignity is therefore bestowed by God, not achieved or earned. The psalmist's poetic language witnesses to God's marvelous creativity, but also to God's concern for the weak and still-developing: "Thou didst knit me together in my mother's womb" (Ps. 139:13). The God who from all the mighty peoples of the ancient world could set, His hand on Israel is not likely to judge worth in the comparative terms of our world (cf. Deut. 7:6-8). Indeed, the God of Israel was identified as One who had shown steadfast love to a weak and enslaved people. Hence, Israel could say:

> Who is like the Lord our God. . .?
> He raises the poor from the dust,
> and lifts the needy from the ash heap (Ps. 113:5, 7).

From the conviction that God has vindicated Israel in her weakness an ethical imperative arose:

> Open your mouth for the dumb,
> for the rights of all who are left desolate.
> Open your mouth, judge righteously,
> maintain the rights of the poor and needy (Prov. 31:8-9).

Christians, belonging to the new Israel, reason in precisely the same way. They confess that Christ has died for the weak and the ungodly (Rom. 5:6) and that God has chosen what is weak in this world (1 Cor. 1:27). Such knowledge gives content to Christ's command that we are to love as He has loved us (John 15:12). We too must value the poor and the weak, those too powerless to speak for themselves, those easily disposed of because they seem to contribute little. This suggests a second principle.

2. *Human lives are entrusted by God to our care.*

The Christian belief that human life is not to be taken rests not only on our conviction that human lives are valuable (because valued by God) but also on the truth that life is not ours to take. In the Decalog is a command which calls upon us to respect the lives of our fellow human beings: "You shall not kill" (Ex. 20:13). As Luther's explanation of this commandment in his Small Catechism makes clear, the command requires not only respect for the neighbor's life ("that we may not hurt nor harm our neighbor in his body") but also care and concern that the neighbor's life be preserved ("help and befriend him in every bodily need"). Similarly, in his Large Catechism Luther explains that this commandment means that God

> wishes to have all people defended, delivered, and protected from the wickedness and violence of others, and he has set up this commandment as a wall, fortress, and refuge about our neighbor so that no one may do him bodily harm or injury (LC 1, 185).

To this Luther adds:

> Not only is murder forbidden, but also everything that may lead to murder . . . we should neither use nor sanction any means or methods whereby anyone may be harmed. . . .(LC 1, 186, 188).

To be sure, the mainstream of Christian tradition has, in its understanding of just war and justice in war, permitted the soldier in service to legitimate government to harm and even kill an enemy soldier. This has been understood as a permitted exercise of government's God-given right to use force to preserve ordered peace and justice within human society. (Also given to government is the right to take the life of the evildoer as retributive justice; cf. Rom. 13:4.[18]) The received Christian tradition has, however, placed limits upon what may be done even in a just war. Most important, it has insisted that the enemy, when he lays down his arms and surrenders—when, that is, he ceases any longer to threaten other human lives—cannot be harmed. Ceasing to be an aggressor, he can be neither harmed nor killed. Of course, throughout the church's history some Christians have felt that only a pacifist stance and witness was compatible with Christian teaching and Christian love—a feeling which is again present within our own day. These Christians will refuse to take human lives under any circumstances. But granted the legitimacy of warfare in certain situations, the use of force is warranted only by a threat to life or some value equal to life. In all other circumstances the strict prohibition of the Fifth Commandment applies.

It has become increasingly common in our society to speak as if taking life—whether of the unborn through abortion, of the handicapped or retarded child through benign neglect or infanticide, or of the suffering and the senile through euthanasia—were a way of serving the well-being of those whose lives we take. Against all such misuse of language Christians insist that the task entrusted us by God is to help and befriend our neighbor in every bodily need, not to rush the neighbor out of existence and beyond the realm of bodily need. This leads quite naturally to a third principle.

3. *There are limits to human freedom*

It is the same apostle Paul who exhorts us that "as we have opportunity let us do good to all men" (Gal. 6:10) who in another context indignantly rejects the suggestion that he might have taught that we should do evil that good may come of it (Rom. 3:8). The juxtaposition of these two passages sets before us a perennial difficulty of the moral life. We ought to serve the well-being of our neighbors—as often as possible, as many neighbors as possible. But we are also forbidden to engage in certain activities (as when, for example, the Fifth Commandment forbids unjustified killing). Yet, there may be occasions in life when it seems that serving the greater good of our neighbors requires the use of a forbidden means to that good.

It is important, when contemplating such possibilities, to retain a firm grasp on our creatureliness. Ours is not the role of a deity, but the limited role of a creature. We are indeed to do all the good we can for as many neighbors as possible, but this means all the good we *morally* can do within the limits set by God's law. We are not, even if our motives are praiseworthy, to do evil that good may come of it.

This means, we recognize, that some good and desirable ends cannot be achieved, because the means to those ends are forbidden us. It may also mean on some occasions that a good end must be achieved more slowly and less directly in order to remain within the limits set by God's will. Certainly the prohibition of unjustified killing constitutes a strict limit on the ways in which we may attempt to do good. Recognizing that our capacity to accomplish the good we desire is limited not only by our abilities but also by moral precept, we are driven to be and become a people of hope, who trust that God can bring good out of evil and may accomplish what we are unable to do. This suggests a final theological principle.

4. *Moved by their hope in God, Christians must be a people glad to receive children into the human family.*

It may be through our children—and sometimes only through our children—that God finds a way to teach us how to love those who are not what we wish them to be and whose presence is neither convenient nor timely. In our society, however, a different attitude has become commonplace. The child is often perceived as a burden, as a threat to our plans and purposes, a danger to our chances for self-fulfillment. We can, of course, understand the experiences which may underlie that perception. The presence of children may sap our energy, deplete our resources, and tax our patience.

Nevertheless, as Christians we understand the presence of children among us in a special way. The divine blessing—"be fruitful and multiply"—spoken at the creation continues to be effective in our world (Gen. 1:28). And the presence of children is a sign of God's continuing "yes" to His creation, a manifestation of God's unwillingness to abandon us or to withdraw from the time and history in which we live (1 Sam. 1:1-2:11). Moreover, this God who through our sexual powers continues to create new human beings is One who has demonstrated in Jesus Christ His indefectible love toward us. In Him, as St. Paul writes, God's Word to us is always "yes" (2 Cor. 1:19). We welcome children into our midst, therefore, as a renewed act of trust in the God who has taken the dangers and problems of human life upon Himself and shared our suffering (Mark 10:13-16).

This means that our willingness to welcome children—to help and befriend these small neighbors in their every bodily need—is one way in which we express our confidence in God's goodness and mercy, and our hope that in the future His promises will continue to find their "yes" in Jesus. In welcoming a child we testify that our hope for fulfillment rests in God, and we express our trust that He is not powerless in the face of life's difficulties and dangers. We value the lives of children because God values them; we refrain from harming them because God forbids such harm; but more important still, we seek to become people who receive them with joy and thanksgiving (Ps. 127).

The Scriptural principles offered here compel us to regard abortion on demand not only as a sin against the Fifth Commandment forbidding the destruction of human life, but also as a grievous offense against the First—that we worship the one true God and cling to Him alone. The act of abortion clearly manifests a refusal to honor God as the Creator and to seek Him above all else in time of need. It, too, belongs in the list of those offenses that illustrate man's rebellion against the Creator (Rom. 1:26-32), summoning wrath from which only God Himself can—and does—deliver us.[19]

B. Ethical Reflections

Though it cannot deal in advance with every imaginable case, ethical reflection seeks to bridge the gap between general statements of Biblical principle and particular actions. As such, it performs a vital and necessary role in Christian theology. The attempt to make precise judgments about right and wrong behavior will always be regarded by some as an unwarranted limiting of Christian freedom. But it is, in fact, the necessary charting of the course of the Christian life, within which course Christians are free to serve their neighbors in the countless ways which love discerns but law can never specify. In that spirit we offer the following ethical reflections with respect to abortion.

1. The unborn child developing within the mother's body[20] is clearly a human being entitled to our care and protection. We now know so much about this developmental process that a refusal to grant that the child is an individual human being must amount almost to willful self-deception. When we consider that within eight weeks of gestational development electrical activity of the brain can be detected and that within the first twelve weeks of pregnancy all major organ systems have begun to develop, we should be at least as awestruck as was the psalmist who marveled that God knit us together in our mother's womb. This young human being may be weak and unable to speak in his own behalf. He may as yet have achieved nothing as we ordinarily measure achievement. But the lives of these small human beings are valued by God and entrusted to our care. This moral judgment gains in precision when we consider the following related points:

   a. We know too much about the unique identity of the unborn child to imagine that he can properly be called "a part" of his mother's body. He has his own genotype, his own developing body. The unborn child can and does respond to stimuli and is already beginning to relate to his mother. He is simply an unborn human being undergoing a period of development in the environment natural to him at this stage of his life. He is neither an aggressor nor a usurper.

   b. Naturally, the unborn child's life is dependent upon his mother. But so is the newborn baby dependent upon others for care, so are we all dependent on each other; so may we all be dependent upon others for care when we are ill and dying. Moreover, the ideal of "independent" life is one which ought to be seriously questioned by us. Our society has seen and experienced some of the dangers which an ideology of isolated individualism can bring. It is mistaken, therefore, to regard viability (the time at which the unborn child is able to live outside the uterus) as a morally significant dividing line. Aside from the fact that the time of viability is relative to the present state of medical science and will change as medical progress continues, the supposed importance of viability depends on imagining that only the lives of human beings who can live independently of others' help are entitled to protection. That is, we think, a supposition which will be rejected by those who think through its possible consequences, and it is surely no part of a Christian ideal for human existence.

   c. The unborn child does not become entitled to our care and protection only if he is "wanted." His dignity rests in his creation for life with God. That dignity does not come into or fade out of existence according to the wants of others. Moreover, we cannot be a people who welcome children into our midst if they must always be "wanted." The ethical task is not to welcome only those children whom we want, but to discipline and shape our wants so that we care for those given us. And finally, it must simply be said with candor: A willingness to abort the unborn on the grounds that they are "unwanted" by adult society is a raw exercise of power by the strong over the weak. Both the requirements of justice and the claims of Christian love compel such a judgment.

d. The fact that a child will be born retarded and/or disabled cannot justify withdrawing our protection for his life. To hold otherwise would require that we also justify infanticide of retarded and disabled newborns—a conclusion from which some at least will still shrink. The glaring weaknesses of this justification for abortion will become increasingly apparent as our ability increases to operate on the unborn within the womb to correct some defects. It will then be apparent that, if we choose to abort some and provide therapy for others, we consider the value of their lives to depend entirely on our own choosing. If, however, instead of looking for value in the lives of such children by comparing them with others who are "normal," we will instead learn to value the lives they have—even as God values them—we will be renewed in our commitment to care for them.

e. There are circumstances in life in which an abortion might be considered a means toward achieving some good end. For example, abortions are often sought to assist family planning goals, to minimize instances in which children may suffer abuse, to control the costs of caring for an increasing poor population, to make it possible for women to continue pursuing careers, to ease the burden on women or families with problems—all, quite probably, desirable goals. But however desirable such goals may be, they cannot justify killing a human being in order to attain them. These are instances in which the means to an admittedly good end is prohibited us. Naturally, we can and should try to achieve these goals by other means. Certainly there are other ways to try to deal with family planning, with poverty and unwanted children, with opportunities for women to pursue vocations—if only we have the will to seek those other ways. Our long-term aim should be to move toward a society in which the choice for abortion is a choice no one feels compelled or drawn to make.

2. We have emphasized as strongly as possible the protection to which the unborn child is entitled. We do not overlook, however, the fact that in the gestation and birth of children mothers bear by far the greatest burdens. The child's life is dependent upon his mother in a unique manner, a manner which calls for an act of self-spending on her part. Indeed, we may even say that in the manner of human gestation and birth we see a deeper truth than our attachment to independence and individualism can reach. The life-giving burden carried by mothers, and only by mothers, must be kept clearly in view throughout our ethical reflection. This fact alone gives the mother's claims a certain preeminence in those cases where the life of the unborn child and the equal life of the mother come into conflict.

In the rare situations of conflict we must recognize the permissibility of abortion. Despite the progress of medical science, there are still unusual circumstances in which a mother will die if an abortion is not performed. There are also cases (e.g., some instances of chronic heart or kidney disease in which pregnancy increases the strain on heart or kidneys) in which the danger to the mother's life is greatly increased if no abortion is performed. Even in such circumstances a mother may choose to risk her own life as an act of love, but such an act of self-giving cannot be required. It must be freely given, not imposed.

Very difficult and painful situations arise in cases of pregnancies which result from rape or incest. Even if such wrongful acts do not result in pregnancy, the most sensitive kind of pastoral counseling is required. Christian love manifests itself in deep compassion for those who are the unwilling victims of exploitation and violation. Guilt, fear, anger, hatred, self-loathing, and other emotional and spiritual upheavals must be dealt with wisely and mercifully. Although conception almost never occurs as a result of forcible intercourse, when it does, the life of the new human being is as valuable and as worthy of protection as any other newly begun life. Thus, the evil and violent circumstances in which a child is conceived do not in and of themselves constitute valid grounds for recommending or approving an abortion. There is a necessity for a concentrated and sustained ministry to the woman who finds herself in such tragic circumstances. There must be concern for her physical, spiritual, and emotional needs as well as for the life and future of the child. Comfort can be taken from St. Paul's exhortation that God promises to bring good out of even the greatest evils that befall us (Rom. 8:28).

3. Ethical reflection must always pay attention to the possible *consequences* of actions we endorse. One possible result of permissive abortion becomes evident when we set out in simple syllogistic form the argument which underlies opposition to abortion.

> *Major premise:* The lives of human beings—whatever their stage of development or achievement—are entitled to equal care and protection.
>
> *Minor premise:* The unborn child is a human being.
>
> *Conclusion:* The life of the unborn child is entitled to equal care and protection.

It is a commonplace of logic that, if we change the conclusion, one of the premises of an argument must also be changed. If, as is certainly the case in our society, the conclusion is no longer affirmed, our commitment to one of the premises is likely to erode. However much some may at present deny the minor premise, it is difficult to believe that it will in the long run be rejected. The more we know of fetal development, and the greater the possibilities become for fetal therapy, the more difficult it will be to deny the persuasive force of the minor premise. We are more likely to see an erosion of our commitment to the major premise. In short, we might predict that our society would begin to abandon the view that entitles all human beings to equal care and protection of their lives—that we would abandon this and replace it with judgments of comparative worth. When we consider decisions presently being made about infants born with defects and decisions made about care for the retarded and senile, it is hard not to believe that some of those consequences are already upon us. People who are untroubled by permissive abortion are not likely forever to resist other judgments of the comparative worth of lives.

4. Finally, we must emphasize the proper use of these ethical reflections within the theological task, the life of the church, and the life of the individual Christian. In the delicate administration of Law and Gospel to those troubled by decisions related to abortion, the Christian pastor in particular should realize that his task does not consist in the mere articulation of moral judgments. Nor ought he to announce God's forgiveness to those who are impenitent. The Law in all its severity and the Gospel in all its sweetness are to be applied with sensitivity to all those who are crying for help through a personal crisis. It is important to understand that a request for an abortion is, in a sense, the mother's serious plea for her life. A Christian women may wish to be freed from a burden she feels she cannot bear and still live. However, the means by which she seeks to affirm her own life is wrong. The Christian pastor must try to help her see and face this painful contradiction in her feelings and affirmations, and finally lead her, under the blessing of God, to accept her burden in the faith that all things work together for good with those who love God and who are called according to His purpose (Rom. 8:28-30).

IV. Conclusion

A. *Reflections for Those Giving Spiritual Care*

The task of ethical reflection and the application of moral judgments to the life of the individual Christian falls not only to Christian pastors but also to Christian counselors, physicians, and—perhaps in some cases more so—to others closely associated with the person seeking help. With the promotion and growing acceptance of abortion as a matter of private choice and constitutional right, fewer women are seeking professional or ministerial counseling in their deliberations about abortion. Today, advice and guidance concerning abortion decisions come primarily from peers, friends, and family—if, indeed, the pregnant woman consults anyone at all. Certainly, any serious counseling that is done is likely to have been done before a woman goes to an abortion clinic. The remarks that follow, therefore, are addressed not only to pastors and to Christian physicians and counselors, but also to anyone who may suddenly be faced with the challenge and opportunity of counseling with a woman or a couple contemplating abortion.

1. *The Contemporary Setting*

   a. Women are being conditioned to want and feel the need for abortions. Data from many countries indicates that a change from restrictive to permissive abortion laws gives rise to a group of women who seek abortions when they would not previously have done so. The subjectively felt stress which leads many women to seek an abortion can be understood correctly only if this social influence is recognized and taken into account.

   b. Overlooked in the abortion dilemma is the distress often experienced by the father of the child to be aborted. Numerous studies have reported that men may have difficulties with an abortion experience and may suffer painful role conflict. Since abortion is legally the choice of the woman alone, she may, in effect, choose motherhood, while he may not choose fatherhood. Some men, thwarted in their desire and need to protect their offspring, report persistent dreams about the destroyed child and considerable guilt and sadness.[21]

   c. A near constant which must be remembered in counseling women who are considering (or have had) an abortion is their low self-esteem. Many have difficulty appreciating the dignity and value of their own lives. They may have a poor self-image or may have experienced rejection at a crucial moment in their lives. It is understandable, then, that they may have difficulty affirming the dignity and value of the child within them. The pain they know takes precedence over the unseen child they do not know. For such women an abortion may only reinforce their negative feelings about themselves.[22]

2. *Counseling Considerations*

   a. Abortion counseling should be crisis counseling. Abortion is an irreversible action often chosen at a time when careful, unhurried reflection is difficult. In such circumstances all of us may make decisions which are not best for us and which we may later regret. The distressed woman or frightened teenager facing pressures of time, economics, and even coercion from those with vested interests may be ill-suited to make a constructive and wise decision. It is imperative, therefore, that she be involved in an exploration of her situation and her alternatives.

   b. It is important to identify accurately the real reason or reasons an abortion is being considered. For example, is it the *condition* of pregnancy or the *result* of pregnancy (the child) which is the source of anxiety? If the pregnancy itself is at issue, this may be because of lack of money for medical care, an existing health problem complicated by pregnancy, loss of employment, other inconveniences due to pregnancy, embarrassment, or rejection by one's spouse or partner when he becomes aware of the pregnancy. If the child to be born is the issue, this may be because of the woman's inability (financially, socially, or emotionally) to care for him, due to fear of single parenthood or fear of a child with mental or motor disabilities. Only by isolating the real problem, exploring its dimensions, and considering its possible resolution will the woman's interests, as well as the child's, be fostered and protected.

   c. Be aware of potential risks. Those who stand to benefit financially from an abortion are least likely to inform the distressed woman of possible physical problems which can result. Medical risks include more than immediate dangers. An abortion increases a woman's chances of having in the future an ectopic pregnancy, a spontaneous miscarriage, or a premature delivery. Hence, it is important to remember that more than a present crisis is at stake.

d. Know about available resources. Experiencing the limits to our ability to help women facing the stress of untimely pregnancy, we may be quickly drawn to assume that abortion is the only possible or reasonable solution. But a variety of agencies, organizations, and volunteer groups are available to offer a pregnant woman the support system needed to meet her personal, medical, and legal needs. These options can become possibilities for choice only as she is made aware of others who want to help her.

e. Be sensitive to the problem of guilt. Since abortion has become legally and socially acceptable, problems of guilt may be dismissed by some as part of an outmoded value system. Such dismissal is not likely to be a real service, however. When many women experience depression, nightmares, and difficulties in relationships following abortion, it will do little good to suggest that such guilt is irrational or unjustified because abortion was their legal right.[23] The problem is the guilt itself, and the verdict of conscience on these occasions is to be taken seriously. Such a women needs counseling which will lead her to sincere confession and to the renewal of hope offered by the powerful word of the Gospel.

B. Response in the Political Sphere

We should not underestimate the depth of division on the issue of abortion which exists within our country, nor should we imagine that any quick and easy solution to that division is possible. While we may grieve over the drastic relaxation of legal restraints on abortion, we cannot, upon serious reflection, be surprised by it. We find in it yet one more example of the growing disposition of an increasingly secular society to resolve moral dilemmas through pragmatic considerations of public policy and one more instance of the perennial tendency of the strong to oppress the weak. The judgments courts make about legality or illegality do not settle moral issues and are not determinative for Christian conscience. If abortion was sinful before 1973, it continues to be sinful in the decade that has followed *Roe v. Wade*. And even if abortion were made illegal tomorrow, the divisions among our people would still need healing and the moral issues would need to be addressed. It is to the moral issues that Christians can and should speak.

We should not acquiesce in the notion that defenders of abortion are merely "pro-choice." There are some issues with respect to which it is not sufficient to be "pro-choice." Just as the Kansas-Nebraska Act of 1854—permitting new states entering the Union the choice whether to be slave or free—was not a tenable solution to the problem of slavery, so also a so-called "pro-choice" position on abortion is not adequate; for it does not recognize the justified claims of the unborn child upon us.

There is also no reason to acquiesce in the notion that abortion opponents are illegitimately attempting to foist a private, religiously grounded view upon the whole of a society which does not share these religious beliefs. Much Christian opposition to abortion is based upon (1) our increasing knowledge about the facts of fetal development, and (2) a commitment to justice and an unwillingness to make comparative judgments assessing the relative value of human lives. These aspects of our viewpoint are certainly held by many who do not share our religious commitments. Beyond this, however, we reject the prevailing view in our society that considers religion good only as long as it remains a purely private matter. This is a distorted notion of the function of religious faith in the believer's life, and we ought not permit others to define for us the nature and extent of our religious commitment. However one arrives at the view that the unborn are, in fact, human beings deserving of protection, it is difficult to see how such a view could possibly be responsibly held as a purely private opinion.

We do not, of course, imagine that all matters of morality are fit subjects for legislation. Lust and gluttony are among the seven deadly sins; yet we would not suppose that they should be prohibited by statute. But those matters of morality which impinge upon civic order, which touch the common good, are appropriate subjects of legislation. In such matters we can, do, and ought to legislate morality. Just as we believe that racial discrimination ought to be opposed not merely in private but also in the public sphere, even so we believe that laws to provide protection for all human lives are appropriate and necessary. When the common good is involved, law and morality must join hands.

For what should we labor in the public sphere? We have seen in our discussion of "The Legal Perspective" that court decisions following *Roe v. Wade,* although clarifying some questions in helpful ways, have left little room for limitation of abortion. It is probably true that any large gains will have to await either a different membership of the Supreme Court or a constitutional amendment. There have been within Congress attempts to settle the problem legislatively by passing a law which defines the legal meaning of "person." (The advantage of such an approach is that, as ordinary legislation, it would require only a simple majority.) The legality of this attempt is greatly disputed, however, and there is no doubt that a constitutional amendment would offer a more lasting resolution.

Proposals for such an amendment have come in several forms. Some propose amendments which specify when individual human life begins and thereby offer protection for the rights of the unborn. Others propose an amendment which states simply that the Constitution does not secure a right to an abortion—hereby returning us to the situation which prevailed prior to *Roe v. Wade* and permitting the several states to regulate abortion to whatever degree they wish. The advantage of the first kind of amendment is that it would provide a more uniform and sweeping solution. In our current political climate, however, it would likely be viewed by many as imposed rather than agreed upon, and might well be the source of new divisions. The second kind of proposed amendment, which would return the abortion issue to the states, would permit the people through their legislatures to debate at length what their policy with respect to abortion should be. Undoubtedly, however, it would make for a less uniform and less restrictive policy.

In truth, our greatest hope may lie in the possibility that the Supreme Court, perhaps with some new justices, perhaps impelled by medical advance, will find it necessary to extend greater protection to unborn human beings. The way in which this may occur was, in fact, suggested by Justice Sandra O'Connor in her dissenting opinion in the 1983 decision, *Akron v. Akron Center for Reproductive Health.* She noted that "the Roe framework . . . is clearly on a collision course with itself." As abortion becomes a safer procedure, states will be less justified in claiming to limit abortion in ways that protect maternal health. But at the same time, medical progress will move farther back into pregnancy the time at which the fetus is viable, the point at which *Roe v. Wade* had permitted the states to legitimate interest in protecting fetal life. We can hope that the direction pointed to in Justice O'Connor's dissent, which takes seriously the need for more stringent protection of fetal life, will in the future be taken by a majority of the Court.

There is currently a "great debate" concerning whose good shall count in the common good. Shall the good of the unborn child count in the common life we share? Shall the rights and protections we all claim flow back evenly upon all, also upon the unborn child? We are, in fact, determining what the outer limits of the human community among us shall be. When such issues are being debated in our public life, Christians ought to be first to speak on behalf of those who are weak and unable to speak for themselves. We confess as a cardinal tenet of our faith that "God chose what is weak in the world to shame the strong'' (1 Cor. 1:27). If that ''religious'' belief does not shape the whole of our life, including also our life in the political sphere, we have not begun to fathom either its power or its depth.

Appendix

Suggestions for Response at the Congregational and Individual Levels

The Christian response to the problem of abortion cannot be limited to public protest; Christians must also commit themselves to an ongoing ministry of supportive care for those who are faced with the kind of burdens that often prompt women to contemplate an abortion. Congregations and individuals interested in pursuing such commitment may wish to consider the following avenues of support for human life:

1. Designate a pro-life resource and contact person within the congregation to coordinate pro-life activity and education. Such a person may be responsible for informing the congregation on pro-life issues through bulletin inserts, a column in the congregational newsletter, pamphlets and tracts available, books for the church and/or school libraries.

2. Address the life issues from the pulpit and in Bible classes.

3. Make information available to all members of the congregation on the needs of pro-life organizations.

4. Organize a ''care'' group within the congregation to help mothers after the birth of the baby. Sensitize members to the plight of the woman who must try to raise a child in poverty, without a husband, often without help or support from family. Teenagers ostracized from peer groups need a listening ear from a friend. Some need parenting skills, assistance to obtain medical care, and other basic necessities. Provide infant and maternity clothes for mothers, as well as for organizations that provide supportive services for crisis pregnancies.

5. Discover ways to be supportive of parents whose teenage daughter becomes pregnant. Elders and spiritual care committees in particular need training for dealing with this situation.

6. Form prayer circles to pray for the unborn, mothers with a troubled conscience, children with handicaps and burdens in the home, the elderly and senile, and others whose value is viewed as diminished because they are unwanted or imperfect.

7. Conduct or sponsor youth workshops on life issues and sexuality for the community. Provide for sex education in the congregation for parents, youth, and children.

8. Establish a local ''Lutherans for Life'' chapter.

9. Celebrate a ''Life Sunday'' during the year to develop a Christian concern for mothers and unborn children.

10. Include a pro-life unit in confirmation classes and premarital counseling sessions.

11. Enlist the Christian day school in projects such as compositions, posters, poetry, and drama that convey a pro-life message.

12. Inquire about governmental and community sources of funding for the support of single mothers.

13. Establish contacts with pro-life leaders in your area and discuss ways of carrying our cooperative programs regarding pro-life issues.

14. Invite pro-life professionals (medical, legal, theological) to address groups within the congregation.

15. Provide home care for unwed mothers seeking temporary assistance during moments of crisis.

16. Write to congressmen and senators expressing the pro-life position on life issues.

Endnotes

[1] In the medical and legal sections of this report the biological terms "embryo" and "fetus" are often used in referring to the unborn child, while in the remaining sections care is exercised to speak of the unborn in terms more indicative of a new human being.

[2] For stylistic reasons the masculine pronoun will generally be used from this point when reference is made to the unborn child.

[3] Hymie Gordon, M.D., Mayo Clinic, Rochester, Minn., Personal Memorandum on file in CTCR office.

[4] Ibid.

[5] C. Everett Koop, now U.S. Surgeon General, has written the following regarding the IUD: "You should know that when the IUD first came on the market, it was known as the IUCD, which stood for 'Intrauterine contraceptive device.' However, it was recognized even then that the IUD was not a contraceptive device, but an abortifacient. It prevented the implantation of the already fertilized egg on the prepared wall of the Womb (uterus).

Early in the use of the IUD, women were not mentally comfortable with it because many felt it was producing an abortion every time a fertilized egg attempted implantation on the wall of the uterus. Then one of the unthinkables happened: The American College of Obstetricians and Gynecologists changed the definition of pregnancy! Whereas formally all textbooks of obstetrics in this country properly defined pregnancy as 'the period of time between conception and delivery,' the definition was changed to 'that time from implantation to delivery.' You can see, therefore, that the effect of the IUD took place before pregnancy by the new definition, and this avoided any possible controversy. The IUD is not a contraceptive device' it is an abortifacient."—Francis A. Schaeffer, C. Everett Koop, John Buchfuehrer, and Franky Schaeffer V, *Plan of Action - An Action Alternative Handbook for Whatever Happened to the Human Race* (Old Tappan, N.J.: Fleming H. Revell Company, 1980), p. 80.

[6] John S. Robertson, "The Right to Procreate and In Utero Fetal Therapy," *The Journal of Legal Medicine,* 3 (1982), p. 352.

[7] Forziatti v. Board of Regulation. 12E 2d 789. This and the two following paragraphs follow closely the argument and language of David A. Frenkel (Ministry of Health, Jerusalem, Israel), in *Journal of Medical Ethics* (London), V (June 1979), pp. 53-56.

[8] The Hippocratic Oath reads in part: "I will give no deadly drug to any, though it be asked of me, nor will I counsel such, and especially I will not aid a woman to procure abortions" (*Encyclopedia Britannica,* 15th ed., s.v. "Medicine, History of," by John Walford Todd, *Macropaedia,* Vol. 11, p. 827). The "Declaration of Geneva," adopted by the General Assembly of the World Medical Association at Geneva, Switzerland, September 1948, states in part: "I will maintain the utmost respect for human life, from the time of conception; even under threat, I will not use any medical knowledge contrary to the laws of humanity."—*Ethics of Medicine,* eds. Stanley Joel Keiser, Arthur J. Dyck, and William Curran (Cambridge and London: The MIT Press, 1977), p. 5.

[9] Fifteenth ed., *Macropaedia,* Vol. 11, p. 849.

[10] In 1859 the American Medical Association called abortion "the slaughter of countless children; no mere misdemeanor, no attempt upon the life of the mother, but the wanton and murderous destruction of her child; such unwarrantable destruction of human life. . . ." In 1871 the AMA said concerning doctors who performed abortions: "The members of the profession should shrink with horror from all intercourse with them, professionally or otherwise; these men should be marked as Cain was marked; they should be made the outcasts of society; it becomes the duty of every physician in the

United States . . . to resort to every honorable and legal means in his power to crush out from among us this pest of society.''—Quoted in William Brennan's *Medical Holocausts 1: Exterminative Medicine in Nazi Germany and Contemporary America,* eds. Richard S. Haugh and Eva M. Hirsch (New York: Nordland Publishing International, Inc., 1980), pp. 331-32.

[11] Constance A. Nathanson and Marshall H. Becker, ''The Influence of Physicians' Attitudes on Abortion Performance, Patient Management and Professional Fees,'' *Family Planning Perspectives,* IX (July/August, 1977), p. 158; cf. pp. 158 and 163 for the brief quotations that follow from this source.

[12] The American College of Obstetricians and Gynecologists, the professional association of those physicians who are most frequently called upon to deal with questions relating to abortion, send out to its membership an occasional newsletter release under the title ''Statement of Policy as Issued by the Executive Board of ACOG.'' Perusal of these mailings more than suggests a cautious reticence on the part of ACOG in dealing directly and intensively with the *ethics* of abortion itself. For example, the statements dealing with abortion, even when labeled ''ethical considerations,'' are characteristically devoted to matters many of which are only peripherally germane to ethics: due care in verifying diagnoses of pregnancy; adequate facilities, equipment, and personnel ''to assure the highest standards of patient care''; problems of conflict between the pregnant woman's health interests and the welfare of the fetus; the special problem of unanticipated delivery of live infants by abortion; the careful consideration of alternatives to abortion, and the suggestion that the fetus has a qualitatively different nature and value from that of other human tissue and organs because of its potential for developing into ''an obvious human being.'' The policy statements acknowledge that ''prognoses often involve medical, social, and economic factors which impact adversely on the health of the woman; and while abortion may be one option . . . other alternatives may, in fact, be equally or more appropriate in solving these problems.'' Alternative options which the policy statements recommend, without explicitly pronouncing upon the ethical considerations involved in abortion, include: education in family life, contraception, reproductive responsibility, and parenting skills; provision of supportive counsel; job protection for pregnant women; changes in employment practices whose present effect is to punish women for being or becoming pregnant; more supportive attitudes toward those who elect abortion or out-of-wedlock birth; improved adoption services; accumulation and evaluation of data concerning experience with abortion and its alternatives.

[13] As in its 1971 report on ''Abortion: Theological, Legal, and Medical Aspects,'' the Commission has here limited its discussion to legal developments in the United States.

[14] See footnote 16.

[15] Recent evidence presents a serious challenge to the Court's premise and also raises questions about the validity of comparing two entirely different classes of pregnant women: healthy and diseased. The death of a healthy woman from a legal abortion is totally preventable simply by not aborting. The death from childbearing of a woman with a disorder is most often unpreventable because of medical inability to understand or control the disease process which takes her life.—M. J. Bulfin, ''Deaths and Near Deaths with Legal Abortions.'' presented at the Oct. 28, 1975, convention of the American College of Obstetricians and Gynecologists. ''Abortion and Maternal Deaths,'' *British Medical Journal* 2 (July 10, 1976), p. 70. ''Most Mother, Child Mortality Seen in Small High-Risk Groups,'' *O.B. Gyn News* 16 (May 15, 1981), p. 13.

[16] The word ''health'' as defined by the Court was not limited to the usual understanding of the word (i.e., the absence of sickness or disease). Rather, the Court defined ''health'' in terms so broad as to encompass a woman's preferred life-style and social well-being. Factors which relate to health, said the Court, are ''physical, emotional, psychological, familial, and the woman's age''—all of which are ''relevant to the well-being of the

patient'' (*Doe v. Bolton*, IV-C). Health also includes "distress associated with the unwanted child," "continuing difficulties and stigma of unwed motherhood"; when pregnancy "will tax mental and physical health of child care" or will "force upon a woman a distressful life and future" (*Roe v. Wade*, VIII).

[17] We refer to the child in the womb as a *human being* but refrain from referring to that child as a *person* though we have no objection to the use of personal language in that context. We do this simply for the sake of clarity and to avoid unnecessary and futile disputes. In the contemporary meaning used by some, a person is a being aware of itself as a self-conscious self, capable of relating to other selves and envisioning for itself a future. On the basis of such an understanding, some would deny that the life of the unborn child is *personal life*. The more traditional sense given by Christian theologians to the term "person" would predicate of any member of the human species, any individual sharing our common nature—whether or not that nature is at any moment developed to its fruition in the life of that individual. Human nature has a capacity to know, love, desire, and relate to others. We share in that human nature even though we do not exercise all the functions of which it is capable. Thus, the contemporary understanding adopted by some will designate as a person only one presently exercising certain characteristic human capacities; it understands personal life in functional terms. The more traditional understanding of Christian theologians regards personhood as an endowment which comes with our nature, even if at some stages of life we are unable to exercise characteristic human capacities. Obviously, some important philosophical disputes—chiefly, the debate between nominalists and realists—are involved here. We bypass these arguments and simply refer to the unborn child as a *human being*. Whatever we may say of personal qualities, human beings do not come into existence part by part as do the artifacts we make. Human beings come into existence and then gradually unfold what they already are. It is human beings who are made in God's image and valued by God—and whose inherent dignity ought also to be valued by us.

[18] Cf. CTCR's 1976 "Report on Capital Punishment."

[19] Early Christian writers specifically condemned abortion as a violation of the Biblical prohibition against killing. The first century *Epistle of Barnabas* states: "You shall not murder a child by abortion, or kill it when it is born" (19:5 Goodspeed Translation). Similarly, the *Didache* (about A.D. 100-20) says: "Do not murder a child by abortion or kill a newborn infant" (2:2 LCC Translation). The ancient church father Tertullian (about A.D. 160-220) wrote in his *Apologeticum* (about 197): "For us, since homicide is forbidden, it is not even permitted while the blood is being formed into a man to dissolve the conceptus in the uterus. For to prevent its being born is an acceleration of homicide, and there is no difference whether one snuffs out a life already born or disturbs one that is in the process of being born" (IX, 8.)

[20] Here we have set aside the medical/legal designations "embryo/fetus" and emphasize the creation of a new human being within the womb of the mother.

[21] Vincent M. Rue, Testimony before Senate Subcommittee (November 4, 1981). Cf. "Sharing the Pain of Abortion," *Time* (Sept. 26, 1983), p. 78.

[22] David Mall and Walter F. Watts, M.D. eds., *The Psychological Aspects of Abortion* (Washington, D.C.: University Publications of America, 1979), p. 121.

[23] R. Illsey and M. Hall, "Psychosocial Research in Abortion: Selected Issues," in *Abortion in Psychosocial Perspective: Trends in Transnational Research*, ed. H. David et al. (New York: Springer, 1978), pp. 11-34.

Notes: *This longer statement by the Lutheran Church—Missouri Synod (approximately 2,660,000 members in 1986) provided a fuller picture of how this church arrived at its final position, which was anti-abortion except to save the life of the mother. Abortion was not allowed as an alternative even in cases of rape or incest because abortion was considered an act against God as creator of that life. Additionally, a constitutional act to protect the unborn was urged.*

METHODIST CONFERENCE (ENGLAND)

STATEMENT ON ABORTION (1976)

Introduction

1. The question of abortion continues to exercise the thought, conscience and compassion of men and women. The area of the debate at this stage is limited to the period between conception and birth.

2. Abortion has at once moral, medical, legal, sociological, philosophical, demographic and psychological aspects. In addition, the Christian will seek to bring to the discussion insights and emphases which derive from his faith.

Theological Aspects

3. The Christian believes that man is a creature of God, made in the divine image, and that human life, though marred, has eternal as well as physical and material dimensions. All human life should therefore be reverenced. The fetus is undoubtedly part of the continuum of human existence, but the Christian will wish to study further the extent to which a fetus is a person. Man is made for relationships, being called to respond to God and to enter into a living relationship with Him. Commanded to love their neighbours, Christians must reflect in human relationships their response to God's love. Although the fetus possesses a degree of individual identity, it lacks independence and the ability to respond to relationships. All *persons* are always our 'neighbours'; other beings may call forth our loving care. In considering the matter of abortion, therefore, the Christian asks what persons, or beings who are properly to be treated wholly or in part as persons, are involved and how they will be affected by a decision to permit or forbid abortion.

Abortion

4. It is of the essence of the Christian Gospel to stand by and care for those who are facing crises and to help them to make responsible decisions of doctors and nurses who find themselves unable to take decisions about their situation. It also respects the conscientious part in carrying out abortions.

5. In considering the question of abortion, Christians must never overlook the reality of human sin. This impairs judgement with the result that the abortion decision may be made in a context of selfishness, carelessness or exploitation. Human sin is also seen in attitudes and institutions which foster any debasing of human sexuality or are complacent to social injustice and deprivation. In facing these dimensions of failure and sin, Christians will work for an experience of spiritual renewal and a deeper understanding of the nature of human responsibility in the response made to the abortion.

The Issues Involved

6. On one side of the abortion debate is the view which seeks to uphold the value and importance of all forms of human life by asserting that the fetus has an inviolable right to life and that there must be no external interference with the process which will lead to the birth of a living human being. The other side of the debate emphasises the interests of the mother. The fetus is totally dependent on her for at least the first twenty weeks of the pregnancy and, it is therefore argued, she has a total right to decide whether or not to continue the pregnancy. It is further argued that a child has the right to be born healthy and wanted.

7. Both views make points of real value. On the one hand, the significance of human life must not be diminished; on the other hand, abortion is unique because of the total physical dependence of the fetus on the mother, to whose life, capacities or existing responsibilities the fetus may pose a threat of which she is acutely aware. It is necessary

both to face this stark conflict of interests and to acknowledge that others are also involved—the father, the existing children of the family, the extended family, and society generally.

8. From the time of fertilisation, the fetus is a separate organism, biologically identifiable as belonging to the human race and containing all the genetic information. It will naturally develop into a new living human individual. A few days after fertilisation, implantation (or nidation) has taken place; it is significant that in the period before nidation a very large number of fertilised ova perish. At some time after the third month, the 'quickening' occurs—an event which is of significant, perhaps crucial, moment for the mother. Not earlier than the 20th week, the fetus becomes viable, *i.e.*, able to survive outside the womb if brought to birth.

9. There is never any moment from conception onwards when the fetus totally lacks human significance—a fact which may be overlooked in the pressure for abortion on demand. However the degree of this significance manifestly increases. At the very least this suggests that no pregnancy should be terminated after the point when the aborted fetus would be viable. This stage has been reached by the 28th week and possibly by the 24th or even earlier. It would, in fact, be best to restrict all abortions to the first twenty weeks of pregnancy except where there is a direct physical threat to the life of the mother or when new information about serious abnormality in the fetus becomes available after the twentieth week. There is indeed also a strong argument on physical, psychological and practical grounds to carry out abortions in the first three months wherever possible.

10. Because every fetus has significance, the abortion decision must neither be taken lightly nor made under duress. It is for this reason, as well as in her own long-term interests, that the mother should receive adequate counselling. This should enable her to understand what is involved in abortion, what are the alternatives to it and what are the considerations she should weigh before asking for a termination. The skills of social workers and the particular technique of counselling, as well as the responsible medical judgement of doctor and consultant, must therefore be engaged. The provision of this service should be a duty laid by administrative regulations on those approving abortions whether in the NHS or the private abortion clinics. This is another reason why abortion on demand is to be rejected.

The Abortion Act 1967

11. It is again to preserve the awareness of the significance of the fetus that the present form of the Abortion Act 1967 is of value. It retained the basic statement that abortion is unlawful, but indicated criteria which sufficiently altered the situation as to make abortion permissible. The intention behind the Act is therefore to be welcomed as it reflects a sensitivity to the value of human life and also enables serious personal and social factors to be considered.

12. These factors include, for example, the occasion when a pregnancy may pose a direct threat to the life or health of the mother. The probability of the birth of a severely abnormal child (where this may be predicted or diagnosed with an appreciable degree of accuracy) also provides a situation in which parents should be allowed to seek an abortion. It is right to consider the whole environment within which the mother is living or is likely to live. This will include the children for whom she is already responsible and there will be occasions when she is unable to add to heavy responsibilities she is already carrying. Again, there are social conditions in our country which are offensive to the Christian conscience, particularly those connected with bad housing and family poverty. These conditions must be improved; meanwhile it is clear that abortion is often sought as a reponse to the prospect of bearing a child in these and similarly intolerable situations. In the particular circumstances indicated in this paragraph, abortion is often morally justifiable.

13. The Abortion Act is nevertheless imperfect and requires clarification and amendment either by legislation or administrative regulations. Abortions should be limited to the first twenty weeks of pregnancy save in the exceptional cases to which reference has been made. Counselling must be offered in all cases. The profit motive must be reduced. There must be further consideration of the clause which allows abortion when the risks of continuing the pregnancy are greater than the risks in terminating it. This clause can be interpreted to justify abortion on demand. Unless the medical profession or suitable administrative regulations can ensure that this clause is not used alone to authorise abortion on demand, the difficult task of amending the Act at this point must be attempted. There is little doubt that the responsible interpretation of the Act and the proper provision of abortion is more likely to be secured if a high proportion of terminations are carried out in NHS hospitals and not in private abortion clinics. The Methodist Church urged this in 1966. It again emphasises its concern.

14. Abortion must not be regarded as an alternative to contraception, nor is it to be justified merely as a method of birth control. The termination of any form of human life can never be regarded superficially and abortion should not be available on demand, but should remain subject to a legal framework, to responsible counselling and to medical judgement. The Church, with others, must help to provide more adequate counselling opportunities. Society must also be sensitive to the burden it places on medical personnel, and not least upon nurses, by permitting abortion very freely. It must fully respect the conscience of those in the medical profession who feel unable to carry out terminations; though, on their part, they have a responsibility to put women who approach them in touch with alternative sources of advice.

15. The problems raised by abortion can be finally resolved only by a new and sustained effort to understand the nature of human sexuality and to encourage expressions of sexual relationships which are joyous, sensitive and responsible, and which do not tend to exploit others. Christians believe that in conception and birth, parents are pro-creators with God of new human life. They also affirm in the whole of their sexual relationships that identity-in-mutuality which is inherent in marriage and which argues so strongly for the permanence of the marriage commitment. In an imperfect world, where both individuals and society will often fail, abortion may be seen as a necessary way of mitigating the results of these failures. It does not remove the urgent need to seek remedies for the causes of these failures.

Notes: *This statement from the Methodist Conference (England) indicates some of the particular concerns raised by the issue in that country. In England, the Abortion Act of 1967 had a similar impact as the 1973 Roe v. Wade decision in the United States. The Abortion Act's slant, however, is to basically rule abortion illegal but with permissable exceptions which can be interpreted very broadly. The Methodist Conference would like to tighten these exceptions, especially after the first 20 weeks of pregnancy (when the fetus becomes viable). In this statement, the conference attempted to balance the arguments on behalf of the fetus with those on behalf of the possible conflicting interests of the established lives of the family, especially the mother.*

MUSIC SQUARE CHURCH

GUILTY BY ASSOCIATION (1984)

I predicted in the last literature that I wrote (entitled ''Tricked'') that these satanic, Soviet agents who have been given charge of many Federal and State Departments would attack me viciously through the media and Federal and State court system for exposing their plot to destroy our national defense and economy by condoning the murders (what they call abortions) of millions of our American youth and the annihilation of tens of thousands of our

Protestant and Eastern Orthodox Churches

women by deceiving them into thinking that abortion is safe. Not only did they attack me that way, but they still are after me. The women think that abortion is safe because women's deaths from abortion have been coded on the death certificates so that no one can tell how many there really are. These codes are D.E., D.C., hemorrhage, complications, dissection, etc.

The diabolical Supreme Court backed by the Federal and the State governments ruled in 1973 that an unborn child is a "non-person", and in our endeavor to rescue that which they call a "non-person", a great wave of false concern (harassment) arose from the Department of (Socialistic, Soviet) Child Welfare Services stating their concern (harassment). They insist that we have a day care center when we do not. In other words the government is now saying that these fetuses are persons and they have initiated an all-out campaign against us, under the guise of concern, to stop our efforts in the salvation of these millions of children's lives and tens of thousands of women's lives. Their efforts (harassments) to discourage us keep getting stronger and more powerful as our efforts of reaching out to save these children and women get stronger. But God has commanded us: "Open thy mouth for the dumb in the cause of all such as are appointed to destruction. Open thy mouth, judge righteously, and plead the cause of the poor and needy." (Proverbs 31:8, 9) "And moreover I saw under the sun the place of judgment, that wickedness was there; and the place of righteousness, that iniquity was there." (Ecclesiastes 3:16), God says that no weapon that is formed against us shall prosper; and every tongue that shall rise against us we shall condemn (Isaiah 54:17). ". . . When the enemy shall come in like a flood (against us), the spirit of the Lord shall lift up a standard against him" (God's enemies-Isaiah 59:19). And Jesus is still on the throne and also says one of us shall chase a thousand and two of us shall chase ten thousand and there's plenty of us, so move out of the way, Satan, here we come and we're not gonna be moved!! "He only is my rock and my salvation: he is my defense; I shall not be moved" (Psalm 62:6). For God said, ". . . greater is he that is in you, (Christ) than he that is in the world" (Satan) (1 John 4:4). We're Joel's Army, ". . . a great people and a strong; there hath not been ever the like . . ." (Joel 2:2) proclaiming the truths and goodness of God loud and strong and the lies and the evil of Satan. If as in their persecutions against us they now deem these pregnancies are persons instead of what the Supreme Court calls non-persons, then let's compel our government, which is supposed to be by the people and for the people, to make laws against the murdering of these millions of innocent women and children, and charge them for condoning the murders of these millions, which has exceeded the number of deaths in all world wars combined. This is the law of God. "If thou seest the oppression of the poor, and violent perverting of judgment and justice in a province, marvel not at the matter: for he that is higher than the highest regardeth; and there be higher than they." (That do these wicked things-Ecclesiastes 5:8) If we don't we shall stand judged according to His Word, guilty by condoning this slaughter, in other words, guilty by association. "If men strive, and hurt a woman with child, so that her fruit depart from her, and yet no mischief follow: he shall be surely punished, according as the woman's husband will lay upon him; and he shall pay as the judges determine. And if any mischief follow, then thou shalt give life for life," (Exodus 21:22, 23). Here are three of the seven things that the Lord God hates, "A proud look, a lying tongue, and hands that shed innocent blood," (Proverbs 6:16, 17). And I can't think of anything more innocent than an unborn child, can you?

Krushchev and Brezhnev said that the best revolutionaries are youths without morals, and that is why their agents in America enthusiastically and unrestrained by courts (our one world judicial system) opened multitudes of porno parlors and planned parenthood groups and cleverly compelled our school system to instill perversion (which they call sex education) into our children's brains, hearts and souls that they may have many revolutionists (our children). Satan is satisfied.

Notes: *This statement is an excerpt from a pamphlet written by Tony Alamo, co-founder of the Music Square Church (approximately 400 members). Alamo said the legalization of abortion was a Soviet plot to destroy the national defense, economy, and morals.*

NATIONAL ASSOCIATION OF EVANGELICALS

STATEMENT ON ABORTION (1973)

Abortion—1973

We reaffirm, as evangelicals united, our position that the moral issue of abortion is more than a question of the freedom of a woman to control the reproductive functions of her own body. It is rather a question of those circumstances under which a human being may be permitted to take the life of another. We believe that all life is a gift of God, so that neither the life of the unborn child nor the mother may be lightly taken. We believe that God Himself, in Scripture, has told us what our attitude should be towards the unborn. Several times it is specifically stated that He conferred divine blessing upon unborn infants. He also provided penalties for actions which result in the death of the unborn.

Therefore, we deplore in the strongest possible terms the decision of the U.S. Supreme Court which has made it legal to terminate a pregnancy for no better reason than personal convenience or sociological considerations. We reaffirm our conviction that abortion on demand for social adjustment or to solve economic problems is morally wrong. At the same time we recognize the necessity for therapeutic abortions to safeguard the health or the life of the mother, as in the case of tubular pregnancies. Other pregnancies, such as those resulting from rape or incest, may require deliberate termination, but the decision should be made only after there has been medical, psychological and religious counselling of the most sensitive kind.

Notes: *The National Association of Evangelicals is an interdenominational association of evangelical Protestant religious groups. Its statement on abortion deplored the legality of easily obtained abortions and said abortions should be allowed only when medically necessary and possibly in cases of rape or incest.*

NATIONAL ASSOCIATION OF FREE WILL BAPTISTS

RESOLUTION ON ABORTION (1978)

IV. Abortion

Whereas God is in control of all things both in heaven and in earth (1 Timothy 6:15), and

Whereas God is the source of all life (Genesis 2.7, Acts 17:28), and

Whereas the human race is created by Him in His image (Genesis 1:27), and

Whereas life in the womb is one and the same that emerges in birth (Psalm 139:13-16), and

Whereas the indiscriminate killing of an innocent baby in the womb is being encouraged in our age as a method of birth control, and

Whereas this is direct contradiction to the sacredness of life taught in God's Holy Word,

Be it resolved that the National Association of Free Will Baptists express its abhorrence to "abortion on demand" as a means of birth control. Rather it takes the position that illegitimate pregnancies under whatever circumstances are symptoms of the underlying attitudes of rebellion, immorality, and irresponsibility. To cover such sins by killing innocent babies only serves the purpose of deepening the guilt and prolonging the application of the appropriate remedy (Proverbs 28:13). (Adopted)

Ralph Hampton, Chairman
A.B. Brown
Clarence Burton
Eugene Hales
Ben Scott

Notes: *This statement from the National Association of Free Will Baptists (approximately 200,387 members) condemned abortion as the killing of an innocent baby and said that "illegitimate pregnancies under whatever circumstances are symptoms of the underlying attitudes of rebellion, immorality, and irresponsibility."*

NATIONAL ORGANIZATION OF EPISCOPALIANS FOR LIFE

PRIVACY OR LIFE: WHICH IS MORE SACRED? (1987)

In 1973 the Supreme Court answered this question but in a manner which needs to be challenged. The Court argued that an unborn child has no rights to life because the child is not a "person in the whole sense." This was a conclusion that the Court had to reach or else there would have been no case. The 14th Amendment clearly states that "no person shall be deprived of life."

For centuries, however, English common law recognized the unborn as full persons in the whole sense, with rights to inherit property, to be given parental support and to be protected against parental neglect. If human beings must first be born to be recognized as persons, then the unborn who have property rights granted *by* the state are unprotected *against* the state. Moreover, no one has ever shown any compelling government interest in excluding the unborn from protection under the 5th Amendment (due process) and the 14th Amendment (equal protection). Why shouldn't every benefit of doubt be given to the offspring of human beings? Why should the rights we take for granted be given to us "contingent upon live birth?"

The Court said that in the 19th century "prevailing legal practices were far freer than they are today." The curious thing is that the Court argues that "a state's real concern in enacting a criminal abortion law was to protect the pregnant woman, that is, to restrain her from submitting to a procedure that placed her life in serious jeopardy." If it is true that anti-abortion laws were to protect mothers from dangerous surgery then why was the law limited to abortion? All surgery was dangerous in the 19th century but there was no law prohibiting gall bladder operations.

The Court also noted that "ancient religion" did not bar abortion, but the fact is that both Judaism and Christianity did. Paganism may have permitted it, but are we to conclude that paganism is a better model? Even paganism was not totally accepting, as the now famous Hippocratic oath, later adopted by the Christian world, clearly shows.

Justice Brandeis once defined privacy as "the right to be let alone." Yet privacy must not be exalted as a right more sacred than life itself. Precious as personal liberty is to Americans, the right to life is more precious. The dead have no liberties to enjoy! We can't help but challenge the Court's ruling that the right of personal liberty "is broad enough to encompass a woman's decision whether or not to terminate her pregnancy." The right to privacy under the 14th Amendment relates to such things as unreasonable searches and seizures, and to electronic surveillance. It cannot be stretched to have any bearing on the issue of abortion.

Christians cannot help but be uncomfortable with the Court's definition of what makes for "meaningful life." Such a topic raises moral and spiritual issues. The question is no longer whether or not the fetus is a human being but whether or not the fetus has any *value*. The Court could not in good conscience say that there is a person "in the whole sense" in the womb but that such a person has no value. That might imply that the taking of life could be one solution to social and economic problems. So the Court compromised by stating that the unborn child has only relative worth. Of more value is a "sense of well being" on the part of the mother, the implication being that pregnancy is a kind of disease. The paramount consideration is the amount of stress pregnancy brings, either by "the stigma of unwed motherhood'' or by having her ''mental and physical being taxed by child care.'' This is a subjective and ambiguous definition of health which varies according to an individual's frame of reference.

Episcopalians are reminded in the sacrament of baptism that we are to ''respect the dignity of every human being'' (Book of Common Prayer, p. 305). Surely this means that human life has absolute, God-given worth. The value of human life and the value of human privacy cannot be compared. Our own House of Bishops rightly stated in their recent study that ''the privacy argument holds only to the extent that what a person does in privacy does not violate another person.'' An abortion is most certainly such a violation. We cannot in good conscience live under the authority and mandate of Scripture and at the same time adopt a utilitarian approach which merely asks ''what is the useful thing to do in this case?''

Notes: *This article, ''Privacy or Life: Which is More Sacred?'' written by Rev. Dr. Albert S. Lawrence, Jr., was taken from* The Noel News *(Sept. 1987), the newsletter of the minority anti-abortion lobby within the Episcopal Church, the National Organization of Episcopalians for Life. The article argues that the pregnant mother's right to decide matters privately is superceded by the fetus' right to life.*

ORTHODOX CHURCH IN AMERICA

RESOLUTION ON ABORTION (1986)

BE IT RESOLVED THAT the Eighth All-American Council of the Orthodox Church in America strongly reaffirms the historical teaching of the Holy Orthodox Church on the sanctity of all human life. We especially condemn the act of willful abortion of children as an act of murder and urge that the life of the unborn be protected by means of the adoption of a human life amendment to the United States Constitution.

Notes: *This statement from the Eighth All-American Council of the Orthodox Church in America (approximately 1,000,000 members in 1978) condemned abortion as murder and urged the passing of a constitutional amendment to protect the unborn.*

PRESBYTERIAN CHURCH (U.S.A.)

STATEMENT ON ABORTION (1869)

This Assembly regards the destruction by parents of their own offspring before birth with abhorrence, as a crime against God and against nature.

Notes: *This statement was taken from the Minutes of the General Assembly Presbyterians— Old School (which is now a part of the Presbyterian Church (U.S.A.), and is the one statement from the nineteenth century provided in this collection. It was issued at a time when the leadership of the American Medical Association was changing many of the state laws to criminalize prequickening abortions, which had been legal up to that point.*

PRESBYTERIAN CHURCH (U.S.A.)

SEXUALITY AND THE HUMAN COMMUNITY (1970)

6. Abortion

In various human societies, primitive and modern, abortion has been utilized as a common means of birth control. In some, its use has been restricted to therapeutic situations where abortion is resorted to only as a means of preserving the life and health of the mother.

The extremely conservative attitude towards abortion which has prevailed in both Protestant and Roman Catholic churches during the last century has, in general, been based on the attitude that human life exists from the instant of the penetration of an ovum by a sperm, and that the cellular, foetal, and embryonic life that proceed from that moment all have equal spiritual status and deserve equal legal and moral protection.

A careful examination of the Judaeo-Christian tradition on the matter of abortion reveals that this attitude, while old, has not always prevailed, nor did it even enjoy status as the official teaching of the Roman Catholic Church until 1869 (except for a three-year period between the promulgation and the revocation of a papal bull *Effraenatum* in the 16th century.)[15] Various theological and hermeneutic traditions have concluded that no "person" exists in the form of nascent life until after forty days, or after eighty days, or after the birth process begins, or after one day following birth, or in the case of premature infants after thirty days following birth. St. Augustine taught, in the 5th century, that an ensouled human life was present after the foetus had quickened (thus after eighty days), even though Tertullian and St. Gregory of Nyssa had earlier held the position that the soul entered the body at conception.

The continuing view of most rabbinical teachings during the post-Biblical era has been that abortion, while a grave proceeding, is not specifically forbidden in the Bible or the Talmud. Indeed, Exodus 21:22 and other instances of the Old Testament laws concerning homicide suggest that the foetus is not to be regarded as a person, but as a part of (or property of) the mother, and that foeticide is not homicide.

With few exceptions, the structure of civil law in the United States reflects the most conservative interpretation of the meaning of abortion, permitting it only under circumstances which seem clearly to involve a choice between the life of the mother and the life of the child, in which instance the attending physician is permitted to favor the life of the mother. In a few cases, states have passed more liberal legislation embodying the recommendations of the American Medical Association. These permit exceptions to the normal prohibition against abortion only in cases where pregnancy threatens the health or life of the mother, where there is medical evidence that the infant may be born with incapacitating physical deformity or mental deficiency, and where a pregnancy resulting from rape or incest may constitute a threat to the mental or physical health of the mother.

The main positions concerning abortion in our society are three:

1. Abortion should be permitted only when the mother's life is clearly endangered, and even then must be regarded as justifiable homicide, no matter what stage of development the pregnancy has reached. This is the position taken by the Roman Catholic Church and by the report of the General Assembly Committee on Responsible Marriage and Parenthood of 1962.

2. Abortion should be permitted under more liberally conceived conditions, such as those outlined by the American Law Institute and adopted by the American Medical Association in 1967. In this position, the question of when a human life with protected rights is involved is not formally faced, although the practical tendency of hospital abortion committees and of physicians performing abortions is to make a distinction between the problem of termination of pregnancy in the first trimester and the problems presented in subsequent trimesters, dealing with the latter more conservatively. It should be noted that there are specific medical reasons for that conservatism, aside from any philosophical or theological ones.

3. Abortion should be permitted at any stage and for any reason decided upon by a woman in consultation with her physician. This position also is not ordinarily accompanied by any explicit address to the question of when, in the development of a pregnancy, there is a human life with rights to be protected, although it clearly presumes the ancient Jewish assertion that a "person" does not exist until after birth. Justification of this position,

therefore, rests on an assertion of the bodily rights of the woman, who should not be compelled to carry to term a pregnancy she does not want.

Our committee takes the position that the first alternative rests on a substantialist theological conception about the entry of a soul into a body which is without Biblical support and has neither philosophical warrant nor any wide currency today, except in some Roman Catholic theological circles. The Roman Catholic requirement (Canon 747) that all living foetuses be baptized in order that, having been denied life in this world, they be not denied eternal salvation as well, is one that we submit would have little appeal to or support by the theologians of our tradition. Furthermore, this first alternative perpetuates a punitive attitude toward sexual activity and one of its possible consequences which does not represent the affirmative regard for sex to which we are committed.

The second of these alternatives is also unsupportable in our estimation. As a form of liberalization of abortion practice, it relieves society and the medical profession of some of the responsibilities they have had to assume in the past for permitting tragedies which could easily have been avoided. But the American Law Institute recommendations adopted by the American Medical Association perpetuate the assumption that abortion is justifiable homicide. Those recommendations only extend the conditions under which it may be committed. There are several problems it does not address at all.

It does nothing to resolve the foeticide/homicide question, thereby effecting none of the attitude changes which might be desirable.

By continuing to assume that abortion is a medico-legal problem, it confines the freedom of moral discretion of the woman and the therapeutic discretion of the physician. It leaves the law as the final moral arbiter of what is proper medical practice.

It does not deal with the problem of the bodily rights of the woman, and does not grant her the right not to bear an unwanted child.

It does not allow for consideration of the emotional, social, or economic welfare of other members of a family into which an unwanted child will be born. The majority of women seeking abortions are those with families of multiple children who wish to limit their family's size.

It does nothing to affect the problem of illegal abortions, a major socio-medical disease, which leaves an important moral and medical problem to be solved by criminals, quack practitioners, and a handful of reputable physicians who are willing to risk their practice and their reputation to perform this procedure at the edge or outside of the presently prescribed boundaries.

It does nothing to relieve the burden which the present structure of laws and practice puts on the poor and on those who are unsophisticated about the ways of medicine and the law. Far more abortions are performed in private than in public hospitals in our country, and medically safe illegal abortions are only available to those who can afford their considerable cost. Further, the procedure for qualifying for a legal therapeutic abortion is complex and expensive, often involving consultations with several psychiatrists and other physicians. Legal abortions outside the United States also involve prohibitive expense.

The liberalization proposals advanced by the American Medical Association do nothing to insure the right of all children to be born as wanted children. Since child abuse is a major problem in pediatric medicine, this lack is serious from both a medical and a moral standpoint.

Our committee's position is that abortion should be taken out of the realm of the law altogether and be made a matter of the careful ethical decision of a woman, her physician and her pastor or other counselor.[16] In the later stages of pregnancy, serious consideration must be given to the competing claims of the developing fetus as well as to the increased risk to the life of the mother in surgical abortion.

We would underscore the need for discriminating counsel about the ethical aspects of a decision for abortion, especially in view of the potential panic associated with many unwanted pregnancies. Ample opportunity must be provided to consider both the alternative means of resolving problem pregnancies and the possible effects of a contemplated abortion on both parties to the conception and on other family members. And since some unwanted pregnancies are established accidentally and others by "intentional accident," the psychological and ethical significance of the conception needs to be understood as well.

In any case we do not think that abortion should be relied upon as a means of limiting family size. Contraceptive procedures are more desirable for many and obvious reasons. But when through misinformation, miscalculation, technical failure, or other reasons, contraception fails and an unwanted pregnancy is established, we do not think it either compassionate or just to insist that available help be withheld.

We also urge Christians to acknowledge and support the work of agencies and organizations which now offer counsel and help to women with problem pregnancies, such as the various Planned Parenthood Associations, Family Service Agencies, and Clergy Consultation Services, as well as those groups which responsibly work for the repeal of abortion laws.

As laws change and hospital abortions become more readily available, we ask that adequate protection be given to those who object to abortion by reason of conscience including physicians, nurses, and prospective mothers.

Endnotes

[15] *Birth Control in Jewish Law,* David M. Feldman, New York University Press, 1968. p. 269.

[16] In November 1968, the American Public Health Association adopted a resolution calling for the repeal of restrictive laws on abortion so that pregnant women may have abortions performed by qualified practioners of medicine and osteopathy. The resolution is based on a belief in the right of individuals to decide the number and spacing of their children, and recognition that contraceptives are not always obtainable, used , or, if used, always effective.

Notes: *This excerpt from the booklet, "Sexuality and the Human Community", published in 1970 by the General Assembly of the United Presbyterian Church in the U.S.A., was the first formal discussion of abortion since the church's statement in 1869, and it represented an almost complete reversal from the earlier statement. The 1970 position advocated a liberalization of the laws to permit abortion to be a private matter between the woman and other counselors. It argued against theological positions that believed the beginning of a human person came at the moment of conception and supported other positions just as theologically valid and traditionally supported, including "the ancient Jewish position that a 'person' does not exist until after birth." The United Presbyterian Church in the U.S.A. merged with the Presbyterian Church in the United States in 1983 and formed the Presbyterian Church (U.S.A.).*

PRESBYTERIAN CHURCH (U.S.A.)

COVENANT AND CREATION: THEOLOGICAL REFLECTIONS ON CONTRACEPTION AND ABORTION (1983)

A. Introduction: Responsibility in Creation and Covenant

When I look at thy heavens, the work of thy fingers,
the moon and the stars which thou hast established,
what is man that thou art mindful of him,

and the son of man that thou dost care for him?
Yet thou hast made him little less than God,
and dost crown him with glory and honor,
thou has given him dominion over the works of thy hands,
thou has put all things under his feet,
all sheep and oxen, and also the beasts of the field, the birds of the air, and the fish of the sea,
whatever passes along the paths of the sea,
O Lord, our Lord, how majestic is thy name in all the earth!

(Psalm 8:3-9.)

The psalmist sings of the honor given to humankind, the honor that reflects human dominion over all that has been created. The very first chapter of Genesis sets forth this honor as a responsibility: ''Be fruitful and multiply, and fill the earth and subdue it; and have dominion over every living thing that moves upon the earth . . . (Genesis 1:28) Our stewardship of creation is our exercise of that dominion. We are called not to dominate, to exercise power for its own sake, but to care for that which God has made.

John Calvin, in the *Institutes of the Christian Religion,* describes the combination of providence and stewardship that forms the basis of our analysis. While we would today reject Calvin's exclusively masculine language in reference to God, we are grateful for this clear and strong affirmation of human freedom and responsibility in God's provision for us.

> For he who has set the limits to our life has at the same time entrusted to us its care: He has provided means and helps to preserve it; He has also made us able to foresee dangers; that they may not overwhelm us unaware, he has offered precautions and remedies. Now it is very clear what our duty is: Thus if the Lord has committed to us the protection of our life, our duty is to protect it; if He offers helps, to use them; if He forewarns us of dangers, not to plunge headlong; if He makes remedies available, not to neglect them. (1. 17.4.)

This paper will examine the issues related to contraception and abortion as an aspect of our care for creation. It will do so out of a profound respect for human life. Like the psalmist quoted above, we know that the value and dignity of human life are bestowed by God our Creator who calls us into a covenant relationship with him and with each other. Our study is based on a deep appreciation for the human family, for the ties that bind people together into long-term commitments and through which joys and sorrows, blessings and burdens may be shared. This study reflects an attitude of respect for the values and teachings of other religious groups. It was developed by the Task Force on Science, Medicine, and Human Values of the Advisory Council on Church and Society. The task force examined many different theological statements on abortion and contraception, interviewed physicians and researchers, and searched for a way it could best serve the church through a paper on contraception and abortion.

We affirm that the decision to bear a child may be described as being a decision to intitiate a covenant with that child. Through this covenant the parent(s) commit themselves to providing those resources of nurture and protection needed to bring that child to maturity. The covenant, begun in the decision to become pregnant (or to continue the pregnancy), is shared in baptism when the child is brought into the fellowship of the covenant community.

The Use of Contraception and Abortion

For the most part, Protestants have affirmed the role of contraception as a responsible exercise of stewardship vis-a-vis natural processes. Limiting the size of a particular family or limiting population growth in a whole population is generally understood to be a kind of caring for the next generation. The most desirable means of limiting natural human fertility is being able to prevent pregnancy. However, in the exceptional case in which a woman is pregnant and judges that it would be irresponsible to bring a child into the world given the limitations of her situation, this paper will affirm that it can be an act of faithfulness before

God to take responsibility for intervening in the natural process of pregnancy by terminating it.

There is a tendency to feel that it is more virtuous to continue a pregnancy without considering the possibility of abortion. However, Calvin asserts, we cannot reduce stewardship to a kind of wonder or awe in the face of the natural world. The pregnant woman has a responsibility to take seriously the relative merits of each course of action open to her. A woman who considers abortion and then opts to continue her pregnancy should never be made to feel guilty that she has pondered the question of abortion. It is better to give birth intentionally than to feel that the diagnosis of pregnancy constitutes an absolute obligation to bear a child. In most pregnancies the question of abortion will never arise, but when it does, the choice of abortion can be an expression of responsibility.

We understand readily that it is moral for a husband and wife who wish to engage in sexual relations, but who are not in possession of sufficient resources—emotional, physical, financial, etc.—to care for a child born at that time, to use contraception. The use of contraception in such a case enables the couple to enjoy the gift of intimate physical communion in their relationship while being responsible about the procreative power of their intimacy. The ability to exercise responsibility in this case is the ability to project future possibilities, to assess both the prospective strengths and limitations in a concrete situation, and to decide whether one can follow through if a commitment is made. Our ability to project both human needs and human limitations, and to make reasoned moral choices based on the work of the projective human consciousness, is an important part of the distinctive humanness of which biblical authors spoke when they affirmed that we humans are created ''in the image of God.''

The decision to bear a child means committing one's human resources for the purpose of sustaining and, in many ways, continuing to create this human life over a period of 18-25 years. Bearing children is a process of covenant-initiation that calls for courage, love, patience, and strength. In addition to these gifts of the Spirit, these covenants also require the various fruits of our labor in a money economy, the economic as well as spiritual resources appropriate to the nurture of a human life. The magnitude of the commitment to be a human parent cannot be overestimated, and should not be understated. Unfortunately, because the roles and functions of active parenting are not assigned a money value in our economy, the personal and social value of this work, performed primarily by women, is underestimated and even ignored.

Parenting may give us a sense that as human beings we can be God-like participants in creating a covenant. However, the question of abortion arises fundamentally out of the experiences of our finitude. The decision to terminate a pregnancy is a question of one's covenant responsibility to accept the limits of human resources. Much as we would like to have the power to follow through on the consequences of all our actions, we do not. When someone can discern that it would not be good for a child to be born as the result of a particular pregnancy, she has a responsibility to take her human limitations seriously and to act accordingly.

There was a time when being pregnant meant following the process to its natural conclusion, childbirth. When a child was born, there was no choice but to make the best of the situation, which could be extremely difficult for children as well as for their parents. We now have the medical skill to intervene, without threatening the life of a pregnant woman, in the development of a pregnancy. Thus, we are called to consider the ethical significance of each of the options set before us.

This frame of reference for deciding about an abortion is fundamental to our Calvinist tradition of Christian responsibility and freedom. Affirming human responsibility for procreative processes is an affirmation of human freedom. The freedom to do what one judges most appropriate in an abortion decision is qualified by the fact that the purpose of such decisions is the responsible exercise of stewardship. Even when we misuse our freedom, God's forgiving grace is offered.

The responsibilities set before us in God's covenant with us would be overwhelming if it were not for the power of the gospel. The gospel says that we have God's grace in deciding which course of action to take. We have important responsibilities, but we can trust, the gospel assures us, in the grace of God empowering us in the exercise of our free will to discern the appropriate course of action in a morally complex choice. If it were not for the assurance of God's Spirit informing human action in the exercise of conscience, we could not claim that we have the freedom to use modern medical skill to direct human procreation.

The Calvinist affirmation of conscience as one of the primary junctures at which the power of the Holy Spirit breaks through into human experience is grounded in both (a) the Old Testament call to human responsibility, as set forth in the biblical witness to God's covenant with us, and (b) the New Testament assurance of the work of the Holy Spirit as our enabler and guide in the exercise of human freedom before God. Our own Book of Order reminds us that "God alone is Lord of the conscience. . . ." (G-1.0301.) The Calvinist frame of reference speaks to the complexity of the human experience and of our being responsible for our actions before God. It speaks profoundly to that aspect of our humanness and has done so for centuries.

B. Contraception: A Question of Social Justice

One of the most significant moral questions that the study of elective abortion puts before our church is the question of the relationship of abortion and contraception. How do contraceptive technology and contraceptive practice relate to the incidence of surgical abortion? To date, most reflection on the morality of abortion has been limited to the questions of personal morality that arise after pregnancy and to intervention in the continuation of this natural process. If we regard abortion as a social and ethical issue as well as a personal question, we must examine abortion policy and practice in relation to "contraceptive" policy and practice.

According to Charles Westoff and Jane DeLong, a large percentage of induced abortions in the United States each year are performed for women who have become pregnant because of contraceptive failure.[1] In most of these instances, the women will choose to continue their pregnancies and give birth. However, some women decide to terminate the pregnancy by surgical abortion for the reasons that lead them to use contraceptives. There are several ways by which the abortions resulting from contraceptive failure could be reduced. Above all, it is important for us as a church to "demythologize" the assumption that contraceptives always work and its corollary, that when a contraceptive fails, it is the fault of the user. When we consider that all but 5-10 percent of the surgical abortions performed each year could be prevented by the development and use of more effective contraception, we should examine contraceptive failure and work to make contraceptive practice as effective as humanly possible.

First, we should review the rates of effectiveness of the various means of controlling or diminishing fertility. The table below gives ranges:

Number of Pregnancies Per Year Among 100 Fertile Women Who Use Method [2]

Method:	
Abortion	0
Abstinence	0
Hysterectomy	0.0001
Tubal Ligation	0.04
Vasectomy (use by partner)	0.15+
Oral Contraceptive (combined)	4-10
Condom and Spermicidal Agent	5
*I.U.D.	5

I.M. Long-Acting Program	5-10
Condom	10
Diaphragm (with Spermicide)	17
Spermicidal Foam	22
Spermicidal Suppository	20-25
Coitus Interruptus	20-25
Various Methods of Fertility Awareness	20-25
Lactation	40
Douche	40
Chance (sexually active)	90

Considered over against unprotected sexual intercourse, the several methods of contraception that medical science has developed within the last century do comprise a significant advance. However, our expectations for contraceptive performance significantly exceed their actual effectiveness.

If we view the moral (or ethical) problem of abortion in social perspective, we discover that the moral question posed by the numbers of surgical abortions performed annually in the United States is more forcefully described as the problem of contraception. As a church we must speak, as forcefully as possible, to the relation of contraceptive technology and practice to the need for surgical abortion. If we refer back to the table above, we learn that the term "birth control" (or "fertility control") is 100 percent accurately employed only in the cases of surgical abortion is and abstinence. It is patently absurd to claim that "abortion is not a method of birth control." Abortion is chosen in tens of thousands of cases annually in the United States alone because of the unfortunate fact that it is the only 100 percent (i.e., genuinely) effective method of preventing birth that medicine can currently offer. All other methods that we employ to prevent pregnancy or birth are only relatively effective; they merely reduce or diminish fertility.

Ninety percent effectiveness is considered good performance in contraception technique. Yet, if one in ten American cars manufactured this year did not last for at least twelve months, i.e., was broken down and could not be repaired because of defects in manufacture, there would be a national outcry against that industry. The commitment to purchase a car, significant as it may be, is not of the same order of magnitude as the commitment to bear and rear a human child. Of course, in any comprehensive analysis, purchasing a car or a home and choosing to bear a child cannot be compared. The useful comparison here is between our attitudes and standards from one industry to another. An important moral question for our society and our churches is raised by the discovery of the dramatically different standards that are popularly assumed in the respective cases. Recent advances in contraceptive technology have created a public consciousness that regards contraception as virtually perfect, while its "effectiveness" is far from reliable. To assume that the failures of contemporary "family planning" are attributable to user error, or to assume that present contraceptive technology is satisfactory, is to ignore our social responsibility and to allow a minority of individuals to bear the burden of our unwillingness to address the problem.

This matter is complicated when we realize that contraceptive "effectiveness" is sometimes cited from "theoretical effectiveness" rates as well as "actual use effectiveness" rates. The theoretical and actual rates can vary as widely as 15 to 20 percentage points, particularly when age-specific fertility is factored into the actual rate.[4] For many of us, it is surprising to learn that combined use of a condom and a spermicidal agent, neither of which requires a prescription, has virtually as few failures as The Pill in actual use. The "effectiveness" rates for the higher risk methods and those which are available only with a prescription are usually quoted from the statistics for "theoretical effectiveness." Even health professionals often under-estimate the value of the nonprescription, low health-risk methods.

As we consider our standards for the contraceptive industry on an individual basis, our evaluations may vary widely. But if we consider the data from a national perspective, the need for changes in contraceptive practice and technology becomes clear. If every female of childbearing age (15-45) used the most effective contraceptive method that is available presently and it functioned at the 1.1 percent rate, which is observed at an age-specific fertility of 35 years + ,[5] there would be at least $450,000 unintentional pregnancies each year. It is irresponsible for the church not to address the question of the relationship of our expectations for medical science in the area of family planning over against the actual performance of contemporary contraceptive technology. In the moral cases of rape or incest, the personal immorality of the aggressor is clear. In the case of women who are pregnant against their wills because of contraceptive failure, the immorality is far less focused because the responsibility is diffused among the various parts of the health care delivery system: the pharmaceutical industry, medical professionals, and the general public as a whole.

There is concensus among our members that methods which prevent fertilization or implantation are preferable to surgical intervention in pregnancy. There are, then, several important moral questions before our church. Is our view of the ''effectiveness'' of present family planning technology an accurate understanding of contraceptive or abortifacient use in actual practice? This question, to which we have spoken above, brings us to the conclusion that it is morally unacceptable simply to let contraceptive technology remain as is. Significant change is needed.

How can the failure rate of nonsurgical means of contraception be significantly reduced. Here are some important steps we can take: (a) As a church we have a responsibility to call for significant changes in contraceptive policy and practice. We should call upon policymakers in government and industry to form a rational policy for all members of our society in the area of contraception. For example, if it is possible to develop an oral contraceptive that is 85-90 percent effective for the female sexual partner, then it should be possible to develop a similarly effective prescription for the other (male) partner. If these two prescription drugs were understood as one contraceptive method, i.e., to be used by both partners together, the effectiveness would be well above the 99 percent mark. In other words, the annual figure of more than 450,000 unintentional pregnancies, which we mentioned above, could be greatly reduced. Sexual partners and medical professionals would welcome this significant diminution in the need for abortion services. It is time for the churches to call for the development and marketing of a range of effective male contraceptives. (b) It is incumbent upon us as a church to reeducate our own membership, to create an awareness that family planning cannot be the concern of either sexual partner individually. This project should be an integral part of the teaching ministry of the church. Our churches can be the place where people come to understand that it is technologically impossible for pregnancy to be effectively prevented by either partner alone. (c) Even before the pharmaceutical industry can make an oral contraceptive for males widely available, we can advise our members to use two or three different methods at once if they intend to prevent pregnancy.

C. When Contraception Fails: The Unanticipated Pregnancy

There is no point in the course of pregnancy before which the moral issue of abortion is insignificant. Because a human pregnancy is the development of a form of human life, the pregnant woman has a moral responsibility to choose whether it is responsible to give birth. An unintended pregnancy may become a wanted pregnancy. In many unintended pregnancies, this is the case.

However, a number of unintended pregnancies remain unwanted. This does not arise out of a casual attitude, a callousness, a disregard for children on the part of these pregnant women. Rather, the women whose unintended pregnancies become wanted pregnancies and the women who choose to terminate an unintended pregnancy may have each exercised their human responsibility to consider prospectively the resources needed by a particular human child in a particular situation. The former group may have found that although they had not made preparations in advance of becoming pregnant, they can reasonably expect to be able to provide the various resources that the nurture of a human child requires. The decision may be that of making the child available for adoption. The latter group may have made the best possible projection of resources necessary for the birth and nurture of a human child. Unlike the members of the former group, their consideration may result in the discovery of significant limitations in their resources. Having reached the conclusion that they are not in a position to care for a human child in that context, or to bring the child to birth so it could be placed for adoption, the decision to terminate the pregnancy can be an expression of human responsibility no less than another's decision to give birth.

These two groups are not exhaustive; there is a third possibility: the woman who discovers her unintended pregnancy and does not find the affirmation of her freedom and responsibility from either her religious community or from within herself. In this case, she continues her pregnancy because she feels compelled or coerced to do so, continues to be ambivalent about her course of action, and finds herself cut off from any spiritual or personal means of resolving her ambivalence. This third group is susceptible to the distortions of human intimacy cited in the abortion rights debate—increased occurrence of physical and emotional abuse, psychosis and schizophrenia, suicide. Our church is called at this time to speak clearly about our respect for all women and to assist them to make a conscious, responsible choice regarding unintended pregnancy.

Having outlined choices regarding unintended pregnancy, the question arises concerning their relationship to the developmental character of pregnancy. The church can offer clear guidelines regarding abortion in each trimester of pregnancy. If possible, an abortion should take place within the first trimester of pregnancy. This guideline does not stem from moral or theological perspectives, as we affirm that there is no point within the first two trimesters (i.e., before viability) at which abortion is a less or more significant moral question than at any other. The grounds for recommending that abortions be performed as early as possible are twofold:

1. The surgical procedures used to perform abortions during the first trimester are statistically safer.

2. On experiential grounds, first trimester abortion is preferable. During the first trimester, the surgical procedure is one of evacuating the uterus, i.e., it is experienced as surgery. During the second trimester, the pregnancy can only be terminated by processes that involve the expulsion of the fetus by uterine contractions, i.e., it is experienced as a process of labor and delivery.

There are two cases in which abortion cannot be performed until the second trimester of pregnancy: (1) Each year there are a small number of women of menopausal age who do not discover that they are pregnant until the second trimester. (2) Diagnosis of a genetic disorder by amniocentesis currently cannot occur until well into the second trimester.[3]

The current practice in the United States regarding abortion is almost entirely consonant with these guidelines. With ten years of experience with elective abortion, the percentage of first trimester terminations of pregnancy has leveled off at 94 percent. Of the remaining 6 percent, many are abortions sought by women of menopausal age; one half are chosen because of a diagnosis of serious genetic disorder, and the remainder are performed for women who either did not seek or did not have access to medical care in the first trimester. The latter group is composed primarily of teenagers who are ambivalent about being pregnant and fearful of disclosing their pregnancy to a friend, family member, or a professional who could be of aid. The physicians, clergy, demographers, and attorneys, with whom the justices of the Supreme Court consulted in the early 1970's, before handing down their 1973 decision led the Court to establish a national policy that would generate this pattern of usage.

By allowing the states to restrict the performance of abortion to hospitals only in the second trimester, the Court established a financial incentive for first trimester abortions. (In 1973, only 38 percent of all abortions were performed in the first trimester; by 1978, the number of first trimester abortions had leveled off at above 90 percent.)[6] At the same time, restricting second trimester abortions to certain facilities, as states have done, continues the protective intent of the law regarding abortion. None of the persons whose circumstances point to a second trimester abortion is burdened with the additional expense of seeking the permission of the judiciary on a case-by-case basis. (The Court's ruling regarding the third trimester will be addressed later.)

As we think about the implications of third trimester abortions we must also take into account the developmental character of pregnancy. To speak only of the absolute dependency of the fetus and of the physical autonomy of the neonate is not to exhaust the full range of possibilities. Later in pregnancy, although the fetus continues to be an integral part of the woman's body, i.e., continues its dependence on her, the fetus is sufficiently developed to survive as a physically autonomous human being. Although the fetus is still in fact dependent on the woman's body, that dependence is no longer absolute. At this point the moral question shifts from dominion (human responsibility for directing the natural order) toward inviolability. The fetus at this stage has similar moral claim to inviolability as does any human being already born. In other words, the responsibilities set before us in regard to the fetus begin to shift at the point of fetal viability. Prior to viability, human responsibility is stewardship of natural processes under the guidance of the Holy Spirit. Once the fetus is viable, even though in actual fact it does not exist outside the womb, its potential for physically autonomous human life means that Exodus 20:13 can be applied, as it is applied to the whole human community. The only moral exception to the Sixth Commandment in regard to the fetus during the last trimester of pregnancy is the endangerment of the mother's life. In such instances the difficult moral dilemma of self-defense presents itself.

The natural point of viability, after which the weight and organic development of the fetus permit its survival outside the womb, coincides roughly with the end of the second trimester, and thus with the end of the period during which elective abortion is permitted by the 1973 Supreme Court decision. We can affirm this decision, then, for religious reasons as well as medical, as it upholds the inviolability of autonomous human life. The Court's decision was, of course, not based on a particular religious perspective. Finding no clear consensus in this sensitive area, the Supreme Court based its decision on the legal tradition of intent to protect the safety of the pregnant patient.

In the last few years, the ability of the medical profession to aid the very small newborn to sustain life outside the womb has progressed wonderfully. Extrapolating from this progress, we can imagine the theoretical possibility that the point of "viability" could be moved back indefinitely. However, it is unlikely, barring a complete revolution in medical science, that this theoretical possibility will ever be the case. It is unlikely that an environment for fetal development that would be an acceptable substitute for the human uterus will be developed. If we wish to stay within the realm in which physicians can offer predictive judgments, we know that the low birth weight neonate, aided by intense oxygenation, temperature control, and a (relatively) sterile environment (i.e., an "incubator"), who survives a period of days or weeks of hospitalization will probably grow to be a healthy child and adult. When more intense, "heroic," measures are employed, neonatologists are unable to predict whether the neonate will later develop serious neurological problems. It is known that these infants, for whom extraordinary life support systems have been used, develop neurological disorders in a significantly greater number than the whole population.[8] Thus, extraordinary means should be used only at the discretion of the physician and the parents. In view of the impossibility of predicting the future possibility of disease resulting from incomplete development of the fetus's nervous system, it would not be helpful to press too rapidly toward an earlier point of viability for its own sake. It would appear that there is a natural point in the development of the fetus's nervous system before which its survival outside of the uterus will not be a practical possiblity.

Our understanding of what constitutes moral practice in the use of surgical abortion is not based on a set of categories, such as social and economic resources of the parents, emotional stress, rape and incest, life endangerment, etc. Because the factors entering into any particular abortion decision are so complex, a single rule regarding Christian practice in the use of abortion is probably not possible. It is statistically likely that virtually 100 percent of all women whose lives are endangered by pregnancy will choose abortion. It is statistically a bit less likely that every woman who is a victim of rape will choose surgical abortion; it is statistically far less likely that a woman or couple who perceive the pregnancy as a cause for financial or emotional stress on the family will actually choose to terminate that pregnancy. Yet the moral claim of each person to choose abortion is no less strong in these situations. The morality (or immorality) of a particular abortion is not contingent on the kind of problem that prompts its consideration, but on the seriousness of that problem in the particular case. We affirm the value of decision-making empowered by the Holy Spirit. Because we understand the morality of abortion to be a question of stewardship of life, the responsible decision to opt for abortion arises from analysis of the projected resources for caregiving in a specific situation and cannot be made without regard to these kinds of human resources.

D. Moral, Legal, and Medical Histories Regarding Abortion

In providing a resource to the church to assist the church's reflection on the use and morality of abortion, it is important to describe the developments that have converged in the late twentieth century. The history of these various developments is woven from a fabric of medical, legal, and theological information. To explore the Christian ethical significance of abortion, we need to be familiar with (1) the legal and medical understanding about abortion as well as (2) the difference between legal or medical thinking about abortion and theological or moral thinking. A brief look at the variety of points of view concerning abortion, as expressed at various times in history and from various professional perspectives, can help us in formulating a contemporary position on the abortion question. Because the medical history of abortion is less complex and is basic to understanding the legal and moral history, we shall deal with medical developments first and then review legal and moral issues.

1. Medical Developments That Generated the Possibility of Safe Elective Abortion

It is important to note the several developments and their timing in medicine relating specifically to abortion. Our examination of the twists and turns of medical progress that we take for granted today and the time lags between one advance and another, enables us to understand the legal history of abortion as such and to avoid making uncritical assumptions that presuppose a long history of moral prohibitions against abortion. (See Appendix A.)

Before developments in medicine in the nineteenth century, all known methods of terminating pregnancy were a serious threat to a woman's life. No chemical or surgical means available could offer any assurance of the woman's health. Any medication or instrument that could be used to cause a miscarriage was forbidden to physicians as early as the Hippocratic Oath. As Hippocrates taught, to use either a drug or a surgical tool with intent to produce an abortion was also seriously to risk the patient's life. Never to risk life is the ethical mandate that guided physicians in ancient Greece. The physician's professional responsibility to his (or her) patient has continued to this day. The intent of the United States Supreme Court's 1973 decision is to respect the professional responsibility of physicians.

There were no significant medical discoveries related to the performance of abortions until the nineteenth century. The first was that infection could be prevented. Any surgery, abortion included, carried with it three chances in eight that the patient would die, and three quarters of these deaths were from postoperative infection. The work of Pasteur and Lister (1857-1867) made physicians aware that bacteria cause infection and that antiseptics could be used to prevent it. These ideas were accepted in this country in the mid-1880's.

However, the problem related to surgical abortion remained, there was no way to treat internal infection, even in the later decades of the nineteenth century.

An equally significant development in the history of surgery was the discovery of anesthesia in the 1840's. Until that time many patients died of shock on the operating table. These two developments, the use of antiseptics to control infection and the development of anesthesia to prevent shock, changed surgery considerably! Along with two other subsequent advances, they made surgical abortion a safe medical procedure.

The first of these additional developments was the discovery of a process of suturing the uterus that allowed doctors to halt uterine hemorrhage. This was first used in 1883. This new technique is best known to us as the one that made Caesarean sections possible as elective procedures. Before this time, performing a Caesarean section meant the doctor had chosen to save the life of the baby and sacrifice the life of its mother. (The converse of this choice, craniotomy, meant taking the neonate's life in order to spare the woman. In either case, a terribly difficult choice had to be made and, yet, these were the best options available for many centuries.)

The last step was the advent of the so-called "miracle" antibiotics (penicillin, sulfa, etc.) in the midtwentieth century, which made it possible to treat an internal infection. Before this time, uterine infection was especially dangerous because it could not be treated. Thus, within the last forty years, we have witnessed the first period in history in which surgical abortion is a safe medical procedure. As a result, voluntary abortion is a realistic possibility for the first time.

2. Medical Developments That Changed Our Understanding of the Religious and Moral Issues in Family Planning

The understanding of how reproduction takes place has changed as dramatically as surgery in the last 100 years. It was not until 1875 that the German embryologist, Baer, postulated that human reproduction results from the combination of egg and sperm; his discovery was not accepted within the medical profession until after World War I. Until that time, it was believed that sperm contained complete miniature human beings (called an homunculus) and that the role of the woman's body in the reproductive process was simply to provide a fertile environment in which the human "seed" could grow. The word for "seeds" in Greek, as in the parable of the sower and the seeds or the parable of the seed growing secretly, is *ta sperma*, from which medicine has received its English language word, "sperm."

The debate over Baer's hypothesis was similar to the debate over Darwin's hypothesis. Were we humans "merely animals," reproducing by the methods of mammalian reproduction? The discovery that mammalian reproduction involves the meeting of gametes (the sperm and the egg) had occurred in the nineteenth century. However, many church leaders and church members refused to believe that observations of animal biology could be applicable to human reproduction. Baer's hypothesis, not proven by observation until the late 1960's, remained in disfavor throughout his lifetime and beyond, in favor of the traditional understanding of human reproduction formulated from Aristotle, derived by observing the reproductive capacities of plants using seeds. Botanists now know and school children are now taught that even most plants reproduce by sexual methods of reproduction. However, these scientific paradigms that we take for granted today were generated within the last fifty years! For the better part of the Christian era, faithful Christians made decisions based on information that has now been shown to be inaccurate. When new information is discovered scientifically, or when a whole new paradigm for scientific understanding emerges, these scientific developments may also bring about the need for changes in our theological or ethical interpretation of human actions.

We must note as we look at any religious or legal evaluation of contraception or abortion before the 1930's that the fetus was viewed as the property of the male, which happened to be found within the uterus only for the purpose and time period of gestation. Thus, as the female was understood to have no active or positive contribution in the creation of the new human being, the "ownership" of the fetus and the right to determine what should be done to, with, or for a child were the father's and not the mother's. An example of this previous understanding of the family as property is the fact that wives and children are given their husband's or father's names. Thus, when we look at the laws in the second half of the nineteeth century against women using the (then) new developments in barrier methods of contraception and intrauterine devices, we should remember that the law was grounded on the assumption that decisions made by one person (the woman) regarded the property of another (the man).

In previous historical periods, faithful persons made ethical decisions on the basis of the science of their day. Future generations may look at our wisdom and call it folly because we lack the scientific sophistication of that later day. There is one criterion that remains regardless of the state of the medical or scientific art, and we share this criterion with the whole history of Christianity both past and future. It is important that abortion decisions be informed by the best medical knowledge and that our decisions be made in the context of our faith.

At the time when the prohibition of contraception and abortion was formulated by Catholic and Protestant church leaders, all parties engaged in the question accepted Aristotle's embryology. Thus, when they spoke of "conception," they were not making the distinction that we do today between the two gametes (egg and sperm) and the zygote (fertilized egg). The "act of conception" in those nineteenth-century documents is what we in the twentieth century call sexual intercourse. In the nineteenth century, when Christian churches proscribed any intervention in the natural process of human reproduction "after conception," they were saying that only abstinence (or what would develop later as a program of periodic abstinence) was permissible for Christians as a means of limiting the number of births.

3. Moral Judgments and Social Consensus Regarding Abortion Throughout Judeo-Christian History: Protection and Prohibition

Because historical evidence is limited and sporadic, it is difficult to discern prevailing attitudes toward abortion more than 100 or 200 years back into history. Abortion is mentioned in a restrictive or prohibitive injunction, but there are also large gaps in time for which we have no reliable records.

The case of medieval England may well be the most nearly typical historical situation we have. There was no law regarding abortion specifically, so the legal historian is forced to assume that in view of the serious danger that abortion presented to a woman's life, there was no need to threaten punishment for abortions. At the close of the medieval period, when the common law tradition was being codified, a law regarding abortion was written into that code. British common law regarded the attempt to induce abortion, whether effective or not, as a crime of the abortionist. In the event of the woman's death, the person who performed the abortion was held guilty of homicide, the murder of the patient. In the event that the patient lived, which was probably the rarer case, for medical reasons outlined above, the abortionist was guilty only of à misdemeanor. Much later, when the American republic was being formed, British common law was carried forward in colonial courts uninterrupted and was amended during the course of constitutional development. This law, which regarded abortion per se as a misdemeanor (while holding the death of the pregnant woman or girl to be murder), became United States law when our Constitution was adopted in 1789.

During the long period of British precedence and even after the American adoption of British precedent, surgeons were not physicians. At the time these laws were written, surgeons, for the most part, were barbers. They were the men who owned the finest, sharpest blades. Surgery and the practice of medicine were not unified until the nineteenth century, when advances in anesthesia and antisepsis made possible the modern scientific practice of surgery as an integral part of the medical profession. Thus, the British law and early American law, while not aimed at doctors, may well have been drafted to discourage the barber-surgeon from performing abortions.

It is more likely, however, that those who were brought to trial under an antiabortion law, the group at whom the law was aimed primarily, were the practitioners of what we now call the areas of "gynecology" and "obstetrics." Within Christian history until about two hundred years ago, it was considered immoral for a male physician to attend a female patient in labor or birth or for the purpose of an examination of her reproductive organs, except in a life-threatening emergency. The Empress Maria-Theresa of Austria, a progressive woman of the Enlightenment, was one of the first women known to have asked a male physician to attend her as an obstetrician. She also instituted a program of childbirth in the hospital in Vienna, where women would be attended by male doctors. Until this time, the persons attending women during pregnancy, labor, and childbirth were women. A woman might have been in the care of a member of her extended family, or a neighbor, or a friend who had more experience than she in giving and attending birth. Until the transition from midwifery to obstetrics with male physicians was complete, the antiabortion laws were aimed at these women who served as companions of and consultants to women in their childbearing years. The protective intent of the law was both well-intentioned and useful; it was grounded in the knowledge of the medical realities of the time and protected the patient from an unwise practitioner, and the practitioner from the demands of a desperate patient.

This long-standing European and American legal tradition prohibiting induced abortion served much the same purpose with regard to the same groups of women and men, patients and providers, be they midwives, surgeons, or physicians, for almost the whole course of the Christian era, until the midnineteenth century. Despite the many changes that have occurred since 1800, the protective intent of antiabortion law, which had been the foundation of the law in this area from the medieval era to the present, remained the sole or most basic ground for laws governing abortion in the United States until 1976. During that same period of nearly two thousand years, there have been a number of shifts in the church's perspective on the theological question of abortion. Let us turn now to the specifically religious history of this issue.

The earliest mention of an artificially induced termination of pregnancy occurs in the Old Testament. There is one mention in the law code (Exodus 21:22-25) of accidentally induced miscarriage. If a pregnant woman is injured and she miscarries, the man who struck her is obligated to pay her husband compensation for the loss of his property. If the woman herself is harmed or dies, the law of an "eye for an eye" applies. Clearly, the implication of this law was that the Hebrews considered inducing a miscarriage not to be a homicide, not even manslaughter. Rather, the law protects the property rights of the husband. It is clear in this law, which occurs in a series of laws regarding damage or loss of various kinds of property, that the induction of a miscarriage, in this case unintentional, was not considered to be the moral equivalent of homicide. The placement of this prescription of a fine for property damages together with similar offenses and penalties was not inadvertent. If this act had been considered murderous, it would be found within a series of interpretations of the Sixth Commandment.

There are two basic reasons why the authors of the Bible were not concerned about abortion as a voluntary procedure. First, abortion was obviously not a realistic medical possibility. There are three Old Testament references that provide a reliable indication that the Hebrews did not practice even the unsophisticated and dangerous methods of voluntary abortion known to their contemporaries. Jeremiah laments the intolerable character of his existence by wishing that he had died in the womb: "So my mother would have been my grave, and her womb for ever great."(Jer. 20:17.) The third chapter of Job is a similar lament cursing the day of his birth, i.e., cursing his existence. The actual message of the lament is not pertinent here; however, one of the details is significant. One of the most common unsophisticated methods of abortion was beating the stomach of a woman late in her pregnancy until the fetus died. At this time, the woman's body will begin labor and expel the fetus. Today midwives and doctors know of this natural reaction of the woman's uterus to produce abortion, and historical references to this practice indicate that it has long been known to the gynecological "experts" in many cultures. Jeremiah is clearly unaware that labor automatically follows the fetus's death. Neither do any of his redactors nor do Job and his editors correct this misunderstanding. Thus, it is probable that the Hebrews did not practice voluntary abortion.

As the texts in Jeremiah and Job indicate, the Hebrews were unaware of induced abortion. In Ezekiel 16:3-5 the practice of "exposing" newborns as a means of controlling fertility is described. Ezekiel obviously disapproves of this practice; it is a Canaanite practice abhorred by the Hebrews. While the texts from Jeremiah and Job demonstrate that the writers of the Hebrew Scriptures did not have knowledge of any method of controlling birth, Ezekiel's reference to exposure informs us that the Hebrew writers were familiar with this practice. They chose, for the obvious reason of faithfulness to the Sixth Commandment, to disapprove absolutely.

A clear indication that abortions were taking place in biblical times would be either a prohibition or invective against it. Even as late as New Testament times, we find no injunction against abortion. The earliest Christian prohibition of abortion in the "Didache," a set of guidelines for the life of a Christian community near Antioch. The admonition against abortion in this list of prohibitions was probably addressed to those who might perform abortions. Its purpose was for the protection of their would-be patients. (It would be nearly fifteen hundred years after the writing of the "Didache" before a Christian theologian would clearly advocate the extension of the fetus's life in order to make possible its baptism as his reasoning for the prohibition of abortions.)

The Hebrews and the early Christians were not concerned with methods of controlling birth because they were perennially aware of being too few in number. Had any forms of birth control been available to them, they probably would have been uninterested in limiting their natural fertility. Our contemporary situation differs radically from the situation of persons in Old or New Testament times. Underpopulation is no longer a threat to the continued existence of either our religious community and its tradition or our society as a whole. To find guidance in determining what is responsible in planning our families, we cannot go directly to biblical references on childbearing. We need to find our own theological framework for understanding voluntary decisions about abortions, not adopt theirs. We find this framework in the biblical model of freedom and responsibility, not by looking to Scripture for references about abortion per se.

There was a significant shift in thinking about sexuality from the Hebrew, then Jewish (scriptural), perspective, which viewed our sexuality as a part of our humanness and therefore as part of God's gift of creation, to a more ascetic view of sexuality, under the influence of Hellenistic (neo-Platonist) philosophers. For them sexuality and sexual activity were inherently evil, a human characteristic that resulted from our "fallen" condition in this world and, thus, a characteristic that would not be a part of our wholeness in the life to come. Within the New Testament, the Pauline epistles already reflect this view. This devaluation of sexuality by the early Christian writers can be understood in view of their position as a marginalized people who disdained involvements, interests, and engagement with this world and held to hopes for the coming of the Kingdom of God. The integration of Platonistic thinking within Christian theology began by the end of the first century A.D., when Justin Martyr set up his school of Christian philosophy in Rome. It can be said to conclude in the time of Constantine, who established Christianity as the official religion of the Roman Empire, thus ending an era of marginalization for the Christian communities and initiating acceptance within the culture and of standardization of doctrine (orthodoxy).

Augustine's writings in this area are typical of his time, neither the most deeply misogynistic, nor among the least severe in his negative evaluation of human capacity for passion. Humanity is tainted with original sin, according to Augustine, because human life is conceived "in passion." As a result of this reasoning, sexuality came to be regarded as sinful because it is pleasurable, but justifiable because it is necessary for procreation. This Augustinian interpretation has probably been one of the most influential ideas in the history of Christianity. The notion that sexual relationships are justifiable only for procreative purposes is profoundly influential even today in thinking about contraception and abortion.

The creation of a single standard of orthodoxy for the Western church under its leaders in Rome generated the next steps in the development of the church's prohibition of abortion and contraception. In preparation for the great council of the whole church that Constantine gathered at Nicaea, there were several regional gatherings (also called councils or synods) of bishops, which Constantine sponsored as well. Two of those meetings addressed the moral question of women who sought or obtained abortions. At the Councils of Elvira and Ancyra, punishments of excommunication for a specific period of time were established. Note that in neither case was the punishment for homicide recommended. In addition, it is much more illuminating for our history to note that not all abortions were condemned: only those sought by unmarried women and "adulteresses," who were "seeking to hide their fornication." Not only does this text indicate that there has not been an absolute condemnation of abortion as a violation of the Sixth Commandment within the church's history. The illustrations of Elvira and Ancyra inform us that while the prohibition of abortion within the medical or health care community had a protective intent, the church had its own different motivations for limiting or, later, prohibiting abortions, even as early as the third or fourth century.

During the era that followed Constantine's establishment of a catholic church, i.e., the medieval period, the new Christian orthodoxy was clarified and refined. Again, to find a clear statement of the thinking typical of his time, we look at writings of the eminent, synthetic theologian at the close of the era. In the work of Thomas Aquinas we discover a new teaching about abortion; the question of the morality of abortion became a corollary to the question of salvation. Following Aristotle's belief that the human soul was infused into the fetus at sometime between the fortieth and ninetieth day, Thomas wrote that abortion was permissible before 40 days for a male fetus or 80 days for a female fetus. After 40 or 80 days, the fetus had an eternal, human soul and required baptism for its salvation.

His convictions about the soul and its genesis were entirely in line with those of the scientists and physicians of his day. Throughout the Middle Ages the physical formation of the fetus was identified with its animation: When the fetal body developed a human shape, physicians assumed that this shape indicated that it was now in possession of a human soul. The Aristotelian teaching on how life begins could be briefly described as follows: Life in every form, be it vegetable, animal, or human, was made to be a living being, rather than an inanimate object, because of that which gave it a particular form, the form of a spaniel, or of a zinnia, or of a man, which formative power or principle Aristotle called its soul (*anima*). Aristotle, and biologists following him, identified three major categories of soul: "vegetable soul" (which caused plants to be); "animal soul" (which caused animals to be); and "rational soul" (which caused humans to be). His term "*Homo sapiens*" for human being states simply that we are *Homo* ("being") *sapiens* ("knowing" or "reasoning"): the being that is able to reason. For Aristotle and his intellectual heirs, the characteristically human faculty *par excellence* was our ability to reason: our intelligence.

In the two higher categories, the being was said to be in possession of the higher soul appropriate to its apparent form, as well as one or both of the lower kinds of soul. In other words, plant life had only a "vegetable soul"; animals had both "vegetable" and "animal souls"; and people were understood to have all three souls—"vegetable," and "animal," and "rational souls."

When Aquinas integrated the newly rediscovered scientific writings of Aristotle in his theological work, he chose to identify the "rational" or human soul in Aristotle with the traditional Christian concept of an eternal soul. Thus, in an Aristotelian or Thomistic framework, the fetus was understood to be alive at every stage. However, the seed (sperm) had only vegetable soul, as it had only the form of vegetable life. The early stage of fetal life *in utero* was formed by both vegetable and animal soul, and after a period of gestation, the fetus was said to be infused with a rational or eternal soul.

Aristotle was an empiricist. He taught that the scientist-philosopher could observe the point during pregnancy when the rational soul was infused into the fetus. The observable criterion for human life was the appearance of external genitalia. The "form" of the fetus was unmistakable human at the point in fetal development when there was an empirically verifiable feature that would indicate one of the qualities unique to humans, in this case, the ability to reproduce itself. Greek physicians had fixed the points at which the external genitalia are visible quite accurately by observing stillbirths. The belief in "delayed animation," based on Aristotle's theory, which Aquinas espoused, prohibited all abortions after the 40th or 80th day of gestation to insure the salvation of the fetal soul. This belief in delayed animation became the doctrine of the Roman Catholic Church at the Council of Trent (1545-63): "Whereas no human body, when the order of nature is followed, can be informed by the soul of man except after the prescribed interval of time." This remained the Catholic belief about human ensoulment until 1869, and abortion was permissible or forbidden on the basis of this Thomistic reasoning. While a variety of motivations for opposition to abortion remain, although protection on medical grounds is no longer needed, the most fundamental doctrinal ground for religious opposition to abortion rights in the current debate is the principle of Thomas Aquinas permitting and prohibiting abortion. Of ultimate significance in a Thomistic theological framework is the baptism of the live fetus or neonate being the guarantee of the salvation of its soul. In opposing the baptism of infants and affirming it as a Sacrament of repentance, Calvin takes a different view on God's providential care for the fetus and neonate. (*Institutes,* IV, Ch XVI.20.)

Before 1869, there was only one very brief period during which abortion was prohibited absolutely without any qualification. Pope Sixtus V (1521-1590), in his Bull, Effraenatum, forbade abortion at any point during pregnancy and made it an offense punishable by irrevocable excommunication. Sixtus had been elected to the Papacy in a struggle between a "Libertine" party and a "Puritan" party fighting for control of the church. By this fiat, and several others, he successfully excluded a significant number of his opposition from their positions of ecclesiastical power. His purpose was to punish persons he considered sexually indulgent. The identification of sexual self-discipline with Christian piety was a legacy he had received from ancient Christian philosophers, notably St. Augustine. Sixtus's teachings on sexual morality were rescinded four years later by his successor.

With the sole exception of this fiat, some form of delayed animation theory was the foundation for theological reasoning about the morality of abortion until the late nineteenth century. In some cases Thomas's own rule was applied, which forbade abortion for all practical purposes, as pregnancy could hardly have been definitely diagnosed before 40 days of gestation. Thus, Thomas's rule enjoyed a congruence with the medical need for protective restrictions. After the Reformation there was no single body of church law; various European nations dealt with abortion in their own ecclesiastical and secular legal codes. Movement was another empirically observable criterion for life, which St. Thomas adopted from Aristotle. This criterion was also a basis for a perspective on abortion documented in the English common law. The fetus was considered to have come alive, and therefore to be inviolable, after "quickening," the first time the woman could feel the fetus moving.

In English law, quickening was used as an observable criterion for abortion decisions. Before that time, there was no offense for terminating pregnancy under the King's ecclesiastical law. As in Thomas's model, after the point when the fetus "came alive," i.e., possessed an eternal soul, as evidenced by intrauterine movement, abortion was forbidden in order that baptism could be performed. For example, a pregnant woman prisoner who was convicted of a capital crime could be executed immediately unless the "moment of quickening'' had passed. If the fetus had already ''quickened,'' a postponement of her execution was required until after birth, because, as it was the King (or Queen) who ordered the sentence, the death of the unbaptized fetus would be ''on the King's (or Queen's) head,'' i.e., the monarch's responsibility before God. After her child was born, the baby was baptized and its mother was executed, in both cases as swiftly as possible. This particular British law is important to us today as we look back into our own history because it clearly defines the purpose of the religious prohibition on abortions and thus discloses to us the primary theological motivation in restricting the termination of pregnancies.

The nineteenth century saw significant changes in the theological evaluation of the morality of abortion, bringing various elements of this history to the particular configuration of attitudes and theory that is often assumed to be the churches' singular interpretation of the morality of abortion throughout Christian history.

The earliest phase of these nineteenth century changes began in the 1820's, and 1830's, in response to the first of the medical advances that were discussed earlier. In the 1820's, Horace Wells discovered the anesthetic property of nitrous oxide. Soon after, a variety of other chemical substances such as cholorform and ether were also identified, which made it possible for the surgeon to work while his patient was in a sleeplike state, free of pain. When anesthesia was discovered, the attitude of the general public about surgery changed rapidly and for the first time, patients began to request surgery. Medical professionals and other highly educated persons recognized, however, that although the dangers of surgery had been diminished considerably they had by no means been removed. A great deal of debate emerged as to what system of accountability would protect the patient in this new age when surgery had become painless and was perceived to be a simple matter, but when, in fact, the risks continued to be considerable. Were laws needed to require of all doctors and hospitals that they bring their testimony regarding the ''relative safety'' of each surgical case before the courts and that surgery could be performed only with the court's permission? Or, as surgeons and other doctors argued, was the best course of action to entrust the decision-making power to the members of the medical profession, who, as professionals, would be accountable to themselves and to their peers? It was from this debate that the statutory limitations on the performance of surgical abortion emerged.

The first of these laws was passed by the New York legislature. In 1828, it considered a bill limiting all surgery to cases where the surgery was necessary to preserve the life of the patient. (The ''relative safety text'' was a standard procedure in hospitals in New York at the time.) Two years later the legislators passed a bill that singled out abortion, as it was the only surgical procedure that was performed on the basis of extramedical pressure. The New York legislators deemed it wise to regulate the performance of abortion in order to prevent surgeons from performing a surgical procedure without the woman's considering the risk to her life. When other state legislatures introduced regulations that singled out abortion from other surgical procedures, the protective intent that was clearly expressed in the debate preceding the passage of the New York law became the implied, if not explicitly stated, intent of the laws adopted.

In the second half of the nineteenth century, there was a series of changes in the church's teaching about human intervention in the reproductive process. The opinion underlying the changes in religious teaching was that the natural function of sexuality was procreation. The 1869 General Assembly of the Presbyterian Church in the United States of America stated that to thwart that end was a ''crime against God and against nature.'' These changes in theological perspective included laws against both abortion and contraception. Catholic and Protestant moralists have differed in the twentieth century over the ethical significance of contraceptive means of controlling birth, but in the late 1860's virtually all branches of the Christian church condemned any attempt to control birth as categorically immoral.

Changes in the theological treatment of the moral issues were probably brought about by a combination of the several factors rather than any one of them. First, medical science was developing new methods of contraception. During the nineteenth century, "pessaries" or cervical caps (the forerunner of the twentieth century diaphragm) and intrauterine devices were developed. I.U.D.'s, usually made of iron, were manufactured in the nineteenth century in Germany, and the ability of such devices to prevent pregnancy was established. Although the nineteenth century "contraceptives" were not as effective as today's, the scientific advance generated a great deal of public interest and a wholly new set of expectations never known before in the history of the world. There are several facets of the churches' response to these developments. First, and probably foremost, it appeared inherently immoral to both Protestant and Catholic clergy that women might have the power to decide the fate of the homunculus contained within the man's sperm. Even as late as 1869, Aristotle's theory that the (nascent) miniature human being was contained within each individual human seed (sperm) was accepted as scientific fact. It is easy to understand indignation at the suggestion of women being given the freedom to thwart the process of reproduction. In view of the legal strictures that had already governed the performance of surgical abortion for nearly forty years,we could probably infer that the ecclesiastical invective in 1869 against any intervention by a woman after "conception" (intercourse) was against the newly developing nonsurgical methods of controlling fertility! Before this time, antiabortion injunctions or legislation were intended to stop the persons who would be performers of abortion. In 1869, for the first time, we find theological invective against women, who would be the users of the new "contraceptive" devices.

In addition, on both sides of the North Atlantic, several related visions of social change began to emerge, under the label of "the women's movement" or "feminism." Radical women were proposing that females should have access to higher education, should be franchised to vote and hold elective office, that females would not be harmed by physical activity in sports and would benefit from wearing clothing more conducive to the health of their internal organs, as well as some other ideas that have yet to be accepted in our culture. There was, no doubt, some fear of and probably considerable resistance to the new medical developments that could give women the power to determine their lives in unprecedented measure.

Antiabortion legislation again enjoyed a wave of popularity. As noted earlier, antisepsis was not common medical practice until the 1880's. During the intervening period there was a second wave of vigorous campaigns, especially throughout the Western states to stop practitioners, both licensed and unlicensed, from performing abortions. While abortion had become a painless operation, its danger had not diminished because of the intrauterine infections introduced by nonsterile techniques. By the end of the 1870's, practically every state in the union had an antiabortion law. In both the first and second waves of antiabortion legislation, the form of the laws indicates that they were motivated by the medical necessity of protecting the patient from the practitioner. In contrast, the religious objections to any form of contraception or abortion inveighed against the women themselves. No doubt, in this second phase of legislative activity, there were coalitions of various people interested in a common end for various reasons. However, even though the antiabortion laws were passed during the nationwide lobbying effort funded by Alfred Comstock that outlawed contraception, other "unnatural" sexual acts, and the sale of prurient literature, these laws continued to take the form of the earlier New York State law. Under these laws, most of which stood until the Supreme Court Decision in the case of Roe v. Wade in 1973, the abortionist, not the woman, could be tried and found guilty of the crime of abortion. These antiabortion laws were not intended to punish or inhibit sexual promiscuity, as might be suggested, because there was no exclusion for women who were married or victims of rape or incest. Most significantly, whether or not the woman was pregnant, the abortionist was guilty of abortion, if her or she introduced any chemical substance or instrument into her womb with the intent to produce an abortion. These laws were written to protect the prospective patient in a time when a popular but quite mistaken assumption was that surgical abortion was a relatively safe procedure. That the abortionist might be licensed to practice medicine was not a defense against criminal conviction for abortion; these laws were written to let doctors (and others) know that they must inform their patients how very dangerous an abortion would be.

Long after other surgery had ceased to be life-threatening, the possibility of infection of the uterus, which could not be cleaned and dressed as other surgical wounds, continued to make abortion a dangerous surgical procedure. Thus, perceptions and attitudes about surgery in general had changed, and the memory of the certain threat to life that it once posed had faded many years before we came to the midtwentieth century reconsideration of the legal status of abortion. In the nineteenth century, we find the idea that contraception and abortion could be part of medical service. There had always been ways of trying to abort or of trying not to conceive, but in the nineteenth century the transition of medicine from a palliative act to a curative act, grounded in a scientific understanding of the human body, generated expectations in the area of family planning long before the technology was sufficiently refined or widely available. The ecclesiastical reponse in the nineteenth century to the possibility of safe and effective contraception or abortion was the condemnation of birth control as "murder."

Between then and now there has been an extraordinary change in attitudes toward contraception. Although all church bodies do not affirm the use of contraceptive means of limiting fertility, most Protestant churches do, recognizing that women chose contraception, even when it was still illegal, out of a concern for their health and safety and for their children. The emergence of decriminalized contraception is a fascinating history in itself, which did not end in this country until the 1958 Supreme Court Decision Griswold v. Connecticut, which struck down state laws forbidding the prescription, sale, and use of contraceptives to and by married persons. A significant theological change occurred at the same time, namely, sexuality was now understood to be a gift from God in both its procreative and communicative functions. It was appropriate for couples to engage in sexual intimacy, using contraceptives, thereby separating one function from the other.

E. An Analysis of Four Questions and Concepts Assumed to Be Necessary for Understanding the Morality of Abortion

Our reflection seeks to establish a framework within which faithful Christians can understand when abortion can be considered a responsible ethical option and when it is an irresponsible choice. The following section presents four concepts often employed in discussion of the morality of abortion. All have nineteenth century roots and need to be tested in the light of twentieth century knowledge about reproduction. The purposes of these analyses are to clarify concepts that are sources of confusion among participants in the current debate and to function as a resource for dialogue and reflection. The areas for investigation are headed by the following four propositions:

1. The question of the morality of abortion is not dependent on an analysis based on a theory of a conflict of rights.

2. The question of the morality of abortion is not dependent on the question of the inviolability of autonomous human life.

3. The question of the morality of abortion is not dependent on the question of when human life begins.

4. The question of the morality of abortion is not dependent on the question of the morality of sexual activity.

1. The Question of the Morality of Abortion Is Not Dependent on an Analysis Based on a Theory of a Conflict of Rights.

The attempt to develop a universal formula that will enable us to analyze the significance or value of the fetus over against the significance or value of the pregnant woman is logically a conundrum and a theologically unhelpful abstraction. Because the 1973 Supreme Court Decision Roe v. Wade remained agnostic on this question, recognizing a plurality of views on the status of fetal life, a great deal of discussion has emerged from those who place an absolute value on the fetus over against the pregnant woman. Opponents of the Court's decision hold that in place of the explicit agnosticism of the judiciary, the Court should have been guided by an absolute conviction of the value of fetal life and therefore should have established an unqualified guarantee of its right to protection under the law. The transcript of the Court's decision exhibits a genuine sensitivity to the profound importance of theological convictions with regard to this question and, at the same time, an unwavering respect for the variety of sincerely held beliefs among United States citizens and the variety of perspectives found in the several strands of our theological and philosophical heritage. The text of their decision states:

> Texas urges that, apart from the Fourteenth Amendment, life begins at conception and is present throughout pregnancy, and that, therefore, the State has a compelling interest in protecting that life from and after conception. We need not resolve the difficult question of when life begins. When those trained in the respective disciplines of medicine, philosophy, and theology are unable to arrive at any consensus, the judiciary, at this point in the development of man's knowledge, is not in a position to speculate as to the answer.

The Court's refusal to affirm any one of these traditions or any one of the variety of present convictions grows out of its traditional posture of respect for religious liberty. In other words, the Court has invoked the constitutional right to privacy on this level: United States citizens who are members of the Jewish faith, members of a Protestant communion, baptized in the Roman Catholic or Orthodox churches, followers of Islam, members of other religious groups, and those who have chosen not to affiliate with a religion have the freedom before the law to choose their course of action according to the teachings of their own faith and according to their own conscience. In order to guarantee religious liberty, the Court chose to recognize no more (and no fewer) rights of a fetus than had been already established by earlier precedents in the law. Because the Court explicitly omitted affirming an absolute right-to-life of each fetus, individuals and groups that hold this particular conviction have objected strenuously to the decision. For our purposes, it does not suffice to say that our theological understanding of the morality of abortion differs.

There are several inadequacies in a theory that views the morality of abortion as an issue involving a conflict of rights or a conflict of interests. From a psychological perspective, the work of Carol Gilligan at Harvard demonstrates that the highly abstract quality of this theory is a typically masculine pattern of logic superimposed on a decision-making process that falls primarily to women. This theory itself and even its theological cousin, the doctrine of immediate ensoulment, do not have a long history within our Judeo-Christian tradition. The doctrine of immediate ensoulment, which holds that an eternal soul is infused in the fetus "from the moment of conception" and thus implies that from that point the fetus has need of baptism if its soul is to enjoy salvation, was established in 1869. The prior history of ensoulment and the various reflections on delayed animation served as guides to the church (or churches) by identifying a stage in the fetus's development after which its protection should be guaranteed in order that it might be baptized. The theological point was a moot one, however, in view of the life-threatening danger of abortifacient techniques or postabortion complications. Before the development of these speculative theologies of animation, early Christian teachings simply restated the long-standing notion of viewing the fetus, although located within the woman's body, as the property of its father.

In this century a liberalization of this absolutist teaching on animation has emerged. As late as the 1930's, Catholic clergy were counseling women carrying an ectopic pregnancy not to avail themselves of the lifesaving medical techniques available to them, on the theological grounds outlined above regarding animation and baptism. By the midtwentieth century, however, many Catholic theologians (and probably most Catholic priests) had come to affirm the morality of terminating an ectopic pregnancy (or any other life-threatening pregnancy) based on the "just war" theory of Thomas Aquinas. Thomas taught that war is never justified in itself; but when an unjust aggressor initiated an attack upon a Christian country, the Christian monarch was morally justified in responding to the aggression by engaging in the war for the purpose of his own or his country's defense. The midtwentieth century liberalization of the absolute prohibition on human intervention in the reproductive process reasoned that in a similar fashion, the woman whose life is threatened by an "unjust aggressor," i.e., the fetus, would be morally justified in choosing to terminate her pregnancy.[2] This moral reasoning fit hand-in-glove with the legal exception to the prohibition of abortion, based on a relative safety test.

Particularly within the last twenty-five years, we have witnessed the convergence of these elements in the interpretation of the moral significance of abortion. The myth has emerged that Christian moral analysis of abortion has always hinged on assessing the relative merits of the interests of two opposing parties. In the case of a pregnancy that endangers a woman's life or health, certainly the consideration of the question of abortion can take this logical form. Both the doctor and the patient must consider the tension between the two values in conflict: the intrinsic worth and potential of the fetus and the value of the woman's life. This tension could be described as a conflict of interests, but that sort of reductionist analysis does not do justice to the complexity of the concerns that enter into the decision that the woman, her physician, and her family must make. To develop a moral analysis that treats the question of every abortion primarily as a conflict of rights is to assume that the woman who chooses an abortion is unequivocally selfish, that she has no concern for the fetal life within her body, that her only concern is for herself. In an era when a relative safety test was medically necessary, moral reasoning that reduced the question of abortion to an analogy of war or interpersonal conflict could suffice. Subsequent to the development of medical skill, which makes elective abortion possible, a theory that limits our analysis of the morality of abortion to a conflict-of-rights model expresses a fundamental contempt for women, who do indeed care for children as well as themselves. In a time when elective abortion is possible, such a moral theory is no longer adequate because the constraints of its logic do not allow us to consider the possibility that there may be other, morally legitimate reasons for choosing to terminate a pregnancy.

The right-to-life theory does justice neither to the social realities that should be considered nor to the personal realities that should be considered nor to the personal realities that are present in the process of moral deliberation in the actual case. Responsible women and their families who are actually considering the possibility of abortion do not experience their dilemma as a conflict of rights or interests. On the contrary, women who are in the process of weighing a concrete choice to terminate or to continue a pregnancy experience themselves as located within, perhaps even the center of, a nexus of responsibilities. Let us consider, for example, a woman and her husband who have two children and have learned of their present pregnancy that a genetic disorder such as Down's syndrome has been diagnosed. As she (or they) reflect on the choice that the physician's report has set before them, she will undoubtedly take into consideration not only a projection of what the extraordinary needs of a Down's syndrome child might be but also the needs of the two children she already has. She may choose, based on her projection of what this particular situation calls for and of the various strengths and resources that she has to offer (taking into account the limits of her strength as well), to terminate the pregnancy. If she already has three or four children, she may be more likely to feel certain that she cannot take on the additional responsibility of bearing and rearing a Down's syndrome child. If this is her first pregnancy, she may feel more readily able to conclude that she could give the appropriate care that such a child needs. Another factor that enters into her decision would be family income level. If they are an affluent family and can afford professional child care in their home, her projection of the boundaries of the resources that she can offer her child(ren) will be quite different than that of the woman who will be able to supplement her own physical and emotional strengths with only occasional help or none at all.

A conflict-of-rights theory falls short of its goal of enabling us to understand the moral significance of the choice for or against abortion, because it cannot account for the personal, social, and economic realities of this existence. It excludes even the ''spiritual'' realities that we enjoy in this life, such as integrity, concern, and a sense of responsibility. These theories, propounded by both secular and religious people, which attempt to decide the moral problem of abortion by setting ''fetal rights'' over against ''maternal rights,'' cannot go beyond their own symmetry. We are left with the abstract equivalency of the woman's humanity and the fetal humanity. Neither can be denied.

If the humanity of the fetus is absolutized, then the woman is reduced to a vessel in its service. In response to this theory, a counter argument arises that, in a similarly absolutist fashion, denies any significant value to fetal human life and refuses to allow that abortion is a moral question. We need to understand the problem in all of its facets in order to receive guidance.

The exposition of this particular theory often includes one or two derivative arguments: one from organogenesis and one from fetal innocence.

The argument from organogenesis, which identifies the appearance of various organs or biological systems at certain points in pregnancy, is intended to persuade us of the humanity of the fetus by an appeal to sentiment. Our identification of these fetal developments with what we know to be parts of our physical selves has a persuasive immediacy but, on consideration, we realize that it too reduces our humanity to the point where it no longer has meaning. If I see pictures of a developing fetus, identifying its heart with mine, its eyes with mine, etc., and later realize that it was of another species—perhaps the arms were not quite right, they turn out to be wings, and I suddenly recognize that it is a fetal bat, for example— the deceptive capacity of this argument from organogenesis becomes clear. While the fetus may be human, we cannot reduce the complexity of what it means to be human—a complexity that we can only express in its fullness by the language of faith, e.g., to be ''made in God's image''—to the single dimension of a biological reality. Even the kicking of the fetus during the latter part of the pregnancy, which gives parents such joy as they eagerly anticipate a birth, we now know to be caused by the fact that the nervous system, one of the later fetal developments, is not yet sufficiently formed to control the voluntary muscle system. These kicks may cause us to imagine a child at play, or one who is communicating with us, when in fact the fetus is not yet sufficiently developed to hold its arms or legs still. For prospective parents to enjoy this phenomenon is entirely appropriate. However, it is not legitimate for us to judge ourselves and one another on the basis of this kind of one-dimensional reasoning.

The argument that the fetus is morally innocent is similarly intended to persuade us that the fetus should be absolutized over against its ''competitor.'' Christians who reason ethically within a Thomistic tradition use the analogy of the fetus as an ''aggressor'' when abortion is being considered because the woman's life is endangered by her pregnancy. Conversely, in all cases when abortion is being considered for a reason other than life-endangerment (if one is using an analogy to Aquinas's just war theory to explain the moral significance of abortion), the fetus is not an ''aggressor,'' therefore, it is ''innocent.'' If we reason about abortion by analogy to war, fetal innocence is implicit in this theory. However, there are two additional points about the ''innocence'' of the fetus, which call into question the value of this concept as an answer to the theological or philosophical question as to the morality of using one of the chemical, mechanical, or surgical techniques of abortion now available to us.

a. The phrase ''innocent fetus'' can be used in dialogue or debate in the popular sense of these terms, i.e., without clarifying the fact that the theological claim regarding innocence in this case is limited to its converse relationship to Thomistic moral theory. When this language is employed, without reference to the larger theological framework of which it is a part, the listener might well assume—and probably often does—that the fetus's innocence is being contrasted with the woman's sinfulness. We all know that pregnancy results from sexual activity. Thus, references to an ''innocent fetus,'' when that technical term is lifted out of the sophisticated and subtle theological argument of which it is rightfully a part, imply a moral judgment of the pregnant woman. The connotative power of this term makes it useful in a prejudicial way and gives it a theological meaning entirely different from the original meaning. This theory, which implies guilt, does not do justice, for example, in a case of rape or incest.

b. The Christian doctrine of original sin, as formulated by Augustine, defines human sinfulness in a manner that is entirely incompatible with the connotative use of a concept of fetal innocence. Augustine's teachings regarding original sin speak of our human condition and hold that humanity is tainted with sin, not as a result of our actions, but by virtue of our very humanness. In Augustinian language, we are subject to original sin because we are descended from Adam and Eve and conceived in passion. In other words, regardless of whether the fetus has ever committed a human act, i.e., made a conscious moral choice and acted on it, the category of innocence does not apply. In the Classical Christian understanding of innocence and sin, neither the woman nor the fetus is less or more sinful than the other. Unless we take the severely ascetic view that pregnancy is a punishment for sexual activity, or the view that sin consists only in immoral acts, then it is heretical to posit on the innocence of the fetus over against the woman in any fundamental theological sense.

In summary, a moral theory of abortion that takes as its model a conflict of rights or interests between two persons is inadequate to describe the process of moral reflection by which thoughtful persons weigh a variety of responsibilities as stewards of the world that God created. This theory does not allow us to differentiate between a responsible and an irresponsible choice. The theory precludes the possibility of a choice, except in the case of self-defense. This type of theory cannot help but exclude every other factor in the concrete situation. If there are factors other than life endangerment that warrant abortion, a conflict model does not provide an adequate frame of reference.

2. The Question of the Morality of Abortion Is Not Dependent on the Question of the Inviolability of Autonomous Human Life.

It is sometimes assumed that the question of the morality of abortion is exhausted by reference to Exodus 21:13. ("Thou shall Not Kill.") The Roman Catholic Church's response (c. 1869) to the demand for abortion, generated by the discovery of anesthesia, used the term "murder." This recent religious history has often become a filter through which we have viewed (and unknowingly interpreted) the long history of moral, legal, and medical perspectives on abortion. Abortion, prohibited as "murder" to physicians for the sake of the women who were their patients, when filtered through this recent stratum of religious history, appears to have been a proscription against intervention in the pregnancy in order to protect fetal life. By the midtwentieth century, a general awareness of the original protective intent of the traditions of medical ethics, legal limitations, and religious proscriptions had been lost.

If we examine the whole of Exodus, Chapters 20-21, we discover that the Decalogue, which expresses the generic case of God's intention for human relationships, is followed immediately by a series of "ordinances" that detail specific behaviors in specific contexts. Among these concrete applications of the broad rubrics of divine intention, we find the sole mention of artificially induced miscarriage in the Hebrew Scriptures. Chapter 21 relativizes the general proscription of Chapter 20, so far as pregnancy is concerned. The word "ratsack" (to murder) appears only four times in the Old Testament in addition to its use in the Decalogue. (Num. 35:27; Deut. 4:42 and 5:17; I Kings 21:19; and Hosea 4:2) Old Testament word study does not solve the problem of the morality of abortion, but it does point us toward the fact that direct application of the moral rubric "murder" is a modern judgment, rather than an ancient one.

The fact that various parties in the current abortion debate cannot agree to a single language regarding "personhood" in describing this moral choice demonstrates the uniqueness of the moral question of elective abortion. When we begin to describe the moral choice set before a pregnant woman, some insist on speaking of two "persons," while others speak of only one "person." Unless one believes in a theology of immediate ensoulment and the use of the term "person" is a secular code word for that specific doctrine, speaking of the blastocyst, or the embryo, or even the fetus, reduces the meaning of the word "person" to a point of absurdity. On the other hand, to insist on speaking of only one "person" whose "personhood" is admissible within our conceptual understanding of the moral question of abortion denies what we know by common sense to be the case: that there is something happening within the female's body at that time that can never take place within the male body, and that the word "person" is used interchangeably, i.e., with the same meaning, for both genders. Clearly the use of the term "person," if it is descriptive of the male, cannot suffice to explain the entire significance of the female who is in the process of gestation, if that description is to allow for a projective as well as a present analysis.

The word "person," unlike the terms "body" or "soul," has a meaning that includes both a physical aspect and a spiritual (or at least mental) aspect. If we choose a definition such as Emerson's—"an intelligence served by organs"—it is clear that during the period of gestation, only the woman can be demonstrated beyond any doubt to possess intelligence as well as physical being. But we can conceptually place an anticipatory value on the primitive form (the fetus) of that which is yet to be realized. When we speak of the relationship of the pregnant woman and the fetus that is developing within her body, we are speaking of a unique category of human existence, a relationship that is not strictly analogous to any other. Thus, the moral question of whether and when it is appropriate to intervene in the developmental process of pregnancy is a question that may be compared to other moral questions but cannot be reduced to any one of them.

In the course of its hearings, the Task Force on Science, Medicine, and Human Values received a very special gift in the testimony of a mother whose adult daughter had been murdered a few years earlier. Ms.* testimony before the task force is included in Appendix II. It is unique in several respects. Hers is the only testimony of a woman who made a conscious moral choice to terminate a pregnancy. In this particular case, the physical limitations of her body were such that she was forced to choose between performing the physical tasks required of any mother of two young children and being able to rest in bed without moving in order to prevent a miscarriage. One feature of her statement, in particular, is a paradigm for the abortion decision as exercised by responsible Christian persons. Ms.* wrote in her statement of her two then-living children at her bedside as she was deciding whether she would terminate her pregnancy. She drew an explicit connection between her reponsibilities as mother and primary active parent of the two children and her decision to end her pregnancy. In other words, it was in the interest of her two children to end her pregnancy, to get up out of bed and perform her duties to them as a parent. This sense of responsibility she understood fully and took entirely seriously. In making her decision to induce a miscarriage by performing the physical activities of parenting, she weighed her parental duties against her responsibilities for the fetal life in her uterus. This feature of her particular testimony is paradigmatic for all abortion decision-making. We cannot understand the human significance—the meaning—of a choice regarding abortion, and thus we cannot evaluate such a choice ethically, until we have perceived the integral relationship between the sense of responsibility for human children (which is fundamental to the parenting process and, thus, also to the human relationships within the Christian institution of the family) and the conviction, with regard to a particular pregnancy, that it is ethically preferable that this pregnancy should be terminated.

Two points of medical sociology are worth noting here also: Ms.* did not have adequate medical care. She should have been hospitalized for this process and aided by surgical intervention. Had this been the case her young children would not have witnessed the physical pain that she suffered, nor would she have had to lock them out of the room where she miscarried, in order to spare them from witnessing the event. Physicians and hospitals are now free to offer medical care in this kind of emergency. This story gives the layperson a clue to the difficulties that demographers encounter in estimating the rate of induced abortion in the United States before 1973. A case such as this, in which both the woman and her physician knew that a conscious choice had been made but were prevented legally from reporting the event, illustrates the kind of fundamental problems that inhere in data recorded more than ten years ago.

Her story is unique, too, in a third, very powerful way. By an exceptionally cruel fact of her own personal history, she was able to compare for us the experience of her child being murdered and the experience of an induced abortion. In so doing, she offered a theological tool that enables us to distinguish between abortion and murder, not by saying that one happens during pregnancy and the other later on—but by examining both motive and purpose as well as act, and judging the morality of the choice on the basis of all three. Murder is, by her testimony, an act of hostility, of aggression, an attack. The murderer seeks to dominate and chooses to murder in order to gain the sense of having absolute power over the other person. The responsibly chosen abortion bears no similarity of motive or purpose to the act of murder. Elective abortion, when responsibly used, is intervention in the process of pregnancy precisely because one takes seriously the needs of a human child.

We are speaking of two separate and distinct moral categories when we speak of murder and of elective abortion. Murder can never be a responsible moral choice. The case of intentionally choosing to take the life of another human being for morally acceptable reasons, such as in war or for self-defense, is a justifiable homicide, a "lesser" homicide than the act of murder. Elective abortion can be a responsible choice or it can be chosen irresponsibly. The fundamental difference between the moral categories of abortion and murder is expressed in the theological distinction between dominion and domination. Our dominion over nature means that we are responsible before God not only for ourselves as individual persons but for the whole of nature insofar as we are empowered to direct its design.

Our church's affirmation of elective abortion as a responsible ethical choice may engender a fear that respect for the inviolability of all human life will be lost. This fear is probably the reason why our moral thinking about abortion can jump so swiftly to the moral category of "murder" without taking into account actual experience, i.e., examining motive and purpose in relation to act. When we say that our church affirms elective abortion by virtue of the humanness of the fetus and its physical dependence on the body of the pregnant woman, we are speaking about a different moral category of acts than does the Sixth Commandment.

3. The Question of the Morality of Abortion is not a Question of When Human Life Begins.

The morality of abortion cannot be based on the question of when human life begins. The modern scientific answer to the question of when life begin is that human life and its reproduction are a continuum. In fact, there are forms of human life in the human ova and sperm, in the human zygote (which the joining of the two gametes creates), in the human fetus which develops in the womb, in the human infant.

It is ultimately senseless to ask when in this continuum from one generation to the next a recognizably human form of life can be found. Human life is never absent. Thus the question "When does life begin?" with regard to a particular pregnancy cannot be answered. A more appropriate question might be, "At what point in the reproductive process should intervention be prohibited?" At ovulation, intercourse, fertilization, diagnosis of pregnancy, quickening, or during the first or second trimesters? At what point is abortion no longer a morally defensible option?

Reasoning that seeks to establish a point at which human life "begins," logically excludes the value of the woman's life except as the instrument for creation of new human life. This kind of thinking excludes the consideration of any other concerns, such as the family environment or the prospects for the life of the child. To take the question "when?" as a starting point, thus, is to preclude responsible decision-making in particular cases. The question of abortion warrants a theological framework that informs decision and actions. In short, the question of the morality of abortion is not simply a question of when human life begins; rather it is primarily a question of whether in this particular case one is prepared to give birth to and care for a child.

To reject the notion that the starting point of a decision for abortion is the question of the beginning of human life is not to diminish the importance of the developmental character of human reproduction. If the theological and ethical analysis of abortion is based on the question of when human life "begins," it is logical to conclude either (1) that there is no point in the continuum in which there is a moral right to intervene or (2) that there is an early period in the development of a human pregnancy that is of less or no moral significance. A moral theory of gradualism, suggested by the physically developmental character of pregnancy, leads to the questionable moral conclusion that abortion in the early weeks of pregnancy is a less significant moral question than abortion that is performed later in the gestational process. We assert that there is no point in the development of new human life before which the moral issues are insignificant.*

In the course of midtwentieth century research—in which new plastic intrauterine devices and prescriptions to be taken orally or intramuscularly have been developed—a great deal is being learned about fertility and pregnancy. On the one hand, in the effort to develop a "Pill" that would generate fewer deleterious, even fatal, side effects, the principle of the synergism of combining two hormones was discovered. The second generation of "low-dosage" pills are far less dangerous than their predecessors. Researchers studying the how and why of this synergistic effect discovered that these newer pills do not prevent ovulation in as many as 50 percent of the cases. However, their effectiveness is as good or better than the first generation of oral contraceptives.[2]

By examining the phenomena related to this particular contraceptive (or abortifacient?) technique, embryologists have learned that without any human contraceptive or or abortifacient intervention, the vast majority of all fertilized eggs do not reach full term, i.e., result in a live birth.

In addition, contemporary embryological research discloses that intrauterine devices significantly reduce the number of diagnosed pregnancies but do not prevent sperm and egg from meeting. Thus there is fertility control that is contraceptive and that is abortifacient. The scientific concept of the "moment of conception," the fertilization of egg by sperm, when used to discern the inherent morality (or immorality) of the various methods does not provide clear guidance. One is left either with the unquestioned morality of the traditional "barrier" devices and therefore the use of those alone or with the conviction that as the reproductive process is a continuum, so too the variety of means of intervening in that process lies along a spectrum.

4. The Question of the Morality of Abortion is not Dependent on the Question of the Morality of Sexual Activity.

This statement may seem at first to be the most surprising of the four propositions in this section. Indeed it is difficult to trust the judgment of a woman (or man) who has engaged in sexual activity of which we, as individual Christians or as a church, do not approve, when she (or they) are considering abortion. Thus, it is often easy to confuse our attitudes about sexual activity outside marriage with our judgments concerning the morality of abortion. Let us juxtapose two different thoughts at this point.

First, it is helpful to keep in mind the fact that over 20 percent of the persons who choose to terminate their pregnancies are married couples,[4] who do so for virtually the same reasons that motivate unmarried pregnant women. Abortion can be considered a responsible choice within a Christian ethical framework, when the resources are not available to care for a child appropriately. In other words, the morality of abortion is not defined by judgments on the morality of the relationship that brought about the pregnancy. Decisions concerning abortion involve projective consideration: Can I (or we or others) care adequately for a child? When the church speaks prescriptively, as a moral authority about sexuality in relation to marriage, it speaks of the ideal case. There still exist a great number of persons whose experience falls outside the church's model for marriage and family. What we have said regarding the ideal case, the model understanding of sexual morality, would indicate that sexual partners should be prepared on a variety of levels—emotional, economic, legal, etc.—for the birth of a child before the onset of sexual activity.

Nonetheless, we do consider it appropriate for young couples to marry, even though they are "not ready to have children," with the understanding that they will "be responsible," i.e., they will use birth control. This sexual activity is entirely within the bounds of marital intimacy which our church affirms. If their contraceptive technique fails, do we understand it to be morally appropriate for this couple to consider and perhaps choose to terminate their pregnancy? Do we consider it appropriate for a family that has experienced, through contraceptive failure, eight pregnancies in nine years (or six in six? or three in three?) to consider abortion in the case of an additional, unintended pregnancy? The young, unmarried woman in her teenage years, considering the problem set before her by a pregnancy, considers the same questions as she weighs her responsibilities: Can I provide the necessities of food, clothing, shelter adequate for a human child? Am I emotionally mature enough to be an adequate parent (or single parent)? Can I provide a social context (in my family, marriage, or community) in which a child can be raised with the loving care that will ground him or her emotionally for the adult years? A menopausal woman, who discovers to her surprise that she is pregnant, has similar questions: Do I (still) have the physical and emotional resources to begin a 20-25 year commitment to raise a child? Is it responsible for me to bear a child, when I have doubts that my strength or health may not outlast the period of a new child's dependence on me? The several situations above seem very different to us at first glance, but on closer, or more thorough, inspection, the reasons for considering, and perhaps choosing, abortion are virtually the same.

As we consider the morality for abortion, it is helpful to draw a distinction between sexual ethics, our understanding of the morality of sexual activity, and an area we might call family ethics, the moral responsibilities involved as we make decisions about the contours and chronologies of our families. There has been a significant shift in our understanding of the relationship between marriage and family since the advent of modern expectations regarding contraceptive techniques. We understand sexual intimacy and procreation to be distinct in a manner that was not possible before the birth control movement in this century. Concomitantly, Christians have come to affirm God's gift of sexuality for its intrinsic worth as a profound form of human communication, a special case among the variety of experiences of human intimacy. At the same time, the church has emphasized the importance of confining sexual intimacy to a context in which there is a clear, mutual commitment to the relationship.

Another way to view the proposal that abortion be understood as a question of "family ethics" but not a corollary of sexual morality is to look at attitudes toward abortion in situations when pregnancy has resulted from rape or incest. In cases where the woman or girl has become pregnant as a victim of sexual violence, most persons agree that she should have the option of abortion. There tends to be a great deal more sympathy or sensitivity toward these women because they did not choose to engage in the sexual relationship or, rather, they were powerless to resist sexual assault. While it is desirable that the greatest number of people be sensitive to the trauma that these women have suffered and that their legal right to choose abortion be maintained, we cannot speak of their having a categorical moral right to abort based solely on the fact that they were victims of assault. When considering the morality of abortion, we should not separate women into two categories according to our view of their sexual morality. A married woman does not "earn" the moral right to abortion by virtue of a universal consensus that she is sexually moral; neither does the woman or girl who is a victim of incest or rape have the right to choose abortion by virtue of her sexual moral status. For the victim of sexual violence, the questions are the same. The intensity of the question whether one is able emotionally to care for a child as a result of this particular pregnancy will be exceptionally poignant.

The morality of abortion is a separate question from the morality of sexual activity, but an additional question is unavoidable. As a church and particularly as clergy counseling on abortion, how are we to respond to the woman or girl who fits the stereotype? Who has become pregnant in a sexual relationship of which we (or I) do not approve?

Our theological understanding of the work of the Holy Spirit mediating the grace of God is pertinent here. It has been the teaching of the Christian churches, since Augustine, that God gives us freedom of the will and that we are also guided by the Holy Spirit in the exercise of that free will. When faced with significant moral choices, men and women who prayerfully consider the options set before them can be assured that they are empowered by the gracious work of God's Spirit to make an appropriate moral choice. Our assertion that abortion need not be an absolute prohibition is grounded in the conviction that God's gifts to us include both the power and the freedom to make moral choices concerning even the most serious questions. Our capacity for moral agency is not limited by our own human frailties nor finitude. Thus, it is less than faithful for us to presume that someone—female or male— whose moral choices in the area of sexual activity we cannot affirm, is unable to make a good choice regarding the subsequent moral questions raised by a problem pregnancy. The power of God's Spirit is equally available to all who face this decision.

F. The Church's Ministry

The Christian community, whether the horizons of that community are perceived as the boundaries of the local parish, a denomination, or the church universal, is a covenant community. Not only are individual Christians in a covenant relationship with God, but God is also in relationship with humanity through the communal structures of the church. In an ideal situation, the church is a loving community in which Christians share their concerns about all matters of significance. The New Testament itself celebrates these values as they were expressed in the new church after Christ's resurrection. (Acts 2:42-47.)

Ideally, the support, wisdom, compassion, and respect with which Christians honor one another in other matters would also be available to persons who face decisions about abortion. However, given the heritage of the church's concern for protecting the soul of the unborn infant and its historical theological denigration of the value of sexuality apart from reproductive purposes, it is not surprising that the church is often unable to be a supportive community. It is a tragic sign of the church's sinfulness that our propensity to judge rather than console too often means that persons in need are given the additional burden of isolation. It would be far better if the person concerned could experience the strength that comes from shared sensitivity and caring.

At the same time, it is important to observe that at some point in the decision-making process, the pregnant woman who chooses abortion suddenly reaches a stage without ambivalence: "I can't do anything else. This must be." She may reach this point before or after the formal counseling process has begun. The ambivalence that the individual (or family) experiences arise from her awareness of responsibilities that she will have to assume. She may have struggled and come to a decision that differs from the conviction of her husband. She may even have recognized that this decision will have profound implications for the future of her marriage. Even in these difficult, ambiguous circumstances, the lack of ambivalence comes when she gives weight to each of the pertinent factors, at which time the courage to act appears. We can trust that such a sense of conviction arising in a context of carefully weighed concerns represents sound judgment; our theological task is to elucidate how this judgment can be made.

The abortion decision need not be a tragedy or an agony. Choosing abortion may make us sad, but it need not generate feelings of regret, guilt, or shame. Clergy who counsel with women who are considering abortion have learned that they are not angry or filled with hate, as an aggressor would be; the most elemental feelings are anxiety and fear. They may, in some cases, seem close to panic or terror. "I don't know what I can do." It is precisely because of the humanity of the life developing *in utero* that a projective analysis is needed, and that a decision cannot be avoided. Their sense of human responsibility as stewards of human life calls them to contemplate the possibilities, however few they may be.

Members of the clergy who have witnessed the seriousness, the care, and the concern that women have evidenced in making this decision should begin to speak on behalf of others who must remain silent. Clergy who have the privilege of access to these most private thoughts and most intimate reflections are in a unique position; they can speak aloud the general case without disclosing any confidences. Opportunities for preaching and teaching should be fully used. Of all professional groups, clergy who have been involved for a number of years in abortion counseling have the greatest opportunity to set fact in place of fear. Thus, clergy can witness clearly to the courage in women of all ages making choices regarding pregnancy. When outside the sanctuary of her doctor's or her pastor's office, this woman may hear the voice of moral disapproval. The voice of moral affirmation should also be heard.

It is particularly difficult for parents who have conceived intentionally to learn that examination of the fetus's chromosomes indicates the certainty or probability of a serious genetic disorder. The method of abortion that is available to these couples is experientially similar to childbirth. Often, by the time the diagnosis can be made, the fetus has begun to move in the uterus and the enlargement of the woman's uterus is such that her pregnancy cannot be kept confidential. Thus, this case is a most difficult, even a tragic, situation. As the church, we are called to be compassionate and understanding, to make clear our support of these families. We should be discussing this subject in adult forums, informing ourselves about this "treatment" for genetic disease, so that members of a church know that they can trust others in their Christian community to understand the ethical legitimacy of this relatively new area of medical practice. This subject should be addressed from the pulpit, letting the whole community know that as Presbyterians, we can choose to interpret this decision as a part of our covenant responsibility before God.

Ultimately, it is the responsibility of the pregnant woman and her husband (or partner) to make the choices. In the first instance, they have the choice of whether to do the amniocentesis. After having been informed of the factors of the risk of disease on one hand and risk to the fetus on the other, the couple may choose not to have the test. They may also opt against amniocentesis because they would not choose to terminate the pregnancy in any case. If this is their choice, it should be respected by the church, i.e., both clergy and other church members. If a serious genetic disorder is diagnosed, there remains a second decision to be made: whether to terminate the pregnancy. Some couples may choose amniocentesis, knowing that they would not consider abortion, for the purpose of learning that they can continue the pregnancy with the assurance that none of the problems that could be diagnosed during pregnancy are present. Our church affirms the right of conscience of prospective parents at both points in the decision-making process. The decision to continue or to terminate a pregnancy is ours by virtue of God's gift of responsibility. These decisions must be made by the person or persons who would be most intimately involved in the bearing and rearing of an afflicted child.

Thus, there is no obligatory or even recommended category for considering abortion. Abortion in the case of genetic disorder is not legitimated because we can set a minimum standard for "humanness," a criterion of human normalcy.[1] It is legitimated for the same reason that any abortion is morally legitimate, because the person (or persons) who would be most intimately involved in bearing and rearing a child have discerned that they do not have the resources to care for the special needs of a human child in this particular situation.

G. The Special Problem of Teenage Pregnancy

The increasing number of teenage pregnancies each year is sobering.[1] While the number of pregnancies among teenagers is increasing, the number of teenagers who choose abortion is not increasing as rapidly.[2] Nor is the number of teenagers who choose to put their babies up for adoption.[3] In other words, there is an increasingly large number of teenagers who are choosing single parenthood. There are approximately 1.2 million out-of-wedlock teenage pregnancies each year: 38 percent choose abortion; 13 percent miscarry; the rest carry the pregnancy to term. Only 4 percent give their babies up for adoption or for care by friends or relatives. Public health officials describe these increases as an "epidemic." It is time for the church to clarify its understanding of when and by whom contraception should be employed. The dialogue about this issue is a painful one: one we may wish to avoid. However we have a responsibility to engage in such reflection. Whether or not we approve of a teenager's sexual activity, we can agree that contraception is always preferable to abortion as a means of controlling birth. We may judge the pregnant teenager as unwise or less than virtuous, but we cannot allow our moral analysis to stop there. This "epidemic" is a disastrous phenomenon. Many young women in this generation will become parents without finishing high school. It is difficult enough for an educated single parent to provide for her family but much more difficult for a young woman without education, skills, or a job. The church, as an institution that values the quality of family life, should call for rational social policy that includes sex education and gynecological care for the teenagers and day care, especially infant care, for the children of teenage mothers.

Until recently there were only two options that the churches recommended to pregnant teenagers: marriage or offering the child for adoption (usually following a secret confinement). A third option used by teenagers, far less frequent, was suicide. Today the range of options has been broadened by (1) the decriminalization of abortion and (2) changes in attitude and policy in the schools and public funding. However, no outcome of the teenager's pregnancy is entirely satisfactory. The church teaches that ideally a child should be born in wedlock. However, the prognosis for marriages that occur when the bride or the groom are under 20 is very poor. Do we honor the estate of matrimony or diminish it by commending it to people for whom the projected divorce rate is above 50 percent? Nevertheless, marriage may be a wise choice for some couples.

Given this, we respect the right of a teenage female to decide about her pregnancy as she feels is right. If a pregnant teenager concludes she can neither undergo abortion nor offer her baby for adoption, it is our moral and social responsibility to provide the variety of resources, social, personal, and economic, which her new family requires. Programs such as parenting education, food and nutrition supplements, provision for special health care needs, and the general provision for basic economic needs are the reponsibility of the whole society for each of its members. For young women who choose single parenthood as their option and for their children, the humane society provides that which is needed for a life with dignity.

As we noted, there has been a significant shift within the last twenty years toward single parenting, a shift away from offering the child for adoption. The data regarding this development raises several moral questions, because formerly it was assumed that adoption was the single satisfactory option for the unmarried, pregnant teenager. While the decriminalization of abortion has made that option less dangerous and frightening, a large number of pregnant teenagers still give birth.[4] The fact that today only a handful choose adoption indicates that in the previous era teenagers probably accepted secret pregnancy followed by adoption because of economic and social pressures.

Now, moral questions about the self-evident desirability of adoption as a choice for the teenager are beginning to emerge. Before we can affirm adoption without qualification, we need to examine questions relating to adoption. What are the risks to the health of the mother and child caused by poor or substandard prenatal nutrition and care when carrying to term? What are the psychological consequences of adoption as compared to early abortion and birth? Do we have the right as a state through our laws, as a religious institution in our teachings, or as individuals to coerce another in decisions on bearing children, rearing them, or giving them up for adoption? This is disrespectful of the other's personhood. Much more thorough attention must be given to the options teenagers face so the church can make wise and loving recommendations. The question of adoption should be researched and reflected upon as thoroughly and carefully as is the question of elective abortion.

Neither surgical abortion, nor marriage, nor a generation of yet-to-be-educated and therefore marginalized (single) parents, nor adoption may be an entirely humane solution to teenage pregnancy. However, the church must speak to the change in family structure that teenage pregnancy is generating. Mary Calderone has said that using fear of pregnancy to diminish sexual activity among teenagers is "a cruel and unusual punishment." In the face of the very real possibility of pregnancy resulting from sexual intercourse during the fertile teenage years, our church teaches that it is best to postpone intercourse until the partners marry. However, in the event that a teenage couple engage in sex despite the traditional teachings of the church, they have unequivocal moral responsibility to use effective contraception because new human life should not be created casually.

New information should allay our fears that information will generate activity or that sharing information communicates permission. Social scientists studying sex education programs discover that presentation of realistic data about contraception, in light of its relative ineffectiveness, serves both to delay the onset of sexual activity and to reduce its frequency. Churches should be scrupulously honest with young people about these realities. In addition to setting forth theological and moral reasons for postponing sexual activity until marriage, we must teach about contraception, its possibilities as well as its failings. This would postpone or diminish sexual activity before young people are prepared to start a family, inform them that no method of preventing pregnancy used alone is foolproof. We do not wish to encourage teenagers to engage in sexual activity, but we fail in our ministry with and to them if we do not offer something better than the illusions and misinformation that are still common in our time. We should not fear that speaking about contraceptive information will encourage its use when already we witness the results of not speaking. Our ministry to and with the younger generation requires us to review our responsibilities as a church and address their needs in the best possible way.

(For pastors and church members who would like to study this question further, *Teenage Pregnancy: The Problem That Hasn't Gone Away*, published by the Alan Guttmacher Institute, is recommended.)

H. Public Policy in Relation to Our Theological Perspective

A Christian understanding of abortion should enable a woman to integrate the decision that she makes concerning abortion with her overall image of herself as a responsible person. In the area of public policy the church's stand should reflect respect for other religious traditions and allow full exercise of religious liberty. For example, Jewish teaching does not protect the life of the child until both the head and shoulders have emerged from the vaginal canal. Catholic teaching prohibits almost all abortions. The Presbyterian Church exists within a very pluralistic environment. Its own members hold a variety of views. Public policy that demonstrates respect for a variety of viewpoints protects religious liberty and freedom of conscience.

The legislation, introduced during the 1950's and 1960's, allowed for abortion only after counsel with, and the agreement of, various professionals—a gynecologist, a psychiatrist, a jurist, etc. The woman was encouraged, sometimes even forced, to demonstrate her desperation. On the other hand, the professional was concerned about whether she should be permitted an abortion. In the context of prohibition or modified prohibition, decision-making about abortion falls into a "desperation-permission" syndrome.

In these circumstances, a woman may obtain an abortion performed by a licensed physician by proving to physicians, attorneys, psychiatrists, or several professionals that her situation is sufficiently desperate to warrant an abortion. At the same time, the woman seeking abortion may not sense that she has thought through the values involved in this case and come to an ethical decision herself. Nor do the professionals think they have made the ethical decision in this case. No one has the freedom to make such a choice, and this is the loss. No one has responsibility for the decision. Thus, the "desperation-permission" syndrome under laws that fall short of clearcut decriminalization is a system that tends to suppress conscience.

Elective abortion removes the "desperation-permission" syndrome and puts abortion squarely in the realm of decision-making. Women should not be coerced into bearing an excessive burden of shame or guilt about an abortion. A woman whose decision is respected will often spontaneously feel a sense of sadness for that which could not be. Her feelings of sadness are her affirmation of human life, childbearing, and childrearing.

We affirm Christian freedom and responsibility (Christian conscience) in the process of deciding whether to abort and we have a responsibility to work to maintain a public policy of elective abortion, regulated by the health code, not the criminal code. Our own Presbyterian tradition, which is also part of our nation's heritage, holds that "God alone is Lord of the conscience." We seek national policy that embodies that conviction, carefully guarding the separation of church and state with respect for the freedom of the individual's conscience.

This study does not hold that the moral significance of abortion is established by saying abortion is a "woman's right." However, for the genuine exercise of conscience to take place, women must have the right to make the decision. The freedom to exercise her conscience in this matter is precisely the freedom of which this familiar slogan speaks. The legal right to have an abortion is a necessary prerequisite to the exercise of conscience in abortion decisions, and the practical option to choose an abortion is also necessary. Access to and funds for abortion are essential for decision-making. The efforts reflected in the Hyde Amendment and other funding restrictions are an unacceptable attempt to limit moral choice. This right precedes any right that states may claim for themselves to establish funding methods based on protecting the fetus. Legally speaking, abortion should be a woman's right because, theologically speaking, making a decision about abortion is her responsibility.

There are two levels of freedom and responsibility involved in the dialogue concerning abortion: (1) The freedom and responsibility of a woman before the law and (2) Her freedom and responsibility before God. First, as citizens, we have a responsibility to guarantee every woman the freedom of reproductive choice. Even though many of us will never be faced with a problem pregnancy, the abortion question touches every citizen at this level. Although some might refrain from any use of contraceptives or abortifacients for reasons of conscience, they are morally obligated to respect the freedom of other persons to act on their own religious convictions.

It may be difficult for us to understand one another's passionately held beliefs regarding the morality of contraceptives and abortion. Our commitment is to the right of the person to make his or her own decisions in this very personal area. This commitment implies another: that of tolerance of diversity in convictions. Statutory law often reflects one viewpoint attempting to constrain others. Such legislation may even reflect a dangerous and far-reaching attack on the role of an independent judiciary in our system of government.

Many individuals who state that they would not choose elective abortion nonetheless believe that other citizens should have the right to do so. This posture is a result of having differentiated the two senses in which we speak about "freedom" in this debate, legal and theological. These persons are saying that they would not choose to exercise the theological freedom set before us, but they do recognize and respect the importance of establishing the legal freedom of others to do so.

The Supreme Court's decision to decriminalize abortion moved the regulation of abortion from the criminal code to the health code in each state. The decriminalization of abortion has made safe abortion services available. Decriminalization of abortion forces no one to terminate a pregnancy against the dictates of her conscience. We should preserve this legal climate in which the exercise of conscience is respected and in no way abridged.

The Supreme Court's 1973 decisions in the cases of Roe *v*. Wade and Doe *v*. Bolton recognize a pluralistic religious view. The Court's decision to decriminalize abortion does not coerce anyone to violate a religious principle. Continuing the tradition in American abortion law of the protection of the woman patient, the Court repealed the prohibition against abortion for only the first and second trimesters of pregnancy when abortion is statistically safer than childbirth, allowing the states to limit abortions in the third trimester when abortion presents a greater risk than the natural process of labor.

The passage of the proposed Human Life Amendment or similar statute would reverse the intent of American law regarding abortion: protecting the pregnant woman.

Before the liberalization of antiabortion laws in the midnineteenth century, the physician had to establish the medical necessity of an abortion to preserve the patient's life. As it is difficult to predict early the dangers in the latter stages of pregnancy, the medical community in general has welcomed the decriminalization of abortion because it permits them to speak candidly of the range of potential dangers without fear of criminal prosecution. As a result, physicians may counsel the patient early in pregnancy about a potential danger. Then, if the patient chooses abortion, it can be performed during the first trimester when the surgery is significantly less dangerous than later in pregnancy or at birth. Since 1973, maternal morbidity and mortality have dropped throughout the United States, as evidenced by the fact that there were 359 deaths annually during 1958-62, 160 during 1968-69, and 19 during 1974-78.[1] Average maternal mortality in the United States per year since the Roe *v*. Wade decision is eight deaths, before 1973 the national average was in the hundreds annually. (However, for women whose health care is provided by federal funds and who are required by law to demonstrate the necessity of abortion for medical indications in order to receive medicaid funds, the mortality and morbidity rates remain significantly above average. Their situations de facto are the same as for the general population before 1973.) Our church affirms the increased safety that the present policy of elective abortion provides for women of child-bearing age in the United States.

The present public policy, as established by Roe *v*. Wade, serves to protect the legal rights of women. The right to privacy, under which the Court established the religious freedom of health professionals as well as patients to perform (or refrain from performing) abortions, is the right of individual choice in matters of faith and morals. However, it is not accurate to characterize the right to choose abortion, as exercised presently in the United States, as an entirely private choice. The structure of accountability that is built into the Court's decision and that functions currently is that the decision to terminate a pregnancy must be made by the patient in consultation with her physician. The patient alone cannot, under current law, demand an abortion. There is no guarantee that she will receive an abortion based only on her judgment and without a physician concurring. The court's decision is based on its respect for the medical profession. The accountability of physicians has been deemed sufficient to insure their appropriate behavior in this area and in any other area of practice. For example, no statutes exist that outlaw the performance of abortion for purposes of gender selection. However, the law does establish the right of a physician (or a nurse?) to refuse to perform abortions for such a reason, which is in fact the common posture of medical professionals today.

Abortion is distinct from the decision to have an abortion. Abortion is a medical intervention that is no different in principle from any other surgical or obstetrical intervention. It should be as available, similarly funded and its quality controlled, as other interventions. Not every physician is professionally allowed to do every procedure, nor is every physician morally obligated to perform every procedure. Even within certain seemingly identical groups of physicians, opinions differ. For instance, there is a great deal of controversy about coronary bypass and, therefore, in a given case, certain cardiac surgeons will not perform them but others will. These differences should be medical, not political, questions in cardiac surgery and in abortion. Medicine itself should never be used as a political tool to deny medical help to the most people possible.

The current public policy, which allows the doctor to intervene in order to preserve the health of the woman, reestablishes the traditional principle of protection of the patient for the later portion of pregnancy. And, as before, the principle that protects the patient is also protection for the physician. In the United States today, there is no elective abortion in the third trimester. However, if a medical emergency arises and medical intervention—either the induction of labor or Caesarean section—is needed, the physician has the legal right to act. If a woman develops a significant health risk related to pregnancy, such as toxemia or gestational diabetes, her physician has the legal right to deliver her baby prematurely. In such cases, every effort is made to save both patients, mother and child. But if the doctor or doctors are unable to save the baby as well as its mother, the Supreme Court decision protects the physician from either civil or criminal prosecution. Current medical practice in the third trimester and its status before the law remains virtually the same as in the period before 1973. The change in language from life endangerment to preservation of health means that the physician is not required in every instance of third trimester intervention to go to court and receive specific permission in advance. However, under the provision for preservation of the woman's health, a physician may be required by a court, after the fact, to document the need for the intervention provided by this feature of the 1973 decision. The obstetrician's hands would be tied by legal liabilities at precisely the moments when swift intervention with modern techniques can mean the possibility of not only preserving the mother's life but delivering a healthy baby.

There is one exception in medical practice to the moral principle that elective abortion is permissible before viability, i.e., in the first and second trimester but not after that point. After viability the fetus has a moral right to inviolability, as does any other physically autonomous human being. In extremely rare cases, a genetic disorder may be diagnosed late in pregnancy, which would make physical life impossible outside the womb, such as anencephaly, the lack of development of a brain or brain stem. In this event, our laws and our moral teachings would be cruel and inhuman if they were to force a woman who is carrying a fetus so diseased to continue her pregnancy to its natural completion. In the event of such a diagnosis, it is humane to change the schedule of birthing, i.e., to induce delivery at the patient's discretion, to conclude this pregnancy. Access to medical intervention when the fetus is diagnosed as unable to exist autonomously *ex utero* is a form of compassion through which God, together with pastor, family, and friends, can begin to free the couple from the pain of these memories and give them hope they can have a healthy baby. It is humane for physicians to offer to induce delivery in these rare cases. Thus, the law should safeguard this option.

Appendix II

I come to you today as a woman called to gospel ministry in midlife, who feels that the "matter of abortion" is a highly personal matter since the woman must come to terms with the decision and the consequences of that decision. I am the mother of three children, two living and one dead. I am married to a Presbyterian minister. The rest will develop in the following narrative.

Several years ago, as a nurse working in an outpatient clinic, I was asked by a doctor, an old friend who was the son of my former obstetrician, to assist him in an abortion. It was my first experience and I did it because I trusted his skills and wanted to help him. I met the young, beautiful woman who came from one of the affluent families in town and who seemed very alone to me. As I stood there and held her hand tightly, I watched her face. I felt very uneasy and could not figure out why.

All went well and there were no complications. Both doctor and patient came through fine.

There was only one hitch: I had fainted and when I woke up I was lying beside the table staring at the doctor. "I saw her face. The total horror was too much so I passed out." I was babbling and aware of it. Within half an hour it was all over that hospital. A nurse had fainted at an abortion. How embarrassing!

My "very unprofessional" behavior was the result of a memory—long buried—which had been triggered by the woman's loneliness and agony. Back in 1962 I had spent an agonizing 10 days in bed, alone most of the time, trying to prevent a second so-called "spontaneous abortion," a miscarriage, from occurring. Four months previously, I had passed an intact, well-shaped 6-week fetus. Two trips to the family physician who was a greatly respected member of the medical profession had revealed "no evidence of pregnancy, but keep tabs on the spotting" . . . my obstetrician, gave me a drug that seemed to level off in early evening each day, leaving me in second stage labor contractions for several hours. He did not change the dosage.

Finally, after the 10th day of pain, I deliberately quit taking the drug. I knew instinctively that this was not meant to be. By that time, I was speaking only to God and to my belly and feeling very alone. I had two small children sucking their thumbs and looking worried and annoyed as this thing dragged on and a husband who tried to comfort me during the evening bouts with pain, who went to work each day. The seeds of future discontent and our eventual divorce were sown during that time. He tended to look the other way and laid an amorphous blame on me for not pulling this thing off well. Money was tight and he was tired of diapers and long days and interrupted nights.

Passing the fetus was awful. I was terrified waiting and pushing alone in that bathroom after everybody was asleep. The bloody nondescript pieces were scary. It was not a fetus or a baby at all. It was nothing identifiable at all but I kept the evidence to show the doctor.

Afterwards, in the hospital where I was taken for a D & C, I was placed in the maternity wing, where I could hear babies crying all night and being brought to their mothers for nursing. I begged to be placed on a surgical floor, and this was finally done. For a year after, I cried a lot . . . my small daughter called my favorite spot "the crying chair." I felt guilt and I could not tell anybody at all. I had a terrible ache where both little fetuses had been. But I had, I felt, made a choice all alone, praying for guidance . . . listening to my insides and to the silence of those around me who could not articulate their feelings easily. I felt an obligation not to mess up things for them. Clearly, another child so soon would not do, even though we were not poor, starving, homeless, persecuted, or diseased.

While this was not a surgically induced abortion, nonetheless, my experience contains many of the same elements. Nature and I cooperated and, as it turned out, I was right. I could not know that for sure until it was over. I became very aware of what the act of choosing to abort for any reason really means to a woman.

So I do not come to a decision that we call "pro-choice" easily. First I had to experience the pain of loss myself in order to understand the experience of other women.

I conclude that because the process of gestation and birth is so very personal and such a lonely event, the decision to terminate pregnancy must be allowed to the woman herself. I am fully aware that the loving husband and father-to-be has a say. But even at the last stage of birth, the wife will push that husband away and focus inward on her baby and herself. I love dearly to see the couple sharing the birth moment in the delivery room . . . each helping the process along with training for the big event . . . the safe delivery of a wanted child who will know a happy, safe, nurturing environment. The tears of joy are shared and all are touched by this. It becomes even more meaningful that the choice made by the woman depends upon the possibility of this outcome: a happy one.

I do not believe that anyone who cannot give birth can possibly understand what it means to take on active responsibility for cocreation with the Creator. I do not believe that a Supreme

Court of men or a male President should be given that kind of power, ignorant of the experience itself.

Finally, I want to say something about abortion as murder. I told you that I am the mother of three children . . . two living and one dead. What I did not say is that the dead child was a murdered child. She was shot by a boy who was denied entrance in the U.S. Air Force Nuclear Weapons Program and who had to prove, in another rite of passage, his manhood. He (believed that he) needed to demonstrate his power over another human being by taking her life. I do not believe any woman feels that way when she decides to end a problem pregnancy. Rather she feels she is making a choice from options that seem to leave her no other choice. She is on anything but a power trip, except, and I qualify this, when the conditions around her have violated her so much that her act is an act of counterviolence. Only she can really know that moment. She is, indeed, claiming her selfhood and attempting to survive. Often for the sake of those dependent upon her.

Usually, the woman who ends her pregnancy weeps and she does it alone more often than not. And the ache inside her stays for a very long time; I speak from experience.

Policy Statement

Biblical faith depicts persons as stewards of life, heirs who are responsible for the care of God's world. This responsibility leads persons of faith not only to an exploration of all of creation but also to efforts that maintain order, secure justice, and improve the quality of human life. Because human life, in the biblical sense, is much more than the perpetuation of physical existence, people of faith should commit themselves to improving its quality spiritually, educationally, and culturally as well as medically. This commitment will often necessitate difficult moral choices in the midst of conflicting values.

The church itself should pattern for society a way of life wherein sexuality, conception, birth, and raising children are issues of profound responsibility, fidelity, and care. That way of life inevitably stands in judgment on our present cultural ethos, which extols casual and promiscuous sexuality.

Some of the most difficult moral choices persons face in their care of creation are related to contraception, pregnancy, and abortion. Christians will make these decisions knowing that the value and dignity of human life are bestowed by God the Creator who calls us into a covenant relationship with our God and with each other. Faith in God surely leads to profound respect for human life.

For the most part, Protestants have affirmed the role of contraception as a responsible exercise of stewardship with regard to procreation. Limiting the size of a particular family or limiting population growth in a whole society is generally understood to be a kind of caring for one's family and for the next generation. Contraception is clearly the most morally appropriate way to control fertility and to plan families.

Current contraception technology is far from reliable. The church is called to exercise social responsibility by advocating more effective contraceptives for males as well as females and to educate our own membership that family planning must be the concern and responsibility of both sexual partners. A greater emphasis in church and society on contraception would significantly reduce the possibility of unintended pregnancies.

When, however, an unintended pregnancy occurs or a genetic problem with the fetus is diagnosed, the question of abortion often arises even though it is not the only solution. An understanding of various kinds of circumstances surrounding unintended pregnancies is especially important.

Tragically, many women become pregnant as a result of rape or incest. All too frequently contraceptives fail, even though conscientious efforts to prevent pregnancy have been taken. In addition, the increasing number of teenage pregnancies each year is sobering and presents especially agonizing situations.

There is no point in the course of pregnancy when the moral issue of abortion is insignificant. The serious moral decision is to be made on the basis of the covenantal character of parental responsibility. Bearing children is a process of covenant-initiation that calls for courage, love, patience, and strength. In addition to these gifts of the Spirit, parent-child covenants also require the economic as well as the spiritual resources appropriate to the nurture of a human life. The magnitude of the commitment to be a human parent cannot be overestimated and should not be understated.

The decision to terminate a pregnancy may be an affirmation of one's covenant responsibility to accept the limits of human resources. Because we understand the morality of abortion to be a question of stewardship of life, the responsible decision to choose abortion may arise from analysis of the projected resources for caregiving in a specific situation.

Abortion can therefore be considered a responsible choice within a Christian ethical framework when serious genetic problems arise or when the resources are not adequate to care for a child appropriately. Elective abortion, when responsibly used, is intervention in the process of pregnancy precisely because of the seriousness with which one regards the covenantal responsibility of parenting.

Biblical faith emphasizes the need for personal moral choice and holds that persons stand ultimately accountable to God for their moral choices. The freedom to do what one judges most appropriate in an abortion decision is qualified by the fact that the purpose of such decision is the responsible exercise of stewardship. Even in the face of the most difficult decisions, of which abortion is surely one, the gospel assures us that we can trust in God's Spirit to guide us in our decision. Furthermore, given the fact that such hard choices involve some unpleasant consequences whatever the decision, the gospel reminds us again and again of God's grace, which is sufficient for us in spite of our limitations, and assures us that even if we err in misusing our freedom, God's forgiveness restores us in covenant love. Only in the knowledge of such grace and guidance could we dare to claim the responsibility and freedom to use modern medical skill to intervene in the process of human procreation.

The Calvinist affirmation of conscience as one of the primary junctures at which the power of the Holy Spirit breaks through into human experience is grounded in both (a) the Old Testament call to human responsibility, as set forth in the biblical witness to God's covenant with us, and (b) the New Testament assurance of the work of the Holy Spirit as our enabler and guide in the exercise of human freedom before God. When faced with significant moral choices, women and men who prayerfully consider the options set before them can be assured that they are empowered by the gracious work of God's Spirit to make an appropriate moral choice.

Any decision for an abortion should be made as early as possible, generally within the first trimester of pregnancy, for reasons of the woman's health and safety. Abortions later in pregnancy are an option, particularly in the case of women of menopausal age who do not discover they are pregnant until the second trimester, or women who discover through fetal diagnosis that they are carrying a fetus with a grave genetic disorder, or women who did not seek or have access to medical care during the first trimester. At the point of fetal viability, the responsibilities set before us in regard to the fetus begin to shift. Prior to viability, human responsibility is stewardship of life-in-development under the guidance of the Holy Spirit. Once the fetus is viable, its potential for physically autonomous human life means that the principle of inviolability can be applied.

The church is called to model the just and compassionate community in its ministries to members and its witness to society. The church has responsibility to help make acceptable alternatives available to persons struggling with an unwanted pregnancy if they are to exercise their freedom responsibly. Moreover, the church must seek to support persons as they exercise their moral freedom, which it can fulfill through such means as proclaiming the biblical faith, clarifying alternatives and their probable consequences, and offering support in love to persons struggling with difficult choices. Christians should make their personal decisions in the context of the community of faith.

It is a tragic sign of the church's sinfulness that our propensity to judge rather than stand with persons making such decisions too often means that persons in need must bear the additional burden of isolation. It would be far better if the person concerned could experience the strength that comes from shared sensitivity and caring. The church is called to be the loving and supportive community within whose life persons can best make decisions in conformity with God's purposes revealed in Jesus Christ.

The church should energetically support efforts of family planning, education in contraception and human sexuality, adoption of unwanted children, care for unwed mothers, and, in general, advocate wholesome and responsible stewardship of the human body and its procreative process. As the church is able to give expression to these values and commitments, the need for abortion will be reduced. Whatever a woman's decision may be, the caring support of the church should always be hers.

In the area of public policy the church should call upon policymakers in government and industry to form a rational policy for all members of our society in the area of contraception. This would need to include research and development in contraception knowledge and technique and the provision for unhampered access to contraceptive information and services for males and females of childbearing age.

The church's position on public policy concerning abortion should reflect respect for other religious traditions and advocacy for full exercise of religious liberty. The Presbyterian Church exists within a very pluralistic environment. Its own members hold a variety of views. It is exactly this plurality of beliefs that leads us to the conviction that the decision regarding abortion must remain with the individual, to be made on the basis of conscience and personal religious principles, free from government interference.

Consequently, we have a responsibility to work to maintain a public policy of elective abortion, regulated by the health code, not the criminal code. The legal right to have an abortion is a necessary prerequisite to the exercise of conscience in abortion decisions. Legally speaking, abortion should be a woman's right because, theologically speaking, making a decision about abortion is, above all, her responsibility.

As Presbyterians and U.S. citizens we have a responsibility to guarantee every woman the freedom of reproductive choice. We affirm the intent of existing law in the United States regarding abortion: protecting the pregnant woman. Medical intervention should be made available to all who desire and qualify for it, not just to those who can afford preferential treatment.

In the United States today, the right to choose abortion is a constitutional right, clarified by the United States Supreme Court *Roe v. Wade* decision (1973). We firmly oppose efforts to amend the Constitution in order to prohibit abortion. Under terms of the 1973 decision, elective abortions are confined generally to the first two trimesters of pregnancy. This conforms to the moral principle we affirm that elective abortion should be available before fetal viability but only in the rarest instances after that point, for instance, in rare cases involving medical judgment and late diagnosis of grievous genetic disorders.

The Presbyterian Church believes that society must offer good health care, both pre- and post-natal; day care facilities and homemaker services where needed; maternity and paternity leaves and family service centers; and expert counseling services. In addition, we must work toward a society in which life long respect and dignity for all people is manifest in the opportunities to obtain adequate resources for maintenance of life and health. In these ways the church seeks to strengthen the various alternatives available to women in making decisions about pregnancies.

Obviously the most desirable moral situation is that every pregnancy be intended and trouble-free, but our life experience is very different from this ideal. Abortion is not the only solution for unintended or problematic pregnancies, although it may at times be the most responsible decision.

Thus, the 195th General Assembly (1983):

1. Urges Presbyterian congregations and their individual members to:

   a. Provide a supportive community in which such decisions can be made in a setting of care and concern.

   b. Respect the difficulty of making such decisions.

   c. Affirm women's ability to make responsible decisions, whether the choice be to abort or to carry the pregnancy to term.

   d. Protect the privacy of individuals involved in contraception and abortion decisions.

2. Affirms the church's commitment to minimize the incidence of abortion and encourages sexuality education and the use of contraception to avoid unintentional pregnancies, while recognizing that contraceptives are not absolutely effective; and

   a. Commits this denomination and urges its members to encourage research in and development of contraceptive knowledge and techniques to make this awareness and facility easily available to all and to support legislation and public funding activities that strengthen family life;

   b. Urges Presbyterians to support sexuality education programs in families, churches, schools, and private and public agencies;

   c. Encourages mutual responsibility by men and women for contraception;

   d. Affirms the need for research in and development of a range of contraceptives that can be used by men;

   e. Encourages couples to use more than one method of contraception in order to minimize the possibility of unintended pregnancy due to contraceptive failure;

   f. Affirms the use of voluntary sterilization by couples who have completed their families.

3. Recognizes that negative social attitudes toward women cast doubt on women's ability to make moral decisions and urges ministers and congregations to work to counter these underlying social attitudes and affirm the dignity of women.

4. Recognizes that children may be born who are either unwanted or seriously handicapped; and affirms the church's ongoing responsibility to provide supportive services to families in these situations and to help find appropriate institutional care and adoptive services where needed.

5. Affirms the 1973 *Roe v. Wade* decision of the Supreme court, which decriminalized abortion during the first two trimesters of pregnancy.

6. Celebrates the courage of clergy and others who were willing to risk participation in the Clergy Consultation Service before 1973.

7. Opposes attempts to limit access to abortion by:

   a. Denial of funding for abortions to women who receive federal funding for their medical care.

   b. Restriction of coverage by insurance companies for abortion procedures.

   c. Passage of federal, state, and local legislation that has the effect of harassing women contemplating abortion.

   d. Restriction of federal funding to medical centers and teaching institutions where abortions are performed.

e. Passage of a constitutional amendment or other legislation that would return control over abortion to individual states or prohibit it as a national policy.

f. Restriction of the jurisdiction of the Supreme Court and the federal courts in the area of abortion.

8. Urges the Presbyterian Church through its members, congregations, governing bodies, boards, and agencies, including the Presbyterian Health, Education and Welfare Association, to model the just and compassionate community by:

a. Opposing adoption of all measures that would serve to restrict full and equal access to contraception and abortion services to all women, regardless of race, age, and economic standing.

b. Working actively to restore public funding by federal, state, and local governments for the availability of a full range of reproductive health services for the medically indigent.

c. Supporting funds, such as the Abortion Fund, for use by women who face abortion decisions but who no longer have access to public funding, so they may freely choose an appropriate course of action without coercion or restriction.

d. Challenging Presbyterian doctors and institutions to provide contraception and abortion services at cost or free-of-charge to those who no longer have access to public funding.

e. Providing openness and hospitality to women who need new structures of support while making an abortion decision or awaiting the delivery of a child.

f. Providing continuing support for women who, having made an abortion decision, may have doubts as to the wisdom of their choice or, having delivered a child, are not able to cope with the separation of adoption or the responsibilities of child care.

g. Opposing efforts to use zoning regulations to preclude the establishment of abortion clinics.

9. Recognizes that the issue of teenage pregnancy and premarital sexual activity is sometimes confused with the abortion issue itself. While time, task, and space have not allowed for extensive presentation in this paper, we express our concern by requesting that the General Assembly council, through the appropriate agency, pursue a study of teenage sexuality and responsibilities in light of the covenant of creation.

Endnotes

*While "The Pill" and the intrauterine devices were introduced to the American market as contraceptives and are commonly thought of as such, it is now known that neither of these methods of diminishing fertility acts exclusively to prevent conception. In both cases, the method's effectiveness is attributable in part, if not exclusively, to its action within a few hours or days after conception.[3]

*The name is omitted to protect the privacy of the individual.

Footnotes

Chapter B

[1] Westoff, Charles F., and DeLung, Jane S., "Abortions Preventable by Contraceptive Practice." *Family Planning Perspectives,* Sept.-Oct. 1981, p. 218.

[2] Hatcher, Robert A., *Contraceptive Technology 1980-1981.* New York: Irvington Publishers, Inc., 1981, p. 4.

[3] *Ibid.,* p. 35.

[4] *Ibid.* See pp. 101-116 for a general discussion of this subject.

[5] This number is reached by comparing the number of pregnancies each year with the effectiveness rate of contraception.

Chapter C

[1] Tietze, Christopher, *Induced Abortion: A World Review,* 1981. New York: The Population Council, 1981, p. 86.

[2] *Ibid.,* p. 86.

[3] *Ibid.,* p. 70.

Chapter E

[1] Gilligan, Carol, *In a Different Voice: A Psychological Theory and Women's Development.* Cambridge, MA: Harvard University Press, 1982.

[2] Hatcher, Robert A. *Op. cit.,* p. 53.

[3] Calderone, Mary Steichen, *Manual of Family Planning and Contraceptive Practices.* Baltimore, MD: Williams and Wilkins Co., 1970, p. 338.

[4] Tietze, Christopher, *Op. cit.,* p. 60.

Chapter G

[1] *Teenage Pregnancy: The Problem That Hasn't Gone Away.* New York: The Alan Guttmacher Institute, 1981, p. 4.

[2] *Ibid.,* p. 52.

[3] *Ibid.,* p. 27.

[4] *Ibid.,* p. 17.

[5] *Ibid.,* p. 37.

Chapter H

[1] *Ibid.,* p. 101.

Bibliography

Aquinas,Thomas, *Summa Theologica.* Westminster, MD: Christian Classics, 1982.

Aristotle, *De Animo, In the Version of William of Moerbeke.* New Haven: Yale University Press (1965).

Augustine, Bishop of Hippo, *The Confessions of Saint Augustine,* Books I-X. Translated by F.J. Sheed, Kansas City, Kansas. Sheed, Andrews, McMeel, c 1942.

Calderone, Mary Steichen, *Manual of Family Planning and Contraceptive Practices.* Baltimore, MD: Williams and Wilkins Co., 1970.

Garvey, John and Morriss, Frank, *Catholic Perspectives: Abortion.* Chicago: The Thomas More Press, 1979.

Gilligan, Carol, *In a Different Voice: A Psychological Theory and Women's Development.* Cambridge, MA: Harvard University Press, 1982.

Hatcher, Robert A., *Contraceptive Technology 1980-1981.* New York: Irvington Publishers, Inc., 1980.

The New Dutch Catechism (1969).

Teenage Pregnancy: The Problem That Hasn't Gone Away. New York: The Alan Guttmacher Institute, 1981.

Tietze, Christopher, *Induced Abortion: A World review 1981*. New York, The Population Council, 1981.

Van Eys, Jan, "Genetic Medicine and the Concepts of Health and Disease," *Church and Society*, The United Presbyterian Church, USA, Sept.-Oct. 1982.

Westoff, Charles F., and DeLung, Jane S., "Abortions Preventable by Contraceptive Practice," *Family Planning Perspectives*, Sept.-Oct. 1981.

Notes: *The Presbyterian Church (U.S.A.) was formed in 1983 by a merger of the United Presbyterian Church in the U.S.A. and the Presbyterian Church in the United States. This longer statement by the Presbyterian Church (U.S.A.) which had approximately 3,048,000 members in 1985, closed with an adopted policy statement and resolution which reaffirmed the earlier pro-choice position, at least prior to fetal viability.*

PRESBYTERIAN CHURCH IN AMERICA

STATEMENT ON ABORTION (1978)

Position Paper

1978, p. 71, 6-40 [Note: The 1978 Assembly adopted the following position paper on abortion. Modifications were made in 1979, and clarification of these modifications were made in 1980.]

Report of the Ad Interim Committee on Abortion

Abortion in distinction from miscarriage, is the intentional killing of an unborn child between conception and birth. The moral question raised in any abortion is whether the life of the unborn child is included in the Biblical teaching respecting the sanctity of life. The special protection God gives to human life is founded upon His making man "in His own image" (Gen. 1:26, 27. All scripture quotations are from the new American Standard Bible). So basic is this to His created order that God declares: "Whoever sheds man's blood, by man his blood shall be shed, for in the image of God He made man" (Gen. 9:6). This protection is then summarized in the sixth commandment. "You shall not murder" (Ex. 20:13; cf. *Westminster Shorter Catechism*, pp. 68-69, and *Westminster Larger Catechism*, pp. 135-136, where the requirements and prohibitions of the commandment are set forth).

Scripture Foundation

The clear and absolute declaration of the sixth commandment, founded upon God's making man in His own image, defines for us the most fundamental question which must be answered from Scripture. Is the unborn child a human person in God's image? While Scripture may not provide a precise scientific statement in answer to this question, the theological understanding of man revealed in Scripture leaves no doubt about the continuity of personhood which includes the unborn child. Simply, yet profoundly, the life resulting from conception is designated "man" both before and after birth (Gen. 4:1, Job 3:3). A "man-child" is conceived; the unborn child is not less than a man.

What we see revealed in Scripture is a marvelous truth, often expressed in doxological language, that there is a continuity of the individual man from "before the foundation of the world" into eternity. All life is a gift from our sovereign God. And in words of adoration, Scripture clearly includes prenatal life. In Psalm 139:13-16, David marvels at God's involvement with him (David between conception and birth). "For Thou didst form my inward parts: Thou didst weave me in my mother's womb. I will give thanks to Thee, for I am fearfully and wonderfully made . . . Thine eyes have seen my unformed substance (Hebrew *golem,* embryo, or fetus); And in Thy book they were all written, The days that were ordained for me, When as yet there was not one of them."

In the New Testament we see this same emphasis in Luke 1:24-56. An unborn child of six months is said to express the human emotion of joy. "When Elizabeth heard Mary's greeting, the baby leaped in her womb . . . For behold when the sound of your greeting reached my ears the baby leaped in my womb with joy" (verses 41, 44). And in verse 36 of this passage the baby is designated a "son", implying continuity. This pattern is seen through Scripture where those in the womb are commonly referred to by the same language used of persons already born (cf. Gen. 25:22; Job 3:3; Isa. 44:2, 49:5; Hos. 12:3).

In Psalm 51:5 the continuity extends back to the actual time of conception. "Behold, I was brought forth in iniquity, and in sin my mother conceived me." The point of continuity is David's humanness even at conception. To speak of oneself at conception in terms of personal sinfulness is to affirm one's humanity.

As the Church of Jesus Christ we confess that "God, from all eternity, ordains whatsoever comes to pass." It should not surprise us, therefore, to see this continuity extend even prior to conception. God Himself declares in Jeremiah 1:5: "Before I formed you in the womb I knew you, and before you were born I consecrated you. I have appointed you a prophet to the nations." It was Jeremiah in the womb, not an impersonal organism. God was forming him, as with all His creatures, for his appointed post-natal responsibilities.

The Word of God affirms throughout the continuity of personhood both before and after birth. Abortion, the intentional killing of an unborn child, is to destroy that continuity. Abortion would terminate the life of an individual, a bearer of God's image, who is being divinely formed and prepared for a God-given role in the world.

The continuity of personhood before and after birth is wonderfully underscored in the way Scripture describes the sovereign activity of God in conception and birth. In Genesis 1:28 God gave man the directive to multiply and to fill the earth. In obeying this instruction, man reproduced human beings who were also formed in the image of God (Gen. 5:1-3). This is not to imply the activity of God ceased. As Eve gave birth to Cain, she acknowledged, "I have gotten a manchild with the help of the Lord" (Gen. 4). Psalm 100:3 reminds us that we are the Lord's for He has made us. Psalm 127:3 says, "Children are a gift of the Lord: the fruit of the womb is a reward."

Conception, then, is not a mere human happening. Apart from the sovereign intervention of God, conception (which Scripture designates a divine blessing) does not take place (Gensis 21:1-2; 30:1-2, 22; 1 Samuel 1:19; Job 31:15, 33:4). It would therefore be a willful act of defiance against the Creator intentionally to kill an unborn child whose conception is so intimately a Divine as well as a human act. No child belongs only to man. He is God's child. And His Word must govern the protection and care of that child both before and after birth.

Apart from pro-abortion arguments which seek to place one command of God against another, denying both the inerrancy of Scripture and the absolute ethic therein, the one argument frequently set forth alleged to be based on Scripture centers around Exodus 21: 22-25. This passage, it is claimed, teaches that the unborn child is of less value than a child after birth. Some would claim it to teach that an unborn child was not a human person. We therefore specifically consider this passage because it is the most prominent "proof text" of those promoting abortion.

Instead of devaluing the unborn child or taking lightly his death, the exegetical evidence to the contrary is overwhelming. The 1971 report on abortion of the Orthodox Presbyterian Church contains an extended discussion of Exodus 21: 22-25, and the following is a portion of that report:

The term *yeled* in verse 22 never refers elsewhere to a child lacking recognizable human form, or to one incapable of existing outside the womb. The possibility of such a usage here, as the interpretation in question requires, is still further reduced by the fact that if the writer had wanted to speak of an undeveloped embryo or fetus there may have been other terminology available to him. There was the term *golem* (Ps. 139:16) which *means* "embryo, fetus." But in cases of the death of an unborn child, Scripture regularly designates him, not by *yeled*, not even by *golem*, but by *nefel* (Job 3:16; Psm. 58:8; Eccl. 6:3), "*one untimely born.*" *The use of the yeled* in verse 22, therefore, indicates that the child in view is not the product of a miscarriage, as the interpretation in question supposes; at least this is the most natural interpretation in the absence of decisive consideration to the contrary. . . .

Further: the verb *yatza'* in verse 22 ("go out," translated "depart" in KJV) does not in itself suggest the death of the child in question, and is ordinarily used to describe normal births (Gen. 25:26, 38:28-30; Job 3:11, 10:18; Jer. 1:5, 20:18). With the possible exception of Num. 12:12, which almost certainly refers to a stillborn, it never refers to a miscarriage. The Old Testament term normally used for miscarriage and spontaneous abortion, both in humans and in animals, is not *yatza'* but *shakol* (Ex. 23:26; Hos. 9:14; Gen. 31:38; Job. 2:10; cf. 11 Kings 2:19, 21; Mal. 3:11). The most natural interpretation of the phrase *weyatze' u yeladheyha*, therefore, will find in it not an induced miscarriage, not the death of an unborn child, but an induced premature birth, wherein the child is born alive, but ahead of the anticipated time.

We should also note that the term *ason* ("harm"), found in both verse 22 and verse 23 is indefinite in its reference. The expression "*lah*" ("to her"), which would restrict the harm to the woman in distinction from the child, is missing. Thus the most natural interpretation would regard the "harm" as pertaining either to the woman or to the child. Verse 22 therefore describes a situation where neither mother nor child is "harmed"—i.e. where the mother is uninjured and the child is born alive. Verse 23 described a situation where some harm *is* done—either to mother *or* child *or* both. . . . An induced miscarriage could hardly be described as a situation where there is "no harm". Verse 22, therefore, describes, not an induced miscarriage, but an induced premature birth.

In this light translations using the word "miscarriage" or its equivalent are both inaccurate and misleading. The intent of this passage appears in the following paraphrase: "And if men fight together and hurt a pregnant woman so that her child is born prematurely, yet neither mother or child is harmed, he shall be surely fined, according as the woman's husband shall lay upon him; and he shall pay as the judges determine. But if either mother or child is harmed, then thou shall give life for life, eye for eye, tooth for tooth, hand for hand, foot for foot, etc."

There are two fundamental principles to be drawn from this passage even if one chooses the weaker interpretation in which miscarriage is used and a fine is the severest penalty relating to the child. First, the passage is obviously not a case of deliberate abortion, the intentional killing of an unborn child. It is an accidental premature birth (or miscarriage). If such an accident has a penalty attached to it, any intentional act of this nature would certainly be forbidden. Secondly, a disparity in punishment does not necessarily imply, let alone prove, a disparity between persons and non-persons. At most we can conclude that accidental killing receives a lesser punishment. The passage immediately preceding this one in question (Exodus 21:20-21) presents a situation where a master kills his slave accidentally and escapes without any penalty. We certainly would not seek to prove from this passage that the slave is less than a human person.

Given the positive command regarding the sanctity of life in the sixth commandment, the burden of proof is on those who would deny the preferred exegesis cited above. It is worth noting also that the proper understanding of this passage would, if anything, elevate the value of the unborn child rather than devalue his life. This appears in that the penalty for the accidental killing of an unborn child is death, while Scripture explicitly exempts from a capital punishment those who accidentally kill persons other than a pregnant woman or her unborn child. This is a strong testimony to God's concern for and protection of the unborn child.

Our obedience to the Word of God leaves us with no option regarding how we perceive the unborn child. He is a person, providentially given and cared for by God, with uninterrupted continuity into post-natal life. There are many explicit and implicit passages of Scripture which further support this conclusion. We are not given unlimited or autonomous sovereignty over our own bodies or the bodies of others (cf. 1 Cor. 6:15, 7:7). Scripture repeatedly affirms the joy and blessing of conception, while barrenness is seen as a curse. God's involvement with the unborn child has already been mentioned. We are even told that John the Baptist was "filled with the Holy Spirit, while yet in his mother's womb" (Luke 1:15). These and many other references are adequately set forth in other studies.

Were there to be no support in the whole history of ethical and moral thought, were there no acknowledged confirmation from the medical sciences, were the history of legal opinion to the contrary, we would still have to conclude on the basis of God's Holy Word that the unborn child is a person in the sight of God. He is protected by the sanctity of life graciously given to each individual by the Creator, Who alone places His image upon man and grants them any right to life which they have.

We must again stress, however, that both exegetical options, even the one we think is wrong, have the same result for the question of abortion, which is not accidental. Exodus 21:22-25 offers no support to any who would seek justification for the intentional killing of an unborn child.

Medical Understanding of Abortion

Although the basic considerations of this report are religious and ethical, information provided through scientific means is valuable in helping the believer to understand and to thereby confirm the clear teaching of Scripture. We will begin our consideration of the medical aspects of the abortion issue by looking at the beginning and continuing development of human life. Although there has been much discussion of when life begins, the scientific community does not seem to have much doubt on this issue. The question is usually raised to obscure the real issue, namely, that abortion is the intentional killing of a living unborn child. The conclusion of the First International Conference on Abortion held in Washington, D.C., in October of 1967, was that no point in time could be found between the union of sperm and egg and the birth of the infant which could not be considered human life. The changes described below are merely stages of development and maturation.

Genetically speaking the human being is characterized primarily by the fact that within each cell of our body there are forty-six (46) chromosomes. This fact distinguishes us from other created beings. Man was created by God with a reproductive potential so that he might be able to obey His commandment to multiply and replenish the earth. In this reproductive cycle the sperm from the man and the ovum or egg from the woman is produced by their respective bodies as the end product in their reproductive cycles. Both the egg and sperm will die unless fertilization occurs. After sexual intercourse the sperm traverses the female genital tract until it reaches the Fallopian tube. When the woman in her menstrual cycle ovulates, the ovum travels from the ovary into the Fallopian tube. If sexual intercourse has occurred at the proper time, fertilization will take place. At conception, which is synonymous with fertilization, the sperm permeates the egg, and the twenty-three (23) chromosomes which are in the sperm and the twenty-three (23) chromosomes within the egg align themselves to form a forty-six (46) chromosome human cell unlike that of any other living being. This union of the twenty-three (23) chromosomes from the woman and the twenty-three (23) from the man brings about the beginning of a unique living being. There are no other human beings who have the potential or same characteristics as this one nor will there ever be in the future. The genetic structure established at this moment guides the development of this individual in regards to its sex, its physical characteristics, such as skin color, eye color, hair, weight, height, and many other characteristics. The only thing that is added is time and food.

The development of this unique being begins at this moment of conception and continues until death. The intrauterine development, however, is usually separated into three stages, zygote, embryonic, and fetal. In the zygote stage rapid division of cells occurs as the development and the formation of this human being proceeds. In a few days the zygote moves down the Fallopian tube and in about five or six days implants itself into the mother's uterus which has been prepared for this act by hormonal influences within the mother itself. The zygote stage lasts through the fourth week after conception. After implantation into the mother's uterus the placenta through which the developing baby is nourished is rapidly formed. Within four weeks a precursor to the fully developed heart has formed and is actually pumping blood through the baby's developing body. The next stage is called the embryonic and exists from the fourth to the seventh week after conception. During the embryonic stage all major internal and external structures are developed. At the end of the embryonic stage the head, ears, eyes, nose, mouth, legs, fingers, and toes are recognizable though small. The baby at this point is only about one half inch long. The primitive skeletal system is completely developed by the end of the sixth week, and an electroencephalogram (brain wave detector) can detect brain wave activity as early as forty-three days after conception. During the sixth and seventh weeks the nerves and muscles begin working together for the first time, and the lips become sensitive to touch. The next and last stage of intrauterine development is the fetal which occurs from the eighth week to birth. This stage is so called because of the ease of recognizing human features with the unaided eye. At this point all internal organisms of the adult are present. The stomach produces digestive juices, the liver manufactures red blood cells, and the kidney is eliminating uric acid from the blood. The arms are still very short, but hands with fingers and toes are recognizable, and legs have knees, ankles and toes. From this point in development until age 25-27 years when full growth and development is complete the only major changes will be in size and sophistication of the function parts.

The lines in the hands begin to develop at eight weeks and will remain a distinctive feature of the individual. The eyelids and palms of the hands become sensitive to touch at about eight and one-half weeks. At this point if the eyelids are touched, the child squints, and if the palm is touched, the fingers close in a small fist.

The sex hormones estrogen and androgen have been identified as early as nine weeks. At ten weeks growth hormone is detectable, and at ten and one-half weeks the thyroid and adrenal glands have begun to function. Also at ten weeks it is possible to record the electrocardiogram, and new ultrasonic techniques can be used by the obstetrician to detect the child's heartbeat.

Twelve weeks is a very important milestone in the development of the baby because at this point all organ systems are functioning. The child swallows its surrounding amniotic debris and has bowel movements. The child swims about within the amniotic fluid. The child has inhaling and exhaling respiratory movements moving the amniotic fluid in and out of its lungs preparing itself to breathe air. Thumb sucking is first noted at this age. The fingernails appear also at this time. The child kicks his legs, turns his feet, curls and fans his toes, makes a fist, moves his thumb, bends his wrist, turns his head, squints, frowns, opens his mouth, and presses his lips tightly together. The child even at this point can be taught. If a sharp instrument is inserted through the mother's uterus and touches the baby, the baby would recoil in pain. If this painful stimulus is preceded by a noise, the baby will eventually learn that he is about to get hurt and will recoil in pain prior to the stimulus.

Growth continues very rapidly during the fourth month of life as weight increases six times, and length eight to ten inches. In the fifth month the unborn child will become one foot tall and weigh approximately one pound. Hair begins to grow on the head and eyebrows, and a fringe of eyelashes appear. The child sleeps and wakes just as he will after birth, and he may even be aroused functionally by external vibrations. At eighteen to twenty weeks the mother perceives fetal movement, and this is defined as quickening. From then on the child develops and adds weight and length to the time of birth.

It must be pointed out here that this developing baby is a separate but dependent new life with its own chromosomal pattern and at no stage of development can be considered as an appendage or part of the mother's own body. Physiologically it is the baby that determines the development of the pregnancy not the mother. The baby, however, is highly dependent upon its mother for protection and nourishment.

Another area in which factual information is vital for understanding the true nature of abortion is the means by which it is accomplished. The following is a brief description of the techniques of abortion commonly used today. The technique most commonly used until the twelfth week of pregnancy is suction. Under a great deal of vacuum pressure the contents of the uterine cavity are torn apart and then sucked out. A second procedure also used during the first twelve weeks of pregnancy is called a D&C which stands for dilitation and curettage. In this procedure the cervix is dilated to a point where a curette or knife-like instrument can be inserted into the uterus. After dilitation the baby is torn apart and cut up with a curette and then is scraped out. During the twelfth through the sixteenth week of gestation the prostaglandin infusion method is used. In this procedure, prostaglandin, which is a hormone-like substance, is injected into the mother to stimulate premature labor and subsequent delivery. From the sixteenth through the twentieth week of pregnancy the "salting out" technique is used. In this procedure a sterile, very concentrated and caustic solution of salt is injected into the embryonic cavity which poisons the baby and causes it to die. The mother will go into spontaneous labor about twenty-four hours later and will deliver vaginally. Another method is hysterotomy, used after the twentieth week until birth. In this technique the usual operative procedure of a caesarean section is accomplished except that the intended result is to remove the infant and allow it to die. Virtually all abortions done this way produce live babies who are either allowed or encouraged to die.

Also significant to the discussion are complications which can result from induced abortions. The American College of Obstetricians and Gynecologists has stated, "The inherent risk of a therapeutic abortion is serious and may be life threatening and this fact should be fully appreciated by both the medical profession and the public. In nations where abortions may be obtained on demand considerable morbidity and mortality have been reported." This is supported by a statement issued by the Royal College of Obstetricians and Gynecologists (Great Britain).

> Those without specialist knowledge, and these include members of the medical profession, are influenced in adopting what they regard as the humanitarian attitude to the induction of abortion by a failure to appreciate what is involved. They tend to regard induction of abortion as a trivial operation free from risks. In fact even to the expert working in the best conditions the removal of an early pregnancy after dilating the cervix can be difficult and is not infrequently accompanied by serious complications. This is particularly true in the case of the woman pregnant for the first time. For women who have a serious medical indication for termination of pregnancy, induction of abortion is extremely hazardous and its risks need to be weighted carefully against those involved in leaving the pregnancy undisturbed. Even for the relatively healthy woman, however, the dangers are considerable.

Obviously the worst complication resulting from a legal abortion is death itself. In the majority of countries where legal safeguards from abortion have been eliminated a woman is more likely to die from legal abortion than she is if she were to carry the pregnancy to term. This is true for legal abortions performed on healthy women by licensed physicians in fully accredited medical facilities.

Another complication centers around pelvic infection. Pelvic infection is a common sequel to legal abortion. While the incidence varies from country to country, consensus reveals an astonishing high rate. The incidence of pelvic infection appears to be highest two to three weeks after the abortion at the time when the patient has been lost to follow-up. There is also good evidence to suggest that young women pregnant for the first time are at much greater risk of infection (55% of New York City abortions are performed on women pregnant for the first time.) These infections are the direct result of the instrumentation involved in the abortion technique and are manifested as salpingitis-"infection in the Fallopian tubes or endometritis (infection of the lining of the womb)." When out of control these infections can cause septic shock with rapid death or pelvic thrombophlebitis (inflamation and bloodclot formation in the pelvic veins) with sudden death by pulmonary embolus (bloodclot from the pelvic veins which dislodges and is carried to the lungs). These infections can also result in sterility because they scar the tubes to the point where they do no longer function properly.

Major hemorrhage is another complication and can result in death by exsanguination. Again the incidence is much too high to be acceptable from a medical standpoint. During the first year of California's new abortion law 8% of patients needed one or more blood transfusions. It should be mentioned that every time a blood transfusion is given there are certain inherent risks, for example allergic reactions and hepatitis which have mortality and morbidity in themselves.

The next complication is uterine perforation. The perforation of the uterus can occur as a sequel to dilitation and currettage. This occurs primarily because the surgeon operates by "touch" alone and not under direct vision. Secondly, the pregnant uterus is much softer than the non-pregnant uterus lending itself to easier perforation. The problem with uterine perforation is the fact that peritonitis (inflamation of the abdominal lining) can occur, necessarily leading to an exploratory abdominal operation with its attendant complications and morbidity.

Menstrual disturbances following abortion are not infrequent. This usually means gross irregularity in the appearance of the menstrual period, heavy bleeding with the menses, or complete absence of menstruation. These disturbances may persist for many years and are mostly the result of endouterine adhesions or infection.

Subsequent pathological pregnancies are quite frequent following abortion, and this without question represents one of the most serious complications of induced abortion. Pathological pregnancies are the following: Premature deliveries, ectopic pregnancies and spontaneous abortions and stillborns. The prematurity rate in Czechoslovakia prior to abortion on demand was 5% which was not much different from the United States. Several years later this had increased to 14%. Hungary and Japan have reported similar trends. It should be pointed out that prematurity is the leading cause of infant death in the United States and one of the major contributors to mental and motor retardation. A number of countries have also reported a significant increase in the incidence of ectopic pregnancies (those pregnancies which occur some place other than the womb). In fact, Japan sees ectopic pregnancies in 3.9% of women which is 4-8 times more frequent than in the United States. Another study indicated a tenfold increase in the relative risk for ectopic pregnancy in a woman with a previous induced abortion. Ectopic pregnancies are not infrequently life-threatening because of rupture and hemorrhage. Again tubal malfunction secondary to infection seems to be the prime cause. Spontaneous abortions and fetal death before the onset of labor are reported to be significantly more common following legal abortion in those countries with weak abortion laws. There is a tenfold increase in the rate of second trimester spontaneous abortions. Complicated labor such as prolonged labor, placenta previa, adherent placenta, and excessive bleeding at the time of delivery are also more common when compared to women who have not had legal abortions. Sterility is also a complication which is related to abortion and which does not appear immediately following the abortion. Post-operation sterility has ranged in various reports from 1% to 27.7%. Poland has reported that 6.9% of women were sterile four to five years after abortion, and Japan has reported 9.7% with subsequent sterility on three year follow-up, and other countries have had similar experiences. There is evidence also to suggest that sterility has an adverse psychological effect on the woman. A number of miscellaneous complications occur which deserve mention.

1. The Czech's have reported that 33% of patients had decreased sexual libido nine months after the abortion. Similarly, a study from Poland showed 14% to have decreased libido four to five years after the abortion.

2. Changes in the coagulability of the blood following legal abortions by the salting out method have been reported. In almost every woman undergoing salt abortion intravascular coagulation of the blood occurs.

3. Pregnancies following hysterotomy will need delivery by caesarean section to eliminate the possibility of rupture of hysterotomy scar.

4. Edometriosis is a common sequel to hysterotomy.

5. A particular problem associated with suction curettage is the perforation of the bladder.

The psychiatric sequels of the induced abortion are most difficult to elucidate but are present in a significant degree. Reports on the incidence of emotional difficulties following abortion vary from 0-85%. The true figures obviously lies some place between. The pro-abortionist would have us believe that unless an emotionally unstable woman's pregnancy is terminated her instability will worsen. They fail to mention that there is a significant degree of emotional instability resulting from the abortion.

In summation it seems obvious that abortion is not the simple uncomplicated procedure its proponents would suggest but rather a risky medical procedure which even on humanistic medical grounds should be carried out only with extreme caution, if at all.

Alleged Special Case

At this point we want to consider what is frequently alleged to be a special case in which an exception is granted by those who would otherwise oppose all abortion. This special case is that abortion may sometimes be necessary to save the life of the mother. The situation is one in which the mother's very life is threatened by the continued existence of a pregnancy. It is posed as a question of one life or the other.

It is necessary first of all to reduce the emotional character of this ''special case'' with its accompanying misrepresentation. In many instances one would be led to believe this is an ethical decision faced regularly by physicians and parents. This is not to deny in any way the extremely painful choice when such a decision should confront us. But medically speaking, such a situation would be extremely rare in today's world. Advances in medical technology and in the knowledge and treatment of pregnancy complications have carried us to the point when almost any pregnancy can be carried to term or to the point where premature delivery can be accomplished with good results. The moral and ethical question is more theoretical than practical.

We have seen how the Word of God considers an unborn child as a person, entitled to the same provisions God gives for all human life. The destruction of such life without proper Biblical warrant is a grave sin. The question must therefore be formulated in terms of whether it is ever justifiable under any circumstance to sin, indeed to sin against an absolute prohibition of God Almighty. God's sovereignty and providential care govern all things. Being perfect in holiness and righteousness, hating all sin, God will not place His creature in a situation in which sin would be approved or justified. To so affirm would be to make God the author of sin. If the intentional killing of an unborn child is sin, there is no situation, no special case, that could warrant its being committed.

In explaining the sixth commandment, the *Larger Catechism* question 136, states: ''The sins forbidden in the sixth commandment are, all taking away the life of ourselves, or of others, except in the case of public justice, lawful war, or necessary defense; the neglecting or withdrawing the lawful and necessary means of preservation of life. . . .'' If there is to be Scriptural evidence for abortion, it must be in exception to the sixth commandment through public justice (capital punishment), lawful war, or self-defense. It can easily be seen that an unborn child could not be guilty of a crime requiring the death penalty, nor could the unborn be the object of lawful war, leaving only the alleged possibility of self-defense of the mother as grounds for intentional abortion.

The Scripture speaks to the issue of self-defense in Exodus 22:2-3 asserting that if one is killed while breaking into another's home, the homeowner is not guilty of murder because of the aggression of the thief; yet if the break-in occurs during the day, the owner would be guilty of murder because seeing the thief and comprehending the circumstances, the homeowner could avoid the aggressive confrontation.

So the question is asked, Is the unborn child aggressively attacking the mother, threatening her life? Does the mere presence of the child constitute aggression? There can be no evidence to validate an affirmative answer. To intentionally kill the baby because of an "assumed" health hazard, can not be justified by the self-defense exception to the sixth commandment.

It must be pointed out that there is a vast difference between the *threat* of death to the mother and the *certain* death (intentional) of the baby in the alleged special case for abortion. No man, trained physician or not, is able to say with 100% accuracy that a woman will definitely die because of a pregnancy. The woman's life is not in her own hand or in the hands of her physician, but it rests in the hands of a loving, sovereign God, who is holy and righteous. We do not pretend to understand all that God does, nor would we imply that this is an easy question for one who must face it. Like other areas of the Christian's walk, this calls for us to have a strong faith and trust in God to carry on a pregnancy in these circumstances.

The conclusion drawn from Scripture is that all life is precious to God, and He especially loves the life of the innocent (Exodus 21:20-21; Proverbs 6:16-17; Deuteronomy 19:10; Isaiah 59:1-9). Therefore there can be no abortion, and there is no "special case". Our decision, in this matter as in all of life, must be determined by God's absolute revelation to us in His Word.

Legal Aspects of Abortion

Having affirmed throughout this report the absolute authority of Scripture in forming our decisions, it is nevertheless true that we are aided in our practical implementation of Scriptural teaching by our understanding of various other disciplines. We will be aided in our opposition to abortion if we understand something of the history of legal developments in regard to abortion.

Abortion, with varying degrees of permissiveness, is legal in many of the nations of the world today. That is, women are permitted to abort their babies, and their doctors can perform the operation without risk of prosecution. Generally speaking, however, in the ancient civilizations this was not the case, and the practice of abortion, though fairly wide spread in pre-Christian times, was by no means universally approved and was indeed explicitly condemned as immoral, dangerous, and harmful to the general welfare by the most important pre-Mosaic law codes and by some of the most celebrated thinkers, philosophers, and moralists of pagan Greece and Rome.

Ultimately the Christian influence which was growing in the Empire from the first century on would deter both the practice of infanticide and abortion. It was through the influence of the Church that Valentinian I, in 374 A.D., made infanticide a capital crime. The early Christian Councils, Elvira (306 A.D.), Chalcedon (451 A.D.), and Constantinople (692 A.D.), which served to shape medieval law, either declared abortion an almost unpardonable sin or branded it as manslaughter. The church so influenced secular law in the middle ages, so strengthened the concept of the sanctity of marriage, the home and family, that abortion was forbidden for a period of some six hundred years. Thus the traditional western view of the sacredness of human life was firmly established by centuries of precedent.

A period of legal uncertainty ensued under English Common Law due partly to the natural limitations of the scientific knowledge of that day. Only mild penalties were levied for abortion before "quickening" because it was felt that prior to that time the baby was not actually alive. After "quickening", when life could be felt in the womb and it was known that life was present, severe restrictions and penalties were administered. Apparently there never was a time under Common Law when abortion was not regarded as a crime. By the end of the seventeenth century the abortion of a "quickened" baby was considered murder or "a great crime", a "great misprison" (felony).

Discovery of the ovum in 1827 led to a reassessment of the significance of abortion. Law followed science, and in 1837 Parliament enacted a new abortion statute that effectively protected the unborn child from the moment of conception. The English lawmakers, having been shown biological evidence that life began at conception, were moved to protect that life in every stage of gestation.

In the United States in the nineteenth century several states interpreted the Common Law so as to render abortion criminal at all states of pregnancy. Most states, however, did not prosecute for abortion prior to quickening. No state held that abortion after quickening was not a crime, and almost all of the then existing states enacted abortion statutes. A New York statute of 1829 imposed a second degree manslaughter charge upon any abortionist who caused the death of a quickened child or its mother unless the reason was to preserve the life of the mother. The same law required imprisonment in the county jail not to exceed one year or a fine not to exceed five hundred dollars for any abortive act prior to quickening.

In 1859 the American Medical Association protested that the quickening distinction allowed the fetus rights for civil purposes but still did not protect its life before that took place. They assailed the unwarranted destruction of human life and called upon state legislatures to revise their abortion laws to conform to the new scientific knowledge that life began at conception and should be protected from that point. One by one each state ruled that human life should be equally and fully protected by law, not from quickening, but from its actual beginning at conception.

In 1868 the fourteenth amendment was ratified which forbade the state to "deprive any person of life, liberty, or property, without due process of law; not deny to any person within its jurisdiction the equal protection of the laws." The child in the womb was regarded as a "person" in the legal sense, and for over one hundred years, until 1967, all states fully protected human life from conception until the first permissive abortion law was passed in Colorado.

June, 1970, when New York passed the first law allowing abortion on demand during the first six months of pregnancy, it was the sixteenth state to permit abortion for other than very restrictive reasons. After that only one more state, Florida, legalized abortion, while thirty-three states debated the issue in their legislatures. All of these states finally voted against abortion for any reason except to save the mother's life.

April, 1972, New York repealed their liberalized abortion law, but Governor Nelson Rockefeller vetoed the repeal, and the law remained in force. New York City's Health Services Administration officials reported in February, 1971, that approximately sixty nine thousand abortions were performed during the first six months of legalized abortion in the state, about half of them women from other states. As other states modified and liberalized their laws, the practice of abortion became widespread. Unofficial statistics in 1972 from fifteen states with the most permissive laws indicated that at least four hundred thousand pregnancies were terminated in this manner.

In 1973 the Supreme Court (Roe v. Wade) ruled that the termination of an unwanted pregnancy is properly the decision of the woman and her doctor. This ruling struck down all laws against abortion in all fifty states and evaded the protection clauses of the fourteenth amendment by declaring the unborn child to be a "non-person" in the legal sense, i.e., "legal personhood does not exist prenatally." The new ruling provided for no legal restrictions at all upon abortions in the first three months of pregnancy and no restrictions in the middle three months except those needed to make the procedure safe for the mother. Abortion was even allowed until birth if one licensed physician judged that it was necessary for the mother's health. The Supreme Court's definition of health is revealed in the decision of Doe v. Bolton. It said that abortion could be performed "in the light of all factors—physical, emotional, psychological, familial, and the woman's age—relevant to the well being of the patient. All these factors may relate to health."

The abortion laws of the United States are probably the most liberal in the world. This is evidenced by the fact that about one third of the abortions performed in the United States are paid for by federal funds. Several versions of a constitutional amendment which would protect the life of the unborn have been introduced into Congress, but at this writing none have gotten out of committee for floor debate. A number of states have called for a Constitutional Convention to amend the Constitution with a "Human Life Amendment", but this requires a call by two thirds of the states, and it has not yet been achieved.

A good summary of the current legal situation is set forth in the Christian Action Council's brochure, "Abortion: What Can I Do?":

"There are only four ways in which *Roe v. Wade,* the abortion decision (or any Supreme Court decision) can be overturned:

1. The Supreme Court could reverse its own decision in a subsequent ruling.

2. The President could try to change the Supreme Court's make-up by adding to the Court new Justices who value the sanctity of life.

3. A constitutional amendment can be passed in Congress and then ratified by 3/4 of the state legislatures within seven years (U.S. Constitution, Article 5).

4. A constitutional convention can be called to draft a constitutional amendment and then pass it through 3/4 of the state legislatures within seven years (U.S. Constitution, Article 5).

"We immediately see that (1) is very unlikely. Since 1973 the Supreme Court has reaffirmed its 1973 position. *Planned Parenthood v. Danforth,* July 1, 1976 is even more sweeping. (2) has already been attempted once (by Franklin Roosevelt in 1937 in his Judiciary Reorganization Bill). This effort was viewed as "packing" the Court-i.e. with Justices favorable to the President's positions. It was soundly criticized by both the Congress and the press. With the delicate balance of powers in our federal government, transforming the Supreme Court at the present time does not seem feasible. We can pray that the President will uphold the sanctity of life in nominating replacements when vacancies occur in the Court. (3) and (4) are really the only courses of action available to the ordinary citizen to effect a change in that 1973 decision. Clearly both involve active participation in the democratic process. Therefore, the only effective *Christian* answer to that 1973 Supreme Court decision must be largely a *political* answer. If we do not recognize this, we in effect surrender our rights as citizens."

In all legal discussions we must remember that our authority is not legal precedent. As with the medical testimony, there will be important confirmation of the revelation of God's Law, but there will also be abundant evidence of man's sin affecting civil law. Thus our argument must not be based on legal history but the Word of God. From divine revelation we know when life begins and that it is holy to the Lord. In that light the Christian can concur with the words of Thomas Jefferson: "The care of human life and happiness, and not their destruction, is the first and only legitimate object of good government."

The Church's Relation and Responsibility to the State

It is one thing to point out the Scriptural foundation, the medical understanding, and the legal aspects of abortion. But what relation and responsibility does the church have beyond her own people? Are we indebted to all men by virtue of the Word of God we have on this matter? One thing is clear. God is God; He is Creator; beside Him there is none other. He will not abdicate His throne and submit His laws to a popular vote. The Christian is characterized pre-eminently by obedience, and whenever there is any conflict, there is only one option. "We must obey God rather than man" (Acts 5:29). But has the Church a responsibility to society other than obedience to legitimate authority?

The Church is under orders. The cultural mandate of Genesis 1:28 is given substance by God Himself revealing laws to govern its implementation. Throughout the Old Testament men of God spoke to kings and nations on the basis of revelation. In the New Testament the great King and Head of Church, Jesus Christ, reiterates this mandate in the Great Commission. "All authority has been given to Me in heaven and on earth. Go therefore and make disciples of all nations, . . . teaching them to observe all that I have commanded you" (Matt. 28:18-20). The command is comprehensive, "teaching them to observe *all*" that Christ commands, and implies that we who enjoy His promised presence are to proclaim His Word of both Law and Gospel. "Thus says the Lord" is to be heard until Christ Himself returns.

In light of these comments relating the universality of God's law for His creation, we want to consider more closely the specific New Testament teaching on church and state relations. Roman 13 and 1 Peter 2 are fundamental passages, and we will especially look at Romans 13.

Note specifically Romans 13:1,2:

> Let every person be in subjection to the governing authorities. For there is no authority except from God, and those which exist are established by God. Therefore he who resists authority has opposed the ordinance of God; and they who have opposed will receive condemnation upon themselves.

Here we are commanded to obey the civil authorities. Why? On what grounds is this obligation set forth? The reason is that in so doing we obey God. "There is no authority except from God," and in verse 4 the state is said to be "a minister of God to you for good." The context here is not the Old Testament theocracy, but pagan, corrupt Rome! Caesar, a "minister of God" in regards to civil authority.

Unhappily Caesar falls far short of bringing his sphere of responsibility under God's Law. So also the government of the United States. Yet even in such an imperfect situation two things are clear. They *ought* to conform to God's law, and we are obligated to obey even corrupt governments except where it would cause us to violate God's law. At that point, "We must obey God rather than men." But clearly there is the responsibility of government to obey God's law, and to the extent possible, we as citizens must do all we can to assure the state's conformity to that law.

As regards our own nation, it was within Christian context that our government was founded. The "establishment of religion clause" or the concept of church-state separation was never understood as separating the state from ethical and moral considerations, which is what the law of God provides. The separation of church and state pertains to the separation of two *institutions* and their respective *spheres* or *functions*. This does not mean they have a different moral authority. It means the church cannot require the state to enforce distinctive Christian duties (i.e. participation in sacraments or tithing to a particular church, etc.). The state is not exempt from the authority of God. God's law is directed to both institutions, church and state, as regards their respective functions.

According to Scripture, then, there can be no question but that both church and state are divine institutions. Both owe their authority, not to autonomous human decisions, but to God. Both church and state have their sphere of authority, and within their sphere we are obliged to be in subjection (cf. Rom. 13:1-6; 1 Peter 2:13, 14). In distinguishing these two authorities, however, we must not miss the fullness of the state's purpose. The state as the servant of God has many duties in the service of the spiritual realm. Failure in these duties does not relieve responsiblity for them.

The civil magistrate is responsible to God. He is to discharge his duty according to God's will. The Bible is the supreme revelation of God's will. Because church and state are neither subordinate to the other but to God, the civil magistrate is under obligation to recognize the Bible as authoritative in the exercise of civil magistracy. The Lordship of Christ in all areas of life is fundamental.

Does the state's obligation to rule according to God's revelation have any bearing on the church. Clearly it does. As the repository of God's revelation the church is culpable if she does not inform the state about God's will. John Murray gives a good summary statement.

> To the church is committed the task of proclaiming the whole counsel of God and, therefore, the counsel of God as it bears upon the responsibility of all persons and institutions. While the church is not to discharge the functions of other institutions such as the state and family, nevertheless it is charged to define what the functions of these institutions are, and the lines of demarcation by which they are distinguished. It is also charged to declare and inculcate the duties which devolve upon them. Consequently when the civil magistrate trespasses the limits of his authority, it is incumbent upon the church to expose and condemn such a violation of his authority. When laws are proposed or enacted which are contrary to the law of God, it is the duty of the church to oppose them and expose their iniquity. When the civil magistrate fails to exercise his God given authority in the protection and promotion of the obligations, rights, and liberties of the citizens, the church has the right and duty to condemn such inaction, and by its proclamation of the council of God to confront the civil magistrate with his responsibility and promote the correction of such neglect. The functions of the civil magistrate, therefore, come within the scope of the church's proclamation in every respect in which the Word of God bears upon the proper or improper discharge of these functions, and it is only a misconception of what is involved in the proclamation of the whole counsel of God that leads to the notion that the church has no concern with the political sphere (*Collected Writings of John Murray*, I, 255).

While Scripture alone is our final authority it is also of value to consider this issue in light of our *Westminster Confession of Faith*. There is some confusion today as to whether our speaking out to the civil authorities is consistent with our *Confession*. The specific section which speaks to this states:

> "Synods and councils are to handle, or conclude nothing, but that which is ecclesiastical: and are not to intermeddle with civil affairs which concern the commonwealth, unless by way of humble petition in cases extraordinary; or, by way of advice, for satisfaction of conscience, if they be thereunto required by the civil magistrate" (Chapter XXXI, 5).

Many reacted against the abuse of the church's power in recent decades and operate now in an ecclesiastical isolationism. Yet an abuse in one direction is as bad as an abuse in the other. Fear of the social action movement has caused many of us at times to superficially appeal to the *Confession* and imply that all communicating to the civil government is "intermeddling". While Scripture, and not the *Confession*, is our supreme authority, the *Confession* itself does not permit such isolation.

First of all, such isolationism was not the practice of the Westminster Divines even in their writing of the *Confession* Chapter XXIII is given over exclusively to "The Civil Magistrate" and defines for the state what his duties are. The framers of the *Confession* thought it proper for the Church to declare the prerogatives and limitations of the civil magistrate's jurisdiction. The implication is that the Church has the right and the duty to declare when necessary what God expects of civil governments. The writings and practice of the authors of the *Confession* provide no support for ecclesiastical isolationism.

In Chapter XXXI, 5, we confess that "synods and councils are to handle, or conclude nothing, but that which is ecclesiastical." Again the reaction against abuse has led many to see "ecclesiastical" as restrictive, while in reality it is a broad term. We have just noted above how the sphere of the magistrate's jurisdiction forms about three percent of the content of the church's "ecclesiastical" confession (one of thirty-three chapters). For a General Assembly to deal with ecclesiastical matters only is not restrictive but includes the whole counsel of God. The *Confession* indeed denies the church's right to intermeddle in "civil affairs," but we must not regard God's law as "civil affairs" distinct from the church. Murray is helpful in his reference to this.

> But to declare the whole counsel of God in reference to political matters, as well as other matters, is definitely an ecclesiastical function and was surely considered to be such by the framers of the Confession. Furthermore, the terms used by the Confession . . . indicate that what is regarded as beyond the province of synods and councils is something quite different from proclamation of the whole counsel of God as it bears upon the conduct of civil affairs (*Collected Writings of John Murray*, I, 256-267).

Ignoring the sanctity of life by destroying it through abortion clearly falls within the purview of the church's ecclesiastical responsibility to speak for God to the state.

We need further to note that when the *Confession* forbids intermeddling with civil affairs, there are two exceptions given. The first of these, "unless by way of humble petition in cases extraordinary," apparently gives opportunity for petitioning the state directly in what is specifically commonwealth business. The intent is to grant exceptions in the area beyond the church's ongoing proclamation to civil government. Whatever areas would be envisioned here would not affect the fundamental position of the *Confession*, which is right of the church to address issues in the political sphere if they touch in extraordinary ways moral and spiritual issues. And even if the understanding of "ecclesiastical" given above were in error (which we do not think is the case), surely our church would be obliged to recognize the intentional killing of millions of innocent lives through abortion to be an extraordinary case in which the people of God must speak out. One cannot use the *Westminster Confession* to support ecclesiastical isolationism on the abortion issue.

The other exception given in the *Confession* is "by way of advice, for satisfaction of conscience, if they be thereunto required by the civil magistrate". Perhaps the only thing that need be said here is that such a request by government authorities is highly unlikely in our nation at this point in time.

To speak publicly to our churches and to our government on God's revelation regarding the sanctity of life, even at conception, is contrary neither to the Word of God nor our *Confession*. The church is under orders to proclaim the whole counsel of God. This will necessitate speaking God's truth to the world in general and civil government in particular. We must not say, "Thus says the Lord," where He has not spoken. We must strive for a unified voice when we speak. And we must exercise extreme caution in any corporate pronouncement. Those to whom we speak may not listen. But we are obliged to speak to public sin for the purpose of proclaiming the Word of God, of vindicating God's authority, and honoring the Name of the Lord Jesus Christ.

Conclusion

The fundamental task of the church is the proclamation of God's Word as it bears upon individuals and institutions. The Holy Scripture, which is God's Word written, is graciously given as the power of God unto salvation for those who believe. But it is no less the absolute authority given to regulate any institution or individual as regards the created life which only God has the right to give or take away. On this basis we believe the intentional killing of an unborn child is a violation of God's command and authority. Scripture considers such a child a person and thus covered by Divine protection even as a person after birth. Any medical support or historical precedent can only be of secondary authority when we have a clear Word from God on moral questions. Yet as often is the case, a candid evaluation of secondary authorities supports the teaching of Scripture. All truth is God's truth, and any alleged conflict is thus but a misreading of one area of His truth.

We are convinced Scripture forbids abortion. The premise of the personhood of the unborn child and the premise of the universal validity of the Sixth Commandment, if true, necessitates the conclusion that abortion is wrong. In a day in which situation ethics has left its mark, the question easily arises in the minds of some, "But what if?" The familiar objections are then presented: population control, economic hardships, unwanted children, psychological or physical health of the mother, rape or incest, deformed children, and protection for the mother's life. We have not dealt with these particular cases with the exception of where the mother's life is threatened. Neither have we dealt with frequently raised objections such as "freedom of choice" and dangers of illegal abortions. There are two primary reasons for not going into detail. One is practical. It would unnecessarily enlarge this report, and these objections have been adequately dealt with in the OPC and RPCES Reports and in other readily available sources. The other reason is to emphasize the principle set forth in this report. Abortion is wrong; it is sin. God as the righteous and holy Judge will not permit sin to be justified by human "situations." Thus the practical application in each of these cases is the consistent application of God's absolute prohibition and the comfort derived from the knowledge that our greatest good is dependent upon our obedience to God.

We cannot stress too strongly our authority in this matter. God in His Word speaks of the unborn child as a person and treats him as such, and so must we. The Bible teaches the sanctity of life, and so must we. The Bible, especially in the Sixth Commandment, gives concrete protection to that life which bears the image of God. We must uphold that commandment. There is a danger of weakening our witness by either retreating from an absolute ethic revealed in God's Word or by uncritically associating ourselves with a humanistic philosophy of right to life based on human wisdom. The Church as the repository of God's revelation must speak from that authority and must do so without compromise or equivocation.

> For Thou didst form my inward parts;
> Thou didst weave me in my mother's womb.
> I will give thanks to Thee, for I am
>   fearfully and wonderfully made
> Wonderful are Thy works,
> And my soul knows it very well.
>
> Search me, O God, and know my heart;
> Try me and know my anxious thoughts;
> And see if there be any hurtful way in me,
> and lead me in the everlasting way.

(Psalm 139:13, 14, 23, 24)

Appendix: Selected Resources Organizations

Christian Action Council
788 National Press Council
Washington, D.C. 20045

CAC represents an evangelical Protestant voice, seeking to persuade Christians to involve themselves in constitutional and political discussion, and to persuade legislators to be attentive to Biblical values. Two excellent brochures are available: "Abortion on Demand?" and the very parctical, "Abortion: What Can I Do?"

Citizens For Informed Consent
286 Hollywood Ave.
Akron, Ohio 44313

Having successfully promoted a local ordinance regulating abortion, Citizens For Informed Consent has become a national clearing house for providing information to those wishing to introduce similar restrictive legislation.

Local and National Right to Life Groups

Right to Life is a broader based organization, including those from Judeo Christian background, which has been effective in pro-life efforts. A good source for general information as well as current issues and opportunities.

Audio-Visual

"The First Days of Life," a film available from many Right to Life Committees or Pyramid Films, Box 1048, Santa Monica, CA 90406.

"Crusade for Life" slide/tape program, Box 1433, Whittier, CA 90607.

"Abortion Kills," a slide/tape program by George Knight, Covenant Theological Seminary, 12330 Conway Rd., St. Louis, MO 63141.

Miscellaneous Publications

"Action Line," 788 National Press Bldg., Washington, D.C. 20045. A Christian Action Council Newsletter.

"Human Life Review," Room 540, 150 East 35th St., New York, NY 10016.

"Lifeletter," Box 574, Murray Hill Station, New York, NY 10016.

"National Right to Life News," 1299 Arcade St., St. Paul, MN 55106.

Bejema, Clifford E. *Abortion and the Meaning of Personhood,* Grand Rapids: Baker Book House, 1976.

Brown, Harold O.J., *Death Before Birth,* New York: Nelson, 1978.

Hilger, Thomas W., *Induced Abortion: A Documented Report. Minnesota Citizens Concerned for Life, Inc.* 1976.

Koop, C. Everett. *The Right to Live: The Right to Die.* Wheaton: Tyndale House Publishing, Inc.,1976.

Orthodox Presbyterian Church. *Report of the Committee to Study the Matter of Abortion.* Philadelphia: O.P.C., 1971.

Reformed Presbyterian Church, Evangelical Synod. "Abortion: The Disruption of Continuity." *Minutes of the 153rd General Synod.*

Lookout Mountain, TN, 1975.

Wilke, Dr. & Mrs. J.C. *Handbook on Abortion.* Cincinnati: Hiltz Publishing Co., 1972.

Dr. Carl W. Bogue, Chairman
Rev. Thomas Cheely
Rev. Charles Dunahoo
Rev. William Fitzhenry
Rev. Fred Thompson

Dr. Warren Diven
Mr. Richard L. Kennedy
Dr. William Russell
Dr. William Thompson

Recommendations:

Scripture alone gives us the revelation from God which governs all of life. The commandments are the clearest testimony by which we regulate our life and discipline our church. The Church of Jesus Christ, through the sessions, presbyteries, and General Assembly, is responsible to implement the Law of God in the life and discipline of the Church. Failure to do this is an indication of spiritual decay, for which the Church comes under judgment. Therefore, we recommend to the Sixth General Assembly of the Presbyterian Church in America the following:

1. That because Scripture clearly affirms the sanctity of human life and condemns its arbitrary destruction, we affirm that the intentional killing of an unborn child between conception and birth, for any reason at any time, is clearly a violation of the Sixth Commandment;

2. That presbyteries, sessions, and congregations be encouraged to utilize available resources so that the cruelty and sinfulness of abortion may be fully understood;

3. That the Committee for Christian Education and Publication, under the auspices of the Stated Clerk, be directed to have this report published in an acceptable pamphlet format as soon as possible (expenses to be borne by the General Assembly), and that this publication be sent to each church and pastor, with additional copies available for sale through the Christian Edcuation and Publication Office, in order that Christians may use this as a guide for their own study and for distribution by them to governmental officials and others;

4. That the General Assembly make available through the Christian Education and Publications office a Slide-Tape presentation on abortion based on the presentation by the Ad-Interim Committee on Abortion, accompanied by a copy of this report;

5. That we remind all Christians of their duty to show compassionate love and understanding to families in distress as a result of pregnancies, and to offer these families sympathetic counsel and help for physical needs where required. This duty is especially incumbent upon us as we minister to persons contemplating abortion. Further, that Presbyteries and congregations give every assistance to Christian groups whose purpose is to help pregnant women to have full term pregnancy rather than resorting to abortion. That the Courts of this Church and their members give this assistance through their Deacons, their Sessions, and where possible, through their women's groups;

6. That all members of the Presbyterian Church in America be encouraged to seek to bring about substantial changes in existing legislation so that the human life of an unborn child be recognized and protected, and that special attention be given to informing our elected representatives at all levels of government of God's Word pertaining to abortion and to lift up in prayer these ministers of God in civil affairs;

7. That the Presbyterian Church in America invite those churches with whom we have fraternal relations to unite with us in issuing the following declaration: "We condemn the intentional killing of unborn children." The Sub-Committee on Interchurch Relations shall arrange implementation of this recommendation;

8. That the Stated Clerk of the General Assembly, on behalf of the Presbyterian Church in America, be directed to communicate to the President of the United States, the leaders of Congress, and the Chief Justice of the Supreme Court, this report along with the

following statement: "God declares in Sacred Scripture that civil government, no less than the Church, is a divine institution and owes its authority to God. The Bible is the supreme revelation of God's will and teaches that the unborn child is a human person deserving the full protection of the Sixth Commandment, "You shall not murder". We who love our nation, in the name of God who alone is sovereign, call upon you to renounce the sin of abortion, to repent of the complicity in the mass slaughter of innocent unborn children, who are persons in the sight of God, and to reverse the ruinous direction of both law and practice in this area. The obedience to God which places us in subjection to your rightful authority, requires of us to proclaim the counsel of God as it bears upon the same God-given authority."

Notes: *This longer statement by the Presbyterian Church in America (approximately 159, 105 members in 1986) provided the opportunity to examine the thought that went into the church's position, which is firmly against abortion, with no exceptions. An important theological consideration was noted here, one which challenged the idea that abortion can present a tragic, life against life situation and thus raised the possibility that abortion, otherwise a sin, might be justifiable. "Being perfect in holiness and righteousness, hating all sin, God will not place His creature in a situation in which sin would be approved or justified. To so affirm would be to make God the author of sin. If the intentional killing of an unborn child is sin, there is no situation, no special case, that could warrant its being committed."*

PRESBYTERIAN CHURCH IN AMERICA

AMENDED STATEMENT ON ABORTION (1979)

Position on, Amended 1979, p. 97, 7-37, III, 3. That Overtures 15 (p. 33), 18 (p. 33), 33 (p. 34), be answered by amending Overture 15 to read as follows:

Whereas, the Sixth General Assembly was of one mind in its general consideration of the abortion issue, but was divided on the question whether abortion might be justified if deemed necessary to save a woman's life,

Therefore, be it resolved that the General Assembly revise the Assembly's statement on abortion (*Minutes of the Sixth General Assembly, p. 72*) to read as follows:

1. That because Scripture clearly affirms the sanctity of human life and condemns its arbitrary destruction, we affirm that the intentional killing of an unborn child between conception and birth (abortion) is clearly a violation of the Sixth Commandment in all situations except possibly that in which it appears finally that no other remedy will save the life of the mother. The Assembly is divided as to whether this situation would justify abortion.

An amendment was moved and seconded to add to recommendation 3 following the last word of the last sentence the following sentence:

In every case where it is determined that it is an immediate medical necessity to terminate a pregnancy to preserve the life of the another, all possible efforts are to be made to preserve the lives of both the mother and the child.

Notes: *This 1979 statement slightly amended the 1978 statement to deal with cases where the pregnancy endangered the mother's life—cases which split the church in regards to the permissibility of abortion.*

PRESBYTERIAN CHURCH IN AMERICA

CLARIFIED STATEMENT ON ABORTION (1980)

Position Clarified 1980, p. 97, 8-69, III, 2. The Overture as amended is as follows:

Overture 12: From Evangel Presbytery

Whereas, the General Assembly, as a Court of Jesus Christ, should speak with a united voice in affirming the sanctity of human life under the protection of the Sixth Commandment.

Therefore, Be It Resolved, that the Eighth General Assembly clarifies the action of the Seventh General Assembly and reaffirms the statement of the Sixth General Assembly on abortion:

> "That because Scripture clearly affirms the sanctity of human life and condemns its arbitrary destruction, we affirm that the intentional killing of an unborn child between conception and birth, for any reason at any time, is clearly a violation of the Sixth Commandment."

Adding to this statement are the following affirmations:

> "Concerning crisis pregnancies in which it appears that the premature removal of the unborn child from the mother is a necessary consequence of medical procedure essential to preserving the mother's life, we affirm that:
>
> 1. The Sixth Commandment not only forbids the taking of innocent life for whatever reason, but also requires the preserving of innocent life wherever possible.
>
> 2. The life of the mother as well as her child comes under the full protection of the Sixth Commandment and all moral medical wisdom and skill must be used to preserve her life as well as the life of her child.
>
> 3. To say that we are ever placed in the position of choosing between two sins (killing the child or neglecting the preservation of the mother's life) is to surrender our belief in the sovereign overruling providence of our All-wise and All-holy God (I Cor. 10:13), and to allege that we must "do evil that good may come" . . . a philosophy clearly condemned by Scripture.
>
> 4. An exception is not made even in the extremely rare case in which in the judgment of competent medical authorities, the unborn child's continuing presence inside the mother's body will necessarily lead to the mother's death. In such a case, the premature removal of the unborn child may be justified, provided that all medical wisdom, judgment, and skill are used to preserve the life of the child as well as the life of the mother. This premature removal of the unborn child shall be at that juncture of time where the greatest possibility for recovery is indicated for both mother and child. If life is lost in such a case, and the death occurs not out of criminal negligence, but merely out of the limitations of human knowledge and skill, all has been done morally that could be done. If we cannot save both lives, we are nevertheless morally bound to save the life we can."

Grounds: The concern of the Sixth General Assembly was to stop abortion. The concern of the Seventh General Assembly was to preserve the life of the mother in crisis pregnancies. We believe this overture as amended addresses and reconciles the concerns of the two assemblies.

Notes: *This 1980 statement continued to deal with the controversy surrounding the previous years' statements on whether abortion might be permitted or necessary to save the mother's life. The position was reaffirmed that God does not place people in the position of having to choose between killing the fetus and saving the mother. If an apparent situation like that should arise, the saving of both lives must be attempted.*

149

REFORMED CHURCH IN AMERICA

STATEMENT ON ABORTION (1973)

In response to an overture concerning abortion, the General Synod adopted the following statement:

> We believe the Bible teaches the sanctity of human life. Men are given the precious gift of life from God and are created in the image of God. Therefore, we believe, in principle, that abortion ought not to be practiced at all. However, in this complex society, where many times one form of evil is pitted against another form of evil, there could be exceptions. It is our Christian conviction that abortion performed for personal reasons to insure individual convenience ought not to be permitted.

> We call on all who counsel those with problem pregnancies, especially youth workers, campus pastors and staff members of our church colleges, to uphold the Christian alternatives to abortion.

> We call on our churches to expand their efforts to support agencies providing a ministry of mercy to those seeking alternatives to abortion.

> We call on our members to support efforts for constitutional changes to provide legal protection for the unborn.

> Recognizing the complexity of the issues, we await the further judgment of the Christian Action Commission and the Theological Commission and the added wisdom which its joint report may give us. However, the gravity of the situation today precludes the possibility of silence at this synod.'' (p. 106f)

Notes: *This 1973 statement from the General Synod of the Reformed Church in America (approximately 346,846 members in 1986) condemned abortion for reasons of personal convenience and supported a constitutional amendment which would protect the rights of the unborn.*

REFORMED CHURCH IN AMERICA

STATEMENT ON ABORTION (1974)

The General Synod received the following statement on abortion from the Theological Commission:

> "The Synod recommended that the Theological Commission and the Christian Action Commission prepare a joint report on the matter of abortion. The Commission prepared two papers on the subject but could not arrive at any consensus. However, the Commission has prepared a paper setting forth some of the Biblical data regarding abortion. We feel that this biblical framework will be helpful to the church.

> While the Reformed Church in America holds God's will and word to be the ultimate context of all ethical decision-making, the difficulty which emerges in the present instance is that the Scripture does not speak directly to the abortion issue. In the face of this difficulty, we believe the church should reject such alternatives as dismissing forthwith all further recourse to the Scriptures or giving a prejudiced exegesis of passages and texts which are sufficiently ambiguous to permit differing interpretations even within our Reformed tradition.

> The more arduous but commendable solution is that of making an instrumental use of the Scripture or developing the Old and New Testament context for the discussion of the issue and for all determinations with respect to it. We suggest that the Scripture contributes as pertinent to the issue under discussion the following data:

1. God is the creator of man, the author of human life (Gen. 1:26, 27:2:7; Psalm 8), active in the conception and birth of human life (Gen. 20:18; 30:2; Ruth 4:13; Luke 1:23-26, 36-37), constant in his care for life before birth (Job 31:15; Psalm 22:8, 139:13-16; Isaiah 44:2, 24:49; 49:1, 5, 15; Jeremiah 1:5; Luke 1:23-25; 36-45).

2. Because man is the bearer of God's image, his life comes under the protection of the divine commandment, ''You shall not kill'' (Gen. 9:6; Exod. 20:13; 21:12-14; Matt. 5:21), and his sexual relationships are assigned serious value (1 Cor. 6:16), even a sanctifying value (1 Cor. 7:1 ff; 1 Thess. 4:3-6), which, in turn, involves the rejection of illegitimate sexual relationships (Matt. 5:32 ff; Mark 10:11, 19ff. 1 Cor. 6:9ff). Although Scripture alludes to eunuchs (Acts 8:27ff. Matt. 19:10-12), the New Testament nowhere commands physical sterilization. Only once does the term ektroma appear (1 Cor. 15:8) meaning ''abortion, abortive, or untimely birth,'' but the exegesis of the passage is disputed, and in no case bears importantly on the issue at hand. Nowhere does Scripture intimate that human life be arbitrarily destroyed (Exod. 21:12-16; Romans 13:4).

3. In unwanted pregnancies as in other human relationships, Scripture requires that we honor the law of love which cares for the neighbor, and which requires that we promote not our own interests but the interest of others (Matt. 22:39, Rom. 12:14-21; Phil. 2:3f). In so doing, Scripture also requires that we keep in view the unique destiny of every human life (Matt. 10:28; 25:41; John 3:36, 5:28, 29).

4. Scriptural passages often cited as determining the status of a human fetus as fully human, upon careful exegetical examination prove to be indecisive and not clearly supportive of an absolutist position, either affirmative or negative (Exod. 21:22-25; Job 3:3, 10:8f; Psalm 51:5; 139:13-15; Isaiah 49:1, 5; Luke 1:41ff; Gal. 1:15; Heb. 7:9, 10), and since the above passages are receiving differing interpretations from equally faithful interpreters within the Reformed community, we believe it is not advisable to make the passages bear the weight of an absolute ''yes'' or ''no'' position. Although this may be disappointing to those seeking a specific biblical instruction for the permission or prohibition of abortion, we do affirm that the above passages provide important biblical principles by which every Christian must measure all counsel and practice on this difficult matter. We further affirm that every Christian seeking to be obedient to the whole counsel of God and the leading of the Holy Spirit, will exercise great care to act both in freedom and responsibility in Jesus Christ (Gal. 5:1, 13-15), and will be slow to criticize or condemn those who act in good conscience before their Maker and Redeemer.'' (p. 207f)

In response to an overture concerning abortion, the General Synod reaffirmed the statement of 1973 except for the deletion of the last paragraph, because the Theological Commission had given the Synod biblical guidelines on the subject of abortion. The Synod also added:

1. We support the adoption of ''conscience clauses'' to free medical personnel and agencies from any legal penalties, or limitations of employment, due to unwillingness to be involved in performing abortions.

2. We direct the GSEC to review ways in which RCA programs, personnel, and agencies can assist in publicizing, encouraging, and if possible, assisting financially in providing alternatives to abortion. (p. 100f)

Notes: *This 1974 statement on abortion by the Reformed Church in America included some of the results of a year-long study by the Christian Action Commission and the Theological Commission. Each prepared a paper, but the two could not reach a joint consensus, partly because the Bible ''does not speak directly to the abortion issue.'' The 1973 statement was then reaffirmed, with minor amendments.*

REFORMED PRESBYTERIAN CHURCH OF NORTH AMERICA

RESOLUTION ON ABORTION (1988)

Resolved:

1. That at next year's meeting of Synod we set aside one afternoon to protest the wickedness of abortion by picketing for two hours at Pittsburgh's leading abortion center;

2. That we invite the Orthodox Presbyterian Church's General Assembly to join with us in picketing;

3. That the Beaver Falls and Pittsburgh Reformed Presbyterian Churches be asked to make the necessary signs and banners for the picketing;

4. That we appoint an organizing committee of Bruce Stewart, Kenneth Smith and John White, Chairman from the Presbytery of the Alleghenies, and that the same committee arrange for as much local and national media publicity as possible for this first-ever protest by the total leadership of two denominations;

5. That the rule of Jesus Christ over the United States be acknowledged in a prepared media statement as the motivating dynamic of our protest;

6. That we publicly and insistently call on the national Synods, General Assemblies, Conventions and Conferences of all other Christian Churches to follow an example in likewise protesting the evil of abortion at sites near the locations of their annual meetings in 1989 and beyond until the United States again protects the life of the unborn human beings living within its borders;

7. That Synod's Moderator read this resolution at the beginning of the Carleton International Family Conference general meeting at 7 p.m., Monday, August 8, 1988.

Notes: *This 1988 resolution on abortion from the Reformed Presbyterian Church of North America (approximately 5,146 members in 1985) was strongly opposed to "the wickedness of abortion," and proposed that picketing at abortion locations should occur as a part of each annual meeting.*

SALVATION ARMY

STATEMENT ON ABORTION (1986)

The Salvation Army believes in the sanctity of all human life. It considers each person to be of infinite value, and each life a gift from God to be cherished, nurtured and preserved.

The Salvation Army supports efforts to protect and promote the welfare of weak and defenseless persons including the unborn. It takes seriously the rights and needs of both the fetus and the mother.

The Salvation Army holds to the Christian ideals of chastity before marriage and fidelity within the marriage relationship and, consistent with these ideals, supports measures to prevent crisis pregnancies. It is opposed to abortion on demand or as a means of birth control.

Termination of a pregnancy may be justified in those rare instances where in the judgment of competent medical and allied staff the pregnancy poses a serious threat to the life of the mother or could result in irreversible physical injury to the mother; and in those instances of proven rape or legally defined incest or where reliable diagnostic procedures determine that a fetal anomaly is present which is incompatible with post-natal survival for more than a few weeks, or where there is total or virtual absence of cognitive function.

It is The Salvation Army's experience that when an unwanted pregnancy occurs, it is best to advise that the situation be accepted and that the fetus be carried to term, and to offer supportive help and assistance with planning.

In situations where our counsel has not been accepted and an abortion has taken place, The Salvation Army will continue to show love and compassion and to offer its services and fellowship to those involved.

A serious commitment to the protection and care of the unborn calls us equally to a commitment to the promotion of societal systems that are conducive to wholeness, a reasonable quality of life and the fullest possible development of the potential of all persons of all ages.

Notes: *This 1986 statement by the Salvation Army (approximately 432,893 members in 1986) was against abortion except in particular instances. Instead, it offered support to the mother for carrying the pregnancy to term. Interestingly, a call was made at the same time for "promotion of societal systems that (were) conducive to wholeness. . ."*

SOUTHERN BAPTIST CONVENTION

RESOLUTION ON ABORTION (1971)

Resolution No. 4—On Abortion

WHEREAS, Christians in the American society today are faced with difficult decisions about abortion; and

WHEREAS, Some advocate that there be no abortion legislation, thus making the decision a purely private matter between a woman and her doctor; and

WHEREAS, Others advocate no legal abortion, or would permit abortion only if the life of the mother is threatened;

Therefore, be it *Resolved,* that this Convention express the belief that society has a responsibility to affirm through the laws of the state a high view of the sanctity of human life, including fetal life, in order to protect those who cannot protect themselves; and

Be it further *Resolved,* That we call upon Southern Baptists to work for legislation that will allow the possibility of abortion under such conditions as rape, incest, clear evidence of severe fetal deformity, and carefully ascertained evidence of the likelihood of damage to the emotional, mental, and physical health of the mother.

Notes: *The Southern Baptist Convention, with approximately 14,000,000 members, is the second-largest religious body in the United States, trailing only the Roman Catholic Church. Like many other statements from denominational bodies, its convention resolutions are not binding upon individual members, but rather represent the majority opinion of the representatives to that year's convention. The 1971 resolution, issued prior to Roe v. Wade, called for legal abortion in cases of rape, incest, severe abnormality, or damage to the emotional, mental, and physical health of the mother.*

SOUTHERN BAPTIST CONVENTION

RESOLUTION ON ABORTION (1974)

Resolution No. 5—On Abortion and Sanctity of Human Life

WHEREAS, Southern Baptists have historically held a high view of the sanctity of human life, and

WHEREAS, The messengers to the Southern Baptist Convention meeting in St. Louis in 1971 adopted overwhelmingly a resolution on abortion, and

WHEREAS, That resolution reflected a middle ground between the extreme of abortion on demand and the opposite extreme of all abortion as murder, and

WHEREAS, That resolution dealt responsibly from a Christian perspective with complexities of abortion problems in contemporary society;

Therefore, be it *Resolved,* that we reaffirm the resolution on the subject adopted by the messengers to the St. Louis Southern Baptist Convention meeting in 1971, and

Be it further *Resolved,* that we continue to seek God's guidance through prayer and study in order to bring about solutions to continuing abortion problems in our society.

Notes: *This 1974 statement of the Southern Baptist Convention reaffirmed the 1971 statement as representing "a middle ground between the extreme of abortion on demand and the opposite extreme of all abortion as murder."*

SOUTHERN BAPTIST CONVENTION

RESOLUTION ON ABORTION (1980)

Resolution No. 10—On Abortion

WHEREAS, Southern Baptists have historically affirmed the biblical teaching of the sanctity of all human life, and

WHEREAS, All medical evidence indicates that abortion ends the life of a developing human being, and

WHEREAS, Our national laws permit a policy commonly referred to as "abortion on demand,"

Be it therefore *Resolved,* That the Southern Baptist Convention reaffirm the views of the Scriptures of the sacredness and dignity of all human life, born and unborn, and

Be it further *Resolved,* That opposition be expressed toward all policies that allow "abortion on demand," and

Be it further *Resolved,* That we abhor the use of tax money or public, tax-supported medical facilities for selfish, non-therapeutic abortion, and

Be it finally *Resolved,* That we favor appropriate legislation and/or a constitutional amendment prohibiting abortion except to save the life of the mother.

Notes: *This 1980 resolution by the Southern Baptist Convention mentioned for the first time support for a constitutional amendment prohibiting abortion except when necessary to save the life of the mother.*

SOUTHERN BAPTIST CONVENTION

RESOLUTION ON ABORTION (1982)

WHEREAS, Both medical science and biblical references indicate that human life begins at conception, and

WHEREAS, Southern Baptists have traditionally upheld the sanctity and worth of all human life, both born and pre-born, as being created in the image of God, and

Whereas, Current judicial opinion gives no guarantee of protection of pre-born persons, thus permitting the widespread practice of abortion on demand, which has led to the killing of an estimated four thousand developing human beings daily in the United States, and

WHEREAS, Social acceptance of abortion has begun to dull society's respect for all human life, leading to growing occurrences of infanticide, child abuse, and active euthanasia.

Therefore, be it *Resolved,* That the messengers to the 1982 Southern Baptist Convention affirm that all human life, both born and pre-born, is sacred, bearing the image of God, and is not subject to personal judgments as to "quality of life" based on such subjective criteria as stage of development, abnormality, intelligence level, degree of dependency, cost of medical treatment, or inconvenience to parents.

Be it further *Resolved,* That we abhor the use of federal, state or local tax money; public, tax-supported medical facilities; or Southern Baptist supported medical facilities for the practice of selfish, medically unnecessary abortions and/or the practice of withholding treatment from unwanted or defective newly born infants.

Be it finally *Resolved,* That we support and will work for appropriate legislation and/or constitutional amendment which will prohibit abortions except to save the physical life of the mother, and that we also support and will work for legislation which will prohibit the practice of infanticide.

Notes: *With this 1982 statement by the Southern Baptist Convention, a significant shift had been completed away from the position articulated in the 1971 and 1974 statements. In fact, that earlier position is explicitly negated. The new position stated, that, due to the sacredness of unborn life, it was not legitimate to consider aborting a fetus on the basis of "personal judgments as to 'quality of life' based on such subjective criteria as stage of development, abnormality, intelligence level, degree of dependency, cost of medical treatment, or inconvenience to parents."*

SOUTHERN BAPTIST CONVENTION

RESOLUTION ON ABORTION (1987)

Resolution No. 9—On Abortion

WHEREAS, Southern Baptists have traditionally upheld the sanctity of all innocent human life and have opposed abortion on demand; and

WHEREAS, 4,000 unborn children are being killed daily in America's aborturies;

Therefore, be it *Resolved,* That we, the messengers of the Southern Baptist Convention, meeting in St. Louis, Missouri, June 16-18, 1987, encourage the Christian Life Commission to continue the expansion of program services related to the sanctity of human life and to actively lobby for legislation to protect the lives of the unborn; and

Be it further *Resolved,* That we encourage the Christian Life Commission to continue to make the abortion issue a priority on its agenda; and

Be it further *Resolved,* that we encourage the Home Mission Board to train churches for ministry in crisis pregnancy centers and residential care homes for pregnant women and children; and

Be it further *Resolved,* That we encourage churches, associations, and state conventions to expand their children's homes ministry to include outpatient and residential care for unwed mothers; and

Be it further *Resolved,* That we encourage all agencies and institutions of the SBC to use their resources and program ministries to promote the sanctity of human life; and

Be it further *Resolved,* That we encourage individuals to minister to those who need physical, emotional, and spiritual support in the midst of a crisis pregnancy; and

Be it finally *Resolved,* That we encourage all churches of the SBC to observe Sanctity of Human Life Sunday on the Convention's calendar, January 17, 1988.

Notes: *This 1987 statement of the Southern Baptist Convention gave evidence of the increase in programming to support anti-abortion sentiments and to support those in crisis pregnancy. It also referred to church observance of Sanctity of Human Life Sunday, which in 1988 was held on January 17. The statement that Southern Baptists "have traditionally . . . opposed abortion on demand" implied a consistency of position which may not have included the 1971 and 1974 statements, which did oppose "abortion on demand," but in a different manner.*

UNITED CHURCH OF CANADA

RESOLUTION ON ABORTION (1980)

Preamble

As Christians we wish to affirm:

The sanctity of human life, born or unborn. That life is much more than physical existence.

We also affirm that:

The taking of human life is evil.

Our concern must not be limited to a concern for the unborn but it must also include a concern for the quality of life as a whole.

Life in this imperfect world often places us in complex circumstances of moral dilemma and ambiguity where values ultimate in themselves seem at times to be in conflict with other values and rights.

We are called as a people of God to take responsibility for our lives and the world in which we live. This may involve making grave decisions relating even to life itself.

Each of us is called upon in a freedom that is given by God and within the context of the community of faith to make responsible personal decisions, even when choosing between two wrongs.

As a forgiven people in Christ, it is possible for us to live in the midst of moral dilemmas.

Within our community strong differences of opinion on moral issues are our strength and not our weakness.

1. Massive Contraception Program

a. A child has a right to be wanted, so that it may have some assurance of this essential element in human development. Bringing unwanted children into the world is irresponsible.

b. Thus, family planning, including vasectomy and tubal ligation is Christian duty. Our Canadian society has to make every effort to ensure that contraception is the only completely acceptable form of birth control. Some practice of abortion is inevitable for the next few years while contraceptive techniques are imperfect and contraceptive ignorance is widespread, but the aim of all education, research and social pressure must be always to reduce the incidence of abortion and to promote effective contraception.

c. To anticipate the use of abortion as a form of birth control and therefore neglect to practise contraception is medically and morally deplorable and socially expensive. Such intentional use of abortion, by individuals or governments, is morally wrong.

THEREFORE

i.   We call on all persons to appreciate their own sexuality primarily in terms of personal relationships and only secondarily in terms of physiology, programs, techniques and services; and charge parents, educators and churches to represent adequately sexuality as intimate, awesome and holy.

ii.   We call on all parents to accept the responsibility to discuss sexual attitudes and information with their children as frankly and as fully as necessary, from the time children begin to ask such questions or need such enlightenment.

iii.   We call on all educators, in provincial departments, regional boards and local schools, to arrange for comprehensive programs, appropriate to the developmental stages of the children and young people, in family live, sex education, contraception information, personality development, relationships and the development of their own values as responsible sexual persons.

iv.   We recommend that sexually mature young people should be informed, by parents, congregations, schools, Health Departments, etc., as to where contraception information and prescriptions are available, and should be instructed in the dangers of venereal disease.

v.   We commend the federal Government for making available funds for education in family planning and birth control, ask it to continue to do so, and urge our people to take action to ensure that the fullest possible use is made of these funds by provincial and local departments of health.

vi.   We call on all United Church people, congregations and presbyteries to urge provincial and local governments to make use of funds available to establish family-planning clinics in hospital and Public Health units, and to support the efforts of public or voluntary agencies to develop or expand such facilities.

vii.   We urge congregations to accept their responsibility to carry out programs on family life education, contraception information, personality development, relationships and the development of sexual values, appropriate to the needs of their members of constituencies.

2. Abortion

a.   We affirm the inherent value of human life, both as immature in the foetus and as expressed in the life of the mother and related persons. The foetus is a unique though immature form of human life and, as such, has inherent value. Christians should witness to that value by stressing that abortion is always a moral issue and can only be accepted as the lesser of two evils and should be the most responsible alternative available in each particular situation. Therefore, abortion is acceptable only in certain medical, social and economic situations.

b.   The present law, which requires a hospital therapeutic abortion committee to authorize an abortion, is unjust in principle and unworkable in practice.

c.   We do not support "abortion on demand". We believe that prior to that stage of foetal development when abortion can no longer be performed by D & C suction, abortion should be a personal matter between a woman and her doctor, who should earnestly consider their understanding of the particular situation permitting the woman to bring to bear her moral and religious insights into human life in reaching a decision through a free and responsive exercise of her conscience. After that period of time, abortion should only be performed following consultation with a second doctor.

Because we see theological significance in the process of growing biological development and in the developing human relationships of the foetus, each of which become factors in ethical decision-making, and because the possibility of physical and emotional harm will be reduced, we consider that any interruption in the pregnancy is less objectionable in the early stages.

We further believe that her male partner and/or other supportive people should have a responsibility to both the woman and the foetus and should be involved in the decision wherever possible.

THEREFORE

1. We Urge the Government of Canada to:

   a. Remove from the Criminal Code all sections presently relating to abortion to the extent that they relate to termination of pregnancy within the first twenty weeks;

   b. Enact and enforce penalties for people who without the required medical qualifications perform or attempt to perform abortions or who perform or attempt to perform abortions in places other than those approved for that purpose.

2. We Urge Provincial Governments to:

   a. Enact in their Public Hospitals Act a provision to the effect that consultation with a second doctor is mandatory before performing an abortion after twelve weeks' gestation;

   b. Provide facilities and personnel necessary to meet the need for abortions, and make known the availability of such facilities, and require all hospitals to declare publicly their policy on abortion.

3. In order to protect the foetus and the woman from all ill-advised abortion, and to help the woman make a responsible decision, we urge the federal and provincial governments to co-operate with churches and other helping agencies in the funding and further development of counselling services in all centres where abortions are performed, and in geographic areas where such hospital and medical services are not available. This counselling should include:

   a. Early Pregnancy Counselling

      To help the woman to:

      —understand her own feelings about being pregnant,

      —explore all the options for coping with the pregnancy,

      —carrying the pregnancy to term,

      —giving up or keeping the baby,

      —abortion,

      —articulate her reasons for choosing an abortion or carrying the pregnancy to term,

      —relate to family members or friends to whom she can look for support in her situation.

      To inform the woman about:

      —available community services, should she choose to have and to keep the baby, or have and give up the baby

      —adoption possibilities and procedures

      —abortion procedures and possible mental, spiritual and social ramifications.

   b. Contraceptive Counselling

      Ensure that the client and, if possible, her male partner understand the facts of fertility, are informed about contraception methods and have access to devices and prescriptions.

c. Follow-up Counselling to deal with personal problems that may arise from the operation and to encourage the continued use of contraceptives.

4. Further, as an expression of our Christian concern, we urge churches, governments, and all helping agencies to work through all possible avenues to ensure adequate community support for mothers choosing to give birth, both those giving up and those keeping their babies.

5. We commend members of the medical and nursing profession for their responsible and compassionate involvement in the matter of abortion, while reiterating their right to refuse to participate on grounds of conscience.

    We repeat our request to all hospital boards to grant nurses and other medical personnel the option of non-participation and at the same time refer medical personnel to the Canadian Medical Association code of Ethics in this matter.

    We draw attention to the action of the Society of Obstetricians and Gynaecologists of Canada at their meeting in June, 1971:

    "That for the time being the fees for the performance of termination of pregnancy should not exceed that set in the local and provincial fee schedules."

6. We instruct the Division of Mission in Canada and the Division of Ministry Personnel and Education to develop further the provisions which encourage and enable ministers and lay people to prepare themselves for the counselling of women faced with an abortion dilemma and, where appropriate, their partners or parents.

7. We instruct the Division of Mission in Canada to continue to study the church's position on both birth control and abortion, and to make available to the congregations current statements that will enable the church to maintain a responsive involvement in these important concerns.

Notes: *This statement from the 28th General Council of the United Church of Canada (approximately 2,185,498 members) offered a Canadian viewpoint on abortion. This 1980 statement affirmed that life often involves the weighing of competing values, and that abortion laws should be fairly liberal, at least in the early stages of pregnancy. The United Church of Canada was formed by a merger of the Methodist Church, Canada, the Congregational Union of Canada, the Council of Local Union Churches, most of the Presbyterian Church of Canada, the Canada Conference of the Evangelical United Brethren, and other churches.*

UNITED CHURCH OF CHRIST

SEXUALITY AND ABORTION: A FAITHFUL RESPONSE (1987)

WHEREAS, Scripture teaches that all human life is precious in God's sight and teaches the importance of personal moral freedom, and

WHEREAS, previous General Synods, beginning in 1971, have considered the theological and ethical implications of abortion, and have supported its legal availability, while recognizing its moral ambiguity and urging that alternatives to abortion always be fully and carefully considered, and

WHEREAS, women and men must make decisions about unplanned or unwanted pregnancies that involve their physical, emotional, and spiritual well-being, and

WHEREAS, the United States leads nearly all other developed nations of the world in pregnancy, abortion, and childbearing rates for teen-agers, and

WHEREAS, access to birth control is being jeopardized by decreases in Federal funding for human services, including family planning programs, and certain groups continue their efforts to reverse the Roe vs. Wade decision of 1973, which affirms the right to choose a safe and legal abortion, and

WHEREAS, abortion is a social justice issue, both for parents dealing with pregnancy and parenting under highly stressed circumstances, as well as for our society as a whole, and

WHEREAS, previous General Synods have called upon the church to provide programs of counseling and education about the meaning and nature of human life, sexuality, responsible parenthood, population control, and family life.

THEREFORE, BE IT RESOLVED, that the Sixteenth General Synod:

1. Affirms the sacredness of all of life, and the need to protect and defend human life in particular;

2. Encourages persons facing unplanned pregnancies to consider giving birth and parenting the child or releasing the child for adoption before considering abortion;

3. Upholds the right of men and women to have access to adequately funded family planning services, and to safe, legal abortions as one option among others;

4. Affirms the need for adequately funded support systems, including health and day care services, for those who choose to raise children;

5. Urges that resources on human sexuality being prepared by the Board for Homeland Ministries be used widely in the churches, and that the Resolutions of previous General Synods on sexuality issues be distributed and studied as part of these resources;

6. Urges the United Church of Christ, at all levels, to provide support, resources, and information to persons facing unplanned pregnancies, including counseling of persons who choose to have abortions;

7. Urges the United Church of Christ, at all levels, to provide educational resources and programs to persons, especially young persons, to help reduce the incidence of unplanned and unwanted pregnancies, and to encourage responsible approaches to sexual behaviour;

8. Urges pastors, members, local churches, conferences, and instrumentalities to oppose actively legislation and amendments which seek to revoke or limit access to safe and legal abortions.

Notes: *This statement by the 16th General Synod of the United Church of Christ (approximately 676,000 members in 1986) continued a pro-choice stance while also encouraging persons to consider options other than abortion.*

UNITED CHURCH PEOPLE FOR BIBLICAL WITNESS

AN OPEN LETTER TO THE CHURCH (1981)

We have read in the news that United Church of Christ President Avery Post has "celebrated" at a rally in Washington, DC, the Supreme Court decision to legalize abortion (Keeping You Posted, 16 Feb. '81, p. 1).

In his defense of pro-choice legislation and action, President Post has spoken of pro-abortion choice as an option for justice: "There is a higher ethical principle that is decisive. The principle is the upholding of the freedom of the individual, before God, to decide her personal course of action" (ibid., p. 3).

Several serious problems arise regarding the logical and ethical validity of Dr. Post's appeal. What "higher" ethical principle decisively affirms the right of the stronger to terminate the life of the weaker? We don't know of any; but the implications are enormous. What difference is there between an individual exercising her freedom to terminate a powerless human life, and the advocate of a secular "life-boat" ethic who avers that in order to maintain a desirable standard of living those who have control of the boat must force the less fortunate to drown and abort. This is hardly a higher ethical principle, though it is certainly decisive.

Already our century has witnessed the mass termination of powerless human beings by more powerful egos deciding their own personal course of action at the expense of others. The logic of the higher ethical principle referred to by Dr. Post is only a "high" principle if it can be accorded to all individuals, and if it is recognized that no ethical decision is purely personal, but invariably involves other persons. By her choice to abort her child, a pregnant mother makes a decision on behalf of that child that he or she will never have the opportunity of making any conscious decision of his or her own. It was recognized by Immanuel Kant, and even by Jean-Paul Sartre, neither of whom was writing from a Christian perspective, that a responsible decision by an individual should be such that that person intend the action to be universal. Kant called this highest ethical principle the categorical imperative.

President Post's appeal to the decisiveness of a higher ethical principle does not come close to meeting the standards of such a secular ethic. Even Sartre, the non-theistic existentialist, knew better than that when he argued that the responsible person acts not just for himself but in behalf of everyone. Jesus said it best of all: "Do unto others as you would have them do unto you." If Dr. Post's support of a pro-choice ethic were to be universally practiced, ours might well be the one-generation generation.

There is something far higher at stake than the categorical imperative, however, and that is the biblical ethic which takes its clue from Christ's role as suffering servant. It is an ethic of giving rather than getting. Termination of a pregnancy is essentially an act which says, "I live for myself here and now without commitments." Funding by the church for poor women to have legalized abortions to up-grade their personal lifestyle says to them, "Aspire to the morality of your more well-to-do bourgeois sisters who can really afford to live for themselves." For Dr. Post's ethic is bourgeois and echoes the secular life-boat ethic. Blacks and other minorities have every right to be suspicious of upper-class whites who, however well-intentioned, aspire to limit the newborn in order that the present generation might have a higher standard of living by limiting minority populations. But a higher standard of living, as we are learning, may come at the price of a lower quality of life.

Jesus calls us to love the oppressed and the powerless, and this includes the widow and the orphan, and the most powerless and oppressed of all, the unborn individual who, by abortion, is denied his or her right of choice and is pushed away from the life-boat by the strong-willed to drown in a salty sea.

There are other questions. Since it takes two to conceive a new life, does the father have a voice in the choice to abort? Can it be wholly the private decision of the mother? And what about the biblical injunctions against breaking commitments and covenants? The apostle Paul addresses the case of the man in Corinth who is living with his father's wife (I Cor. 5:1-13) and admonishes the Corinthian church not to celebrate this unethical behavior, but to celebrate Christ's festival with sincerity and truth.

Dr. Post is more on target ethically and biblically when, in the same article, he is reported as having "called for a nationwide effort to stamp out (sic) social evils that cause abortion to be needed: 'rape, the emptiness of casual intimacy, the humiliation of woman's dominance by man, loss of meaning in marriage, the perpetuation of poverty and absence of love.' The family should be supported as 'a place of nurture for God's love,' he said. 'Strong families will alleviate the demeaning qualities of American life and reduce the perceived need for abortion.'" (ibid.).

If Dr. Post would stay close to the biblical themes which underscore the importance of covenant, family, marriage, and self-control, he would advance the cause of Christ on the highest ethical level and do us proud. We pray that he will see the illogic of his pro-abortion stand, and forsake the captivity of a bourgeois ethic.

The question does indeed have to do with love and life for the powerless, down to the little creature aforming in the womb. If a higher standard of living has to be bought at the price of a lower quality of life, then it were better, perhaps, for God to allow the boat to sink. But Christ came to give life, and to give it to the whole world, including future generations.

Celebrate abortion? Only if we are willing to settle for the one-generation generation.

—written by Dr. Royce Gruenler for United Church People for Biblical Witness

—adopted as the statement of the Board of directors on May 1, 1981

Notes: *This statement was written by Dr. Royce Gruenler and was adopted as the statement of the Board of Directors of the United Church People for Biblical Witness, (United Church of Christ), on May 1, 1981. The statement, representing a minority anti-abortion lobby within the church, took U.C.C. President Avery Post to task for the church's pro-choice position, arguing that it promoted selfishness and did not recognize the needs of the fetus or the father.*

UNITED METHODIST CHURCH

STATEMENT ON RESPONSIBLE PARENTHOOD (1968)

Responsible Parenthood

We affirm the principle of responsible parenthood. Each married couple has the right and the duty prayerfully and responsibly to control conception according to the circumstances of their marriage. Married couples are free within the limits of Christian conscience to use those means of birth control which meet the approval of the medical profession. We find no moral distinction between periodic continence and the use of various types of contraception now available.

We favor legislation on abortion along the lines recommended by the American Law Institute and the American Medical Association, allowing termination of pregnancy upon the recommendation of a qualified panel of physicians when it has been clearly determined that the physical or mental health of the mother is seriously threatened, or where substantial medical evidence indicates that a child will be born grossly deformed in mind or body, or where pregnancy has resulted from rape or incest. We recognize that the vast majority of illegal abortions will be unaffected by the above provisions. We favor a program of primary prevention through making conception control advice and means economically available through proper channels. We further urge the Church to continue study of the serious ethical considerations surrounding abortion and other issues of family planning, such as genetic therapy and overpopulation.

We call upon churches to counsel married couples and those approaching marriage on the principle of responsible parenthood. We urge the churches to support public policies which make available contraceptive advice and means to the medically indigent at public expense. We urge our government to increase its commitments to international projects to assist developing nations with family planning upon the request of those nations.

Notes: *This 1968 statement by the United Methodist Church (approximately 9,504,164 members in 1983) recommended reform of the abortion laws according to the suggestions of the American Law Institute and the American Medical Association, along with strict guidelines. The United Methodist Church is the third largest religious group in the United States (behind the Roman Catholic Church and the Southern Baptist Convention), and the* *statements of its quadrennial General Conference speak for the church but are not binding upon individual members.*

UNITED METHODIST CHURCH

STATEMENT ON RESPONSIBLE PARENTHOOD (1976)

Responsible Parenthood

SP 71.A, F, G

We affirm the principle of responsible parenthood. The family in its varying forms constitutes the primary focus of love, acceptance, and nurture, bringing fulfillment to parents and child. Healthful and whole personhood develops as one is loved, responds to love, and in that relationship comes to wholeness as a child of God.

Each couple has the right and the duty prayerfully and responsibly to control conception according to their circumstances. They are in our view free to use those means of birth control considered medically safe. As developing technologies have moved conception and reproduction more and more out of the category of a chance happening and more closely to the realm of responsible choice, the decision whether or not to give birth to children must include acceptance of the responsibility to provide for their mental, physical, and spiritual growth, as well as consideration of the possible effect on quality of life for family and society.

To support the sacred dimensions of personhood, all possible efforts should be made by parents and the community to ensure that each child enters the world with a healthy body, and is born into an environment conducive to realization of his or her full potential.

When, through contraceptive or human failure, an unacceptable pregnancy occurs, we believe that a profound regard for unborn human life must be weighed alongside an equally profound regard for fully developed personhood, particularly when the physical, mental, and emotional health of the pregnant woman and her family show reason to be seriously threatened by the new life just forming. We reject the simplistic answers to the problem of abortion which, on the one hand, regard all abortions as murders, or, on the other hand, regard abortions as medical procedures without moral significance.

When an unacceptable pregnancy occurs, a family, and most of all the pregnant woman, is confronted with the need to make a difficult decision. We believe that continuance of a pregnancy which endangers the life or health of the mother, or poses other serious problems concerning the life, health, or mental capability of the child to be, is not a moral necessity. In such cases, we believe the path of mature Christian judgment may indicate the advisability of abortion. We support the legal right to abortion as established by the 1973 Supreme Court decision. We encourage women in counsel with husbands, doctors, and pastors to make their own responsible decisions concerning the personal and moral questions surrounding the issue of abortion.

We therefore encourage our churches and common society to:

1. Provide to all education on human sexuality and family life in its varying forms, including means of marriage enrichment, rights of children, responsible and joyful expression of sexuality, and changing attitudes toward male and female roles in home and marketplace.

2. Provide counseling opportunities for married couples and those approaching marriage on the principles of responsible parenthood.

3. Build understanding of the problems posed to society by the rapidly growing population of the world, and of the need to place personal decisions concerning childbearing in a context of the well-being of the community.

4. Provide to each pregnant woman accessibility to comprehensive health care and nutrition adequate to assure healthy children.

5. Make information and materials available so all can exercise responsible choice in the area of conception controls. We support the free flow of information on reputable, efficient and safe nonprescription contraceptive techniques through educational programs and through periodicals, radio, television, and other advertising media. We support adequate public funding and increased participation in family planning services by public and private agencies, including church-related institutions, with the goal of making such services accessible to all, regardless of economic status or geographic location.

6. Make provision in law and practice for voluntary sterilization as an appropriate means for some for conception control and family planning.

7. Safeguard the legal option of abortion under standards of sound medical practice, and make abortions available to women without regard to economic status.

8. Monitor carefully the growing genetic and biomedical research, and be prepared to offer sound ethical counsel to those facing birth-planning decisions affected by such research.

9. Assist the states to make provisions in law and practice for treating as adults minors who have, or think they have, venereal diseases, or female minors who are, or think they are, pregnant, thereby eliminating the legal necessity for notifying parents or guardians prior to care and treatment. Parental support is critically important and most desireable on such occasions, but needed treatment ought not be contingent on such support.

10. Understand the family as encompassing a wider range of options than that of the two-generational unit of parents and children (the nuclear family); promote the development of all socially responsible and life-enhancing expressions of the extended family, including families with adopted children, single parents, those with no children, and those who choose to be single.

11. View parenthood in the widest possible framework, recognizing that many children of the world today desperately need functioning parental figures, and also understanding that adults can realize the choice and fulfillment of parenthood through adoption or foster care.

12. Encourage men and women to demonstrate actively their responsibility by creating a family context of nurture and growth in which the children will have the opportunity to share in the mutual love and concern of their parents.

13. Be aware of the fears of many in poor and minority groups and in developing nations about imposed birth planning, oppose any coercive use of such policies and services, and strive to see that family-planning programs respect the dignity of each individual person as well as the cultural diversities of groups.

ADOPTED 1976

Notes: *This 1976 resolution from the United Methodist Church (which was reaffirmed in 1988), supported the legality of abortion and also recognized the moral complexities involved. Regard for the fetus had to be balanced by an equal regard for the environment of birth, including the physical, mental, and emotional health of the pregnant woman and her family.*

UNITED PENTECOSTAL CHURCH INTERNATIONAL

RESOLUTION ON ABORTION (1988)

The following resolution on the issue of abortion was passed at the 1988 General Conference in Salt Lake City. It was also passed that the resolution should be printed in the *Pentecostal Herald*.

Whereas our world has been troubled for a number of years by the corporate sin of abortion, and

Whereas the United Pentecostal Church must confront this moral and ethical challenge to our American society, and

Whereas the Holy Bible does provide insight into this climate of sexual permissiveness prevalent in our generation, and

Whereas the Bible acknowledges God as totally involved in the creation of new life (Jeremiah 1:5, Psalm 139:13-16, Isaiah 44:24), and

Whereas the church of the living God has a responsibility in protecting the rights of the unborn,

Therefore be it resolved that the United Pentecostal Church go on record as opposing abortion on demand.

Be it further resolved that we voice our opposition to any legislation at provincial, state, or national levels which would bring about a climate designed to undermine the sanctity of human life, further destroying the moral fiber of our society.

Be it further resolved that we give ourselves during the time of Global Conquest to earnest prayer for an awakening in our North American society of moral consciousness concerning this issue.

Be it further resolved that we encourage and help provide for proper biblical solutions to this problem and that we continue to reach out to those who have been caught or blighted in any way by the effect or contemplation of abortion.

Be it further resolved that we encourage our ministers and churches to assist and counsel those with unwanted pregnancies concerning Bible alternatives.

Be it further resolved that we again reaffirm that we want to minister with compassion to those who may presently suffer the trauma of having had an abortion.

Notes: *This 1988 resolution on abortion by the General Conference of the United Pentecostal Church International (approximately 400,000 members in the U.S. and Canada) opposed "abortion on demand" as undermining "the moral fiber of our society" and as being against God's will.*

WESLEYAN CHURCH

STATEMENT ON THE SANCTITY OF LIFE (1985)

7. Sanctity of Life

We believe that life is a gift from God and must always be regarded as sacred.

Abortion

The Wesleyan Church seeks to recognize and preserve the sanctity of human life from conception to natural death and, thus, is opposed to the use of induced abortion. However, it recognizes that there may be rare pregnancies where there are grave medical conditions threatening the life of the mother, which could raise a serious question about taking the life of the unborn child. In such a case, a decision should be made only after very prayerful consideration following medical and spiritual counseling. The Wesleyan Church encourages its members to become informed about the abortion issue and to become actively involved locally and nationally in the preparation and passage of appropriate legislation guaranteeing protection of life under law to unborn children. (*Discipline* 187:11)

Notes: *This 1985 statement by the Wesleyan Church (approximately 110,241 members) on the sanctity of life, is excerpted from the larger book,* The Wesleyan Church Speaks on Contemporary Issues. *The statement opposed abortion except in rare instances where the life of the mother is threatened.*

Jewish Groups

The organized Jewish religious communities in the United States involve approximately half of the six million Jewish citizens in the U.S. They are generally divided into three main branches—Orthodox, Conservative, and Reform—which each have approximately one million adherents. Additionally, the Reconstructionist movement claims approximately 40,000 members. The Conservative, Reform, and Reconstructionist groups interpret Jewish tradition to favor the established life of the mother over that of the fetus if there is a conflict. The statements from two Jewish women's organizations are included here to illustrate the particular interest they exhibit in the issue and to show their method of approach to the topic.

CENTRAL CONFERENCE OF AMERICAN RABBIS (REFORM)
STATEMENT ON ABORTION (1967)

Abortion

1. The Central Conference of American Rabbis considers as religiously valid and humane such new legislation that

a. recognizes the preservation of a mother's emotional health to be as important as her physical well-being; and

b. properly considers the danger of anticipated physical or mental damage; and

c. permits abortion in pregnancies resulting from sexual crime, including rape, statutory rape, and incest.

We strongly urge the broad liberalization of abortion laws in the various states, and call upon our members to work toward this end.

Notes: *This 1967 statement by the Central Conference of American rabbis (Reform) urged liberalization of abortion laws and went on to say that it "recognizes the preservation of a mother's emotional health to be as important as her physical well-being."*

CENTRAL CONFERENCE OF AMERICAN RABBIS (REFORM)
RESOLUTION ON ABORTION (1975)

WHEREAS we are heirs of a prophetic tradition which ever sought to repair the damaged world, and

167

WHEREAS in our efforts to restore the world to sanity we affirm the following position which we take, knowing full well the complexity of such an issue, but knowing also that we cannot be silent,

BE IT THEREFORE RESOLVED that as inheritors of and participants in a religious tradition that encompasses all human experience in its scope, we recognize that Jewish tradition has addressed itself to the question of the termination of pregnancy. We believe that in any decision whether or not to terminate a pregnancy, the individual family or woman must weigh the tradition as she struggles to formulate her own religious and moral criteria to reach her own personal decision. We direct the attention of individuals and families involved in such decisions to the sentiments expressed in Jewish legal literature looking favorable on therapeutic abortion. We believe that the proper locus for formulating these religious and moral criteria and for making this decision must be the individual family or woman and not the state or other external agency.

BE IT FURTHER RESOLVED that as we would not impose the historic position of Jewish teaching upon individuals nor legislate it as normative for society at large, so we would not wish the position of any other group imposed upon the Jewish community or the general population.

BE IT FURTHER RESOLVED that in reaffirming previous Central Conference of American Rabbis resolutions, we commend those states that have enacted humane abortion legislation and appeal to other states to do likewise. We affirm the legal right of a family or woman to determine on the basis of its or her own religious moral values whether or not to terminate a particular pregnancy. We oppose all constitutional amendments that would abridge or circumscribe this right.

BE IT FURTHER RESOLVED that we express our concern over the case of Dr. Kenneth Edelin and urge the Social Action Commission of the UAHC-CCAR to file a brief *amicus curiae* in behalf of Dr. Edelin if and when applicable. We further express our shock over the decision of the government of Quebec to prosecute Dr. Henry Morgentaler once again and consider this act of prosecution one of persecution. In view of the deteriorating state of health of Dr. Morgentaler, we urge the Federal Government of Canada to grant him an immediate compassionate pardon.

BE IT FURTHER RESOLVED that, recognizing the role of the UAHC and the CCAR in promoting freedom of choice, we call on the UAHC and the CCAR to support the Religious Coalition for Abortion Rights on a national and statewide level.

Notes: *This 1975 resolution from the 86th Annual Convention of the Central Conference of American Rabbis (Reform) suggested that the criteria for making the decision about abortion should be formulated by the people involved, and not the state.*

NATIONAL COUNCIL OF JEWISH WOMEN

NCJW REAFFIRMS ABORTION AS A CONSTITUTIONAL RIGHT (1989)

New York, NY—On the 16th anniversary of the landmark Supreme Court decision Roe v. Wade, which established abortion as a constitutional right, the National Council of Jewish Women (NCJW) reaffirms its commitment to that position.

Lenore Feldman, National President, stated during a press conference held by the Religious Coalition for Abortion Rights at the National Press Club in Washington, D.C., that "NCJW deplores the insidious chipping away at abortion rights that has been taking place over the past 16 years. We condemn the tactics that have been used to eliminate choice, whether they be governmental or private. We condemn the terrorism of bombing clinics. We condemn the further impoverishment of poor women by restricting Title X and Medicaid funding. We condemn the lack of concern for the health of military personnel, federal employees, Peace Corps workers, and their families by eliminating abortion health benefits. We condemn the constant court battles on the issue of choice. NCJW is extremely distressed by the newest assault on abortion rights which is before the Supreme Court—Reproductive Health Services v. Webster. NCJW will continue to advocate for those abortion rights that have been lost, while at the same time work to prevent further erosion of abortion rights.''

As an organization with a long pro-choice history, NCJW is proud to be one of the first organizations to support the April 9, 1989 March for Women's Equality/Women's Lives in Washington, D.C.

Established in 1893, the National Council of Jewish Women is the oldest Jewish women's volunteer organization in America. NCJW's more than 100,000 members in 200 Sections nationwide are active in the organization's priority areas of women's issues, Jewish life, aging, children and youth, Israel, and constitutional rights.

Notes: *This 1989 statement by the National Council of Jewish Women (an independent group with approximately 100,000 members) affirmed a pro-choice position as a constitutionally protected right.*

NATIONAL FEDERATION OF TEMPLE SISTERHOODS (REFORM)

STATEMENT ON ABORTION (1965)

3. Abortion

While Jewish tradition does not generally favor abortion, it does permit it under special circumstance. Humane considerations motivate us to speak out in the name of our United States members, in favor of needed revisions in the abortion laws of many States. At present, these laws make no distinction between pregnancies which occur voluntarily and those which happen involuntarily, either through force or otherwise. Neither do these laws sufficiently take into account other circumstances, such as threatened disease or deformity of the embryo or fetus, that warrant judiciously considered termination of pregnancy. Each year, more than one million American women, many of them married, seek abortions. Existing State statutes like so many divorce laws, penalize the poor who cannot afford recourse to those services which the more affluent in our society can and do find. But for the poor or affluent alike, the risks of illegal operations yearly take a tragic and needless toll.

Therefore, upon behalf of our United States members, we appeal for liberalization of the abortion laws of the various States and urge our United States constituents to work toward this end.

Notes: *This 1965 statement by the National Federation of Temple Sisterhoods (Reform) was one of the earlier religious statements on abortion, issued eight years before Roe v. Wade. It urged liberalization of the abortion laws to take into account unfortunate circumstances and to remove the risks of illegal operations.*

NATIONAL FEDERATION OF
TEMPLE SISTERHOODS (REFORM)

STATEMENT ON ABORTION (1977)

The Right to Choose—Legal Abortions

We believe that the right to choose on the matter of abortions is a personal decision based on religious, moral or cultural values and beliefs; it should not be determined for others by special interest groups whether religious or otherwise, nor should government be the enforcing agency for their points of view.

THEREFORE, on behalf of United States Sisterhoods assembled in San Francisco, We:

1. Reaffirm our support of the Supreme Court decision of 1973 relating to abortions.

2. Deplore the current trend of Supreme Court opinions to impinge upon women's freedom of choice, and the current trend of Congressional action to reject the funding of non-therapeutic abortions through federal programs. The preferential treatment policy which would permit women of means to travel to a facility for an abortion, while condemning all other women to beat unwanted children is abhorrent.

3. Urge all Sisterhoods to participate at local and state levels, to insure passage of pro-choice legislation, and to deter contrary action; to educate members on the importance of maintaining every woman's right to choose, with special emphasis on its significance to the preservation of religious freedom; include family planning and sex education programs; to cooperate and participate with the Religious Coalition for Abortion Rights and other like-minded groups to create greater awareness of significance of the abortion issue which preserves the rights of freedom of choice; to work against passage of constitutional amendments prohibiting abortion, and for repeal of present restrictive legislation and defeat of prohibitive legislative proposals in Congress.

   Offer encouragement to non-United States affiliates in their efforts to secure similar opportunities for women to exercise their own freedom of conscience and right to choose.

Notes: *This 1977 statement from the National Federation of Temple Sisterhoods (Reform) was issued in the face of increasing restrictions of access to abortion, especially for the poor. It encouraged support of pro-choice legislation and awareness of groups like the Religious Coalition for Abortion Rights.*

RABBINICAL ASSEMBLY (CONSERVATIVE)

RESOLUTION ON ABORTION (1985)

Abortion

WHEREAS Jewish law recognizes a qualitative difference between the life of a fetus and established human life; and

WHEREAS abortion, though never condoned as elective birth control, is mandated by Jewish law when the pregnancy threatens the life or well-being of the mother; and

WHEREAS legislation outlawing abortion would compromise our obligation to preserve the established life, that is the life and well-being of pregnant women;

THEREFORE, BE IT RESOLVED that the Rabbinical Assembly oppose any legislation, including a Constitutional amendment, aimed at outlawing abortion.

Notes: *This 1985 statement by the Rabbinical Assembly (Conservative) "recognizes a*

qualitative difference between the life of a fetus and established human life," and went on to oppose any criminalization of abortion.

RECONSTRUCTIONIST RABBINICAL ASSOCIATION

STATEMENT ON ABORTION (1981)

Jewish tradition affirms the infinite value of human life as it is expressed in the Biblical affirmation that all human beings are created in the Divine image, and judges the decision to abort a fetus to be a most serious matter. Yet a survey of decisions rendered by recognized Halakhic (Jewish legal) authorities over the centuries would counsel several attitudes: First, that abortion of a fetus, though a diminishing of the Divine image, is not judged to be murder at anytime prior to birth. Second, that abortion is warranted, indeed required, when the fetus threatens the life of a woman. Third, that a woman's mental anguish may be viewed as a sufficient ground for abortion.

Moreover, Reconstructionist Judaism affirms the values of democracy, pluralism, and individual freedom in both Jewish and general life, and rejoices in the absence of any theological, religious, or scientific consensus in the United States of America that would make a woman's decision to abort a fetus an issue of public morality to be enacted into public law.

The Supreme Court has supported this latter view when, in 1973, it recognized that the abortion decision is a personal one and removed abortion from the realm of criminal law and made it a legal medical procedure.

Therefore, be it resolved: that the 1981 Annual Convention of the Reconstructionist Rabbinical Association goes on record as

1. affirming the right of American women to choose safe, legal abortion

2. opposing the limiting of Federal and State funding of abortions for poor women

3. opposing those hospital policies and legal harrassments that would limit access to abortion, and

4. opposing anti-abortion legislation, including any constitutional amendment that would make abortion illegal, as threats to both the Establishment and the Free Exercise Clauses of the First Amendment.

Notes: *This 1981 statement from the Reconstructionist Rabbinical Association was reaffirmed in 1982 and again in 1989. It maintained that abortion is not murder at any time prior to birth, and that "a woman's mental anguish may be viewed as a sufficient ground for abortion."*

UNION OF AMERICAN HEBREW CONGREGATIONS (REFORM)

STATEMENT ON ABORTION (1981)

It has been the longstanding position of the *UAHC*, which we again state, to affirm the legal right of a woman to exercise her moral and religious conscience regarding abortion. Our tradition has always upheld the sacredness of life. Similarly, it has upheld the sacredness of the body.

In light of the fierce and increasing campaign in America to deny freedom of choice in regard to abortion,

WE, THEREFORE,

1. REAFFIRM STRONG SUPPORT FOR THE RIGHT OF A WOMAN TO OBTAIN A LEGAL ABORTION IN ACCORDANCE WITH THE 1973 SUPREME COURT DECISION IN *ROE V. WADE* AND *DOE V. BOLTON*.

2. OPPOSE THOSE CONSTITUTIONAL AMENDMENTS AND BILLS INTRODUCED IN THE CONGRESS AND STATE LEGISLATURES WHICH WOULD UNDER-MINE A WOMAN'S CONSTITUTIONAL RIGHT TO CHOOSE ABORTION BY DECLARING A FETUS TO BE A PERSON WITH RIGHTS SUBJECT TO EQUAL PROTECTION UNDER THE CONSTITUTION.

   Such a definition of the origin of human life is incompatible with the teachings of Judaism. Moreover, the practical consequences of such a definition could go much further than merely reversing the 1973 Supreme Court decisions. Certain forms of birth control could be outlawed and the termination of pregnancy could constitute an act of homicide, subject to the charge of murder or manslaughter.

3. EXPRESS DEEP ALARM AT THE SUCCESSFUL MOVES IN CONGRESS AND STATE LEGISLATURES TO DISALLOW FUNDING FOR POOR WOMEN TO RECEIVE MEDICALLY NECESSARY ABORTIONS AND OPPOSE PROPOSED MOVES TO REDUCE FUNDING FOR, AND PROHIBIT, GENETIC SCREENING TO DETECT DEFECTS IN FETAL DEVELOPMENT.

   Such actions would compel a woman to carry every pregnancy to term regardless of the consequences to her physical and psychological health. We are opposed to such restrictions as oppressive to women. Forcing women to bear children at any cost also threatens the stability of the family.

4. OPPOSE ANY LEGISLATION WHICH WOULD DENY FEDERAL COURTS JURISDICTION OVER ABORTION ISSUES.

   Such laws would undermine our constitutional structure. We oppose the procedure and the substance of such legislation which would eliminate the uniform protection of constitutional rights across the nation.

5. CONTINUE TO AFFIRM THE LEGAL RIGHT OF A WOMAN TO ACT IN ACCORDANCE WITH THE MORAL AND RELIGIOUS DICTATES OF HER CONSCIENCE WITH RESPECT TO ABORTION.

Notes: *This 1981 statement by the 56th General Assembly of the Union of American Hebrew Congregations (Reform) reaffirmed the right of women to act according to their consciences with regard to abortion, and opposed any legislation which would give the fetus equal rights as persons—a position "incompatible with the teachings of Judaism."*

Other Religious Bodies

America is now home to hundreds of groups which are neither Christian in the traditional sense (i.e. Catholic, Protestant or Eastern Orthodox) nor Jewish. There is Hinduism and Buddhism from Asia, Islam from the Middle East and elsewhere, the Latter-day Saint tradition native to the United States, and other traditions, both ancient and modern. Only a few of these groups have issued formal statements on social issues like abortion. Presented here are those statements as well as some less formal statements, which may be representative or suggestive of other approaches to abortion. Also included here are statements from two national abortion organizations. While neither group is affiliated with any one church, religious beliefs play a part in both of their statements.

AMERICAN MUSLIM MISSION

THE MAN AND THE WOMAN IN ISLAM (1976)

I am sure that you would not like to be guilty of the henious crime of abortion. To abort a child's life that is growing in the womb of the mother is a deplorable and terrible act. Nobody in their right mind could like such a thought.

You yourself, were born a physical person as a newborn baby with no mark against you. You were as innocent as a blank page of paper. Then you grew up and became a thinking person.

Suppose someone had murdered you in your infancy. You would never have become a person as you are now.

In the Holy Quran there are some instructions that will enable us to know that there are some restrictions or limitations upon the woman and the man in regards to abortion. Many men and women agree to abort life because they fear that there is not enough material provisions in the family or in the community to support the new human life. The Holy Quran, 1400 years ago, recognized this problem and it instructed the people not to kill children for fear of want, for the same God that provided for the parents would provide for the children. It is like a rich man who is properly providing for his wife, but she has to decide whether she should have more children or not.

If the man is rich, he obviously has enough wealth to take care of the physical needs of the wife and all of the children that she can bear him. But she takes it upon herself, without consulting him, to say that there will be no more children. This woman, having no physical problems or health problems, decides against having another child because she determines on her own that the budget is unable to provide the necessary funds for its care. From where did the budget come? It came from the rich husband. So until he says that there is a limit of

173

funds, the woman should avoid taking it upon herself to say that they have enough children and that there will be no more. The Holy Quran says that the Creator of the Heavens and the Earth has an abundance. Until He says that things have run out, we should desist from taking it upon ourselves to say that there will be no more children because the budget is getting too tight.

History shows that men and women who disregard the fear of poverty and who go on and have as many children as they desire always have something for themselves and their children. It is those who worry about what is going to happen tomorrow or next week that always are in some kind of trouble.

Abortion to save or to enrich the family materially is outlawed in Islam. Other justifications for abortion should be dealt with separately as individual cases. You might ask if there is any justification for abortion. Certainly there is. The Holy Quran does not say whether abortion is permissible or not. It only says that you cannot abort to save the budget. However, suppose that we know for sure that if a sister has another child, she will lose her life. Should we take it upon ourselves to decide whether the baby or the mother should live? We are not Almighty God. It is up to that mother to decide for herself whether she wants to sacrifice her life so that the baby will come or whether she wants to keep her life and not have the unborn baby.

The history of the Arabs tells us that when the message of Islam came to Arabia, the men placed so much value upon males that they felt ashamed and they felt that they were less than men if they had many daughters and few sons. They even killed some of their daughters.

If you could read the Holy Quran in the Arabic language, you would really get the full force of the beauty in this saying: "For what sin was she killed? No crime has she committed?" The female children were as innocent as the males, but just because of the selfish ignorance of the father, they were killed so that he could boast of having many sons. On this same thought, the Holy Quran says, "Do not kill your children for fear of want." In this statement the scripture is hitting at the first big sin of the Arabs in having many sons and few daughters.

To have many sons means to have many helpers to do the hard work and many fighters to fight the enemies. In disrespecting his mother and his wife, the man had even lost the respect of the value of his sons. He was their father and they should have been children to him, but he had the thought like a man raising horses, cows, donkeys, and fighting dogs. This is the wrath of truth that falls upon a society when it gets out of contact with reality. Allah, the Creator, is the only concept that can keep people in touch with reality. Anything else eventually will lead you to leave reality.

Do not be guilty of "self abortion." Almighty God never called "man" something short of divine development. When God says that He is going to make a man, He means that He is going to bring the human being through the stages of development from childhood, up to a person of knowledge; and lastly up to a person of divine awareness.

If you refuse to accept the religious experience and the scriptural guidance that will develop your mind to a higher elevation and that will lift your mind out of the womb again, you are guilty of self abortion.

Self abortion is the aborting of your own self before you are born out of the wombs of human development.

On the question of abortion, there are some verses in the Holy Quran that shine light to enable us to see what kinds of abortion are allowed, if any. First, we will refer to Chapter 81, entitled "The Folding Up."

8. When the female (infant),
   Buried alive, is questioned-

9. For what crime
   She was killed;

Other Religious Bodies

Holy Quran Yusuf Ali Translation Sura LXXXI: Verse 8-9

In this Chapter, a deplorable act of the Quarish tribe before they embraced Islam is brought to our eyes. This horrible act was the act of burying the female child alive. It was an act that was done in secret or, as Maulana Yusuf Ali says in his footnote, done in collusion. In the history of the pagan Arabs, or the pre–Islam day Arabs, we learn that the Arabs, as many other primitive societies, were proud of male children in their family and the absence of female children. They disliked having daughters and they prided themselves in being the father of many sons. In this Chapter, The Holy Quran speaks to this ignorant practice and it tells us of the day of judgment and of the female child that was buried alive. This "burying alive" brings to our mind something a little bit deeper than just the act of burying a physical body. Burying alive, as it is used here, also brings to mind the retarding of the females by the males who felt that females were a different creation and that they should not be allowed to go to school or to be taught wisdom with men. There are some Muslims today who feel that women should not be allowed to go to the mosque, but that they should stay at home. They say that women are not to be allowed to socialize or to attend public meetings, even if it be for their moral and spiritual development.

Many of the people who hold these ideas might be innocent, but we are sure that many of them are guilty of using this as an excuse to keep their women ignorant and subservient. On the subject of abortion, it is very difficult to say whether this verse should be admitted in forming judgment on abortion, because it could very well be that this verse is speaking to the social killing and the spiritual killing of the woman more so than to the physical killing of the female child. In this Chapter, the question is put to us, "For what sin was she killed?" The Arabs killed the female child to save themselves from experiencing the embarrassment of shame in the society. We may reason from this knowledge that, if anyone aborts a human life to escape shame in the society, they may be acting against the teachings of the Holy Quran. If a young girl gets pregnant and fears that her parents will punish her or that the society will look down on her because of her having a child out of wedlock, and this fear of shame forces her to seek a doctor to abort the human life, before aborting the life in her womb she should remember that the Holy Quran teaches against the taking of life to save one's self from shame or embarrassment.

The second point to consider is the practice of abortion out of fear of poverty, or the killing of children out of fear of poverty. The Holy Quran says that you should not kill your children out of fear of want, and that Allah provides for you and for them. So, in light of this teaching of the Holy Quran on the taking of a child's life, we may conclude that it is sinful for any parent or any believer to take the life of a child out of fear of want or out of fear of poverty. We may reason still further that the family or the parent who feels that they cannot afford more children are not respecting the teachings that are given on this subject in the Holy Quran. If we are not allowed to kill our children out of fear of want, then we are not allowed to control the size of our family so that our gain or our benefit will increase so that there will be enough material goods for all the members to live a comfortable life. If we are concerned about material comfort for each member of the family, we are manifesting the fear of poverty and want—so such abortion would be considered against the right conduct of a believer in Islam and the Holy Quran.

The third point is that the Holy Quran teaches us to save our life, to preserve our life, and to feel responsible for our own individual life. It also teaches that it is a sin for us to abuse ourselves or to kill ourselves. There are cases wherein the mother, herself, is threatened by the growth of a human life in her womb. Many women have been advised to submit to abortion to save their own life. Many have been told that to carry and deliver the baby would most likely mean the death of the mother and the baby. When this is the case, as we have said in earlier teachings on the subject of abortion, the individual mother whose life is at stake must make the decision for herself. Her husband should give her the right to make the final decision on the question of risking her own life.

Our fourth point on the subject of abortion, as the subject might be influenced by the

175

teachings of the Holy Quran, is that many Muslims feel that under no circumstances should anyone take it upon themselves to abort a life. Many Muslims feel that you should not use any contraceptives or do anything to prevent the sperm from developing into a human life. They feel strongly that to do this would be committing a sin. Those who have these feelings should not be forced to accept a different belief or judgment. If they are convinced that their belief is right and that it is dictated to them by the teachings of the Quran or Islam, they should not be persuaded to give up their belief or position. However, for those who do feel that there are exceptions, we would like to offer some questions that might help us to reason better and to draw better conclusions.

Actually, there is no way to prevent the germs of life from dying or from falling short of their development. In our sleep, and at other times, there are involuntary releases of semen, that is sperm (human life germs). Also, the female during her mensus discharges or releases eggs in her menses, or in the blood. Those eggs, if fertilized by sperm, will feed the sperm and bring about, with the sperm, the development of a human life. The sperm that is lost, if it has been carried to its place in the female womb, would have developed into a human life. We have no control over that. If any sister should be faced with the problem of having children at the risk of losing her own life, she should give this a lot of thought. Before taking a chance on having life begin and grow over months into the latter months of its development in her womb before she starts to worry and go to the doctor to ask if she should have the baby, she should make the decision before she decides to give herself to her husband and allow the germ of life (the sperm) to be received into her womb and the growth process started. She should decide beforehand whether or not she is going to risk her life and also the life that would form in her womb. If she decides that she is not certain whether she is ready to risk a life to have a baby, she should use the safest contraceptive that is available. Some of them are very safe. This would be better than waiting until it is too late, and then aborting a well–formed life in her womb. It would seem to me to be more reasonable, more honorable, and more decent to use contraceptives that are safe rather than go on with an uncertain mind and allow life to begin forming in the womb. You should not wait until you are forced to make a decision and then abort the life in your womb or risk your own life.

I personally approve those contraceptives that have low risk and are proven to be very safe.

In concluding, I ask you to weigh these comments with the other teachings that you have heard on abortion. When you make your decision, be certain that it is your own decision and keep Allah's guidance first. Pray to Him and then do what your conscience guides you to do. May Allah bless us and save us all from mistakes and wrongdoings.

Notes: *This statement is an excerpt from the book,* The Man and the Woman in Islam, *by W.D. Muhammad, Chief Minister of the American Muslim Mission (unknown membership). It indicated that the Holy Quran had little to say about abortion, aside from the prohibition against killing children for fear of want i.e., they would be born into poverty. If the mother's life is at stake, she should make the final decision. While no definitive statement was made concerning other situations, abortion in general was referred to as a "henious crime."*

AQUARIAN EDUCATIONAL GROUP

SEX, FAMILY, AND THE WOMAN IN SOCIETY (1987)

People often say that it is all right to have an abortion up to the sixth month of pregnancy because the child's soul is not yet in its body. This is false. Before conception even takes place, the baby's soul floats in the mother's aura. In the future, people will develop the capability to see it. Conception causes an anchor of a blue light to go from the heart center of the incoming soul to the embryo in the womb.

The incarnating human soul waits in the mother's etheric body for three to four months to enter the body which is forming in his mother's womb. If abortion is performed during this period, he cannot descend into the body, but becomes trapped in the mother's etheric body. In the majority of cases, he cannot return to the Subtle World because he is already rooted in matter. Thus the woman has an entity in her aura which manifests in various ways, causing various disturbances in her consciousness and behavior. The entity may even try to possess her.

If the incarnating human soul does not understand the reason for the abortion, he expresses his dissatisfaction or despair by trying to make her want to be pregnant again. Or if he turns negative toward her, he creates psychological disturbances in her nature.

One can observe very clearly how the behavior of a woman changes after she has an abortion. In any case, it is a very gloomy setback for the human soul to wait in the aura of the woman.

Later, such a human soul leaves the mother-to-be and becomes an inhabitant of the etheric plane, until the years he would have lived—had he incarnated—have passed. Then he tries again for a new birth.

For a human soul coming from higher spheres to lose seventy to eighty years in the etheric plane with its unpleasant inhabitants is a horrible prison. Preventative actions must be taken before pregnancy for the sake of the mother's health and for the sake of the incarnating human soul.

If the aborted human soul stays in the etheric body of the woman for more than three months, and if through intercourse she attracts another human soul into her etheric body, she may have a complicated situation. If the two human souls do not agree with each other and both want to incarnate, they fight for the body during gestation. If there is only one body being formed, they both try to occupy it, which causes various disfigurations in the embryo. But if they agree, usually two eggs are produced and they are born as twins.

We must not assume that twins are only the result of an aborted human soul waiting in the etheric level to incarnate. In the majority of cases, karmic association and the magnetism created by love invite two or more human souls waiting for incarnation. In such cases, the babies are born normal.

Miscarriage occurs when the human soul leaves the aura of the woman (but not the etheric plane, where he remains trapped.) Often this happens as a result of karmic complications between mother and child, where, because of certain psychic events, the incoming soul decides against incarnation and withdraws.

Other times it occurs because of the poor health of the mother, or as the result of accidents, use of drugs and alcohol, wrong physical exercise, and such factors. These cases, too, reflect karmic complications.

Sometimes a miscarriage occurs because the incarnating human soul has an enemy or a lover on the etheric plane who does not want him to leave for incarnation. In such cases, that enemy or lover may keep him from incarnating, or the human soul aborts by himself. For whatever reason he leaves, physiological conditions within the mother change and miscarriage occurs.

Incarnation does not depend on the wishes of the human souls in the subtle planes. Their physical incarnation is dependent upon specific laws, timing, cycles, and other factors. Everyone waits his turn to be born. But sometimes some try to escape incarnation because they do not want to face their karma, or they want to finish the work they are doing there in the Subtle Worlds.

The birth of the human body is the result of the coordination of higher bodies, which reach perfect coordination in seven steps.

When mental coordination reaches the second step, the first step of the coordination of the astral body starts.

When astral body coordination reaches the second step, the first step of etheric coordination starts.

When etheric coordination reaches its second step, physical conception takes place, which develops in three periods:

1. Three and one-half months
2. Three and one-half months
3. Two months

This means that when conception takes place, coordination of the mental body of the embryo has already reached the fourth step of development, the astral body has reached the third step of coordination, and the etheric body has reached the second step of coordination.

This being the case, all the subtle personality vehicles of the embryo, who is only one or two days old, are already in formation and condensation. When abortion takes place, this process of building is wasted, and the building devas in the etheric, astral and mental realms pass through a heavy shock. They then pass the work to those devas who destroy half-built vehicles and clean the debris from the aura of the mother. This cleaning work is not always successful; the debris causes problems in the etheric, astral, mental bodies, and eventually also the physical body as the years pass.

Thus, abortion is a crime not only against the body, but also against the soul of the embryo, who loses the subtle vehicles which were built by building devas or forces of construction.

The aborted human soul lives for a while in his half-built subtle bodies and eventually tries to come back into incarnation. Or, he rejects the process of incarnation as much as he can, since the destruction of his vehicles is equal to the process of dying for him.

Abortion has a serious effect on the woman who has one, as well as on the child she aborted. Abortion encourages people to be:

a. careless about pregnancy;
b. disrespectful of their organs and inclined to enjoy their sexual pleasures at the expense of others;
c. careless about human life;
d. inclined to think that one can easily erase the effect of the crime;
e. irresponsible;
f. immersed in guilt complexes which prevent spiritual advancement;
g. split psychologically.

Those who have abortions often meet destinies similar to that of the aborted ones later, in retribution for those lives they took. Miscarriage itself can be the result of past abortions or a karmic punishment.

These are the first steps toward release to be taken by a woman who has had an abortion:

a. She must really understand her crime.
b. She must ask forgiveness of the one whom she murdered.
c. She must dedicate her life to saving the lives of human beings.
d. She must work hard to prevent abortions by others.

Notes: *Torkam Saraydarian, the leader of the Aquarian Educational Group (unknown membership), an occult group in the Theosophical tradition, wrote Sex,* Family, and the Woman in Society, *from which this statement is excerpted. Going beyond groups who say* *personhood begins at the moment of conception, the group states that "before conception even takes place, the baby's soul floats in the mother's aura." An abortion may cause the soul to be trapped in the aura, causing problems. Abortion is understood as a crime of murder.*

BUDDHIST CHURCHES OF AMERICA

A SHIN BUDDHIST STANCE ON ABORTION (1984)

As the controversy continues to rage in this country, abortion nonetheless has become a wide-spread practice. It is estimated that up to 3 out of every 10 pregnancies now result in abortion. Pro-abortion or "pro-choice" advocates cite the following arguments in support of legalizing abortions:

1. Every woman should have the right to make decisions about her own body (including the fetus in the womb).

2. Every child should be a wanted child because unwanted children create additional stress and misery for the family unit.

3. Since many women are going to choose to have abortions regardless of what the law says, safe and legal abortions should be made available for humanitarian reasons.

Anti-abortion or "pro-life" advocates put forth the following arguments in establishing their position:

1. Life begins at conception. Therefore abortion is the murder of a human being.

2. While deaths of women undergoing abortion are rare, there are a disturbing number of cases of premature births and spontaneous abortions in subsequent pregnancies. Sterility can also result from abortion.

3. Psychological problems (e.g. remorse, guilt, anger) following abortions are more the rule than the exception.

We Jodo Shin Buddhists are not immune from the abortion dilemma. What are some of the considerations that we as Jodo Shin Buddhists might have?

In theistic religions, divine sanction is the ultimate resource in resolving moral dilemmas. Since Buddhism as a religious system is human-centered without dependencies on God or gods, moral or ethical questions involve individual subjectivities and require a meeting of a sense of responsibility and of enlightened self-interest. For instance, in heterosexual relations, the Buddhist emphasis on individual responsibility requires that both man and woman understand the consequences of their actions and take appropriate precautions. Yet those in the grasp of sexual desire are often negligent or what seem to be reliable precautions fail, and we are again faced with the abortion issue.

Within the life of Nembutsu, the truth seeker cannot help but feel compassion for all forms of life. Realizing that all sentient beings have Buddha-nature and are embraced in Oneness within the Great Compassion of Amida Buddha, he holds all forms of life in deepest reverence. As is expressed in the oft-repeated phrase, "Hard is it to be born into human life . . .", Human life is especially precious because it is only the human being among all living forms who can realize Shinjin. And it is indisputable that the human fetus is a manifestation of human life. Therefore abortion, the taking of human life, is fundamentally wrong and must be rejected by Buddhists.

However, the Great Compassion recognizes the complexity of samsaric life and the inability of unenlightened beings to live a truly ethical life, no matter how much they might want to. How can one live even one day without necessitating the taking of life?

The body involuntarily destroys bacteria, viruses and parasites. Eating meat and vegetables requires killing or harvesting. Our clothing and shoes are often made of the physical parts of various life forms. And we exterminate life forms that we consider to be undesirable (e.g. insects, vermin, weeds). Perhaps the more sensitive among us may even assume personal responsibility for the countless human deaths resulting from military conflicts, mass starvation and disasters. It is truly lamentable to Buddhists that living itself requires the taking of many lives.

The abortion issue is a distinct form of this human dilemma. The life of the fetus is precious and must be protected. Yet the woman carrying the fetus may sincerely feel that her physical and/or psychological condition requires the abortion of the fetus. Her pregnancy might be a result of a sexual assault or might be life-threatening to her. Perhaps she knows that the baby, if allowed to be born, will be seriously deformed or disabled. Or she might be convinced that the baby will be born into an unwelcome environment. Who can pass judgment on the morality of such a situation?

Although others may be involved in the decision-making, it is the woman carrying the fetus, and no one else, who must in the end make this most difficult decision and live with it for the rest of her life. As buddhists, we can only encourage her to make a decision that is both thoughtful and compassionate. Gassho, Namu Amida Butsu.

Notes: *This 1984 statement by the Buddhist Churches of America (approximately 100,000 members in 1984) is representative of the American Shin Buddhists affiliated with the Jodo Shinshu Hongwanji denomination of Buddhism. It recognized the sacredness of life on the one hand and the complex dilemmas people find themselves in on the other when it asked the question, "Who can pass judgment on the morality of such a situation?" The answer, in this case, was that the woman who was involved should make the decision.*

CHURCH OF JESUS CHRIST OF LATTER-DAY SAINTS

STATEMENT BY DR. RUSSELL M. NELSON (c. 1986)

For a nation that grieves for its dead, we are inconsistently calloused in allowing millions to be killed before birth, said Dr. Russell Nelson, an internationally known heart surgeon who is now a worldwide leader of The Church of Jesus Christ of Latter-day Saints.

Abortions claim more lives annually than the total number of fatalities from all the wars of the United States, said Dr. Nelson in an address to the general conference of the church.

"For years, I've labored with other doctors here and abroad, struggling to prolong life. It's impossible to describe the grief a physician feels when the life of a patient is lost. Can anyone imagine how we feel when life is destroyed at its roots, as though it were a thing of naught?" said Dr. Nelson.

In fact, a war is being waged on the defenseless and voiceless—the unborn, he added. "Over 55 million abortions were reported worldwide in the year 1974 alone. In the United States, over 1.5 million abortions are performed annually. About 30 percent of all pregnancies now end in abortion."

Dr. Nelson pointed out that as sons and daughters of God, we cherish life as a gift from Him. Scripture declares that the "life of the flesh is in the blood" (Leviticus 17:11). Abortion sheds that innocent blood.

Even in the 16th century, reformer John Calvin understood the sanctity of life as he wrote, "If it seems more disgraceful that a man be killed in his own home than in his field—since for every man his home is his sanctuary—how much more abominable is it . . . to kill a fetus . . . who has not yet been brought into the light."

Acknowledging that the health of the mother is a proper concern in pregnancy, as is pregnancy resulting from rape or incest, Dr. Nelson noted that less than three percent of all abortions are performed for these two reasons. The other 97 percent are for what may be termed "reasons of convenience."

"Some argue abortion because a malformed child may result. But if one is to be deprived of life because of *potential* for developing physical problems, consistency would dictate that those who already have such deficiencies should likewise be terminated. Such irreverence for life is unthinkable!

"Another contention raised is that a woman is free to choose what she does with her own body. To a certain extent this is true for each of us. We are free to think, to plan, and to do. But once an action is taken, we are never free from its consequences. Those considering abortion have already exercised certain choices," said Dr. Nelson.

He used the analogy of an astronaut, who is free to withdraw during the selection process, planning, and preparation for a trip. But once the rocket fuel is ignited, he is no longer free to choose.

"So it is with those who would tamper with the God-given power of procreation. They are free to think and plan otherwise. But their choice is sealed by action." said Dr. Nelson.

The woman's choice for her own body does not validate choice for the body of another, he added. "The consequence of terminating the fetus therein involves the body and life of another. These two individuals have separate brains, hearts, and circulatory systems. To pretend that there is no child and no life there is to deny reality."

The question of when "meaningful life" begins is a moot question, he said. "In biological sciences, it is known that life begins when two germ cells unite to become one cell, bringing together 23 chromosomes from both the father and from the mother. These chromosomes contain thousands of genes. In a marvelous process involving a combination of genetic coding by which all the basic human characteristics of the unborn person are established, a new DNA complex is formed. A continuum of growth results in a new human being.

"The onset of life is not a debatable issue but a fact of science," said Dr. Nelson.

Approximately 22 days after the two cells have united, a heart begins to beat. At 26 days, the circulation of blood begins.

"The Church of Jesus Christ of Latter-day Saints has consistently opposed the practice of abortion," said Dr. Nelson. "One hundred years ago the leaders of the church wrote, 'And we again take this opportunity of warning the Latter-day Saints against those . . . practices of foeticide and infanticide.'

"Life is a gift from our Heavenly Father. It is eternal as He is eternal. Innocent life is not sent by Him to be destroyed."

Notes: *This is an authoritative statement from Dr. Russell M. Nelson, a worldwide leader of the Church of Jesus Christ of Latter-day Saints (approximately 4,300,000 members), that was issued as a press release (undated, c. 1986). Abortion was condemned as the killing of innocent life which was given by God.*

NATIONAL RIGHT TO LIFE COMMITTEE

STATEMENT ON ABORTION (UNDATED)

What of the U.S. Supreme Court Decision?

This has opened all fifty states to abortion on demand until the cord is cut. It prevents any state from forbidding abortion when needed for the life or health of the mother.

By the Court's own definition, the word "health" means . . . "The medical judgment may be exercised in the light of all factors—physical, emotional, psychological, familial, and the woman's age—relevant to the well-being of the patient. All these factors may relate to health" (Doe v. Bolton).

It includes when a pregnancy would:

"Force upon a woman a distressful life and future."

Produce "psychological harm."

"Will tax mental and physical health by child care."

Will bring the distress "associated with the unwanted child."

Will "bring a child into a family already unable psychologically or otherwise to care for it."

Will bring the "continuing difficulties and stigma of unwed motherhood" (Roe v. Wade).

The Dred Scott Decision in 1857 ruled that black people were not "persons" in the eyes of the Constitution. Slaves could be bought, sold, used or even killed as property of the owner. That decision was overturned by the 14th Amendment. Now the court has ruled that unborn people are not "persons" in the eyes of the Constitution. They can be killed at the request of their owners (mothers). This dreadful decision can only be reversed by the court itself or overturned by another constitutional amendment.

But Legalizing Abortion Would Eliminate Criminal Abortions!

This is purely wishful thinking and a completely false statement. Consistent experience has been that when laws are liberalized, the legal abortion rate skyrockets, the illegal abortion rate does not drop, but frequently also rises. The reason consistently given is the relative lack of privacy of the official procedures. (Abortion: Questions & Answers)

Doesn't a Mother Have a Right To Her Own Body?

This is not her body but the body of another human person. Since when have we given to a mother the right to kill her children—born or unborn?

Abortion Is Only a Religious Question, Isn't It?

No. Theology certainly concerns itself with respect for human life. It must turn to science, however, to tell it when life begins. The question of abortion is a basic human question that concerns the entire civilized society in which we live. It is not just a Catholic, or Protestant, or Jewish issue. It is a question of who lives or dies.

Isn't Abortion Another Means of Contraception?

No. Do not confuse abortion with contraception. Contraception prevents new life from beginning. Abortion kills the new life that has already begun.

Why Bring Unwanted Babies Into the World?

An unwanted pregnancy in the early months does not necessarily mean an unwanted baby after delivery. Dr. Edward Lenoski (U of S Cal.) has conclusively shown that 90% of battered children were planned pregnancies.

What About a Girl Who's Been Raped?

Pregnancy from rape is extremely rare. The victim must be supported, loved and helped, but we should never kill an innocent baby for the crime of his father.

What If the Mother Threatens Suicide?

Suicide among pregnant women is almost unknown. In Minnesota, in a 15-year period, there were only 14 maternal suicides. Eleven occurred after delivery. None were illegitimately pregnant. All were psychotic.

Are There After-effects to the Mother?

After legal abortion there is an increase in sterility of 5%, of miscarriages of an additional 10%, of psychiatric aftermath (9 to 59% in England), of Rh trouble later. Tubal pregnancies rise from 0.5 to 3.5% and premature babies from 5 to 15%. There can be perforation of the uterus, blood clots to the lungs, infection, and later fatal hepatitis from blood transfusions. (Abortion: Questions & Answers)

But Isn't It Cruel to Allow a Handicapped Child to Be Born—to a Miserable Life?

The assumption that handicapped people enjoy life less than "normal" ones has recently been shown to be false. A well-documented investigation has shown that there is no difference between handicapped and normal persons in their degree of life satisfaction, outlook of what lies immediately ahead and vulnerability to frustration. "Though it may be both common and fashionable to believe that the malformed enjoys life less than normal, this appears to lack both emperical and theoretical support."

Paul Cameron & D. Van Hoeck, Am. Psychologic Assn. Meeting. 1971

A New Ethic?

For two millenia in our western culture, specifically protected by our laws, and deeply imprinted into the hearts of all men has existed the absolute value of honoring and protecting the right of each person to live. This has been an inalienable, and unequivocal right. The only exceptions have been that of balancing a life for a life in certain situations or by due process of law.

Our new permissive abortion laws represent a complete about-face, a total rejection of one of the core values of western man, and an acceptance of a new ethic in which life has only a relative value. No longer will every human have an absolute right to live simply because he exists. Man will now be allowed to exist only if he measures up to certain standards of independence, physical perfection, or utilitarian usefulness to others. This is a momentous change that strikes at the root of western civilization.

It makes no difference to vaguely assume that human life is more human post-born than pre-born. What is critical is to judge it to be, or not to be, human life. By a measure of "more" or "less" human, one can easily and logically justify infanticide and euthanasia. By the measure of economic and/or social usefulness, the ghastly atrocities of Hitlerian mass murders came to be. One cannot help but be reminded of the anguished comment of a condemned Nazi judge who said to an American judge after the Nuremburg trails: "I never knew it would come to this." The American judge answered simply: *"It came to this the first time you condemned an innocent life."*

Willke, *Handbook on Abortion*

Isn't Abortion Safer Than Childbirth?

In the last stages it is far more dangerous. In the first three months it is probably more dangerous or at least as dangerous as childbirth. Like Venereal Disease, abortion complications and even deaths are substantially underreported. Therefore, even though the reported statistics state that aboriton is much safer, in fact it is probably more dangerous even in early pregnancy.

Isn't It True That Restrictive Abortion Laws Are Unfair to the Poor?

It is probably true that it is safer for a rich person to break almost any law, than for a poor person to do so. Perhaps the poor cannot afford all the heroin they want. Rich people probably can. Does that mean we should make heroin available to everyone? Not everything that money can buy is necessarily good. The solution is not to repeal laws, but to enforce them fairly. Laws restricting abortion can be, and frequently have been, adequately enforced.

What of the Population Explosion?

Fertility in the United States has dropped below the "replacement" level of 2.1 children a family that is necessary to achieve zero population growth. It has been at 1.8 since 1973.

If the current decline in the world birth rate continues "It should be possible to reduce the world crude birth rate to less than 20 and the world population growth rate to less than 1% per annum by 1980" (same as U.S.A.).

World Fertility Trends During the 1960's,
R. Ravenholt, director, off. of population USAID

Constructive Answers

"Choosing abortion as a solution to social problems would seem to indicate that certain individuals and groups of individuals are attempting to maximize their own comforts by enforcing their own prejudices. As a result, pregnant school girls continue to be ostracized, mothers of handicapped children are left to fend for themselves, and the poor are neglected in their struggle to attain equal conditions of life. And the only solution offered these people is abortion. It becomes very disturbing when we think that this destructive medical technique may replace love as the shaper of our families and our society." "We must move toward creating a society in which material pursuits are not the ends of our lives; where no child is hungry or neglected; where even defective children are valuable because they call forth our power to love and serve without reward. Instead of destroying life, we should destroy the conditions which make life intolerable. Then, every child regardless of its capabilities or the circumstances of his birth, could be welcomed, loved, and cared for."

Induced Abortion, A Documented Report, p.134.

Notes: *This statement is taken from material put out by the National Right to Life Committee in Cincinnati, Ohio. The NRLC is the single largest group operating on a national level opposing the 1973 Supreme Court Roe v. Wade decision, which judged freer access to abortion to be a constitutional right. While the group serves as the focus of interdenominational time and energy, it does not present itself as a religious group.*

NEW AGE MOVEMENT

STATEMENT ON ABORTION (1986)

Abortion

LI SUNG: There has always been abortion. Well (in our day) more often, the infant children were left to die, and especially the little girl children. So, in our view, the fetus is not viable or if the time is not appropriate, the soul can return in another vehicle. And so, the act of abortion is not seen as a murder, for the fetus does not have a soul . . . is not fully controlled by the soul until birth. Now the soul will hover above, as it were, to keep an eye on its new body, and then, at the appropriate moment, will join it. And so if the little body is terminated, the soul says, "Well, I must go find a new one." So, we do not agree that has any moral reprehensibility.

QUESTION: Why do some believe that abortion is murder.

LI SUNG: Well, they make up their minds from belief systems, not from their experience, so perhaps their minds are not open to reason. We know of no easy way so that they may see the spirit hover about the little body. They will not believe what they cannot see. And so, they will suffer pain and guilt. It is the tradition of their religious teaching. Yes, if they have abortion, this will be very painful for them for they will feel terrible guilt, *terrible guilt*, they will feel they have murdered someone. But you see, there are certain drawbacks from religious traditions. You humans are forever creating these straight jackets, hmmmm? You cannot let yourselves live natural way, no, you must make up laws or what you call "God's Laws", but God has nothing to do with it. It's always a priestly society who maintains control, that makes up rules. Ah, but one day, some of you will wake up and say, "If there is rule to be from God, I will find it in my heart—not from some pulpit".

Notes: *This message is from the magazine,* Spirit Speaks, *and is an example of a position on abortion obtained from the New Age phenomenon of channeling. Li Sung is an entity who is said to have lived in northern China 1200 years ago. He is channeled by Alan Vaughan, a psychic and author. The statement maintained that abortion was not murder because the fetus did not yet have a soul, nor was it "fully controlled" by a soul until birth. If there was an abortion, the soul simply found another vehicle.*

RELIGIOUS COALITION FOR ABORTION RIGHTS

STATEMENT ON ABORTION (UNDATED)

The Religious Coalition for Abortion Rights is working to preserve your freedom.

Pro-choice people often ask, "Why don't we have a brochure with pictures?" We could. We could print pictures of women who have bled to death from illegal abortions. We could print pictures of rape victims. We could print pictures of babies with fatal birth defects; babies that lived only a few minutes after birth.

But we don't.

Those pictures would shock and upset you.

We'd rather that you take the time to think seriously about the real issue.

THE ISSUE IS FREEDOM. YOU CAN'T TAKE A PICTURE OF FREEDOM.

You've probably seen the garish brochures that anti-choice organizations hand out.

The pictures in those brochures are designed to shock you—and they do!

They are designed to keep you from thinking seriously about the *real* issue.

Sadly, they often do.

THE ISSUE IS FREEDOM!

Freedom of Choice

In 1973, the U.S. Supreme Court ruled in the case of *Roe v. Wade* that the right to privacy is guaranteed by the Constitution. The Court found that the right to privacy extends to a woman's decision regarding her pregnancy.

The Court's decision did NOT "mandate abortion on demand to the moment of birth," as some anti-choice organizations have erroneously claimed. Rather, it placed clear restrictions on the woman and on the state, giving neither an absolute right to "demand" or to prohibit abortions; it established safeguards for the woman's health and for the potential life of the fetus; it recognized the delicate balance between private rights and social responsibility. And—within those limits—it allowed a woman, in consultation with her doctor, family, and spiritual counselors, to *choose* what she may do about an unplanned or problem pregnancy. So . . .

- the 52-year-old woman, who thought she was going through menopause, may choose whether to continue or terminate a pregnancy she thought couldn't possibly happen.

Perhaps she and her spouse would welcome a "September baby." Or perhaps her health is so poor that a pregnancy would threaten her life.

- the victim of rape may choose whether or not to bear the rapist's child. Perhaps she is so emotionally damaged by the rape that her thoughts run constantly to suicide. Or perhaps she feels that she should have the child and give it up for adoption.

- the woman, who discovers through prenatal tests that her baby will be born with multiple birth defects, may choose whether to continue or terminate her pregnancy. Perhaps the tests show that the defects are mild and treatable. Or perhaps they show that the baby has no chance of survival.

Anti-choice organizations would deprive these women—and *all* women, in *all* circumstances—of the right to choose. If these organizations could, they would give these women—and *all* women, in *all* circumstances—only *one* "choice."

What if you were one of these women. Would you rather have your decisions made for you? Or would you rather have the freedom to choose?

RCAR

The Religious Coalition for Abortion Rights is comprised of 31 national religious organizations—Protestant, Catholic, Jewish and others—representing 13 denominations that support the option of legal abortion. Because each denomination approaches the issue of abortion from the unique perspective of its own theology, members hold widely varying views on when abortion is morally justified. But all agree that there are situations in which abortion may be a moral alternative.

Every person, therefore, must have the freedom to make decisions concerning abortion in light of his or her own conscience and religious beliefs, and in accordance with responsible medical practice. Only in this way will the religious liberty we currently enjoy be maintained.

The U.S. Supreme Court recognized that abortion is a personal decision when, in 1973, it removed abortion from the realm of criminal law and made it a legal medical procedure. "We recognize the right of the individual, married or single, to be free from unwarranted governmental intrusion into matters so fundamentally affecting a person as the decision whether to bear or beget a child." the Court held. "That right necessarily includes the right of a woman to decide whether or not to terminate a pregnancy."

Shortly after that Supreme Court decision, the members of RCAR joined together to oppose legislation that would restrict access to legal abortion—legislation such as mandatory waiting periods, consent requirements, and denial of federal or state Medicaid funds for low-income women.

RCAR also opposes attempts to overturn the Supreme Court decision by adding an anti-abortion amendment to the U.S. Constitution. Such an amendment would define the moment of conception as the beginning of human personhood, giving a fertilized egg or a fetus legal standing equal to that of the pregnant woman. Any abortion, even one performed to save the life or health of the woman, might then be legally defined as murder. The IUD and some forms of the birth control pill, which function as early abortifacients, would also become illegal.

The Constitutional amendment prohibiting abortion would not only inflict tremendous suffering on women and their families; it would enact into civil law one particular theology—a theology that is not shared by the majority of western denominations. Many denominations do not believe that equal human personhood begins at conception. And most believe that there are instances in which the decision to seek an abortion, as well as the decision to use the birth control pill or the IUD is in keeping with their own moral precepts.

If the Supreme Court decision is overturned, members of these denominations will be forced by law to abide by the doctrine of another faith group.

Religious liberty is one of our most cherished traditions. If we permit our legislators to enact theology into law, we will significantly diminish that liberty.

The Coalition operates on both the national and state levels. Resources include a newsletter, a legislative network, and publications. For further information, please contact the RCAR office.

Notes: *This statement is from a brochure produced by the Religious Coalition for Abortion Rights, the only national-level religious pro-choice organization. It emphasized freedom of choice, so that one religious view on conception and life would not be legislated into making decisions for those who religiously disagree.*

REORGANIZED CHURCH OF JESUS CHRIST OF LATTER DAY SAINTS

STATEMENT ON ABORTION (1974)

The following affirmations were developed by a committee composed of physicians, social scientists, an attorney, and church officials.

1. We affirm our faith in God and in the fellowship of the church, as the work of God among us and within us and the context within which decisions about abortion should be made.

2. We affirm our shared humanity and common need for redemption and reconciliation to God and to one another.

3. We affirm that parenthood is partnership with God in the creative processes of the universe.

4. We affirm the necessity for parents to make responsible decisions regarding the conception and nurture of their children.

5. We affirm a profound regard for the personhood of the woman in her emotional, mental, and physical health; we also affirm a profound regard and concern for the potential of the unborn fetus.

6. We affirm the inadequacy of simplistic answers that regard all abortions as murder or, on the other hand, regard abortion only as a medical procedure without moral significance.

7. We affirm the right of the woman to make her own decision regarding the continuation or termination of problem pregnancies. Preferably this decision should be made in cooperation with her companion and in consultation with a physician, qualified minister, or professional counselor. This decision should be made in light of the full range of moral, medical, legal, and cultural influences within which the person lives.

8. We affirm the need for skilled counselors to be accessible to the membership of the church to assist persons in their struggle with issues centering in human sexuality, responsible parenthood, and wholeness of family life. There is a need for church leaders to be cognizant of counseling resources within the community to which our members may be referred.

Church leaders recognize that there may be rare occasions which might make it necessary, because of the conditions of the conception or the pregnancy, to terminate a particular pregnancy. Yet for purposes of teaching children and young people what we consider to be moral principles and the law of the church, these teachings must include placing a high value on the preservation of life and proscribe the use of abortion as a means of merely terminating an unwanted pregnancy or as an alternative method of contraception. Just as surely as the church must stand for the sanctity of marriage and forbid adultery and fornication, so must it also stand against any practice which would seem to weaken marriage or promote immorality. We feel the emphasis should be placed on the teaching of values and moral guidelines which accent the positive worth of chastity before marriage, fidelity within marriage, and a reverence for life as Christian principles. If a termination of the pregnancy is chosen, those who share the burden of making the choice must assume responsibility for this act of agency. (Standing High Council Minutes, January 24, 1974)

Notes: *This 1974 statement by the Standing High Council of the Reorganized Church of Jesus Christ of Latter Day Saints (approximately 201,480 members in 1982) supported the legality of abortion and the right of a woman to make her own decision in the matter. It also emphasized the moral importance of the decision and the need to live in ways which would minimize the need for such decisions. This statement was reaffirmed in 1980.*

UNITARIAN UNIVERSALIST ASSOCIATION

RESOLUTION ON ABORTION (1963)

WHEREAS, we as Unitarian Universalists are deeply concerned for dignity and rights of human beings; and

WHEREAS, the laws which narrowly circumscribe or completely prohibit termination of pregnancy by qualified medical practitioners are an affront to human life and dignity; and

WHEREAS, these statutes drive many women in the United States and Canada to seek illegal abortions with increased risk of death, while others must travel to distant lands for lawful relief;

BE IT THEREFORE RESOLVED: That the Unitarian Universalist Association support enactment of a uniform statute making abortion legal if:

1. There would be grave impairment of the physical or mental health of the mother;

2. The child would be born with a serious physical or mental defect;

3. Pregnancy resulted from rape or incest;

4. There exists some other compelling reason—physical, psychological, mental, spiritual, or economic.

Notes: *This 1963 Resolution from the Unitarian Universalist Association (approximately 173,167 members) is one of the earliest modern, official religious statements in the United States to specifically address the issue of abortion. It urged liberalization of the abortion laws to allow abortion in cases of rape, severe defect, or "some other compelling reason."*

UNITARIAN UNIVERSALIST ASSOCIATION

RESOLUTION ON ABORTION (1977)

WHEREAS, attempts are now being made to deny Medicaid funds for abortion and to enact Constitutional Amendments that would limit abortions to life-endangering situations and thus remove this decision from the individual and her physician; and

WHEREAS, such legislation is an infringement of the principle of the separation of church and state as it tries to enact a position on private morality into public law; and

WHEREAS, such anti-abortion legislation would cause the revival of illegal abortion and result in the criminal exploitation of women who are without money or influence, forcing them to resort to unsafe procedures; and

WHEREAS, we affirm the right of each woman to make the decisions concerning her own body and future and we stress the responsibilities and long-term commitment involved in the choice of parenthood;

WHEREAS, the majority of the Supreme Court has ruled on June 20, 1977 that the states are not obligated to expend Medicaid funds for elective abortions, and has also ruled that public hospitals are not obligated to perform abortions;

WHEREAS, there is a strong national movement to have two-thirds of the state legislatures request Congress to convene a Constitutional convention for the purpose of proposing a Constitutional amendment to prohibit abortion;

THEREFORE BE IT RESOLVED: That the 1977 General Assembly of the Unitarian Universalist Association expresses its dismay and regret at the June 20, 1977 decision of the Supreme Court as seriously jeopardizing the right of legal abortion won in the Supreme Court decisions of January, 1973; opposes the denial of Medicaid funds for abortion and any Constitutional amendment prohibiting abortion and urges members of the societies of the Unitarian Universalist Association to write or wire their senators and representatives in Congress and state legislatures to inform them of our position on these issues.

BE IT FURTHER RESOLVED: That the 1977 General Assembly positively affirms its respect for the responsibilities and joys of parenthood, and the member societies of the Unitarian Universalist Association are encouraged to develop workshops and other programs on parenthood and parenting.

BE IT FURTHER RESOLVED: That in 1977 General Assembly urges that federal funds be invested in research to find more effective and safer methods of birth control.

Notes: *This 1977 resolution by the Unitarian Universalist Association condemned the Supreme Court ruling of that year which specified that Medicaid funds did not need to be spent on abortions and that public hospitals were not required to offer abortions.*

UNITARIAN UNIVERSALIST ASSOCIATION

RESOLUTION ON ABORTION (1987)

BECAUSE, Unitarian Universalists believe that the inherent worth and dignity of every person, the right of individual conscience, and respect for human life are inalienable rights due every person; and that the personal right to choose in regard to contraception and abortion is an important aspect of these rights; and

BECAUSE, we believe in tolerance and compassion for persons whose choices may differ from our own; and

BECAUSE, we believe not only in the value of life itself but also in the quality of life; and

WHEREAS, pain, suffering, and loss of life were widespread prior to the legalization of abortion in 1973 by the U.S. Supreme Court (*Roe v. Wade*) and the 1969 amendments to the Criminal Code of Canada; and

WHEREAS, the issue of abortion is morally complex, and abortion must remain a legal option; and

WHEREAS, attempts are now being made to restrict access to birth control and abortion by overriding individual decisions of conscience, and attacks in legislatures, courts, and the streets often result in depriving poor women of their right to medical care; and such legislation is an infringement of the principle of separation of church and state in that it tries to enact private morality into public law; and

WHEREAS, there is a movement to re-criminalize abortion both for women and their health-care providers which could bring back dangerous alternatives to clinically safe abortions;

THEREFORE BE IT RESOLVED: That the 1987 General Assembly of the Unitarian Universalist Association reaffirms its historic position, supporting the right to choose contraception and abortion as legitimate aspects of the right to privacy; and

BE IT FURTHER RESOLVED that:

1. Individual Unitarian Universalists educate themselves, their congregations, and the public about the new moral understandings emergent in the works of feminist theologians and social ethicists; and

2. Unitarian Universalists oppose any move to deny or restrict the distribution of government funds as a means of restricting access to full contraceptive and abortion counseling and/or services, at home or abroad; and

3. Unitarian Universalists actively oppose all legislation, regulation and administrative action, at any level of government, intended to undermine or circumvent the *Roe v. Wade* decision; and

4. Unitarian Universalists communicate their opposition to such attempts to their legislative representatives and to the electorate; and

5. Unitarian Universalists expose and oppose bogus clinics and other tactics that infringe on the free exercise of the right to choose; and

6. Unitarian Universalists promote legislation funding safe abortions for low-income women; and

7. Individual Unitarian Universalists, congregations, and the Unitarian Universalist Association open discussion with those of different mind, and seek opportunities to work productively from shared values to promote family planning and education for responsible sex; and

BE IT FINALLY RESOLVED: That we reaffirm the right to choose contraception and abortion as a legitimate expression of our constitutional rights.

Notes: *This 1987 statement from the Unitarian Universalist Association reaffirmed their pro-choice position and rejection of any moves to restrict access to abortion.*

WICCA

A RITUAL FOR AN ABORTION (1984)

Recently I became pregnant for the second time. This was a very sad situation for me to be in, because I want children very much and cannot afford to give them a good home. I had aborted my first child because of this, and it was a traumatic experience. For over a year I was haunted by feelings of profound loss and guilt, complicated by the fact that our society doesn't allow for grieving in such situations. Even my Craft friends didn't understand what I was going through.

I finally understood what the trouble was: I had forced a soul out of this world without asking permission, and that was why I grieved so. Once I understood this and dealt with it, I was able to heal the pain.

So here I was, pregnant again, and again not wanting to raise a child, emphatically not wanting to repeat the experience I had had before. This time, I know, I wanted to be sure that I had my child's understanding and consent before I forced him out of the world. What I needed to do was perform a psychic abortion.

The night before I was scheduled to have the abortion at a clinic, I set my altar with black, blue and white candles—for banishing, healing and purification. I bathed in an infusion of rosemary, rose petals, and pine, and while I was in the bath I meditated on my body, the changes it was going through, feeling all the signs of pregnancy and remembering how it would feel to be without them.

Once out of the bath, I purified myself before casting the circle. I sat in front of my altar, with my chalice in front of me, and began a slow breathing exercise, slowly gathering all the anger and grief and pain that I was feeling and sending it out the ends of my fingers and into the chalice. All my anger at my body, for becoming pregnant when I didn't want to be; my jealousy of the friends who have husbands and babies, my fear of physical pain, my anger at the company that made a birth control device that didn't work — I breathed it all out of myself and into the chalice, which I visualized as being filled with purple-black, pulsing liquid. Then I took up my wand and pointed it at the cup, visualizing a beam of clear blue light. Gradually, the dark liquid changed to clear, sparkling blue fluid. It was transformed, neutralized, and I felt the last vestige of negative feelings slip away from me.

I then cast the circle and ceased the room with Peace incense. I invoked the Goddess with this invocation:

> Great Mother, Dark Lady -
> You who are the mistress of life and death,
> Of Joy and sorrow-
> Come to me now
> Aid and protect me.
> Be with me now
> As I work this spell,
> And comfort me.

I had never felt the Goddess' presence come into me so strongly. I could feel Her arms surrounding and embracing me, and for the first time since I had learned of my pregnancy I was able to cry tears that weren't for anger or fear or frustration, but simply of sorrow. I cried for a long time, feeling just like I felt when I was a small child and my mother held me. When I had done crying, I didn't feel fatigued, but healed.

I wanted to invoke the Horned God. I don't always call him, but it was important to me to acknowledge the joyful sexuality that had created this child, and the warm support I was getting from my partner. I summoned him with these words:

> Horned One, Dancer in the Woods
> Gentle friend, sweet lover-
> Come to me now.
> Bring your laughter and joy-
> Aid and protect me -
> Cherish me.

I was ready to work the spell. Sitting down, I began to sense my aura. I perceived it as violet, but around my womb there was an egg shaped field of golden light. Slowly, I breathed into the golden light until it surrounded by entire body. It was like being in a cloud of golden mist, very heavy, like thick fog, but warm. I began to concentrate on my child. I had been sure I conceived a male child, and I called him by a name I had chosen as his. Slowly, the mists began to swirl and part, and I could see a child, a small boy about two years old, although his face wasn't clear. I opened myself to him and we communicated, not with words but with feelings.

At first we just enjoyed each others company, sending feelings of love and tenderness to each other. Then I asked if he knew what it was I was going to do. He knew, and he didn't want to go—he was looking forward to being born. But I explained to him that it would not make me happy to give birth to him at this time, and that I couldn't give him the life I wanted him to have. I asked him to leave me. I told him that I wanted to give birth to him someday when I could give him the life he deserved, and that if he needed to be born soon, he would have to choose another mother. He told me he understood. The mists gradually started to close over him. At the same time, he went very far away, like a figure seen through the wrong end of a telescope. I could hear him saying, in words this time, "Goodbye, Mother." Then I was alone, and the mists were drawing down, fading away.

The next day I went to the clinic and had an abortion. That was a month ago. I feel very different than I did a month after my first abortion. I think I felt right about it this time because of this ritual—because I had my child's consent and because I acknowledged to myself the sanctity of my choice. Because I've realized this: if it is holy and sacred to give birth by choice, it is equally sacred to choose not to, and to be able to end a pregnancy easily, safely, and with a total absence of guilt.

Notes: *This 1984 article describing a ritual for an abortion was written by Callista and was taken from a San Francisco Wiccan newsletter,* Cernunnos. *Wicca is a neo-pagan witchcraft movement with diverse parts and no centralized organization. This article described a ritual devised to allow communication with the fetus in order to reach a mutual understanding about the proposed abortion.*

Acknowledgments

"Abortion." Reprinted with permission of the U.S. Catholic Conference. (© April 17, 1969 by the United States Catholic Conference; Washington, D.C.).

"Explosion or Backfire." Reprinted with permission of the U.S. Catholic Conference. (© November 19, 1959 by the United States Catholic Conference; Washington, D.C.).

"Pastoral Plan for Pro-Life Activities." Reprinted with permission of the U.S. Catholic Conference. (© November 20, 1975 by the United States Catholic Conference; Washington, D.C.).

"Respect for the Gift of Life." Reprinted with permission of the Watchtower Bible and Tract Society of New York, Inc., from *True Peace and Security—From What Source?*

"Sex, Family, and the Woman in Society." Reprinted with permission of the Aquarian Educational Group, from *Sex, Family, and the Woman in Society.*

"Statement on Abortion." Reprinted with permission of Molli Nickell, from *Spirit Speaks*, Volume 1, no. 6, p. 41.

"Statement on Abortion." Reprinted with permission of the U.S. Catholic Conference (© October 3, 1985 by the United States Catholic Conference; Washington, D.C.)

Index to Organizations, Statements, and Subjects

Citations in this index refer to page numbers; page numbers rendered in boldface after an organization name indicate the location of that organization's statement(s) within the main text.

Index to Organizations, Statements, and Subjects

Index to Organizations, Statements, and Subjects